Contested City

Social History, Popular Culture, and Politics in Germany
Geoff Eley, Series Editor

Contested City

*Municipal Politics and the Rise of
Nazism in Altona, 1917–1937*

Anthony McElligott

Ann Arbor
THE UNIVERSITY OF MICHIGAN PRESS

Copyright © by the University of Michigan 1998
All rights reserved
Published in the United States of America by
The University of Michigan Press
Manufactured in the United States of America
⊗ Printed on acid-free paper

2001   2000   1999   1998   4   3   2   1

A CIP catalog record for this book is available from the British Library.

Library of Congress Cataloging-in-Publication Data

McElligott, Anthony, 1955–
    Contested city : municipal politics and the rise of Nazism in
Altona, 1917–1937 / Anthony McElligott.
        p.   cm. —   (Social history, popular culture, and politics in
Germany)
    Includes bibliographical references (p.   ) and index.
    ISBN 0-472-10929-4 (acid-free paper)
    1. Hamburg-Altona (Hamburg, Germany)—Politics and government.   2.
Hamburg (Germany)—Politics and government.   3. National
socialism—Germany—Hamburg.   4. Political
parties—Germany—Hamburg.   5. Municipal
government—Germany—Hamburg.   I. Title.   II. Series.
DD901.H28   M42   1998
320.943'515—dc21   98-19712
                                                                         CIP

Contents

Illustrations

Tables

Acknowledgments

A study that has taken a long time to complete necessarily leaves behind it a trail of debts, intellectual and otherwise. My first thanks go to the staffs of the libraries and archives whose cooperation lightened the task of research: Frau Ildiko Barabas and Dr. Klaus Richter at the Staatsarchiv in Hamburg; the late Professor Werner Jochmann, Dr. Ursula Büttner, and the staff at the Forschungsstelle für die Geschichte des Nationalsozialismus in Hamburg; the Landesarchiv in Schleswig; the Stadtarchiv in Kiel; the Landesarchiv in Berlin; the Geheimes Staatsarchiv Preußischer Kulturbesitz in Berlin-Dahlem; the Berlin Document Center; and the Bundesarchiv in Koblenz. The staff of the now defunct Institut für Leninismus-Marxismus beim Zentralparteiarchiv in what used to be East Berlin deserves a special mention for their hospitality in the winter of 1982. A similar expression of thanks goes to Judge Heidkämper and his colleagues at the Ministry of Justice in Hamburg, who for six months in 1982 provided a congenial environment in which to study the then closed files of the Altona *Sondergericht*. In Hull Wendy Munday drew all the maps, her colleague Eddie Meggitt gave invaluable assistance with the computerized maps for the ward elections, and Simon Williams guided me through the universe of computer space.

I would like to gratefully acknowledge the financial support of the British Academy and the King Edward VII British-German Foundation that enabled me to carry out the original research.

Lynn Abrams, Liz Harvey, and my colleagues, Richard Saville and Chris Schmitz, read individual chapters of this book at various stages of completion. Their helpful criticisms have been indispensable. However, they are not responsible for errors of fact and wayward judgment. Those must be my own liability. A deep intellectual debt is owed to my former teachers, Ian Kershaw and John Breuilly, who guided the original research. Geoff Eley and the editors at the Press get sainthoods for patience.

During my long stays in Germany I have developed many friendships. In this respect Professors Hans-Juergen Goertz and Arnold Sywottek at the University of Hamburg have given generously of their time for nearly two decades. The ongoing friendship and collaboration with Elizabeth von Dücker and fellow travelers at the *Stadtteilarchiv Ottensen* have remained an inspiration. Among the many friends and colleagues in Britain and Germany who have discussed different aspects of my work and who have given their encouragement and advice for over a decade and a half, the following deserve a special mention. First and foremost, Richard Evans has been an unswerving pillar of support; Karl Ditt, Dick Geary, Michael and Carmen Grüttner, Elizabeth Harvey, Tim Kirk, Alan and Renate Kramer, and Helga Stachow also deserve a note of thanks. Heinrich von Berenberg-Gossler, Sigrid von Berenberg, Dieter Putzier, and Irmingard Lamersdorf have all listened patiently to my ideas since the beginning, and in different ways they have made my long research stays in Germany very enjoyable. The "bad boys" of Hospitalstraße in the Altona Altstadt, Andreas Fritz and Ecki Schweppe, shared slum life with me. The sharp wit and companionship of Wiltrud Lamersdorf and the rowdy, contested, but happily sane world of our children, Anna, Sophie, and Max, have been constant reminders that there is life beyond the script. This book is as much theirs as it is mine.

Finally, this study is dedicated to the memory of those *Altonaer* who lived through what I have put into words and who, in one way or another, have shared their histories with me.

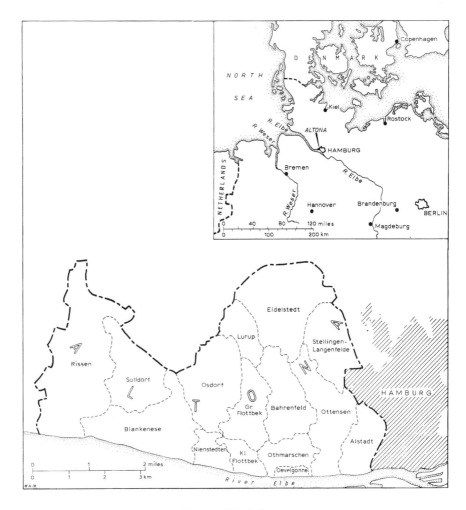

Altona and North Germany

CHAPTER 1

Introduction

At the election for a National Assembly on 19 January 1919, three-quar-ters of the German electorate gave its blessing to the newly established Weimar Republic. Its first president, Friedrich Ebert, in his address to the new parliament, which met for the first time at Weimar on 6 February, noted that the old regime "by the grace of God" had been banished by a republican majority: "The German people are free! Will remain free and will govern themselves from now on."[1]

But the republic's golden egg of 1919 was never laid again. Indeed, within a year signs of disenchantment were visible. At the Reichstag elec-tion in June 1920, for instance, support for the so-called Weimar Parties, represented by the Sozialdemokratische Partei Deutschlands (SPD), Deutsche Demokratische Partei (DDP), and Center Party (Zentrum), had tumbled to 43.6 percent of voter turnout. Even at their peak in 1928, the republican parties only managed to gain an extra 3 percent above the level of 1920, and this was due to a short-lived increase in support for the Social Democrats. In the final three elections between July 1932 and March 1933, just about a third of the electorate gave their endorsement to the republic.[2] The Enabling Act on the 21 March, giving Hitler a free rein over govern-ment, struck the final blow to parliamentary democracy without barely a murmur of protest from the public. What had happened to the hopes and aspirations of 1919? Where did they go?

There are many good studies of the republic that have sought answers to these questions. These works, however, often tackle the problem mainly from the perspective of players on the stage of high politics and from the world of business institutions and industrial interests.[3] Rarely is the his-tory of the republic charted and explained through the experiences of ordi-nary people. The big players, representing the interests of the conservative elites in the higher ministerial bureaucracy, East Elbian landowners, army officers, court politicians, and the organized factions of capital and labor, are clearly important, and, as Edgar Feuchtwanger has recently reminded us, some of them must bear a major part of the weight of responsibility for the demise of the republic.[4] But, by focusing on high politics in this short period, we learn little of how ordinary people experienced the republic from its inception to its demise.[5] They are the focus of my case study of municipal politics in Altona.

The choice of a local study rather than a national or regional approach seems self-evident to social historians interested in the "history of everyday life," or *Alltagsgeschichte*. Readers will note that I am partly following in the trail blazed by William Sheridan Allen's classic study of Northeim three decades ago.[6] Indeed, his book is probably the single most influential investigation for the study of the emergence of Nazism in its local context. Since the publication of Allen's book, and especially since the emergence of *Alltagsgeschichte* in Germany at the beginning of the 1980s, there have been numerous similar studies that have singled out a locality in order to explore the path to Nazism in depth.[7] But, very often, they are not studies of the interaction between municipal politics and people's political choices. Frequently, these everyday life histories merely retread the path to Nazism without taking in the full meaning of the wider landscape, and thus, paradoxically, they tend to leave the politics out of their social histories, to paraphrase the British historians Keith Nield and Geoff Eley.[8]

That is not to say that politics per se are omitted from these local studies, but it is the case that local politics as an analytical tool for deciphering the bigger picture of the Weimar Republic, is. Instead of looking at the impact of politics from the center on life at the periphery, I want to reverse the focus and look at local politics as a way of explaining the national picture. This perspective is not new. The representatives of Weimar's municipalities also thought in this way. Indeed, the man who led Altona for most of the Weimar period, Max Brauer, while in exile told his American students of civics, "the destiny of nations is decided by the destiny of municipal progress."[9] Nonetheless, in spite of the influential works by Herzfeld, Busch, and Hofmann, to name but a handful,[10] few attempts have been made to explore in detail how the politics of Weimar's municipal progress might explain the destiny of interwar Germany.[11]

The city of Altona lies to the immediate west of Hamburg on the river Elbe. Until the mid-nineteenth century it had been Denmark's unofficial capital of Schleswig-Holstein and the second major city after Copenhagen. As a result of war against Denmark and the Austro-Prussian conflict in 1866 and 1867, the city became Prussian. During the eighteenth century Altona had been a center of the German-speaking enlightenment in the north, with a buoyant economy, before its decline during the Napoleonic

Wars. After the political and financial trauma of the successive military upheavals in the 1840s and 1860s, the city underwent a revival with the onset of industrialization in the last quarter of the century.[12]

In 1855 Altona's population had stood at 40,626; by 1885 it had more than doubled, to 104,717. In 1889 and 1890 the developing industrial town of Ottensen-Neumühlen and the smaller communities of Bahrenfeld, Othmarschen, and Oevelgönne were incorporated into Altona, bringing its population to 176,628 by 1910.[13] By the time of the census in 1925 the population had reached 185,653 and grew to nearly a quarter of a million after the incorporation of ten suburbs to the west and north of the city in July 1927. Thus, by the mid-1920s Altona had become the largest city in the province of Schleswig-Holstein, the twelfth largest in Prussia, and came within the category of primary cities of the reich. Denominationally, Altona was a Protestant city typical of north Germany, with a small minority of Catholics (4.5 percent) and Jews (1.2 percent in 1925 and falling to less than 1 percent in 1933).[14] In 1937, by diktat of Hermann Goering, Altona was abruptly incorporated into the city-state of Hamburg.[15]

Meanwhile, Altona had developed into a major center of manufacturing. Its transformation from the later nineteenth century came about with the regional industrialization—centering mainly on the Hamburg harbor—after the inclusion of the two cities in the Customs Union in 1888.[16] Industrial production was thus geared to the capital goods sector, notably shipbuilding and the railways. Metal manufacturing was the largest single sector in Altona and was linked to shipbuilding and harbor-related activities. A total of 12,090 persons were employed in the metal trades, or approximately 15.3 percent of the 66,841 persons employed in Altona in the mid-1920s (the city's economically active population numbered 94,337).[17] Of this number 84.6 percent actually worked in the 685 factories located on land, mainly in Ottensen and Bahrenfeld. This skilled labor force made excavators, ship propellers, engines, boilers, and various other machines and tools and were mostly concentrated in large factories, such as those of the machine builders Menck and Hambrock and the Zeise Iron Works, both of Ottensen, each of which employed a labor force between 400 and 700, depending on the size of their order books.[18]

The second single largest sector in Altona was the food processing industry. This sector employed just over 11,000 persons in approximately 948 factories and workshops or those who were engaged in home-based outwork. The labor force in this sector was predominantly female, especially in the fish processing industry and in the cigarette industry, the two largest employers. In the former branch in 1927 some 2,358 employees, many of them seasonal, were employed in approximately 43 establishments. In the cigarette industry around 2,000 women were employed in four factories in Bahrenfeld, the most important of which was the Reemtsma cigarette factory. Also important were brewing and margarine production, with each branch employing about 1,600 workers in a small number of plants. While brewing was mostly a male industry, food processing was almost entirely female. Thus, A. L. Mohr's margarine factory, which was the largest and most important in this branch, employed mostly women. Other important branches in this sector employing predominantly women were cocoa-chocolate, jam, and marzipan production, with around a thousand workers.[19]

Since the late nineteenth century Altona had gained a reputation as a working-class city. According to the census of 1925, 45 percent of Altona's total population was working-class, and it hovered around that level until the later 1930s. The census differentiated between workers in "characteristic" occupations of mostly skilled, artisanal, and auxiliary trades and "ordinary" workers (i.e., unskilled and casual), who made up nearly half of Altona's working class. This latter grouping mostly found casual employment in the land-based factories or in the harbor area. Their world of work was insecure and their means of gaining an income sometimes dubious, as we shall see in chapter 3. Altona's working class was thus segregated by income and by residential patterns as well as by social and cultural lifestyles that were compounded in part by political behavior, a subject we return to in chapter 6.

The centrality of the harbor complex and the importance of overseas trade for the local economy (a considerable number of firms produced for export, maintaining overseas links rather than attempting to find a niche in the German domestic market) meant there was also a sizable tertiary sector. The largest branch of this sector was banking and related financial services, which employed nearly two-thirds of the 35,082 persons working in this area. While many of these technical and office workers earned markedly differing incomes, the majority of both sexes earned rates at the lower end of the scale. Their growing numbers and low level of remuneration led the sociologist Theodor Geiger to call them *Stehkragenproletariat,* or "white-collar proletariat."[20] But, in spite of the fact that frequently, in terms of income, residence, and family roots, Altona's clerical employees stood in close proximity to the manual working class, they viewed themselves as a distinct social animal from the proletariat.[21]

While much of industrial manufacture in Ottensen and Bahrenfeld was concentrated in medium to large units of production, smaller workshops tended to dominate in the central parts of Altona's Altstadt. These workshops were to be found in the cellars, courtyards, and terraces, to the rear of the tenement blocks built at the end of the nineteenth century. Similar workshops existed in the older quarters of Ottensen near the railway station in subdistricts 24 and 25, and a large number were scattered throughout the suburbs, notably in Blankenese, Eidelstedt and Stellingen-Langenfelde. These craft workshops were particularly numerous: nearly four thousand such workshops employed a total of around fourteen thousand masters and men in the late 1920s; that is, nearly 15 percent of the city's economically active population was dependent on *Handwerk.*[22]

Much more numerous than these artisanal enterprises were the 6,966 small businesses in commerce and transport employing 23,535 persons in 1925. A large number were to be found in retail. In 1925 there were 3,500 small shops, each employing on average 2 people. Nearly half the employees were females.[23] All of these artisanal and commercial enterprises were vulnerable to the slightest fluctuation in the economy. Altona's old *Mittelstand* of petty producers and retailers, like the new *Mittelstand* of employees and newer professions, such as lawyers and technicians, was sometimes hardly distinguishable in social, cultural, and material terms from the pressing proletariat with which it often shared the same physical space at the neighborhood level.[24]

The middle class in Altona was not homogeneous; indeed, it was stratified into broadly three significant groupings of the very wealthy, an educated professional class and a mass of struggling *Mittelstand.* There was only a small haute bourgeoisie of wealthy industrialists and business magnates, such as the Menck family and the millionaire tobacco magnate Philip Reemtsma. In fact, there were only 3 millionaires, with nearly 6 million reichsmark between them, and 23 half- or near-half-millionaires with a combined wealth of 17 million reichsmark. The census of 1925 showed that in Altona only 13 persons had annual incomes over 100,000 reichsmark, while a further 40 had incomes above 50,000 reichsmark. The incorporation of the suburbs in 1927 helped to strengthen the upper end of the wealthy middle classes. But by far the largest group consisted of the city's 11,273 middling self-employed, but of these the greater majority, 66 percent, earned less than 3,000 reichsmark annually.[25] Through their professional and interest associations and clubs, the middle classes represented a collective, if not always harmonious, set of outspoken voices in Altona's civic life both before and after the revolution in 1918. We will take a closer look at the concerns of this *Mittelstand* in chapters 4 and 5.

In conceptualizing this study, the scientific model for analyzing the dynamics of municipal life developed by the German political scientist Erich Becker has proved useful.[26] Becker identified three typologies in his model of the local state. The first, the *authority relationship,* can be described as one embodying a Hegelian understanding of the state as an impartial power detached from society.[27] Writing in the early nineteenth century, in a period of great turmoil, Hegel had argued that national survival depended on ensuring that the state in its objective function of government was "removed from the fight of factions against factions" in society that lead to "the weakening and eventual destruction of the state's power." He proposed that the tasks of government be carried out by a permanent and professional bureaucracy composed of "a small number of talented men who devote themselves completely to political activity and the state's interest."[28] Thus, all active power should reside solely in a central power. In practice this meant that the central government dealt with the affairs of state, while local self-government was largely confined to a depoliticized activity, in which local dignitaries, the *Honoratioren,* under the supervision of a professional civil servant (the mayor) ran the mundane day-to-day affairs.[29]

The mayor and his professional officers acted as a conduit between state and society. They were first and foremost servants of the state, not of society, and made sure that local activities did not breach municipal boundaries to impinge adversely upon the national interest.[30] This ideology was shared by local notables, who were able to enjoy vast social power under this arrangement.[31] For, in exchange for their subservience to the central authority, the state buttressed their local positions. To quote one nineteenth-century German authority on civil society, Rudolph Gneist: "Society can find personal freedom, the moral and spiritual development of the individual, only in permanent subordination to a constant high power."[32]

This largely passive role assigned to municipal life was brought into question by World War I and shattered by the revolution of 1918. These two events mobilized municipal administrations at the front line of national life.[33] Not only did local administrations play a patriotic role during the war; they also found themselves with the responsibility of keeping Germany afloat in the stormy seas of social chaos and revolution, in the midst of which the central authorities had capsized.[34] Thus, it was to the municipal sphere that Germany's postwar leaders looked to reconstruct the national body in 1918.[35]

The collapse of the imperial state in 1918 sparked off a vigorous debate on how best to reconfigure national life in the postwar era. After 1918 it was no longer accepted that local administrations should simply fit into a larger bureaucratic constellation dictated by the central authorities.[36] Instead, a democratically organized local life was envisaged as the *shaping* force of the national system. Democratic constitutionalists argued that the process of reconstruction in Germany could only take place from the bottom up, since the central authorities had been thoroughly discredited.[37] This view, which fits Becker's second typology, the *integrated organism,* found a broad consensus among Social Democrats and liberals, who believed that the reform of local politics was the key to democratizing the nation. Max Quarck, a prominent Social Democrat from Frankfurt, argued that only a fully democratized local authority could cement the republic's national constitution.[38] Indeed, the father of the Weimar Constitution, Hugo Preuss, envisaged a republic firmly anchored in a fully democratized local civic life and largely independent from interference by regional, state, and central bureaucracies.[39] And Erich Koch-Weser, a leading member of the DDP, and himself a former lord mayor of Kassel and reich interior minister, likened municipal administrations to the "foundations and walls" of the democratic house.[40] The thrust of their thinking on the role of the local state was encapsulated in a physiological metaphor employed by a Social Democrat and expert on municipal affairs, Viktor Noack, in his introduction to the party's *Handbook for Local Politicians* (1922):

> In the same way the proficient development of the body depends on the health of the individual cells, so the state can only develop successfully if the communes are viable. The greater the measure of freedom which is granted to the communes within the legal framework of the state, and the smaller the barriers limiting their activities, so much the better for the state.[41]

This vision of how the relationship between local and central administrations should be shaped challenged the entrenched positions of both central bureaucracy and the local *Honoratioren.* And it was to remain one of the underlying structural problems of the republic.[42]

The separation of powers and roles governing local-central relations in Germany and stipulating the inner form of local life had been encapsulated in a variety of municipal codes (*Städteordnungen*) dating from the early and mid-nineteenth century.[43] In Prussia two types of municipal ordinance were in operation, the *Magistratverfassung* and the *Bürgermeisterverfassung.* Under the former constitution a bicameral system was permitted. The representative chamber, elected by a limited franchise, in its turn elected the executive (*Magistrat*) and mayor. In Schleswig-Holstein the executive and mayor were elected by the public, again by a limited franchise. Both chambers participated in the decision-making process. The *Bürgermeisterverfassung* allowed for no such (albeit limited) democracy. The elected chamber was little more than a talking shop with no influence over the mayor, who dictated policy.[44]

Before 1918 there had been general recognition that these ordinances were in need of reform. Indeed, a special commission had been set up in 1917, charged with looking into the whole question of administrative reform at all levels. Although this commission continued its work after 1918, there was not an overhaul of the *Städteordnungen*. The old municipal ordinances remained in place, albeit seriously modified by articles 17 and 127 of the Weimar Constitution. Article 17 introduced proportional representation and thus democratized local government, while Article 127 gave municipalities some protection from outside interference by guaranteeing them "the right to administer their own affairs within the limits of the law."[45] Thus, on the one hand, municipal administrations became more responsive to their local populations. And, on the other hand, Weimar's mayors took the guarantee accorded in Article 127 to heart and sought to establish a measure of autonomy, especially in financial matters, from external bodies. Both of these developments ultimately brought them into conflict with *Länder* and reich administrations.[46]

Thus, the Weimar Constitution brought about a fundamental change in the functioning of local administrations, although this was by no means a uniform phenomenon, even in Prussia. During the 1920s the *Magistratverfassung* crystallized into a redoubt of municipal democracy: both chambers became forums of the people, who expressed their will through political parties, especially in Schleswig-Holstein, where, as noted, both chambers were directly elected. Thus, the municipal sphere was transformed into a politically contested arena. By contrast, the *Bürgermeisterverfassung,* while not banning politics from the administrative sphere, nonetheless, kept it contained. The latter system represented the old authoritarian idea of an ostensibly harmonious self-government in which the mayor, as servant of the state, remained the chief arbiter of local affairs, assisted by his officers, who were untainted by party politics.[47]

Before the storm of revolution in 1918 local life in Germany was controlled by the propertied elites. Their status and power was underwritten by a restrictive franchise in a number of states, notably in the largest, Prussia, where a three-class suffrage had been in place since 1849 and incorporated into the *Städteordnung* of Schleswig-Holstein.[48] Under this system the male electorate was divided into three groups based on the income derived from taxation. The result was a gross inequality in local representation. For it only took a handful of wealthy taxpayers to equal the equivalent tax level of either of the other two larger but economically weaker groups. Nevertheless, working-class incomes rose in the latter years of the nineteenth century, precipitating a rise in working-class voters and councillors. The growth in their numbers challenged the municipal hegemony of the *Honoratioren,* leading Becker to define this as his third typology, the *sociological conflict relationship.*[49]

In order to combat the growing influence of the SPD at municipal elections by the end of the nineteenth century, franchise conditions were tightened. Thus, in 1900 an amendment of the 1853 ordinance allowed Prussia's councils of towns with populations above ten thousand (usually affecting those towns in which industrialization meant a growth in the support for social democracy) to determine the thresholds for each group independently. Many councils, dominated by National Liberals or Progressives, took advantage of this amendment to raise the threshold. Consequently, inequality in the suffrage grew deeper by the turn of the century, as local elites strove to hold on to their monopoly of power, as Wolfgang Hofmann's data suggests:[50]

	Class		
	I	II	III
	(percentage of eligible voters)		
1853–91	3–6	8–20	70–80
1893–1913	0.2–2	4–14	84–94

The efforts to contain the Social Democrats at the local level by and large proved doomed to failure. In the two decades before the outbreak of war in 1914 the SPD fielded increasing numbers of candidates for election to the councils and registered remarkable successes. Between 1909 and 1911 the number of socialist councillors doubled, and, according to SPD sources, by 1913 the party had around 11,500 councillors. In the absence of data relating to the total number of councillors, we cannot say what the proportional strength was, and it is important to note that barely a quarter (23.6 percent) of socialist councillors were based in urban areas. We do know that local administrations continued to remain in the grip of the *Honoratioren.*[51]

This grip was finally broken in early November 1918 when the revolutionary Prussian government, led by the Majority Social Democrat, Paul Hirsch, democratized the local franchise in Prussia, and other states soon followed.[52] Men and women were accorded equal suffrage rights, and the voting age was lowered from twenty-five to twenty years old. The first local elections, held in 1919 and 1920, radically changed the political landscape of Germany's larger towns and cities. The Majority Social Democrats and the Independent Social Democrats together now dominated the local assemblies of the important towns and cities of individual states. In Saxony, for instance, they accounted for 53 percent of council seats in thirteen larger towns (with populations over 20,000); in Baden they gained nearly 37 percent of seats. In Prussia and Bavaria they took about 44 percent of council seats.[53]

This left-wing dominance of local politics persisted throughout the 1920s. For example, in Prussia the Social Democrats accounted for a quarter of council seats in larger towns, until falling to a fifth in the last municipal elections of 12 March 1933. The communists could be assured of between 12 and 15 percent of seats. In a number of towns and cities of the reich the left-wing parties accounted for 50 percent and more of council seats during the 1920s (e.g., Berlin, Magdeburg, Leipzig, Chemnitz, Altona, Offenbach). And even where the Left did not represent the single dominant force in the council, it was strong enough to act as a power broker, as in Bochum.[54]

As well as the humiliating loss of social status, the political displacement of the local elites after 1918 was of crucial importance to local politics, for it raised the question of the exercise of control over the quality of local life and, in particular, over the economy. Business and property interests, for instance, viewed the new administrations with deep suspicion and feared an attempt to *socialize* the economy from below, or what they called "communalization" (*Kommunalisierung*). For taxpayers this policy was rendered visible in the substantial expansion of the local state and its activities since the war, notably in the area of welfare, and contributed to a doubling of the per capita burden of public expenditure between 1913 and 1929.[55] Local politics under the Weimar Republic can be said to be characterized by the fight-back of the middle classes to regain their position lost to them in 1918.

While my approach to municipal politics has been influenced by Becker's first and second typologies, they are not the direct subject of this book. They do, however, provide an overarching conceptual framework to my study and reemerge to form the basis of discussion in the final chapter. More immediately visible to the reader will be Becker's third typology of social conflict. The implications of controlling the local state cannot be underestimated in the political strategy of the SPD or any other party or interest group, for that matter. In the final analysis it was in Weimar's local arena that many socialists, and other progressive forces, saw the possibility of a new democratic dawn. For, as Max Brauer himself put it, "no unit of government deals more frequently with the daily life of the people than local government . . . as a real and potent agency for the improvement of social conditions as well as guardian for the material needs of the people."[56] Under Brauer's stewardship Altona was to gain a reputation among socialists as an "exemplary achievement of Social Democratic municipal politics."[57] This "exemplary achievement," however, did not go uncontested by Altona's displaced *Honoratioren* and their allies, as we shall see in this study.

CHAPTER 2

"Rowdies" in Altona's *Rathaus:* Politics and Conflicts, 1917–1933

It would not be permissible to grant each rowdy the right to vote.
—*Bürgermeister Dr. Franz Schulz, 1907[1]*

In a report on the extraordinary level of political violence in Altona during the summer of 1932, Rudolf Diels at the Prussian Interior Ministry wrote: "There is hardly another city in Prussia in which the political parties define so completely the character of the individual districts as in Altona."[2] Although he was specifically referring to the city's Altstadt, his comments ring true for Altona as a whole. Indeed, over the course of the 1920s the political cleavages in Altona not only deepened but also revealed intractable geographical fault lines.[3]

The social and political topography of the city had taken shape in the half-century before World War I. The Altstadt was dominated by the manual working class but also had a number of mixed, lower-middle-class districts. From the middle decades of the nineteenth century new suburbs sprang up between the Allee and the new Altona-Kiel railway to the north of the city. Here, upon the once open fields of Bahrenfeld, comfortable tenements were colonized by a labor aristocracy of skilled workers and an emerging class of white-collar employees. The districts of Othmarschen and Oevelgönne to the west and south were largely suburbs of the "new" and "old" *Mittelstand.*[4]

After the incorporation of 1927 the differences in the social topography between the fifteen districts of Altona remained as pronounced as they had been before.[5] The political cultures of these districts during the Wilhelmine period were divided between strong support for the SPD, on the one hand, and for the National Liberals or Progressive Party, on the other. How did these districts vote after 1918? As the maps in this chapter will show, the city polarized along an east-west axis: with a predominantly Left tradition in the city's mainly working-class districts of Altstadt, Ottensen, Bahrenfeld, and Lurup and a strident conservative and nationalist culture in the suburbs of Othmarschen, Oevelgönne, Klein Flottbek, Groß Flottbek, Nienstedten, and Blankenese. The remaining districts of Eidelstedt, Stellingen-Langenfelde, Osdorf, Sülldorf, and Rissen accommodated both traditions. This study will go behind the bare data represented in the maps to examine the daily tribulations and struggles of the people of these districts. Before doing so, this chapter briefly looks at the changing configuration of the political landscape in one of Weimar's contested cities.

The Changed Landscape

Before 1918 civic affairs in Altona were largely dominated by the *Honoratioren,* local dignitaries drawn from the city's middle classes. The restrictive Prussian franchise laws meant that approximately a quarter of Altona's adult population could participate in local elections. They were divided into three electoral bands as follows: class 1 (674), class 2 (2,732), and class 3 (32,246).[6] This meant that the propertied classes, however modest, dominated the city assembly. For instance, after the elections of

TABLE 1.   Socio-Occupational Structure of Altona by District, 17 May 1939

	Self-Employed	Family Helper	Civil Servant	White-collar	Manual Worker
Altstadt	11.8	3.2	5.3	19.0	60.1
Ottensen	10.3	3.0	9.7	25.2	51.8
Bahrenfeld	7.9	2.3	10.5	27.2	52.1
Eidelstedt	12.0	4.6	10.2	18.3	54.9
Stellingen	13.4	4.0	5.5	25.2	51.9
Gr.Flottbek	21.3	3.5	10.7	28.9	35.3
Othmarschen	23.6	2.5	7.1	27.7	39.2
Nienstedten	18.4	3.4	6.5	24.2	47.5
Blankenese	17.2	3.1	10.8	25.4	43.4
Sülldorf	14.7	11.5	8.1	20.4	45.3
Rissen	18.2	7.6	7.7	25.6	40.9
Osdorf	11.9	3.9	19.1	14.1	51.0
Lurup	6.3	2.5	4.1	10.2	76.9
Altona	12.4	3.2	7.7	22.1	54.6

Source: AHVW Sondernummer 6 (1 Nov. 1941): 17.
Note: Oevelgönne is included in Othmarschen figures.

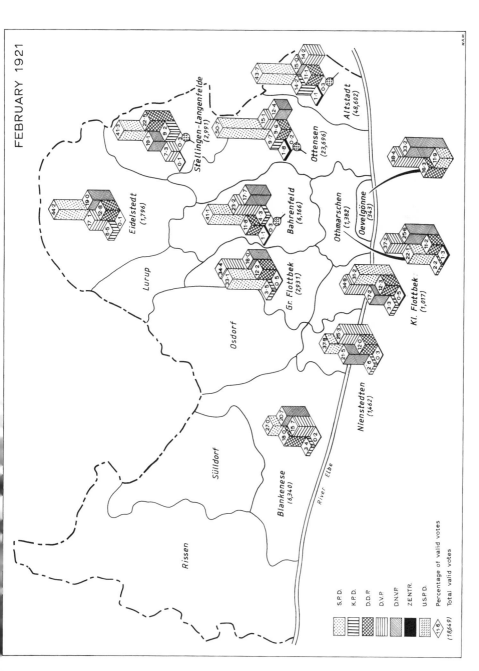

FEBRUARY 1921

Map 1a–f. Voting patterns in Altona: Reichstag elections, 1921–32

Map 1a. February 1921

S.P.D.
K.P.D.
D.D.P.
D.V.P.
D.N.V.P.
ZENTR.
U.S.P.D.

Percentage of valid votes

Total valid votes

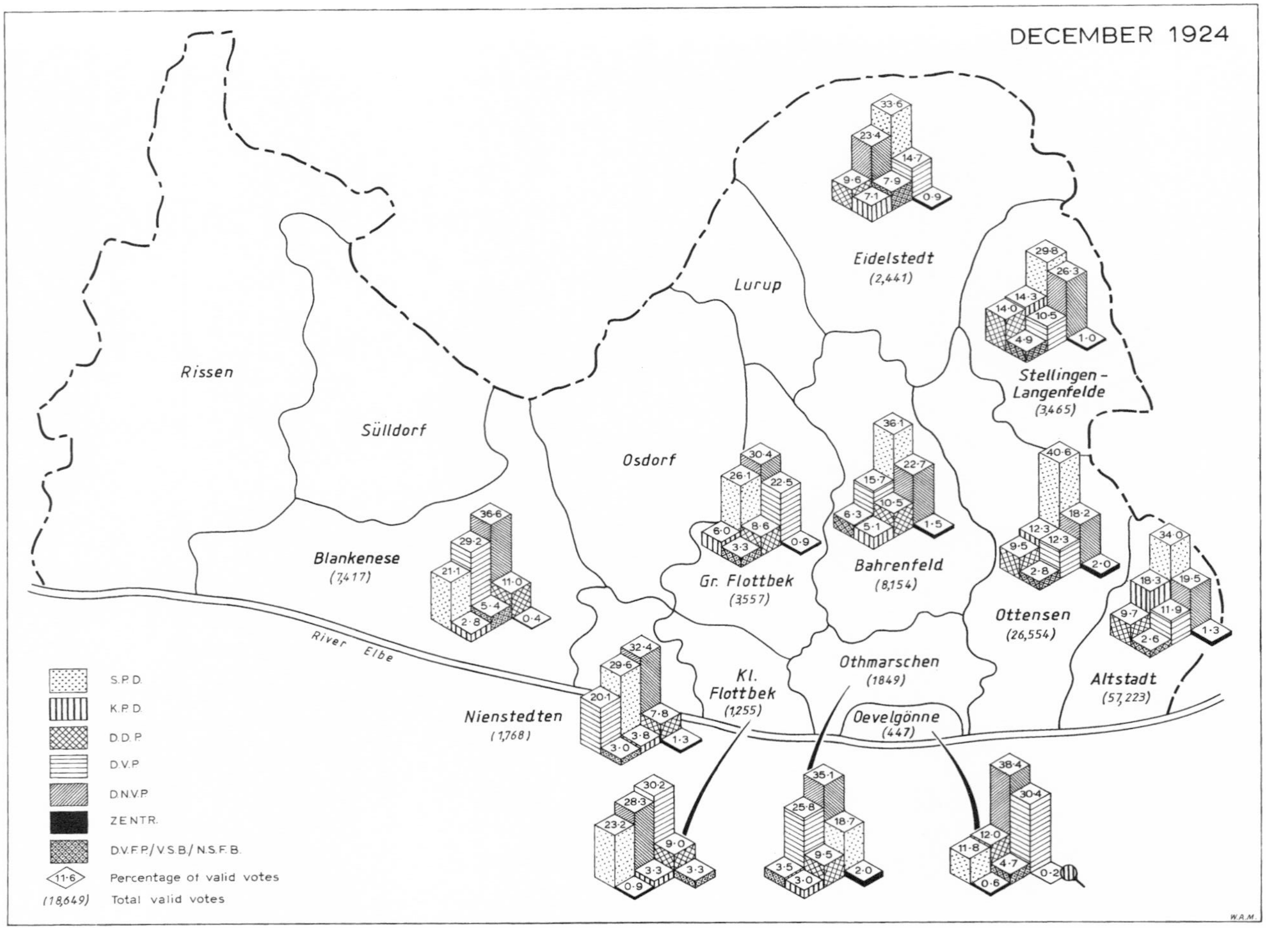

DECEMBER 1924

Map 1b.   Voting patterns in Altona: Reichstag election, December 1924

Legend:
S.P.D.
K.P.D.
D.D.P.
D.V.P.
D.N.V.P.
ZENTR.
DVFP/VSB/NSFB

⟨11·6⟩ Percentage of valid votes
⟨18,649⟩ Total valid votes

Regions shown:
Rissen
Sülldorf
Blankenese (7,417)
River Elbe
Osdorf
Lurup
Eidelstedt (2,441)
Stellingen-Langenfelde (3,465)
Bahrenfeld (8,154)
Gr. Flottbek (3,557)
Nienstedten (1,768)
Kl. Flottbek (1,255)
Othmarschen (1,849)
Oevelgönne (447)
Ottensen (26,554)
Altstadt (57,223)

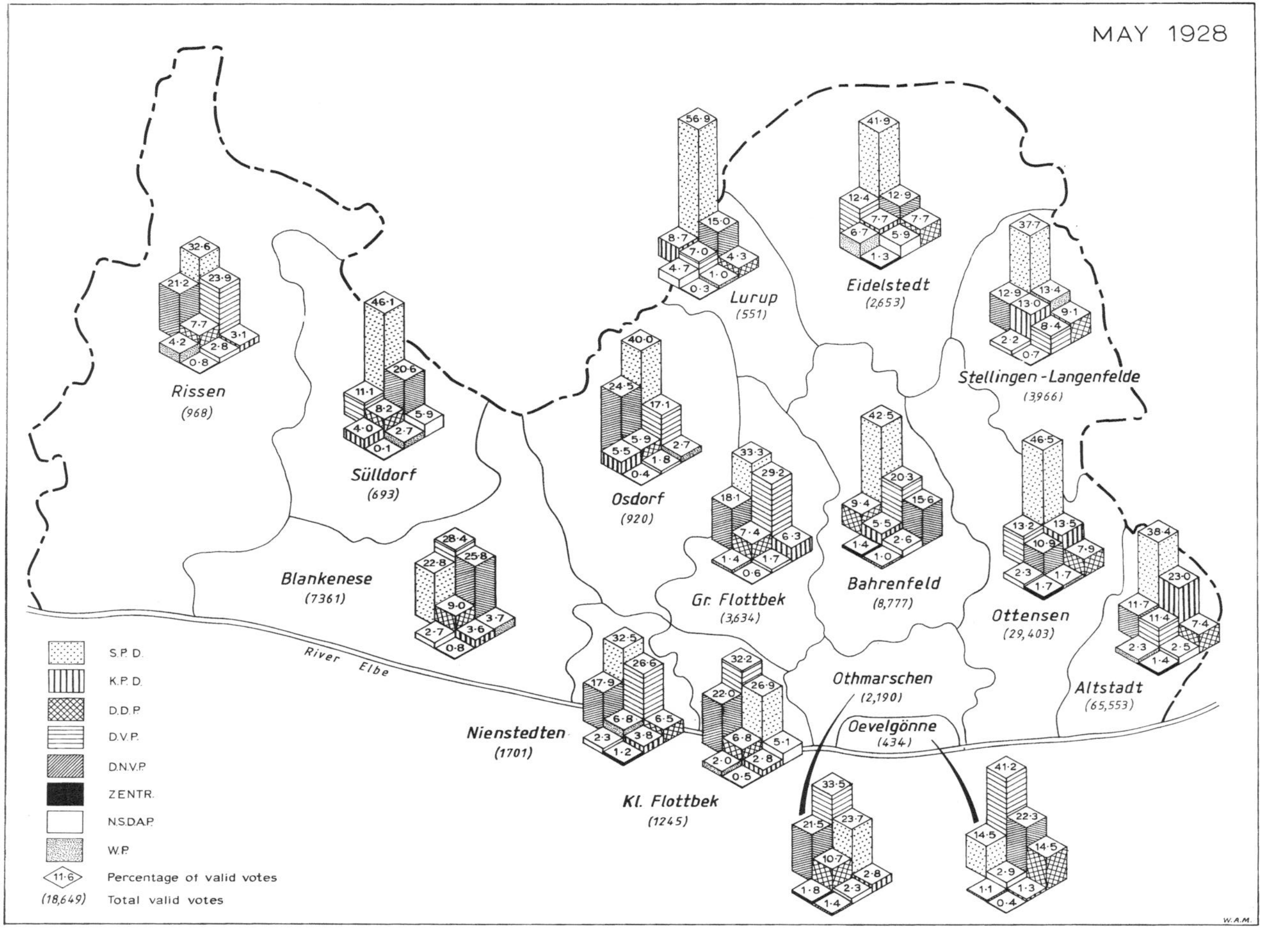

Stellingen - Langenfelde
(3966)

Ottensen
(29,403)

Altstadt
(65,553)

Eidelstedt
(2653)

Bahrenfeld
(8,777)

Othmarschen
(12,190)

Develgönne
(434)

Lurup
(551)

Gr. Flottbek
(3,634)

Osdorf
(920)

Kl. Flottbek
(1245)

Nienstedten
(1701)

Süldorf
(693)

Blankenese
(7361)

River Elbe

Rissen
(968)

W.A.M.

S.P.D.
K.P.D.
D.D.P.
D.V.P.
D.N.V.P.
ZENTR.
N.S.D.A.P.
W.P.

11·6   Percentage of valid votes
(18,649)   Total valid votes

Map 1c.   Voting patterns in Altona: Reichstag election, May 1928

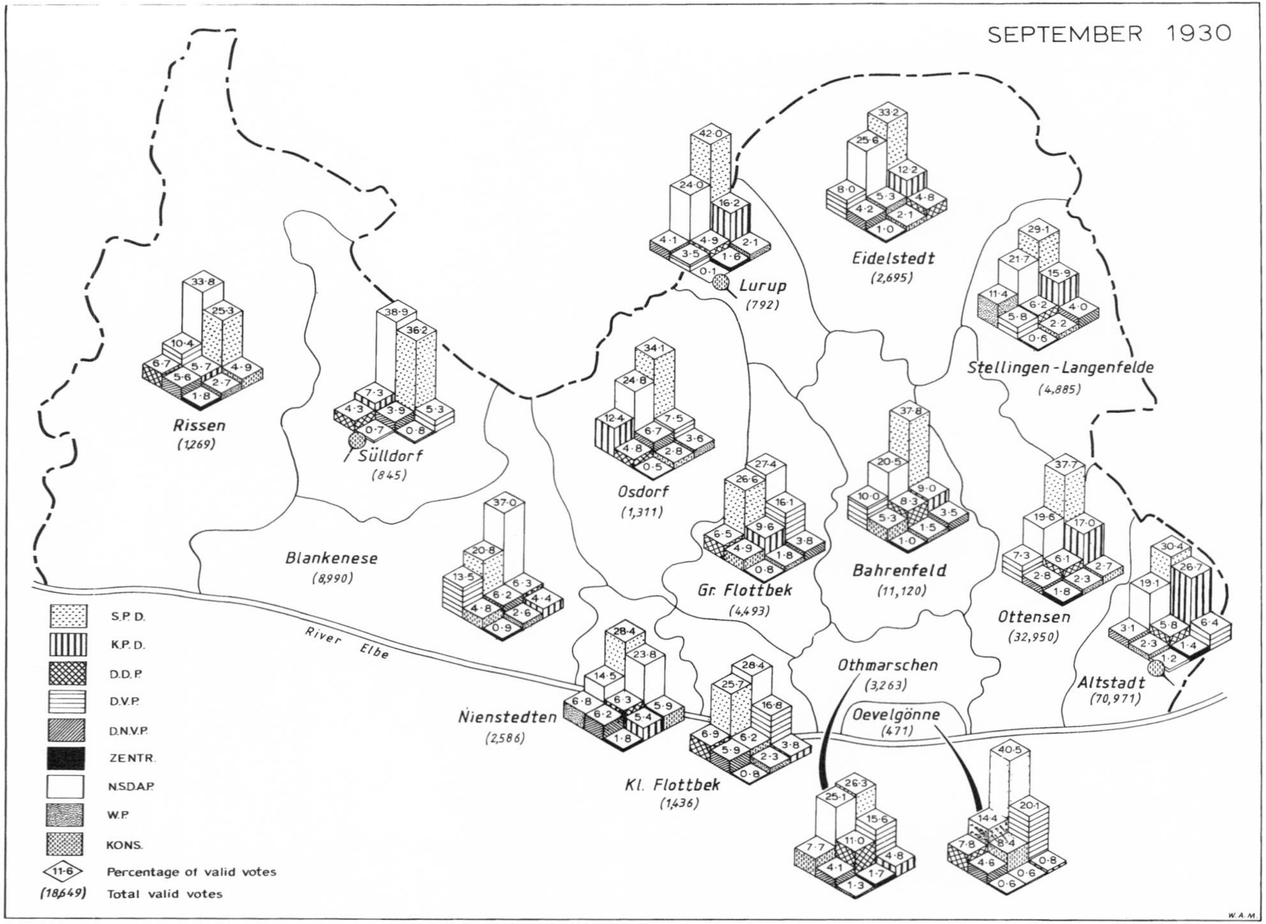
SEPTEMBER 1930
Rissen
(1,269)
Süldorf
(845)
Blankenese
(8,990)
River Elbe
Nienstedten
(2,586)
Osdorf
(1,311)
Lurup
(792)
Eidelstedt
(2,695)
Stellingen-Langenfelde
(4,885)
Gr. Flottbek
(4,493)
Kl. Flottbek
(1,436)
Bahrenfeld
(11,120)
Othmarschen
(3,263)
Oevelgönne
(471)
Ottensen
(32,950)
Altstadt
(70,971)
S.P.D.
K.P.D.
D.D.P.
D.V.P.
D.N.V.P.
ZENTR.
NSDAP
W.P.
KONS.
11·6 Percentage of valid votes
(18,649) Total valid votes
W.A.M.

Map 1d. Voting patterns in Altona: Reichstag election, September 1930

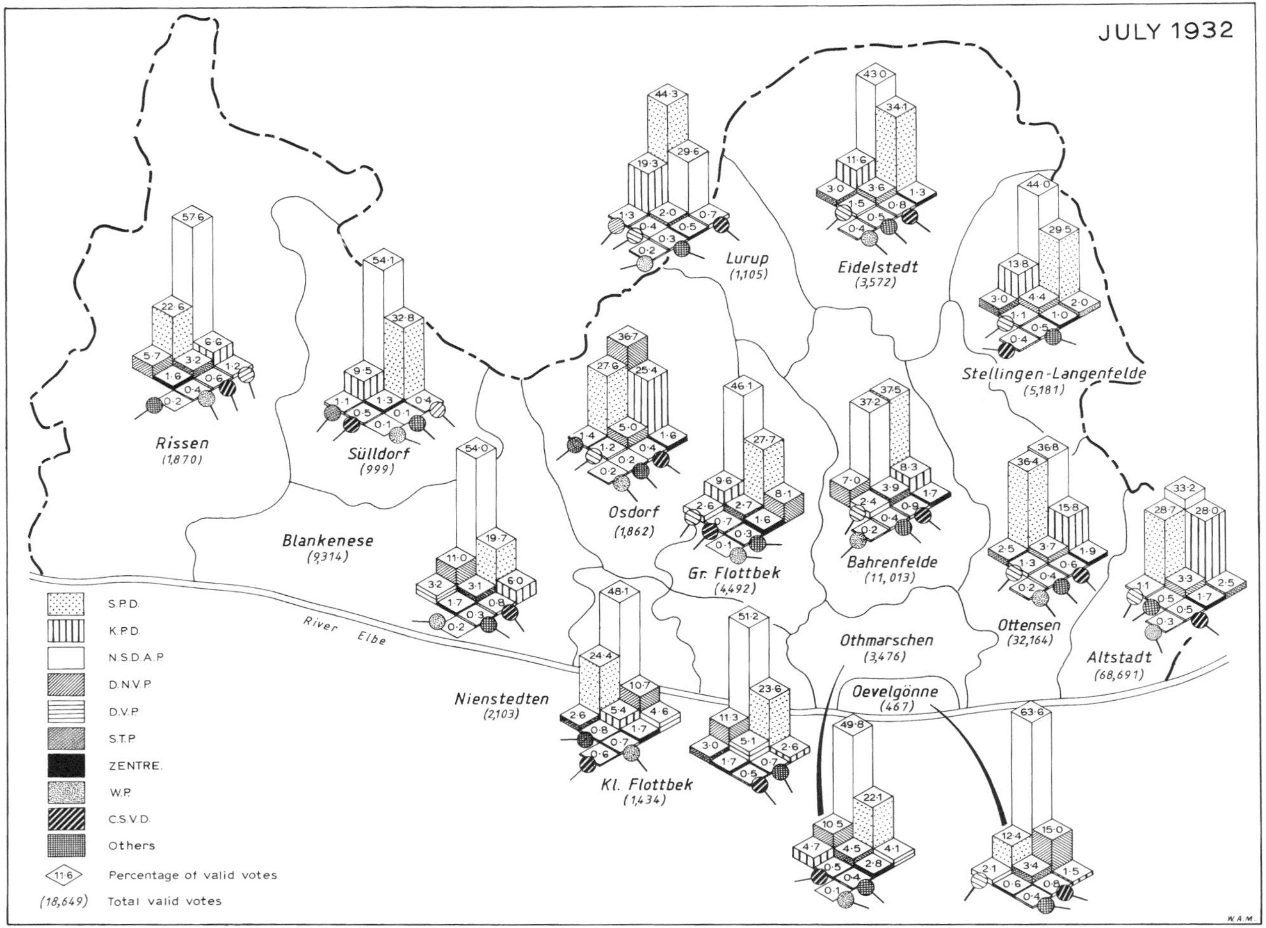

Map 1e. Voting patterns in Altona: Reichstag election, July 1932

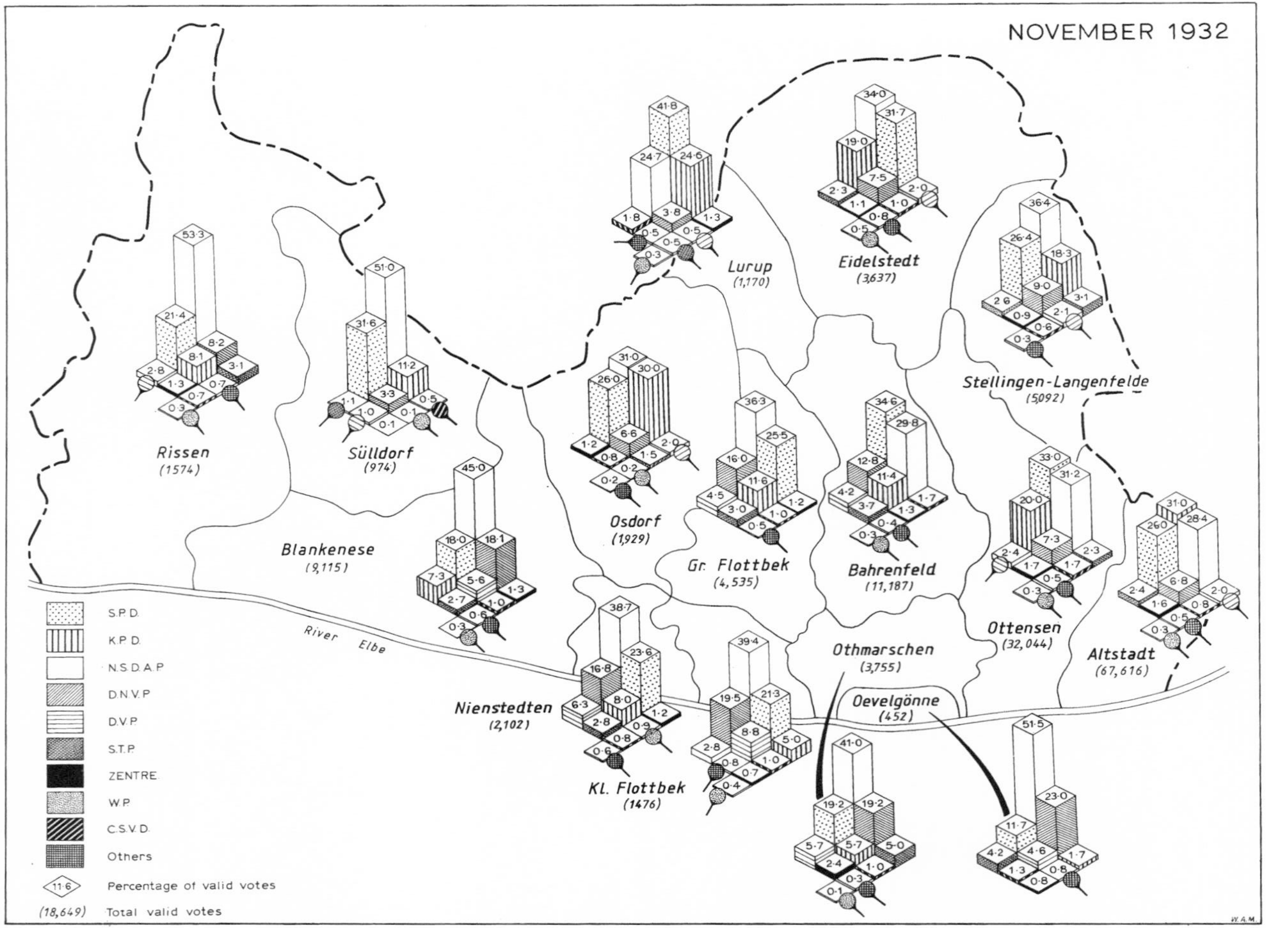

NOVEMBER 1932

Stellingen-Langenfelde
(5092)

Altstadt
(67,616)

Ottensen
(32,044)

Othmarschen
(3,755)

Oevelgönne
(452)

Eidelstedt
(3637)

Bahrenfeld
(11,187)

Lurup
(1,170)

Gr. Flottbek
(4,535)

Osdorf
(1929)

Kl. Flottbek
(1476)

Nienstedten
(2,102)

Sülldorf
(974)

Blankenese
(8,115)

River Elbe

Rissen
(1574)

SPD
KPD
NSDAP
DNVP
DVP
STP
ZENTRE
WP
CSVD
Others

(11·6) Percentage of valid votes

(18,649) Total valid votes

Map 1f. Voting patterns in Altona: Reichstag election, November 1932

1912, of the thirty-five councillors duly chosen, eight belonged to the *Mittelstand* of petty commerce and artisanal trades, five were lawyers, five were rentiers, four were manufacturers, and four were merchants (*Kaufleute*). Another four were described as "full-time" politicians (*Berufspolitiker*). The remaining five were Social Democrats.

In the quarter century before 1914 support for the Social Democrats in Altona had seemed unwavering. In every Reichstag election from 1874 their candidates, Wilhelm Hasenclever and Carl Frohme, won a share of the vote that far outstripped that of their middle-class rivals.[7] By the late 1880s Altona stood alongside Hamburg as one of the foremost centers of social democracy in the reich. And it remained unsurpassed in Prussia as a Social Democratic stronghold.[8] A city councillor, Louise Schroeder, became a Reichstag deputy during the 1920s, and from 1930, she was joined by the city's Social Democrat police president, Otto Eggerstedt. The head of the province, the *Oberpräsident,* was also a former councillor from Altona.[9]

By the turn of the century the threat of an ever-increasing number of Socialists in Altona's *Rathaus* was cause for deep concern among middle-class circles. Before the party's breakthrough in Altona in 1909, the ultra-conservative deputy mayor, Dr. Franz Schulz, had urged his colleagues to support the proposal to raise the qualification threshold of the electoral bands in order to prevent more "working-class rowdies" from getting elected.[10] In spite of this, five socialists were elected in 1909, followed by a further five shortly before the outbreak of war in 1914. The war radically transformed the social and political composition of the council. By its end barely a third of the councillors elected before 1912 still held a seat in the chamber. Shortly before the municipal elections in 1919 there were thus eleven Social Democrat councillors, while the remainder were mostly drawn from the city's professional and manufacturing middle classes. The traditional *Mittelstand* was less well represented.[11]

Though the council was thus modified, until the events of November 1918 the social and political hegemony of Altona's middle classes remained unbroken. During the war the attempt to forge a united home front, the so-called *Burgfrieden,* had cemented the pre-1914 collaboration between Social Democrats and progressive liberals on social issues. For instance, two Social Democrats sat on the important ten-man central commission administering welfare support (*Familienkriegsunterstützung*) to families whose male breadwinners were either at the front or killed.[12] Similarly, Socialists were represented on the rationing and price commissions, ensuring that the poorer members of Altona's working class were fairly treated as consumers within the wartime distribution system.[13]

Collaboration with the SPD was by no means universally welcomed by Altona's middle class, including Lord Mayor Schnackenburg, who did everything in his power to resist the forward march of the Social Democrats. Indeed, the inclusion of the SPD in the local administration contributed to the fissuring of the Wilhelmine *Bürger* bloc and ultimately led to a new configuration in local politics that provided the basis for the future Weimar coalition in Altona. By the summer of 1918 Altona's middle classes had split decisively into conservative and liberal groupings, with liberals and Socialists moving closer to each other. For instance, the liberal councillor Dr. Goerlitz was elected senator to the executive body, the *Magistrat,* in July with the support of Socialist councillors as quid pro quo for liberal support for the SPD senatorial candidate, fifty-three-year-old Hermann Thomas.[14]

The decisive challenge to middle-class control over public affairs came in the critical days of unrest and revolution in late 1918, when, as elsewhere, Socialist leaders in Altona found the responsibility of government thrust upon them.[15] By the late autumn of 1918 the political and social situation in the city was rapidly and visibly deteriorating. In October 1918 Oberbürgermeister Schnackenburg called upon members of the city administration to remain calm at their posts in order to avert a total collapse of law and order.[16] Within a month, however, Altona was in the grip of political revolution and faced the threat of social anarchy as military and police forces initially capitulated to the crowds on the streets. The commanding officer of the local army post, together with his staff, fled the city. The chief of police was nowhere to be found. And Bürgermeister Dr. Schulz, who was widely despised by Altona's working class, went into hiding too. Meanwhile, Oberbürgermeister Schnackenburg lay in bed with influenza.[17]

Crowds of civilians and soldiers—in "a blind rage," according to middle-class observers—took control of the streets on 4 and 5 November. Weapons were stolen from district police stations and used to besiege police headquarters and the courts, from which prisoners were freed. On 6 November a Workers' and Soldiers' Council was formed and the red flag raised over Altona. Oberbürgermeister Schnackenburg was later described as having been "extremely depressed by the situation," and his mental and physical health seemed to collapse with the empire.[18] With the leading forces of the ancien régime either gone or paralyzed, the Social Democrats Sievert, Kirch, Thomas, and Brauer saw to it that the Workers' and Soldiers' Council ensured law and order in the city.[19]

Schnackenburg had fiercely resisted the election of Hermann Thomas to the *Magistrat* in July. Nonetheless, he was a pragmatic and experienced politician and recognized that the days of *Honoratioren* politics were over. He therefore sought an accommodation with the Socialists. A full month before the revolutionary events in Altona, Schnackenburg had spoken of the necessity for "closer contact" with the SPD, no doubt in the hope of averting an escalation of unrest in the city.[20] For their part the Social Democrat leaders were equally keen to ensure that the political rupture did not lead to the total collapse of social order. After quickly occupying key positions on the Greater Hamburg–Altona Workers' and Soldiers' Council from the end of 1918, they set about recovering what they could from the wreckage of the Wilhelmine administration.[21] Schnackenburg remained in office (though he was temporarily seconded to West Prussia between May and September 1919). His continuing tenure of the mayoral office thus offered Altona's middle classes some reassurance that parts of the old civic house might be salvaged.[22]

The upheaval of 1918 brought about a change in the leadership of the city that on first viewing might appear limited but, nonetheless, went deeper than is sometimes recognized by historians.[23] As a consequence of pressure from the SPD, four more Social Democrats were co-opted as ex officio members of the *Magistrat* in mid-November 1918. They were Carl Stoll, Wilhelm Sievert, August Kirch, who was not yet forty years old, and Max Brauer, who at thirty-one symbolized the shift toward a younger political generation. At the same time, council representatives of the new political parties were brought into the meetings of the *Magistrat* for the first time. This act of democratizing the decision-making processes of city government destroyed the last vestiges of *Honoratioren* politics in Altona.[24]

The *Magistrat* consisted of eleven members, including the *Oberbürgermeister* and his deputy, all of whom were elected. Apart from Oberbürgermeister Schnackenburg, who, according to Hoffmann, now aligned himself with the Democrats, only three full-time senators of the prewar *Magistrat* remained. Unlike Schnackenburg, the unloved Bürgermeister Dr. Schulz was unable to reconcile himself to sharing power with Social Democrat "rowdies" and, after bitter exchanges, was forced to resign his post on 1 April 1919.[25] This left the senators Dr. Heydemann, who now deputized for the departed Schulz, Friedrich Schöning (DDP), and the conservative Dr. Wilhelm Harbeck, who was also father of the house (*Dienstälteste*). Schöning and Harbeck retained their prewar portfolios of welfare and municipal personnel and administration, respectively. Three lay senators, Kaufmann Theodor Hampe and Kaufmann Friedrich Marlow and the privatier Emil Groth, survived the early elections and so too provided a link to the prerevolutionary period until the mid-1920s.[26]

In the course of 1919 the Social Democrat's position on the *Magistrat* steadily strengthened, undergoing a process of normalization and professionalization. Thus, Kirch replaced Heydemann, who left to become mayor of Rostock in May 1919, and Brauer took over from Schulz as Bürgermeister and city treasurer in November. And, when Senator Goerlitz became mayor of Oldenburg in 1921, he was replaced in August by another Social Democrat, revolutionary Hamburg's former *Stadtkommandant* and a lawyer by training, Dr. Walther Lamp'l. Meanwhile, among the lay senators Thomas was joined by two more party comrades as a result of the *Magistrat* elections in October 1919.[27]

After further elections in June 1924 the *Magistrat* became even more "politicized."[28] A Communist, thirty-eight-year-old electrician Johannes Köhnsen, was elected honorary senator. Paralleling this breakthrough by the radical Left, a representative of the *völkisch* anti-Semitic Right, Rudolf Sube, a functionary of the right-wing German National Commercial Employee's Association (DHV), was also elected.[29] Their presence, however, did little to hamper the SPD, which was able to rely upon the support of the liberals—an enduring cooperation that was based as much on pragmatism as on good personal links.[30]

The position of the Social Democrat senators was strengthened by the first postwar municipal election on 2 March 1919, based on a free universal suffrage for men and women over the age of twenty. Just over half of the previous council was returned, mostly Social Democrats, unlike many of their middle-class protagonists.[31] Nearly 54 percent of votes cast were for the Socialists, thereby doubling the SPD *Fraktion* to thirty-six, in an enlarged chamber of sixty-six.[32] And their influence was further underpinned by their virtual control of the city's sixty-two subcommittees, which discussed and prepared economic and social policy.[33] Viewed from this perspective, it is understandable that the representatives of middle-

TABLE 2.   Composition of the Magistrat by Political Party, 1918–29

	SPD	DDP	DVP	KPD	BÜRG	NS[a]	Total
1918	1[b]	2[c]	—	—	8[d]	—	11
1919–23	6	3	—	—	3	—	12[e]
1924–26	5	3	—	1	2	1	12
1927–28	5	3	1	1	2	—	12
1929	5	3	1	1	2	—	12

Source: Compiled from StJü Altona (1923), 52, and (1924), 47–48; StJB Altona (1928), 102. Paul-Theodor Hoffman, *Neues Altona,* vol. 1 (Altona, 1929), 40, 44–46.

[a]Völkisch/NSDAP

[b]Plus three exofficio commissars

[c]Includes one co-opted member

[d]Includes two co-opted members

[e]The number of honorary senators was increased to six in an amendment to the city constitution on 14 August 1919.

class interests in Altona felt aggrieved at their loss of influence over the *Rathaus.* Their attempts to break the SPD's grip on the council often proved futile, as we shall see. Indeed, Altona remained one of the few major cities of the Weimar Republic to remain under Socialist control until 1933.

When the new council met for the first time on the 13 March 1919, there was a clear Left majority and an overwhelming one for the Weimar coalition of SPD and DDP, as we can see from table 3. The six Independent Socialist (USPD) councillors, led by the lawyer Dr. Herz, emerged as the SPD's political conscience on the council, while the ten bourgeois councillors already bared their teeth in opposition.[34]

The municipal elections in Altona on 4 May 1924, saw the number of SPD councillors halved from thirty-six to eighteen, thereby reducing their share of seats from over half to a third. This decline mirrored a general trend in towns and cities throughout Prussia, where an absolute and relative decline in the number of Social Democrat councillors from around a third to a fifth took place.[35] The SPD in Altona was able to recoup part of this loss in 1927, but its Achilles' heel was surely the DDP, which suffered

TABLE 3.   **Municipal Elections in Altona, 1919–33 (percentage of valid votes[a])**

Party	1919	1924	1927	1929	1933
SPD	54	33	38	39	25
USPD	9	1	—	—	—
KPD	—	19	17	15	19
DDP/StP	22	12	6	6	2
DVP	11	—	9	—	8
DNVP[b]	3	—	8	—	—
NSDAP	—	9	2	6	43
Center	—	—	1	2	2
WP[c]	—	—	—	6	—
EL/BG[d]	—	23	—	25	—
GL	—	—	15	—	—
WB	—	4	—	—	—
SPL[f]	—	—	5	1	1

Source: Compiled from relevant volumes of StDR, StJü Altona (1923, 1924), StJb Altona (1928), and from relevant volumes of *Amtsblatt der Stadt Altona.*

Note: Percentage of eligible voters who participated in elections are 1919 = 52%; 1924 = 66%; 1927 = 71%; 1929 = 71%; 1933 = 87%.

[a]Percentages are rounded

[b]1933: Kampffront Schwarz-Weiß-Rot

[c]Wirtschaftspartei

[d]Includes the DVP and DNVP on a joint list

[e]Gemeinschaftsliste des Zentralausschusses d. Kommunalen Vereins

[f]Splinter parties: Aufwertungspartei, Volksrechtspartei, Konservative Volkspartei, Christlich-sozialer Volksdienst

permanent stagnation from the mid-1920s, when the number of its councillors was halved. This meant that, in spite of the deep and sometimes bitter differences, the SPD had to rely on the toleration of either the Communists, who formed the second largest group on the council (excluding
the so-called nonparty Einheitslist), or on the shifting and volatile inclina-
tions of individual bourgeois councillors on particular issues.

Universal suffrage also meant, at least in theory, that for the first time
women could break free from the political shadow of their menfolk. Along
with those women already active in local life via the SPD's ancillary organizations or the patriotic associations or attached to the mainly conservative "apolitical" 783-strong *Hausfrauverein,* some became more visibly
active in municipal politics.[36] The elections in Altona in 1919 returned
eight women out of sixty-six councillors to the city council. Although this
appears to be a rather low figure, Altona had a higher proportion of
women among its city councillors than the average for cities of its size (8.7
percent). Even the hostile conditions of March 1933 could not prevent the
election of five women, including two Communists (who were promptly
removed and taken into "protective custody."[37]

TABLE 4.   **Distribution of Seats in Altona City Council, 1919–33 (municipal elections)**

Party	1919	1924	1927	1929	1933
SPD	36	18	26	25	16
KPD	—	10	11	9	8
USPD	6	—	—	—	—
DDP/StP	14	7	3	4	—
Center	—	—	—	—	1
DVP	—	—	5	—	—
DNVP	—	—	5	—	6
BG[a]	10	—	—	16	—
WP[b]	—	2	1	4	—
GL[c]	—	—	9	—	—
EL[d]	—	13	—	—	—
NSDAP	—	5[e]	1	3	30
Total	66	55	61	61	61

Source: Hoffmann, Neues Altona, 50; StJbDS 23 (1928); Mitteilungen des Deutschen Städtetages 11,
no. 9 (1924): cols. 123–24; *Statistische Vierteljahresberichte des Deutschen Städtetages* 2 no. 4 (Dec. 1929):
196.
[a]Bürgerliche Geminschaftsliste (= DVP and DNVP)
[b]Wirtschaftspartei
[c]Gemeinschaftsliste des Zentralausschusses d. Kommunalen Vereins
[d]Einheitsliste
[e]1924, Völkisch-Sozialer-Block.

Some of the women elected in 1919 and 1924 served continuous terms as city councillors. For instance, Dorothea Meyer of the SPD remained a member of the city council between 1919 and March 1933. Her two party colleagues, Marie Deppe and Magda von Hollen, served from 1927 to 1933. Communist councillors appear to have served shorter periods. The opportunities for sexual equality in politics, though limited, were also, until 1933, seized by bourgeois women. The second longest-serving woman on the council was Elisabeth Cimbal (b. 1884), who was elected in May 1924 and remained on the council until the advent of the Nazis (she was primarily a member of the DVP but also a unity list candidate in 1924 and 1929; in 1933 she headed the Unpolitische Frauenliste). Dr. Emilie Kiep-Altenloh served between 1929 and 1932 for the DDP. Kiep-Altenloh and Louise Schroeder (SPD) became members of the Reichstag, and Schroeder was the first woman to serve as a deputy mayor of Berlin after 1945.[38]

But there were limits to political equality, and these become clearer on examination of the public roles assigned to women in Altona. They were not represented in the *Magistrat* and were also grossly underrepresented on the city's powerful subcommittees. Of the total voting membership of 610 (co-opted members could not vote) in 1928, only thirty-seven were women (or roughly 6 percent). Also, a closer look at the composition of the subcommittees reveals a predictable gendered fault line, with women absent from the commissions dealing with financial matters, municipal boundaries, real estate, construction, and the economy, but they were overrepresented on those addressing family-related problems of health and welfare, pensions, and educational matters. This weighting toward "traditional" female roles was reflected in the city administration, in which few women rose to senior posts. In the mid-1920s the city administration had a personnel of just over three thousand, of which a third were female. Barely 2.5 percent were in the category of civil servant (*Beamte*), compared with a third of males. Instead, they occupied mostly subaltern positions, and the overwhelming majority of female employees was to be found in health and primary education and, to some extent, in welfare.[39]

The Working-Class Parties

In spite of the overwhelming popular support for the SPD at the polls in Altona, party membership was actually stagnating. Between 1900 and the outbreak of war membership had doubled to around fourteen thousand. That was still 10 percent of the prewar population, but it then came to a standstill thereafter. By the early 1920s the party was failing to renew itself, notably because of its lackluster appeal among German youth.

Indeed, SPD councillors by the mid-1920s were largely characterized by early middle age, in keeping with the general age profile of the council.[40]

Party membership in Altona was drawn predominantly from the skilled working class and from among petty craft trades and minor professions. Barely a third of members hailed from the un- and semiskilled manual trades. For instance, the party's 1910–11 annual report listed over seventy-five occupations. It showed that of the seventy-two hundred members in Altona-Altstadt over two-thirds were in highly skilled, professional, and independent trades, whereas less than a third of this group was composed of unskilled workers. The leadership in Altona reflected faithfully its skilled and professional rank and file. For instance, Heinrich Thomas, August Kirch, Max Brauer, and Max Behrens were mostly skilled manual workers (printer, glassblower, and factory hand) who also had been employed by the trade union movement. Other leading municipal functionaries, such as Rudolf Katz, Paul Bugdahn, Carl Zanker, and Robert Berendsohn, were either professionals or self-employed businessmen.[41]

While female activists were often described as housewives, there were notable exceptions, such as Louise Schroeder, who was a welfare worker and writer, and Magda von Hollen, a clerical employee.[42] This genus of social respectability dominated the party's council election lists throughout the 1920s and was underlined by residential patterns. For instance, at the municipal elections in 1924, 71 percent of the party's forty-five candidates lived in Ottensen, Bahrenfeld, and Othmarschen, whereas barely a third lived in the Altstadt. Only two candidates from the Altstadt were placed within the first twenty; the rest had to make do with places lower down the list.[43]

The preference given to candidates from the "respectable" working-class districts ignored the party's excellent voting tradition in the "slum" quarters of the Altstadt. Before the war, for instance, subdistricts 9 through 11, 14 through 16, and 18, in the heart of the Altstadt, had been *the* key strongholds of the SPD in Altona, where before 1914 the party could expect between 80 and 90 percent of the vote. These districts remained strongholds of the Left during the 1920s but with the difference that the KPD was either on the heels or neck and neck or had overtaken the SPD as the main political choice. It appears that the Social Democrats too easily gave up the claim to leadership in parts of the Altstadt. In particular, the neighborhoods incorporating Adolf-, Annen-, Christian-, Denner- and Marienstraße in subdistrict 10 (election ward 21) had become, by the early 1920s, staunchly communist. Here the KPD gained its best election results, earning the district the reputation of a "little Moscow." Thus, by the mid-1920s the undisputed strongholds of the SPD were either in Ottensen or had shifted from the inner city to the newer housing areas, such as the model settlement of Steenkamp, where its vote remained steady at around 43 percent between 1924 and 1932.[44]

In its efforts to demarcate itself from the Social Democrats, the KPD claimed that it alone was a bona fide proletarian party. Many of its activists were metalworkers who worked in the shipyards or as casual laborers in the docks. Many of them, like most of the work force from the Vulkan shipyard, lived in the run-down quarters of the Altstadt.[45] Information on the size and makeup of the Communist Party in Altona during the 1920s is sparse. In March 1921 card membership was estimated by the police to be around seventy-six hundred, marshaled into five districts. The Communist *movement,* however, was clearly much larger, ranging from a number of small sects to mass shop floor movements, such as the Communist-influenced anarchosyndicalist General Workers' Union (AUU), which numbered several thousands.[46]

But, in spite of its efforts to establish itself as a proletarian party, the occupational and social composition of the KPD's local activists, as far as its electoral lists show, was not unlike that of the SPD: the proportion of manual workers was in steady decline in the mid-years of the 1920s, whereas employees were increasing. The corps of political candidates in Altona is thus roughly congruent with that for the party nationally. A survey of 89 percent of the national membership in 1928 showed that nearly 74 percent had manual occupations, whereas only 8.3 percent were employed in nonmanual occupations or were self-employed.[47] Indeed, judging from the data presented here, the leadership in Altona appears to have been developing toward a greater balance in terms of occupation and gender as the 1920s drew to a close. For instance, of the ten candidates elected to the council in 1924 six were skilled workers, two were employees, and two were housewives; of the eleven elected in 1927 five were skilled workers, one was unskilled, and, among the others, there was a butcher, a small trader, an employee, a journalist, and a widow. In 1929 there were three skilled and two unskilled workers, the same small trader as in 1927, and three women candidates, a widow, a housewife, and a cleaner.[48]

The KPD's hesitant start nationally meant that it was unable to participate in Altona's first municipal elections in March 1919. As a result of the merger with the USPD in 1921, however, it immediately gained six seats in the council chamber. This number increased to ten in 1924, peaked at eleven in 1927, only to fall after 1929, at a time when grassroots support was on the increase.[49] The party's role in municipal politics was primarily an agitatory one. Some indication of the importance attached to this function is revealed by the fact a third of the regional budget of 279,890 reichsmark for 1927–28 went to agitation and propaganda, much of this arising from extensive municipal work in an effort to increase the number of councillors.[50]

In its parliamentary guidelines published in 1924 the Central Committee in Berlin expressed the view that "every communist councillor is not a maker of law, [but] an agitator of the Party who has been sent into the enemy camp."[51] Once there a councillor was supposed to hold out to the masses an alternative vision of a "people's state" (*Volksstaat*) by pointing to the failures and inadequacies of the present system, the product of a thwarted revolution. The leadership therefore warned against "unnecessary and uncritical co-operation" with the SPD, which it regarded as not a genuine workers' party.[52]

Nevertheless, the dogma of ideological purity did not preclude collaboration in Altona whenever a common cause could be identified. For the Communists, in spite of allegedly being in the habit of discharging an "unending stream of propaganda speeches" and of "foaming at the mouth," could also play a more pragmatic part in the council when called upon to do so, especially under a succession of leaders such as Wilhelm Reimers, Karl Rokohl, and John Schehr.[53]

In spite of its public image, the KPD was not a revolutionary party. In Altona its reputation as an insurgent party was largely due to its close association with particular quarters of the city, particularly in the Altstadt, where the *Lumpenproletariat* were said to lead disorderly and ungovernable lives (see chap. 3).[54] An early sign of the KPD's appeal among the residents of the Altstadt came during the Reichstag election in February 1921. The party won more than nine thousand votes, about 11 percent of the total, and two-thirds of these were gained in the Altstadt.[55] The gap between the KPD's citywide support and that in the Altstadt remained after this date and even grew wider throughout the period.

Support for the KPD in the Altstadt was not just a consequence of political volatility. High levels were registered in the good times as well as bad, suggesting a deeper relationship than simply a cynical manipulation of material distress.[56] For example, at the Reichstag elections in 1928, it took 23 percent of the vote in the Altstadt, compared with around 16.3 percent citywide. More striking was the continuous high level of support it gained within particular wards of the Altstadt, thus reinforcing the impression of a ghettoization of the party's appeal, as maps 2a–f demonstrate.

These exceptionally stable pockets of support for the Communists can perhaps be explained by what the contemporary Italian theorist Antonio Gramsci referred to as the organic relationship between party and base. For instance, nearly 80 percent of the party's forty-nine candidates in 1924 hailed from the same Altstadt neighborhoods with the highest level

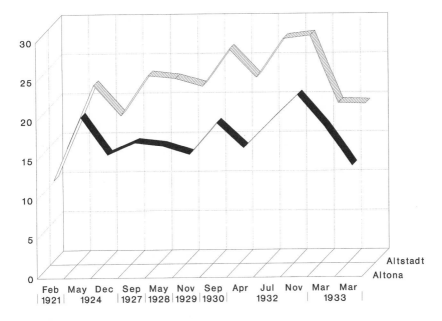

Fig. 1.   KPD votes in Altona and Altstadt, 1921–33

of votes.[57] Before 1927 the party did not even field candidates in the suburbs of Nienstedten, Eidelstedt, Klein Flottbek, Rissen, and Lurup. The
latter district eventually became a bastion of the KPD, after large numbers
of mostly unemployed persons and their families had moved onto allot-
ments in so-called wild settlements during the Depression, becoming, after
1933, the focus for an underground network of resistance.[58] Like the SPD,
Communists came from the milieux over which they claimed leadership.

The Fragmented Middle: Personalities and Politics

Before the war the DDP's forerunner, the Freisinnige Volkspartei, had
been the major platform of the middle classes in Altona, drawing over a
quarter of the votes in the 1907 and 1912 elections.[59] The new Deutsche
Demokratische Partei was able to retain its predecessor's prewar vote level
at the election for the National Assembly. But, as we saw, its share of the
vote in Altona collapsed to 10 percent during the Reichstag elections in
February 1921. It hovered at that level in 1924, fell again at the municipal
elections of 1927 and 1929, recovered slightly in 1928, and practically disappeared thereafter. Its position became so bleak that, at the municipal
elections in March 1933, it joined with the Center Party on a single ticket

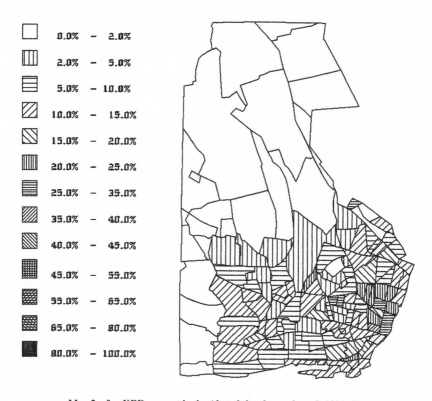

□	0.0% – 2.0%
⊞	2.0% – 5.0%
⊟	5.0% – 10.0%
▨	10.0% – 15.0%
◩	15.0% – 20.0%
▥	20.0% – 25.0%
▤	25.0% – 35.0%
▨	35.0% – 40.0%
▧	40.0% – 45.0%
▦	45.0% – 55.0%
▩	55.0% – 65.0%
▩	65.0% – 80.0%
■	80.0% – 100.0%

Map 2a–f.   KPD support in the Altstadt by electoral ward, 1921–32
Map 2a.   1921

in the hope of getting votes.[60] In March 1933 it failed to get into the chamber, which would have been futile anyway. Its dismal performance generally was attributed to the sharpening of class conflict since the war, and its attempt to redefine itself by swinging to the Right in 1930 came too late and proved to be ineffectual. In Altona the DDP was too closely associated with the alleged municipal malaise, and the nationalist press even accused it of class betrayal.[61]

Nonetheless, in spite of its electoral catastrophe, the DDP did comparatively well in Altona when measured against other Prussian municipalities. After the local elections in 1919 it had an impressive fourteen seats in the council. And, even though this was halved after the municipal elections in 1924 and again in 1927, its share of council seats in 1929 was 6.5 percent, or three times that for Prussian cities of a similar size. As with the other parties in Altona, the DDP had its liberal enclaves in the city. For

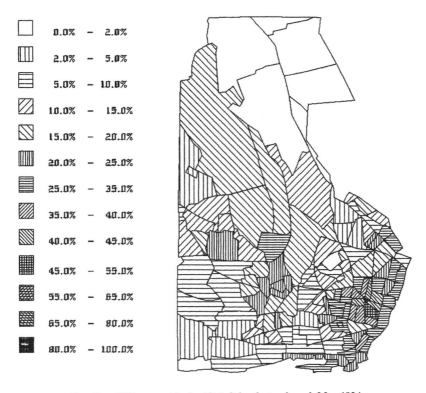

☐	0.0% – 2.0%
▦	2.0% – 5.0%
▤	5.0% – 10.0%
▨	10.0% – 15.0%
▨	15.0% – 20.0%
▥	20.0% – 25.0%
▤	25.0% – 35.0%
▨	35.0% – 40.0%
▨	40.0% – 45.0%
▦	45.0% – 55.0%
▩	55.0% – 65.0%
▩	65.0% – 80.0%
▰	80.0% – 100.0%

Map 2b.   KPD support in the Altstadt by electoral ward, May 1924

instance, in the model housing suburb of Steenkamp, its vote remained fairly steady at around 9 percent until 1932 and then declined less rapidly than in other districts, where its collapse came earlier and was more catastrophic.[62]

The émigré political scientist Sigmund Neumann has described the DVP as "liberal but not democratic."[63] Its idea of self-government was molded by the nineteenth-century experience of the German *Bildungsbürgertum.* Certainly, its program, published in 1919, mingled progressive social ideals with conservative, indeed revanchist, political aims, such as the return of the emperor and the restoration of the old reich colors. But, while the party propagated "a strongly anchored state, supported . . . finally . . . by unavoidable means of power," it also firmly believed in "extensive self-government . . . at all levels of public life."[64] Embedded in the ideology of the corporate state, Altona's DVP set out its municipal

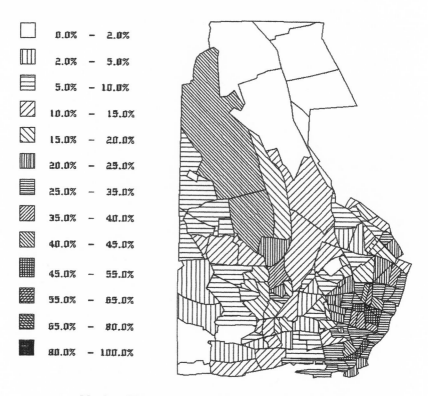

☐   0.0% – 2.0%

▥   2.0% – 5.0%

▤   5.0% – 10.0%

▨   10.0% – 15.0%

◨   15.0% – 20.0%

▥   20.0% – 25.0%

▤   25.0% – 35.0%

▨   35.0% – 40.0%

◨   40.0% – 45.0%

▦   45.0% – 55.0%

▦   55.0% – 65.0%

▦   65.0% – 80.0%

■   80.0% – 100.0%

Map 2c.   KPD support in the Altstadt by electoral ward, 1928

philosophy during the 1927 election campaign and declared, "the municipality is not only an economic community, a joint-stock company, but also a political and moral organism" within the body politic.[65] Altona's professors and state counselors, who made up the party's leadership, saw themselves very much in a Hegelian tradition of local conservative authority of an essentially *Honoratioren* nature. In their view it was they, the educated men of the DVP, who were intellectually and socially best equipped to provide the necessary disinterested political and moral leadership in municipal matters, missing since 1918. Hence, in 1927 they called upon the city's electorate to "vote personalities."[66]

The DVP had strongholds in the more middle-class districts of Altona, including parts of the older inner city, such as the Königstraße, Allee, and Mörkenstraße, where a number of their councillors lived or worked. The party's most tenacious support, however, came from voters

☐	0.0% – 2.0%
▥	2.0% – 5.0%
▤	5.0% – 10.0%
▨	10.0% – 15.0%
▧	15.0% – 20.0%
▥	20.0% – 25.0%
▤	25.0% – 35.0%
▨	35.0% – 40.0%
▨	40.0% – 45.0%
▦	45.0% – 55.0%
▦	55.0% – 65.0%
▦	65.0% – 80.0%
■	80.0% – 100.0%

Map 2d.   KPD support in the Altstadt by electoral ward, 1930

in the western suburbs of Klein Flottbek, Othmarschen, and Nienstedten. In these three districts the DVP usually achieved levels of voter support that doubled its citywide performance during the various Reichstag elections. But the party's elitism militated against its broadening its popular appeal and thus helping it to overcome its geographical and social ghettoization. It remained conspicuously a party of industry and especially the *Bildungsbürgertum,* whose "ponderous academic style," according to Peter Fritzsche, and *Honoratioren* political language eventually jarred unharmoniously with the discordant notes of Weimar politics, especially during the economic crisis.[67] There were more academics and representatives of industry and finance among their candidates than among those of the DNVP, whose election lists, while not excluding the occasional *Oberleutnant* or *Regierungsrat,* appear to have had a deeper anchor in Altona's *Mittelstand.*[68]

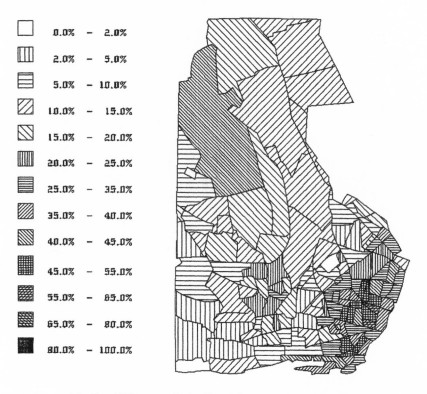

☐	0.0% – 2.0%
⊞	2.0% – 5.0%
⊟	5.0% – 10.0%
▨	10.0% – 15.0%
◩	15.0% – 20.0%
⦀	20.0% – 25.0%
▤	25.0% – 35.0%
▨	35.0% – 40.0%
◩	40.0% – 45.0%
▦	45.0% – 55.0%
▦	55.0% – 65.0%
▩	65.0% – 80.0%
■	80.0% – 100.0%

Map 2e.   KPD support in the Altstadt by electoral ward, July 1932

Driven by an uncompromising ideological impulse, the DNVP retained an active interest in the more mundane day-to-day matters of local life. The DNVP was thus able to tap a greater reservoir of support than the DVP among a broad cross-section of Altona's citizens. Many of its candidates gave occupations that placed them squarely within the *Mittelstand,* and quite a few of them lived in socially mixed neighborhoods, of the type that formed the traditional backbone of the DNVP's urban support. Of its fifty-six candidates for election in 1927 over half lived in the Altstadt, Ottensen, and Bahrenfeld, and over half of these were domiciled in the Altstadt, albeit in better-situated parts of it. The DNVP was, therefore, more of a *Volkspartei,* or, "people's party."[69]

The widespread distribution of support for the DNVP is borne out by the 1924 election results themselves. It took upwards of a fifth of the bal-

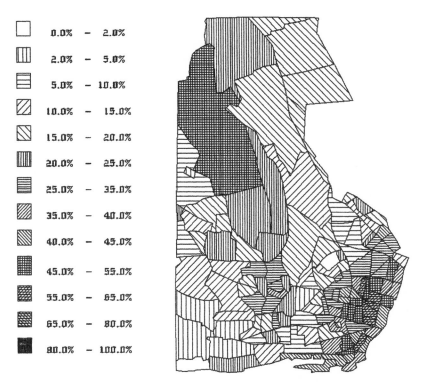

☐	0.0%	– 2.0%
▥	2.0%	– 5.0%
▤	5.0%	– 10.0%
▨	10.0%	– 15.0%
▨	15.0%	– 20.0%
▥	20.0%	– 25.0%
▤	25.0%	– 35.0%
▨	35.0%	– 40.0%
▨	40.0%	– 45.0%
▦	45.0%	– 55.0%
▦	55.0%	– 65.0%
▦	65.0%	– 80.0%
■	80.0%	– 100.0%

Map 2f. KPD support in the Altstadt by electoral ward, Nov. 1932

lot in thirty-three wards in the Altstadt and nineteen in Ottensen and Bahrenfeld, compared with the DVP's thin performance of only ten and eight, respectively. Endorsement for the party was clearly derived from the *Mittelstand,* which was heavily represented in these three districts. The nationalists' uncompromising politics during the occupation of the Ruhr in 1923 won it widespread support among *völkisch* voters in May 1924 in a number of *Mittelstand* wards in Ottensen and the Altstadt and among some working-class voters, for example in Eidelstedt.[70]

This sprinkling of working-class voters notwithstanding, the main brace of support came from the suburbs, namely Othmarschen, Oevel-gönne, Blankenese, Klein Flottbek, and Nienstedten, where traditionally nationalist-based conservatism was strongest. Together the DVP and DNVP constituted the main force of opposition in municipal politics in these suburbs of Greater Altona, either agitating independently, as in 1927, or, more typically, under a unity banner and with strongholds that could deliver up to 60 percent of votes.[71]

Party politics was not necessarily incompatible with the ideology and practice of local *Honoratioren* apoliticism. Apart from 1919 and 1927 the city's municipal elections were contested either by sectional interest groups, such as Richard Galster's Economic Bloc and later the Business Party, or by unity lists. Altona's local personalities found themselves adept at moving easily between these and a national party or back again, as in 1919, when, after having campaigned under the banner of the DVP and DNVP, elected candidates took their seats in the council as the Citizens' Association, or the Bürgerliche Gemeinschaft (tables 3 and 4).

Between 1919 and 1924 the unity lists had spanned the whole spectrum of Altona's middle classes, embracing professionals such as architects, lawyers, and teachers or small-scale retailers, property owners, master craftsmen, as well as more substantial industrial and financial interests. The departure of the DVP and DNVP from the alliance in 1927 made the Gemeinschaftsliste des Zentralausschusses der kommunalen Vereine zu Altona (Joint List of the Central Committee of Altona Civic Associations [GZkV]) look more *mittelständisch,* in spite of representatives from the League of German Architects and the teaching profession.

The main candidates, Christoph Gehrke, Heinrich Ahrendt, and Ernst Seehase, were chairman, deputy chairman, and treasurer of the Altona House and Property Association, while among the other candidates were also the chairmen and representatives of the associations for dairy retailers, grocers' shops, publicans, manufacturers. There were also candidates from the district-based civic associations, such as the Kommunalverein der Norderteil (Altstadt), and similar associations from Ottensen and Bahrenfeld. Many of these associations had been established between the 1870s and 1900s. The GZkV's candidates represented a male-dominated public sphere of associational life in old Altona. Women were simply not represented, as they had been in 1924, when four of them campaigned; they were only to feature again in 1929, when the DVP and DNVP rejoined the bloc, giving once again a broader social configuration to middle-class politics.[72]

Challengers

The problem facing Altona's middle classes during the 1920s was how to reconstruct their political fortunes in a form best suited to meet the challenge of socialist municipalism. Although they had dominated the

Rathaus before the revolution, they had lacked any ideological coherence other than the belief that they should govern the city. This conviction, of course, did not disappear in the postwar period. But, after the dust of revolutionary change had settled, they found that they had fragmented into a number of fluid and fractious groups. The number of splinter groups contesting the local elections increased from three in 1924 to a peak of eight in 1927, halved to four in 1929, and rose again in 1933 to six.[73] Their conundrum was how to regroup in such conditions in order to recapture the *Rathaus.*

The purpose of unity lists, therefore, was not so much a sentimental throwback to prewar *Honoratioren* politics but, rather, to find an effective means for challenging Brauer's regime. The leaders of the alliances emphasized the "natural common sense" of the propertied and productive citizen, placing this above what they perceived as the negative wrangle of partisan politics. Their own aims were anything but "apolitical," however, and boiled down to little else than an attempt to restore middle-class political hegemony in Altona. A local lawyer named Heinrich Ahrendt, who had offices in the Königstraße, formulated the aim of alliance politics at a meeting of the city's communal associations on 17 February 1924, as follows:

> All of us are agreed on the point that the influence of the Social Democrats in the city council must be done away with. To achieve this however, we must stand together as a man. Only a strong unity can in this respect bring advantage. . . . For this reason also, all citizens must put aside their special interests and work together at the problem.[74]

Ahrendt's exhortation came at an important moment for Altona's middle classes. Not only were council elections looming in May; there were also to be elections for the *Magistrat* in March. And, since Lord Mayor Schnackenburg was gravely ill (he died of typhus little more than a week after the meeting at which Ahrendt spoke), the question of his successor was now raised. Brauer had come forward as the main candidate of the Social Democrats and the liberals.

Up to this point in the republic's early and tumultuous history Altona's conservatives had seemed relatively quiescent on the question of socialist leadership.[75] The SPD had proven remarkably iron-handed in maintaining public order and, as such, had been useful in damming the flood tide of revolution.[76] The partial stabilization of political and social life by early 1924 signaled an opportunity to try and regain the initiative.

In order to coordinate an effective challenge to the SPD, the leaders of Altona's thirteen citizen groups, representing between seven and ten thousand members, among them the prominent Bürgerverein 1848, the Communal Association of the North District (Altstadt), the Ottensen Bürgerverein 1867, and the Altona Property Owners' Association, grouped themselves into the Zentralausschuss der kommunalen Vereine zu Altona, led by Ahrendt.

The committee called for a boycott of the *Magistrat* election. A notice in the conservative *Hamburger Nachrichten* advised readers in Altona on how to obstruct the elections on technical grounds, mainly by lodging protests against the list of candidates.[77] Yet, at the last minute, the organizers of the boycott changed their minds and, instead, urged their followers to register their protest by spoiling ballot papers on 30 March. Indeed, this tactic seems to have worked because 7,398 voters spoiled the two ballot papers for lord mayor and town planning senator, for which post the main candidate was Gustav Oelsner (the former municipal architect from Kattowitz and of Jewish background).[78] Brauer received the overwhelming majority of the valid ballot, receiving 12,915 votes, while his party friends and fellow candidates for the post, August Kirch and Walther Lamp'l, each received 85 and 343. Oelsner took more than 57 percent of the valid ballot, far outstripping his nearest rival.[79]

The turnout on 30 March had been extremely low; of the city's 137,496 eligible voters only 20,741 voted, or just 15 percent of the electorate. One of the leaders of the Ottensen Bürgerverein, retired *Justizrat* Dr. Türck, interpreted this low turnout as equaling a no vote and claimed that this invalidated Brauer's election. According to Türck, if Brauer became Oberbürgermeister, he would neither be able to garner the trust of all citizens nor be in a position to represent the city credibly in its external business. Such low levels of voter participation in *Magistrat* elections were not unusual, however. At the elections of 1919, for instance, voter participation had barely risen above 4 percent for Schnackenburg and other candidates of the city's Bürgertum. And yet the embattled positions in 1924 actually had the highest participation rates.[80]

The second round of *Magistrat* elections in June displayed a similar but smaller spoiling of ballot papers when it came to choosing the deputy mayor. The candidate, Dr. Ebert (a member of the DDP from Kiel), had the support of the SPD and was able to gain a majority similar to Oelsner's. The election of other *Magistrat* members on 29 June, including two members of the Bürger bloc and a Communist, elicited a very low participation rate, between 2 and 4 percent. These contrasted with rates ranging between 6 and 12 percent for the two socialist and two liberal candidates. Thus, if one followed the logic of the leaders of the Bürgervereine, their "nationally minded" candidates also lacked the confidence of a sizable number of Altona's citizens.

This did not deter the protesters. Under the Schleswig-Holstein municipal ordinance of 1869 the election of an *Oberbürgermeister* had to be confirmed by the head of the provincial administration, Dr. Johannsen, who also happened to be a member of the DVP.[81] The opposition used the period between the election result and Brauer's confirmation in office, scheduled for 17 May, to mobilize a petition against his election on apparent breaches of procedure. In mid-April Türck, together with Carl Bischoff, a post office inspector who was also chairman of the Bürgerverein 1867; a local lawyer, Carl Sieveking of Flottbecker Chaussee; and the Kaufmann Korndörffer; and two high school teachers, Professors Roll and Johannes Stolting, submitted a formal objection to Brauer's election.[82]

The dissenters produced a number of arguments that they believed invalidated Brauer's election under paragraphs 45 and 31 of the Schleswig-Holstein *Städteordnung* of 1869. They argued, for instance, that Brauer lacked the prerequisite legal training necessary for the post, that his brief period in office as deputy mayor did not furnish him with enough experience to compensate for the lack of formal qualifications. They complained that the post had not been publicly advertised as required. The other two contestants, Dr. Lamp'l and August Kirch, were described as straw candidates whose presence was a ploy to block bona fide challengers. Moreover, they alleged, the list of candidates was the result of a backroom deal between the SPD and Justizrat Dr. Otto Löwenthal, the leader of the liberal group on the council, whereby, if the liberals agreed to the post of lord mayor going to the Social Democrats, candidates for *Bausenator* and deputy *Bürgermeister* would be DDP choices.

Türck and his colleagues also claimed that the selection committee had been aware of these goings-on but had manifestly failed to protect the wishes and interests of all citizens. They asserted that the distribution of high office in Altona had been thus subjected to a "downright horse trade" and that citizens had been "robbed in broad daylight" of their constitutional right to choose their executive. In their view this was not only "injurious" to the people of Altona but also damaged the democratic principles upon which the republic had been founded.[83]

The complainants did not restrict their arguments to purely legalistic or procedural points. Brauer's middle-class critics stated that it was public knowledge that the lord mayor–designate intended to stand as a candidate in the forthcoming Reichstag elections in May. Indeed, on his election Brauer had expressed confidence that he could serve the public and retain his political role:

It is stated in the wonderful Weimar Constitution: The civil servant is servant of all, not of a political party. I do and will continue to feel as a servant of all, however, without ceasing to be a political person.[84]

Because Brauer was such a "dynamic party man," he stood a good chance of getting elected. Should this happen, the time and energy required to manage Altona's affairs properly would be heavily compromised, given that Brauer was already a member of the Prussian State Council, the Provincial Diet, and sat on the supervisory boards of three public utilities.

Türck alleged that Brauer had already demonstrated his political unsuitability for high office by publicly defending the regional SPD's accord with the Danish socialist party over the northern part of Schleswig-Holstein that had been ceded to Denmark in 1920. The SPD's behavior had raised "great indignation" among the "nationally minded citizens of the province" against such a "treacherous act." Türck and his compatriots saw in Brauer a "Social Democrat extremist of internationalist leanings." His failure to defend German national interests meant that, as a future Oberbürgermeister, he would neither command trust nor the respect necessary for cooperation with other provincial administrators.[85]

A large section of the middle classes, however, were prepared to give Brauer the chance to prove himself. For some Brauer was the right man to lead Altona in changed and difficult times. The liberal *Hamburger Fremdenblatt,* in a retrospective of the events of 1924, emphasized Brauer's strength of character and intelligence as well as his leadership acumen as reasons for choosing him as Oberbürgermeister. Brauer had the wherewithal, it was believed, to lead the city into a new progressive era of social and economic reconstruction and to create out of "old Altona" a "New Altona."[86] In 1924 not only did the local mood look forward in expectation of positive change, but the *Honoratioren* class and its allies were themselves unsure of their own unity. These were the reasons making the attempt to dislodge Brauer premature.

Humiliation

As we shall see in chapter 4, the incorporation of ten parish communities in July 1927, necessitated new local elections. A new "Greater Altona" council was inaugurated on 3 October 1927 and got off to a controversial start. In spite of the splintering of the bourgeois camp as a result of the incorporation campaign, the DNVP, DVP, and GZkV combined in an effort to oust Brauer from office by tabling a motion of no confidence against him. Heinrich Ahrendt from the GZkV, as leader of the largest group, brought the motion, cosigned by the leaders of the DNVP and

DVP, Dr. Paul Heidke a government counselor, and Dr. Wilhelm Schramm, the headmaster of the boys secondary school in Blankenese. The objection this time was that Brauer had stepped outside the boundaries of mayoral propriety by taking part in the SPD's election campaign. As in 1924, the argument ran that, because of his overt political partisanship, Brauer did not have the confidence of the council nor, by extension, that of a large section of Altona's citizens.

This motion was inadmissible under the Schleswig-Holstein *Städteordnung* of 1869, regulating municipal politics. Nevertheless, the Social Democrat speaker of the chamber, Paul Bugdahn, decided to allow a discussion "out of consideration for parliamentarism" and to put the motion to a vote by roll call.[87] Bugdahn was confident that this action would provide uncontestable affirmation of Brauer's public leadership. The members of the three factions naturally voted for the motion, except Frau Cimbal (DVP), who, unusually, was absent from the chamber that day. The bourgeois bloc in the council was a minority, anyway, but the lack of Cimbal's vote, together with the abstentions of both the single Nazi councillor, Hinrich Lohse, and Ernst Heinrich from the Business Party, further reduced the credibility of the motion. Against the eighteen votes in favor of the motion the Socialists, the Democrats, and the Communists, in a rare show of unity, combined to produce an overwhelming thirty-nine votes against the motion. Thus, the opposition's second attempt to oust Brauer had failed.

But that was not the end of the story. Bugdahn had allowed the vote to go ahead, not only to publicly affirm Brauer's position but also as a ploy to strike back at the opposition by administering the same unpleasant medicine. Brauer opened the counterattack in an article in the regional Social Democrat paper, *Hamburger Echo:*

> The introduction of a vote of confidence or no confidence in the city assembly is based on the erroneous assumption that the *Magistrat* is a constitutional position like that of the Reich Chancellor—and needs the confidence of parliament. . . . The incorporation of many areas into Altona has exposed quite a few strange flowerings of opinion. Confusing Altona with an independent state is in this respect the latest development. If individual members of the *Magistrat* needed the confidence of the majority in the city assembly, then Herr Bauermeister and Herr Frahm, who, according to proportional representation, should be elected as honorary senators, would never be active in the *Magistrat.* In the case of paid senators, we are dealing with civil servants. Their appointment is usually through an election by the city assembly; in Schleswig-Holstein by the general public.[88]

A Social Democrat councillor from Othmarschen, Wilhelm Dörr,[89] therefore brought a motion directed against the leader of the DVP, Dr. Schramm, the cosignatory of the no-confidence motion. Schramm was a long-standing and vociferous opponent to the Socialists, and the SPD must have been pleased to have gotten him in their sights. Dörr claimed that the attempt to remove Brauer had revealed a woeful ignorance of civics; therefore, the SPD was demanding that the Provincial Schools *Collegium,* the governing body overseeing secondary education, deprive Dr. Schramm's right to teach civics in Blankenese's schools.[90]

The motion censuring Schramm was carried by a combined SPD and KPD majority (the DDP abstained). The opposition parties left the chamber before voting began.[91] Schramm was facing public humiliation at the hands of the Left, leaving him fighting for his personal reputation. He appealed to his party colleague Dr. Johannsen, the *Regierungspräsident,* for public redress, but this simply fueled the fires of public ridicule. The *Echo* commented with irrepressible *schadenfreude:*

> Dr. Schramm is a hell of a cheeky guy. He is of the opinion that he is naturally entitled to move for a vote of "no confidence" against the Lord Mayor, or to use Dr. Schramm's own language, to attack the professional honour of the leading civil servant when he acts outside his office. But the Social Democratic council group are not allowed to turn the tables and do the same to him. For when that happens it is called "unconstitutional."

The writer continued:

> The *Regierungspräsident* finds himself in a dilemma here: if he grants Schramm's wish and faults the SPD motion, then he has to equally fault the motion for a vote of "no confidence" signed by Dr. Schramm. To do that will be terribly difficult for him; and if he does not do so then he cannot fault the SPD motion. So what should he do? The best thing would be to keep out of this, but then Dr. Schramm will be disgraced. However, [Schramm] will be equally disgraced if his appeal results in a faulting of his motion for a vote. . . . Whatever the choice, Dr. Schramm has disgraced himself.[92]

It was not the first time that Altona's middle-class opposition had been made to look foolish as well as impotent. With tactical wisdom Lohse had kept the NSDAP at a distance from the protest, preferring instead to wait for the opportunity to make a more serious onslaught against Brauer.[93]

Immobilized

In spite of public humiliation and previous setbacks, Altona's middle-class opposition was optimistic in 1929 that all it needed was one final united push to remove the SPD from power. For that purpose the various bourgeois factions reconstituted themselves as the *Bürgerliche Gemeinschaft* in time for the Prussian local elections set for 17 November. Campaign slogans such as "United Citizenry against Marxism and Its Corrupting Aims" and "Economic Individualism against Economic Collectivism!" reflected the wider issues but also spoke to economic conflicts specific to Altona (see chap. 5).[94] Yet, unlike elsewhere in Prussia, the election results in November showed a drop in support in Altona for alliance politics in general.

The attempt to maintain the alliance of 1929 came up against a number of serious impediments, not the least of which was the rapidly desperate economic situation, as local propertied and business interests were hit hard by tax hikes. As we shall see in chapter 5, the nature of the tax squeeze tore a rent through the alliance. Another factor was a growing mood of disillusion with the status quo of middle-class politics, already in evidence in the Reichstag elections the previous year.

This situation brought the Business Party to momentary prominence.[95] Overall, the Business Party took around 6 percent of the vote. But its achievement in some districts could be quite remarkable. Indeed, the party experienced a marked increase of votes in those areas characterized by a very strong handicraft and small trades sector. In Stellingen-Langenfelde it came in a strong second to the SPD with a stunning 22.6 percent. In Eidelstedt and Blankenese it increased its share of the vote, enabling it to take third place, as it did in Rissen and Lurup (though in these districts it did so with a stationary vote). The contemporary prognosis was that the Business Party was able to siphon off votes from the Bürgerliche Gemeinschaft and the DVP, whose supporters were unhappy about the alliance with Hugenberg's DNVP, as well as attract some new voters.[96] Its success meant that it could return four councillors, making the party *salonfähig* (politically viable). This led to wild speculation on the possibility of collaboration with the liberals and Social Democrats, who, in the worsening economic and political climate, were increasingly unable to rely on support from the Communists.[97]

From late 1929 Altona's alliance politics became increasingly marginal to resolving disputes in the *Rathaus.* Their impotence was made public in yet another assault on Brauer's regime that backfired in early 1930. The issue this time was Brauer's austerity budget for 1930, which foresaw increases in the tax burden for property and business (see chap. 5). The entire bourgeois bloc tried to obstruct the budget by bringing in five hundred amendments to tax proposals, believed to hit the *Mittelstand* unfairly. Brauer calculated that each amendment would require about ten minutes discussion time, at which rate about five weeks would be needed to debate the budget.

To cut through this difficulty Brauer called an extraordinary council meeting for Sunday, 13 April, at ten o'clock in the morning. This was Palm Sunday, an important date in the religious calendar, when children were traditionally confirmed. After initial protests the bloc sought a compromise and offered 1 P.M. as an alternative, since this would allow members to attend church. Angered by the bloc's original intransigence, Brauer would not move from his original order. Because of the significance of the day—and the fact that Brauer was a Socialist—the godlessness of his action was received "as a provocation in wide circles of Altona's population." In editorials published in the *Altonaer Tageblatt* and the *Norddeutsche Nachrichten* Brauer was nicknamed the "Palm Sunday Dictator." And the *Altonaer Tageblatt* published the following sarcastic ditty, entitled: "We have the Power!" after the new *Regierungspräsident,* Waldemar Abegg, refused to intervene on behalf of the bloc.

> The council meets on Sundays too,
> even when it is Palmdays!
> Why all the passion?!
> That is with us our fashion;
> It is necessary to the last
> that we perspire with the budget.
> After all there's no law busted.
> That's why: stay seated, seated, seated!
>
> What troubles us church and organ?
> Why should we be bothered by protests!
> We're the strongest council faction;
> so "here's to you," steadfast! steadfast!
> Whoever will not on Sunday counsel
> should stay at home.
> We'll start the budget quietly,
> eventually alone!
>
> We have the power, we're so powerful,
> "one for all, all for one!"
> In our bones there's marrow still

one feels it, that is sure!
And if, as often, the spirit fails
then our lungs will be our cure.
So, at least we'll be stalwart
as the taxes procreate![98]

The 1929 municipal election had revealed the limits to voters' patience with "apolitical" unity lists in politically charged times. Indeed, the DNVP's anti-Young campaign had repoliticized politics at a local level, contributing to a rightward shift among the electorate, a development that partly contributed to the prising open of a latent Right-Left fissure in the DVP.[99] Nor was support for unity politics helped by the revelation sometime later that a deal was being struck with the hated SPD to get Dr. Schramm (no less) a seat on the *Magistrat* as quid pro quo for agreeing to an early reelection of Kirch and Lamp'l.[100] Meanwhile, the DNVP, which had been uncompromising in its opposition to Brauer and yet equally compromised by the goings-on over Schramm's election to the *Magistrat,* had already began its own descent into dissolution.[101]

The impotence of the middle classes in the face of a confident administration rekindled a "yearning for concentration" in order to find the means to overturn Brauer.[102] The earlier strong endorsement by the electorate in Altona for unity lists had revealed a desire for a *Sammlung* of the *Mitte* from the NSDAP to "the doorstep of the SPD that was also in evidence elsewhere."[103] Before 1930 this desire had remained elusive, for the problems that had hitherto confronted Altona's middle classes were issues that either divided or did not affect them uniformly. As a consequence, middle-class mobilization remained both partial and disunited.[104] This situation began to alter during the Depression, when in Altona local peculiarities blended with the universally felt harsh consequences of the economic crisis. The NSDAP was able to insinuate itself into the political vacuum that had began to open as a result of these developments.

A New Bloc: The Nazis

The early history of the NSDAP in Altona is difficult to reconstruct because of the fragmentary nature of the sources. For example, early reports do not necessarily make a clear distinction between the city and its larger neighbor, Hamburg.[105] Nor is the fledgling Nazi movement easily distinguishable from the many other right-wing *völkisch* groups on the scene at the time. For example, a proto-Nazi group was established in the city in March 1922 under the name of German Worker's League (Deutscher Arbeiterbund), led by a master glazer, Rudolf Mohr. The league had links to other extreme nationalist anti-Semitic organizations, such as the Deutsche-Völkische Arbeitsgemeinschaft, led by a local businessman, Werner Dietz, and later also joined the Völkisch-Sozialer Block.[106]

The membership of these proto-Nazi groups was small and fluid. Mohr's Workers' League, for instance, had about fifty members, and they tended to drift to other groups in search of a political *Heimat,* as the wider political terrain shifted. While membership remained limited, there was a wider *völkisch* culture in Altona, such as the Stadtring der Vaterländischen Verbände, and it was from this as well as groups such as those led by Mohr and Dietz that the Nazi Party was to emerge. Its early membership in Altona is not known, but on its refounding in early 1925 it numbered 121 members.[107]

A career through these early organizations was the usual experience of the so-called old fighters, who formed the nucleus of the early Nazi Party in Altona. Werner Dietz, founder-member of the DVA, played a leading role in the early NSDAP until a criminal incident and party intrigue dispatched him into the political wilderness in 1925.[108] Another old fighter with a similar and somewhat colorful background was Wilhelm von Allwörden, the owner of a cigar shop in Ottensen.[109] Allwörden found his way into the Nazi Party in 1925 after an early career in Armin zur Treue und Einigkeit (1922–24) and the Deutsche-Völkische Freiheitsbewegung (1924–25), which voted to join the NSDAP en masse at the party's refounding in Neumünster in early 1925. He was elected to the city council in 1929 and during the 1930s became a member of the Hamburg senate.

Similarly, Wilhelm Sieh, an employee in the legal department of the Hamburg Metropolitan Transport Authority, had served both in the army and in a number of paramilitary organizations before joining the Nazis. Sieh was born on 19 May 1892 in Great Wisch, county of Steinburg (Schleswig-Holstein), the son of Hans Friedrich Sieh, a local primary school teacher. After attending the Meldorf grammar school, until the upper second grade, he joined the lower court in Meldorf, from April to October 1911, as an auditor, moving to the preparatory college in Lunden before commencing a commercial traineeship at the Hamburg Overhead Railway Company in Hamburg on 7 December 1911. As a war volunteer in 1917, he was twice badly wounded and finally discharged on 1 August 1919 as a war invalid with 50 percent disability. He immediately joined the Völkischer Schutz und Trutzbund until its ban. In 1923 he graduated to the Free Corps Roßbach and, when that was disbanded, moved to the Völkisch-Sozialer-Block in early 1924 and from here made the smooth transition to the newly reconstituted Nazi Party in June 1925, of which he became party member number 7,540.[110]

The bank clerk and Altona's first Nazi Oberbürgermeister, Emil Brix, who at one time had been a member of the notorious Roßbach Free Corps, made a similar switch to the early Nazi movement at the same time as a fellow traveler through the early *völkisch* movement in Altona, Werner Schmalmack, a violinist.[111] These men were born in the last decade of the nineteenth century and were in their middle twenties at the moment of their entry into active politics. Men such as these, according to Rudolf Rietzler in his study of the Nazi Party's early history in Schleswig-Holstein, "as far as discipline and strength is concerned," formed "a steadfast group of National Socialists who provided a durable infrastructure that could absorb the weight of the mass movement" after 1930.[112]

The Nazis' entry into local politics took place during the municipal elections of 1924, under the aegis of the Völkisch-Sozialer Block. The VSB gained 9 percent of the vote overall, with particular pockets of strength in the Altstadt and Ottensen. This was among the highest levels of support in the reich. It was thus able to return five members to the council.[113] This rather large and loose alliance of anti-Semitic councillors had become by December a tight Nazi faction as nonparty members, such as the headmaster Johannes Laß who had led the VSB during the election, and a master decorator (*Malermeister*), Karl Johannsen, were forced out.[114] The leadership went to Hinrich Lohse, who was also *Gauleiter*. Between 1924 and 1927, however, the NSDAP experienced problems relating to personnel, organization, and, notably, political strategy.[115] As a result, the number of Nazi councillors was cut back to one in 1927.

Before the onset of the Depression the Nazi faction on the council played a fairly undistinguished role, largely due to the lack of a coherent municipal strategy. Instead, much of its energy went on waging virulent and noisy campaigns to discredit Brauer and his colleagues in city government.[116] The NSDAP's implacable hostility toward socialism provided Nazi councillors with the ideological raison d'être to join forces with other councillors in opposing Brauer's policies. Thus, it cooperated with bourgeois councillors on issues such as the house rent tax and even voted with the Communists on the issue of free public transport for war veterans. It mounted campaigns jointly with the bourgeois bloc against individual SPD politicians close to Brauer and added its voice to criticism of the *Magistrat* over the distribution of public contracts. Nevertheless, it sought to establish a separate political identity from that of other opposition conservative groups in the council. In some respects following a similar strategy to the KPD, the Altona NSDAP exploited its council crusades as a means to attract new recruits.[117]

Nazi membership in Altona was mostly confined to social groups from lower-middle-class backgrounds. The minutes of the conference of

1 March 1925 in Neumünster, which reconstituted the *Gau* Schleswig-Holstein, clearly show the middle-class background of the thirty delegates. Their social homogeneity was largely duplicated among the party's electoral candidates for office in Altona. The party fielded twenty-one candidates in 1927, half of whom had occupations that placed them within the new middle class of white-collar employees. The majority of the other half were easily identifiable as hailing from the "old *Mittelstand*" of petty retailers and craftsmen. And before and after 1933 middle-class activists dominated the Nazi faction in the council assembly.[118] But, unlike other parties, the Nazi electoral lists did not show the same geographical concentration.

Throughout the 1920s the NSDAP only ever fielded a very small minority of manual workers. In 1924, for instance, there was only one candidate described as a "manual worker" (*Arbeiter*), placed twelfth on a list of twenty. In 1927 there was again only one working-class candidate out of twenty-one (this time placed at second position). In 1929 four out of thirty-seven candidates gave manual occupations, but only two of these were located within the first fifteen positions. This low placement matched the diminishing proportion of "workers" on the candidate lists, from approximately a quarter in 1927–29 to barely one-fifteenth by 1933. These Nazi workers should not be confused with industrial workers. Rather, they tended to occupy low-skill manual positions outside Altona's manufacturing sector. For instance, one was a porter, another a messenger, another a cabman, and another a gardener. Of the handful of working-class Nazis only one ever came to prominence. This was Bruno Stamer, who first joined the Altona Nazis in 1924 and was among the first wave of re-joiners in June 1925.[119]

Stamer was not a typical worker, nor was he typical of the local leadership. He was born in 1900 in Altona; his father was a train driver and Social Democrat. Although he completed an apprenticeship as an electrician, he never practiced his trade. At various times he described himself as a factory worker or window cleaner. In the early postwar years he had flirted with communism, but after a youthful spell in the KPD (1921–23) Stamer embarked upon an exemplary career in the NSDAP. When Gauleiter Hinrich Lohse resigned from Altona's council in June 1928 in order to concentrate his energies among the farmers of Schleswig-Holstein, Stamer took his place.[120] He was elected in 1929 to the provincial assembly in Kiel, and in 1930 he was able to join Lohse in the Reichstag. His working-class credentials qualified him to become the *Gau* spokesman on trade union affairs and social policy. He continued with this role after 1933, as regional leader of the Deutsche Arbeitsfront (German Labor League [DAF]), until he fell from grace in 1936. Stamer's career ended as a consequence of personal as well as more broadly based rivalries between the mainly working-class DAF and the *Mittelstand* Nationalsozialistische Handels- und Gewerberorganisation (National Socialist Commerce and Crafts Organization [NS-HAGO]), headed by a local draper, Max Boge, whose intrigues brought down Stamer. His fall reflected the deep-lying class tensions within the Altona party and was not an isolated case.[121]

The petit bourgeois character of the NSDAP cadre in Altona was mirrored in the party's wider membership up to March 1933. In 1929 the Nazi Party in Altona consisted of only a few hundred activists. Between this date and coming to power the size of the party never exceeded more than around 1,300 members. As with the early movement, details about the party as it expanded are sporadic. Nonetheless, information gleaned from a variety of sources relating to between 200 and 250 people who joined the party in 1931–32, and who made up between 15 and 20 percent of the membership in Altona at that time, is summarized in table 5.[122]

As we can see, Altona's middle classes were overrepresented in the local party, while the contrary was true of the working class. Moreover, manual workers tended to come less from the larger manufacturing establishments than from the numerous smaller workshops or were employed in the more seasonal or vulnerable trades such as construction and transport. Thus, the NSDAP in Altona may on first viewing look like a *Volkspartei*, but closer examination shows that it failed to broaden its appeal to reach Altona's industrial working class in the way it is said to have done nation-

TABLE 5.   **Nazi Members in Altona by Occupation**

	Economic Active Population by Occupation (1925)	Nazis by Occupation	
		Dec. 1931	March 1933
		N 181	N 249
Self-employed (including artisans/traders)	14.0	14.3	25.6
White-collar/civil servant/professional	28.7	49.2	24.4
Working class	49.6	29.9	34.4
skilled		15.5	17.8
unskilled		14.4	16.6
Others/unknown	7.7	2.8	15.6
Housewives		3.8	—

Source: Anthony McElligott, "Kommunalpolitische Entwicklungen in Altona vonn Weimar zum Dritten Reich," in Stadtteilarchiv Ottensen, ed., "*Ohne uns hätten sie das gar nicht machen können, Nazi-Zeit und Nachkrieg in Altona und Ottensen* (Hamburg, 1985), 22.

ally.[123] Indeed, a bulletin from the *Gau* propaganda office in early 1931 reported how "hefty counter-measures from the marxists" in Altona were preventing any satisfactory recruitment of workers.[124]

The 1927 local election had marked the low point of the party's fortunes in Altona. Its urban and electoral strategy was in confusion, and, as if to underline the point, the *Gau* offices left the city within the year for Halstenbeck in the rural province. But the fortunes of the party in Altona soon showed signs of recovery, and by the following July the *Gau* head-quarters were once again to be found in the city.[125] The growth in membership in Altona was part of a wider regional success. The number of local branches throughout the province increased fivefold, from 45 in 1927 to 201 by the time of the *Gau* conference in April 1929. By this date membership in Altona stood at approximately three hundred, together with an eighty-man strong SA. The party continued its steady (if somewhat uneven) growth into the spring of 1930.[126]

Against a background of spreading economic crisis, a rapprochement between nationalists and Nazis (and epitomized by the collaboration over the anti-Young campaign) took place that kindled a greater interest in the NSDAP among Altona's middle classes. Indeed, after 1929 there was a shift among the local *Stahlhelm* toward greater collaboration with the SA that paralleled the swing to the NSDAP among DNVP voters.[127] In the six weeks leading up to the local elections on 17 November, the NSDAP held numerous meetings in Altona, far outstripping all other parties and attracting audiences numbering thousands.[128] The NSDAP was able to benefit from these factors in the municipal elections. It took nearly 6 percent of the city votes but with notable variation that ranged between as much as 10 percent in Eidelstedt and as little as 3 percent in Osdorf. The Nazis made a notable comeback in wards that had shown strong support for the Völkisch-Sozialer Block in May 1924.[129] Significantly, the party gained directly from the DNVP and other conservative groups, as it had done in the Reichstag election in 1928. Henceforth, the party was to reposition itself as the fulcrum of the much desired bourgeois unity.

In the course of 1930 and following the announcement of elections in September, the regional party mounted vigorous propaganda campaigns throughout Schleswig-Holstein that took politics onto the streets. Altona once again became the nerve center of Nazi activities in the struggle for the streets, which eventually characterized political life in Altona by 1932, and which we will explore in greater detail in chapter 6.[130] Meetings in Altona attracted large numbers who flocked to hear Gregor Strasser and even the former kaiser's son, Prince August Wilhelm, speak. Departing from its 1929 alliance with the Nationalists, the NSDAP now sought to promote a distinct program of its own. The party's speakers drew crowds on subjects

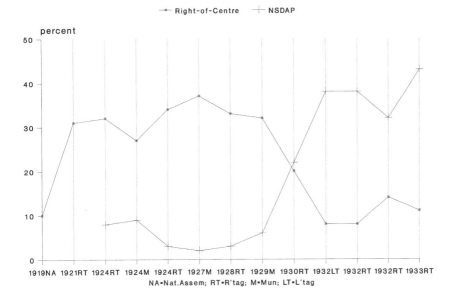

Fig. 2.   Middle-class party transfers to NSDAP, 1921–33

such as "What Does Hitler Want?"; "What Does the NSDAP Want?"; "What Will 1930 Bring Us?"; and "On Dictatorship." Between May and early September the NSDAP more than tripled the number of its meetings, from 68 to 239. The size of these meetings swelled too, attracting audiences of between 500 and 2,000.[131]

This activity paid off, for in the Reichstag election in September the party took over a fifth of the vote in Altona. Even though its result was still 6 percent below that for the province and trailed far behind rural strongholds such as Norderdithmarschen, it was nonetheless 3 percent above the national average.[132]

Commenting on the Nazis' success in the city, the liberal daily, the *Altonaer Nachrichten,* stated in resignation, "what the entire public in the last weeks has come to expect has happened."[133] The Nazi "landslide" was quite phenomenal in individual districts of the city. Oevelgönne, Blankenese, Sülldorf, and Rissen displayed levels of support for the NSDAP of between 34 and 40 percent, while both Groß and Klein Flottbek produced 27 and 28 percent respectively.

These largely mixed middle-class areas were to provide the bulk of Nazi support for the remainder of the period. The savaging of the bour-

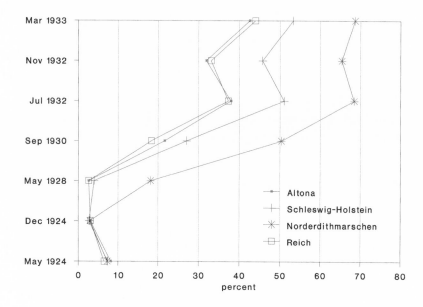

Fig. 3. Nazi votes in Altona and Schleswig-Holstein, 1924–33, compared to Reich and rural

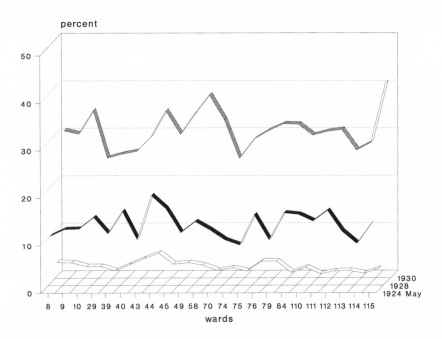

Fig. 4. Nazi votes in Altona by electoral ward, 1924–30 (selected electoral wards)

geois parties by the NSDAP, led both the liberal and Left press to speak of a "terrible crisis" in parliament.[134]

On the voters themselves James Pollock, a political scientist at the University of Michigan, noted:

> It is not difficult to explain why it [the NSDAP] gained. But it is very difficult to explain why it gained so much. . . . The election gave effective expression to the real feelings of the generality of Germans, even though it may reflect on their political intelligence.[135]

Closer to home, the Social Democrats drew on Marx's 18th Brumaire to provide an analysis of the elections. The *Hamburger Echo* concluded that the result was "an expression of the political rootlessness of the bourgeoisie."[136] The editors were forgetting themselves, however. Two years earlier the *Hamburger Echo* had placed the NSDAP firmly *within* the mainstream of bourgeois politics.[137] And this is where the party properly belonged, for, as the Altona case shows, the 1930 result reflected the onset of a *realignment* rather than a *dissolution* of bourgeois politics.[138] The NSDAP offered a new alliance transcending the divisions among the middle classes, overcoming both sectional interests and its district-based ghettoization. Altona's middle classes were turning to what they hoped would prove to be a far more resilient and successful *fronde* against Brauer and the system he personified. Rather than being "very difficult to explain," the emergence and ultimate success of the Nazis can be better understood by studying the dynamics of municipal politics.

CHAPTER 3

A Clash of Cultures: Slum Life and Welfare, 1918–1932

We know that we give social progress the biggest push in our municipal work.
—*Oberbürgermeister Max Brauer*[1]

In his memoirs published shortly after World War II Altona's archivist and chronicler, Paul-Theodor Hoffmann, portrayed the stark difference in the quality of life between interwar Ottensen and the Altstadt. He wrote how

> the chimneys of the factory and industrial areas were fiery with the noise of work near the Altona railway station in Ottensen and Bahrenfeld, where Altona's heart pulsated in time to Hamburg's gigantic work-rhythm. Close by were the small alleys in which old women sat knitting either at the window or together with cats sunning themselves in front of the door; there were pleasant looking court-yards with blossoming red hawthorn and laburnum. . . . Next to this, proletarian poverty: miserable grey streets from the *Gründerzeit* with ugly tenements betraying the wholly anti-social capitalist, profiteer-ing way of exploitation. . . . Something heavy and forlorn always hung over this part of the city.[2]

Although similar poverty-stricken areas existed in Ottensen, contempo-raries considered the worst problems of inner-city decay, such as prostitu-tion, petty crime, and violence, to be most pressing in the Altstadt.

Throughout the period under consideration in this study the physical and moral improvement of the inhabitants of the rundown neighborhoods was regarded as the linchpin of municipal policy. From the 1880s progres-sive mayors such as Franz Adickes had set their sights on transforming the city into one in which the laboring population would live in conditions that "guarantee their physical and moral health and industriousness."[3] "The priority," argued Hoffmann in the later 1920s, "is to create and safeguard the most essential conditions for the existence of those people who are living on the dark side of life, that is, the financially weak and oppressed."[4] The Social Democrats shared this aim. Max Brauer had declared that he wished to create out of "a poor people's city" a sturdy and modern "new Altona" as a symbol of republican and Social Democratic endeavor.[5] Brauer's goal was underpinned not only by his political philosophy but also by his personal experience. He told the assembled deputies at the council's opening on 17 May 1924:

> I was born in Altona. Altona is my home town. I grew up here as a child of the working class; went through primary school in order to become a worker. I got to know the loathsome social conditions of the lower classes through my own experience. Unemployment, poor housing, everything that oppresses the broad mass of our population, is known to me. Like many young workers, I have hungered and thirsted after education and knowledge.[6]

Thus, the improvement in the condition of Altona's working class, and in particular those of the Altstadt, went to the heart of Brauer's municipal and political agenda.

During the nineteenth century urban reformers in Germany, like their counterparts elsewhere, had been content merely to "control and contain an existing situation with the minimum amount of interference."[7] The collapse of the Wilhelmine order, triggered by the devastating experience of war, pushed reformers further along the road from simply the "sanitation" of the working class to its "civilization." Detlev Peukert has argued that social policy was "constitutionalized" under the Weimar Republic, turning the physical and spiritual worlds of the working class into the property of the state to shape and regulate.[8] The German philosopher Jürgen Habermas has referred to this process as one of colonization of the individual's private sphere, as the state attempted to shape civil society.[9] As we shall see, a crusading social policy toward the poor in Altona was accompanied by a policing instinct. As Charles Tilly once remarked in a different context, the poorer sections of society consisted of "naturally unruly people who had to be checked, trained and civilized."[10]

The Poor People's City

Between 1905 and 1913 Altona's population increased by around 16,000 to 184,634, mostly due to migration (migrants constituted nearly 60 percent of the population in 1890). The trend continued during World War I: between 1914 and 1918 around forty thousand migrants made their way to Altona from the surrounding regions, principally from Hamburg and the provinces of Schleswig-Holstein and Hannover. Split almost evenly between the sexes, this influx of migrant population was to continue into the 1930s.[11] The majority of immigrants were single, low-skilled, and tended to concentrate into the older housing of the city's Altstadt, so that by the mid-1920s its neighborhoods were brimming with a population of around 118,000.[12]

Incomers looking for cheap accommodations were attracted to the older subdistricts of the Altstadt, notably those to the south and east. Consequently, population density was high. On average there were 271.8 persons per hectare in the Altstadt, and this was therefore almost three and a quarter times that for the city, which itself was double that for the reich.[13]

The advantage of these areas was that they were close to the work opportunities afforded by the harbor and docks and the service industries that these gave rise to. Thus, in subdistricts 1 to 3 (the harbor area) steam- and electric-powered grain mills and wood mills and warehouses towered above the tenements that straddled either side of the low steps rising from the quayside, offering employment to residents. The sailors' bars and raw entertainment dives that lined the waterfront and the leisure industries of Hamburg's St. Pauli area, which sprawled over into subdistricts 9 to 11, also held out the prospect of work.[14] Itinerant hawkers, mostly outside the normal relations of labor and production, also established themselves here and included a Gypsy population in the Kleine and Große Papagoyenstraße and Sandberg. Housing in these districts, such as that around the Langestraße, Große Marienstraße, or Kleine Freiheit, was both cheap and convenient for work. But the human price levied upon residents was a harsh one. Paul-Theodor Hoffmann observed:

> The Hamburg harbor lying opposite makes it desirable for the workers employed there to settle in the nearby Altona Altstadt. So the people there crowd together in a frightful manner and thus increase public hygiene problems. Whereas there are about 200 persons to the hectare in a healthy density ratio, there are 300 to 700 persons to the hectare here; in the area of Lohmühlenstraße and Schauenbürgerstraße even 800.[15]

Officially, at least eight subdistricts within the Altstadt had average densities in the mid-1920s ranging from 400 to nearly 700 persons per hectare of total area. In reality the number of thickly populated districts was closer to thirteen when calculated on the basis of built-up area, a truer indicator of

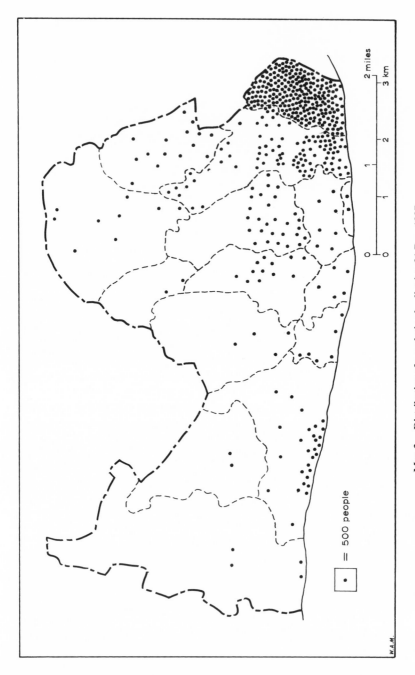

Map 3. Distribution of population by district, 31 Dec. 1927

= 500 people

2 miles

3 km

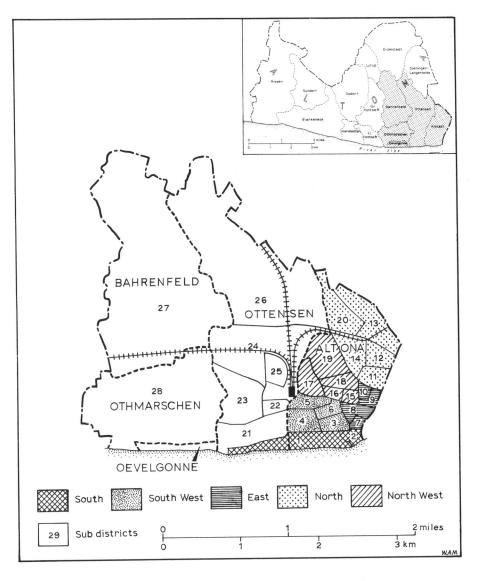

Map 4. The twenty-nine subdistricts of Altona (pre-1927 borders)

density levels. Thus, in subdistrict 11 a population of over ten thousand shared eleven hectares; in subdistrict 18 nearly nine thousand persons rubbed shoulders on twelve hectares of living space. These districts, like those of subdistricts 10, 15, and 16 or the areas adjacent to the Haupt-kirche (subdistricts 3 and 8), were considered by contemporaries to be the social blackspots of the Altstadt.[16]

The only other part of the city to share similar characteristics was an area covered by subdistricts 22, 24, and 25 in Ottensen, where approximately fifteen thousand persons also lived in conditions of dire poverty. In the dilapidated sidestreets and courtyards of these neighborhoods, especially those closest to the railway station, the residents displayed the same social symptoms of bitter destitution typical of the worst areas of the Alt-stadt.[17]

Many parts of the Altstadt and of Ottensen were permeated with small factory workshops and fish smokeries, each adding to the cacophony of inner-city noise and environmental pollution.[18] But it was not only the close proximity of industrial and residential accommodation and the attendant health risks that worried observers. The quality of accommodation itself was a problem. The Altstadt's housing stock was generally not very good, built along narrow streets or around cramped courts. In the southern neighborhoods of the Altstadt, between Breitestraße and the quayside, some of the housing dated from the early eighteenth century, when the city had been rebuilt after the Swedish Fire of 1713.

In 1910 official estimates put the number of people living in cellars and attics or in back courts at nearly nine thousand.[19] The pressure on housing during World War I exacerbated this situation, as officials soon discovered at the first postwar housing census carried out in May 1918. They found that nearly three thousand dwellings, mostly in the Altstadt, were unoccupied. A closer inspection of nearly half of these found that 28 percent were thoroughly uninhabitable, and a further 42.5 percent were inadequate for human use. A further report on twenty-four hundred apartments found that only eight hundred were in a condition allowing for immediate occupation, a thousand were in need of repair, while six hundred were either attic or cellar dwellings unfit for human habitation. Although the number of cellar dwellings had been reduced by the mid-1920s, the overall problem of a large number of poor-quality apartments had actually increased slightly.[20] Particular subdistricts in the Altstadt (i.e., subdistricts 9, 10, 12–14,16, and 18) had heavy concentrations of the poorer category of court dwellings, somewhere between a fifth and a third of housing in each subdistrict, and thus far above the Altstadt average of 13 percent.[21]

The housing office also found that the smaller the apartment the

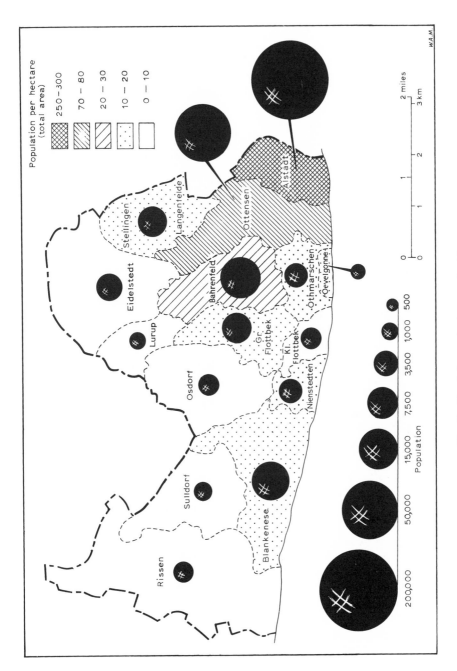

Population per hectare
(total area)

250 – 300
70 – 80
20 – 30
10 – 20
0 – 10

Alstadt

Ottensen

Langenfelde

Stellingen

Bahrenfeld

Eidelstedt

Othmarschen

Oevelgonne

Lurup

Gr.
Flottbek

Kl.
Flottbek

Osdorf

Nienstedten

Sulldorf

Blankenese

Rissen

W.A.M.

2 miles
3 km

2

1

1

0
0

500
1,000
3,500
7,500
15,000
50,000
200,000
Population

Map 5. Population per hectare, greater Altona

greater the level of overcrowding. Of approximately a thousand dwellings in the Altstadt inspected by the office in the early years of the republic, a quarter were overcrowded; around 12 percent were insanitary; nearly 18 percent lacked sufficient lighting and ventilation; over 5 percent were vermin infested; 7.4 percent provided inadequate privacy for the sexes; close to 15 percent were found to be damp and dirty; and nearly 16 percent lacked beds.[22]

The number of occupants to a room in such dwellings was usually about two or three times that found in larger flats, although this situation was to improve a little by the mid-1920s.[23] Again, the problem related to the Altstadt's "blackspots." For instance, in subdistricts 9, 10, 11 over a third of housing in the 1920s was either shared by two or more families or had a single subtenant. By far the larger part of sharers and subtenants were not related either by blood or marriage, thus raising the specter of the "dissolution" of the family.[24]

Poor housing bred poor health. For example, respiratory illnesses and tuberculosis accounted for a fifth of cases at the city hospital in the Allee throughout the 1920s. By comparison less than a tenth of patients at Blankenese's hospital had such problems. Moreover, a third of deaths of those between the ages of fifteen and forty-five were due to these illnesses.[25] A vivid example of the sort of conditions encountered by housing officials in the Altstadt is provided by the following report from a social worker's case diary from November 1919:

> At my visit I found a cellar flat in many ways unfit for human beings. It comprised two rooms and an absolutely dark cupboard. The first room, which one reached by the main door of the flat, was aired only through this door. Because the windows had fallen out and wooden boards had been nailed in their place, the room was as good as dark. . . . The second room is inhabited, that is, solely by the 52 year old E. The room is very low; the windows are in part missing. The unbelievable dirt which exists here has a frightening effect. The walls are totally black. The man himself, in his face, on his hands and on his clothes, was so black, that one must assume that he works all day in coal dust. E. is unable to work since a year and a half. He has tuberculosis and suffers from open sores on his feet. He receives a sick pension and a small support from welfare, 40 RM monthly. The man is wholly unable to look after himself, he needs a carer (*Pfleger*). There is little point arranging another flat for him.[26]

Nearly twenty years later, in 1937, an investigation into housing and social conditions in the Altstadt produced a rather bleak picture (which the Nazi authorities were reluctant to accept).[27] The findings of sixty individual reports on cellar dwellings in the Altstadt showed that the mostly father-less families of 337 elementary school children had to survive on incomes below the "existence minimum," housed in "overcrowded and inadequate apartments," which in view of the shortage of housing had become a "nec-essary evil."[28]

Poor housing, if not the cause, was certainly an important factor con-tributing to poor health and early death, especially among infants of the poorest and most vulnerable households. A report in May 1934 identified three main causes of infant mortality: premature birth, diarrhea with vomit-ing, and frailty (*Lebensschwäche*). Indeed, during the mid-years of the republic frailty accounted for between 35 and 48 percent of infant mortality.

The mothers of such infants were mostly young and frequently single and resided in areas notorious for their impoverished conditions. Not sur-prisingly, the data for 1923 show that three-quarters of children who died before fifteen years of age came from proletarian backgrounds, whereas children from middle-class households, notably from Mittelstand and employee families, accounted for just 16 percent.[29] For example, the num-ber of still-born babies and incidence of infant mortality was usually higher in the poor neighborhoods of south, north, and east districts of the Altstadt (subdistricts 1 and 2 and 7–10). These districts also had the high-est levels of illegitimate births in the city. Conversely, in the neighbor-hoods of the southwest district (subdistricts 4 and 5), where, according to Kaufmann, the best residential streets of the Altstadt were to be found, infant mortality stood at just one-tenth of all deaths and thus was well below both Altstadt and city levels.[30]

The social and spatial distribution of poverty at neighborhood level was accentuated during periods of economic crisis. The number of Altona's poverty-stricken inhabitants had increased greatly as a result of the war and inflation and had spread beyond the poorer working class to encompass parts of a struggling lower middle class. In the ten years of war and inflation the number of persons with annual incomes in excess of 5,000 marks, and therefore liable to taxation, was halved, mostly at the lower end.[31] Women especially, were badly affected by the war and its aftermath. They formed the overwhelming majority of the 40,969 recipients of family war welfare (*Kriegsfamilienunterstützung*) on 1 April 1917. Their menfolk were either at the front or had been killed, and they were left to struggle both during and after the war with their children.[32]

The introduction of wartime kitchens in 1917 providing cheap mid-day and evening meals was taken up eagerly by a large number of inhabi-tants. By the spring of 1917 an estimated thirty thousand persons, or roughly 16 percent of the population, were being fed by publicly run agencies, either at one of the city's eleven kitchens or at the *Mittelstand* kitchen for the impoverished middle class.[33] While some recipients may have been driven onto public support because of the coal, gas, and potato shortages, the majority ate there not from contingency but because of the permanence of their indigent condition.[34]

Throughout this period local authorities were faced with the problem of having to feed large numbers of impoverished and hungry citizens trapped by financial and material hardship. War and inflation had left behind a sizable number of invalids, widows, and orphans in need of support. Such was the neediness among the elderly and children that the authorities sought to increase the number of public canteens in Ottensen, Bahrenfeld, and the Altstadt's north district.[35]

The spatial configuration of the hunger crisis persisted into the years of inflation and economic instability. In the first quarter of 1923 the municipal welfare office administered approximately 64,731,393 marks in material and money benefits to residents in the Altstadt.[36] An examination of the distribution of 57,927 food tokens dispensed between January and the end of March, and accounting for nearly a third of this cost, shows that by far the greatest demand for municipal poor relief came from subdistrict 3 in the area just south of the Hauptkirche, where 56 percent of residents made requests for tokens. In others—such as subdistricts 1, 6, and 15—demand for food tokens ranged between 15 and 35 percent of the resident population over the three months in question. Five other districts showed percentage levels of between 12 and 22. Worst off appear to have been subdistricts 11 through 14 and also 20, where fifty-five cases of malnutrition were reported to the city's chief of welfare, Senator Schöning, in early 1923.[37]

By contrast, the socially and materially better-off subdistricts of the Altstadt—notably 4, 5, 8, 17, and 19—drew less upon municipal aid. In Ottensen a similar divergence between hungry and bountiful areas existed. Thus, in subdistricts 22, 23, and 24 requests for food relief ranged between 12 and 20 percent of their resident populations, whereas in subdistrict 25 less than 14 percent of local inhabitants made requests, and in subdistrict 26 the number of requests was negligible.

The stabilization of the economy in 1924 did little to alleviate the hardship of many of Altona's citizens. For many their well-being continued to depend on a charitable wholesome midday meal. The Speiseanstalt von 1830—which provided the bulk of cheap meals after the withdrawal of the war canteens in September 1920—was still supplying a large number of subsidized meals in the mid-1920s, somewhere between 500- and 600-liter portions daily.[38]

The Depression years recalled the hunger and hardship of the war and inflation years. The demand for some sort of publicly provided meal, especially for the unemployed and their families, rose steeply, so that in March 1933 over fifteen thousand meals were served at the Altstadt's soup kitchen in the Blumenstraße, and the opening of a second canteen in Ottensen to meet an expected doubling in need was being planned.[39] The situation among children was particularly bad. Pastor Hansen, the headmaster of the VI Boys Primary School in the Altstadt's Lucienstraße, reported that at least four hundred pupils in his school, whose catchment area took in children from subdistricts 1 and 2, were generally undernourished, and he expressed his concern that this would affect both their physical and intellectual development. The children had been examined by the city medical officer, who found that at least seventy-two children were suffering from "extreme malnutrition through lack of available food."[40]

The children of impoverished families not only lacked food during difficult times; they often lacked decent clothing at most times. The files of the Poor Commission from the last two decades of the previous century and the first decade of this one are voluminous and detail the perennial material needs of Altona's indigent folk.[41] A particular problem related to the lack of decent clothing among Altona's school population. A report commissioned in 1937 on social conditions in the Altstadt found "that some pupils could not attend school in winter because of the lack of overcoats; that there is a whole group of children who only have a single shirt or single suit and dress to call their own; that in winter many pupils only have shoes made of remnants (*Zeugschuhe*) or cheap plimsolls or own one pair of boots," and, when these had to be repaired, then attendance suffered.[42]

Prevented from attending school for lack of adequate clothing, such children also found that they were inadequately kitted out when they came to finally leave school. Again, the same subdistricts appear. For instance, the city's three main welfare offices covering the Altstadt and Ottensen, together with the four suburban branches, provided financial support for clothing for 267 Easter school leavers and confirmants in 1933. The cost of clothing provision for these Easter confirmants totaled 3,996 reichsmark, averaging 15 reichsmark each. Welfare Offices 1 and 2 covering the Altstadt dealt with 164 cases (or over 60 percent), accounting for 63 percent of the overall cost. The third main office covered parts of the Altstadt and Ottensen-Bahrenfeld and handled about a quarter of the children. And, again, in 1935 around 50 percent of the thousand Easter confirmants in need of clothing (a suit for the boys and a dress for the girls, together with shoes, socks, and underwear for both sexes) came from the Altstadt.[43]

As part of a campaign to offset the social problems brought on by the war, city and charity organizations took in large numbers of poor children, many of them orphaned, frequently sending them to the country. During the 1920s groups of poor and undernourished children were regularly sent to holiday camps in the country or on the island of Trischen in the North Sea in order to rebuild their physical and mental reserves.[44] The municipal authority was not the only body involved. The Altona branch of the Workers' Welfare association frequently sought substantial financial support from the city administration, regional government, and private firms, in order to set up day nurseries for working mothers or to send children from the Altstadt to various recreation camps for a fortnight, including to the municipal-owned children's home in Neugraben (Heide), or to holiday work placements at farms in the surrounding countryside.[45]

Similarly, the Isrealitische Humane Women's Association in Altona dispensed recreational charity during the summer months in the city's stadium to around two hundred Jewish children from the poor Jewish neighborhood around the Parallelstraße, near the harbor. The association believed that team games in the "sun, light and air" would "mean colonization in a spiritual sense, implanting new values into childish hearts and minds," thus facilitating future integration into the community.[46] These programs continued after 1933 and indeed may even have expanded under the auspices of the National Socialist People's Welfare. Hundreds of children (but excluding Jewish children), sometimes accompanied by their mothers, were sent on *Kindertransports* into the country for recuperation.[47] By the later 1930s poverty had seeped beyond its traditional milieu in the city's slum districts into bordering social groups. By 1938 the families of impoverished white-collar employees joined with their poor working-class neighbors on recuperative excursions into the countryside.[48]

Officials and charities throughout the period voiced their deep concern at the social conditions prevailing in the Altstadt. Particularly worrying to those in authority was the long-term effect of such conditions upon the lives of the young. A common worry held by Altona's administrators (whether republicans or Nazis) was that the awful living conditions in the slum districts would produce physically, mentally, and socially inadequate citizens.[49] At stake was not only the well-being of the individual and the integrity of the family but also the future of German society as a whole. The director of the city housing office, Dr. Otto Fischer, gave expression to the general apprehension in an article published in the city gazette in 1928:

> the stamp of inferiority is imprinted on the youth growing up in these apartments [and] destroying their inner self-value, which in later life renders adjustment and assimilation into public and community life nigh impossible.[50]

Lumpen People of the "Abruzzenviertel"

At the International Housing and Town Planning Congress held in Berlin in 1931, Dr. Jürgen Brandt, a planning officer from Hamburg, provided an analysis on the evolution of slums:

> Slums develop mostly because certain older neighborhoods are stymied in their development as a result of the confined property conditions . . . the street network is inadequate; the buildings have poor lighting and ventilation and scant hygiene facilities. The better-off tenants therefore move away to the newer suburbs, and the desirable businesses follow them, the social niveau of residents sinks; the properties lose in value, causing the situation of the property-owners to worsen; the buildings fall into disrepair, since large sums for repairs and refurbishment are no longer economical; the rents plunge and finally the economic decline of the entire district can no longer be halted.

It was the duty of planners to revive these ailing districts back to economic health in order to sustain the well-being of the city. But the motive for paying attention to the slums was not only economic. Brandt continued:

> A reason for clearance programs is the fact that in individual districts danger areas of a social, health or political nature develop, which necessitate public intervention. On the one hand, the restless and darker elements of the population, especially prostitutes and their following, gather in the slum quarters; on the other hand, many unproductive families with children, especially large families, also reside there. The worst social nuisance results from this cheek-by-jowl cohabitation of these most disparate elements.[51]

This typology found widespread acceptance throughout Altona's administration and among those who came into contact with the Altstadt. Heinz Kaufmann, an empirical sociologist working in the city's statistical office, referred to the residents of the poorest districts as the "flotsam of the big city." An official in the city's buildings department (*Baupflegeamt*) described the residents of the slums in a short report of 1919, as "parasites" (*Schmarotzer*) and insolent (*Wanzen*) and nothing other than "totally propertyless people, devoid of culture," who "live badly and spoil their homes completely, and doubtlessly after a corresponding time, even causing and bringing about the ruin of the city."[52]

This apocalyptic vision was shared by Altona's Senator Schöning, who had responsibility for welfare. Schöning believed that in the "vast and morally endangered quarter" of the Altstadt there lurked "very many trouble-making elements."[53] A view also held by the police. Recalling his experiences in quelling disturbances in Altona-Hamburg, the later head of the Greater Hamburg Ordnungspolizei, Lothar Danner, likened the Altstadt to the wild, harsh terrain of the Abruzzo in Italy, whose inhabitants were notorious for their social banditry, when he dubbed this part of Altona "Abruzzenviertel."[54] As we shall see, contemporaries (both republicans and Nazis) stigmatized these Altona citizens as feckless and criminally inclined "asocials" who had to learn the educative value of reform and discipline.[55]

For Max Brauer the principal aim of municipal policy in Altona was to reduce the poor's dependence upon the welfare state, so that the individual could take responsibility for his or her own destiny.[56] Of course, the guiding hand of benevolent welfare was supposed to direct this process of emancipation. The organizational fabric of the municipal welfare system had been first woven during the days of poor relief before 1914, when the city was divided into twenty-nine districts, each with a representative (*Bezirksvorsteher*) responsible for dealing with applications for assistance (see map 4). This structure, with its network of mostly *mittelständisch* male *Bezirksvorsteher,* remained in place after 1918 and again, after 1933, functioning as the basis for the welfare management of the population.[57]

The gulf between the values of the republican welfare state and those of the poor was nowhere more in evidence than over the issues of work, welfare, and shelter. Here the vision frequently clashed with the social reality of the poor, as very often the latter pursued their own strategies of self-help. And, typically, such practices brought the participants into conflict with the city welfare authorities and sometimes with the police. The boundary between social respectability and a dissolute and criminal lifestyle said to characterize Altona's slum neighborhoods was fixed in the popular imagination by the experience of two particular waves of plunder during and soon after World War I. In both cases, at a time of great hunger and when impoverished residents of the Altstadt felt severely disadvantaged by the regulated market, crowds formed in last resort to protest for fairer access to food and items of clothing. During the first wave, in 1917, the contested point was the freedom to purchase bread with money rather than with ration cards, while in 1920 rising prices forced people onto the streets. In both cases the state was openly defied and even put on the defensive by the city's "unruly" people.[58]

The first wave of plunder, in February 1917, lasted six days, over which period two hundred bakeries in the Altstadt and Ottensen were subjected to theft or forced sales to the tune of nearly forty thousand marks.

Map 6. "Abruzzen" quarter of the Alstadt (n.d.)

Police sources show that over 65 percent of the plundering clustered around certain neighborhoods in the Altstadt and that the majority of the two hundred people detained by the security forces also came from here.[59] The crowds, consisting mostly of women and youths but with men in the rear, descended on particular shops and demanded that the owners sell "bread without ration cards." Shopkeepers were usually given cash for the bread, and only in those cases where a shopkeeper refused to comply did the crowd take loaves without paying or cause damage to the premises.[60] The experience of Wilhelm Schlüter, a master baker, is a good illustration. He faced the full fury of the mob, as he called them, when he refused to meet their demand for bread. The crowd rushed the front of his shop, demolishing windows and door, emptied his shelves, and, for good measure, set about looting his flat at the rear. His personal losses far outweighed those of his stock.[61]

The second major wave of plunder to shock the city took place in June 1920. Unlike the February incident, rioting took place almost exclusively in the districts neighboring St Pauli and spread beyond bakeries to include fish stalls, small grocery shops, department stores, and shoe and clothing businesses.[62] The weekend of trouble began on Friday the twenty-sixth, when a group of young men strode along the Reeperbahn crossing from Hamburg into Altona via the Reichenstraße and finally into the Große Bergstraße, where they smashed the windows of a shoe shop and stole its contents. Hangers-on and curious onlookers joined in. When the police finally arrived, they managed to arrest fifteen persons. And it was these arrests that sparked off the further rioting and looting over the weekend.

At first the crowds targeted shoe shops in particular. In one case, where a shop had closed its doors early on Saturday, the crowd demanded it reopen, "then they pushed their way in, some stood behind the counter and proceeded to sell the stock at reduced prices."[63] The crowd left behind 421 marks as payment for one hundred and fifty pairs of shoes and slippers valued by the owner at over 17,000 marks. The crowd extended its activities over the rest of the weekend to food shops and suppliers, demanding fair prices. The fish smokery of Tolgreve and Company in the Kleine Freiheit was relieved of a large quantity of its stock at a much reduced price. And Wilhelmine Sellhorn's small dairy goods shop was besieged by a large crowd late on Monday evening and was forced to sell ninety-five pounds of margarine at half-price.[64]

These waves of popular theft and collective defiance no doubt hardened the attitudes of the authorities toward the "lumpen" crowds (see chap. 6). For the present the behavior of Altstadt residents during the shortage years of the war and early postwar years notched into the public mind the danger of a menacing poverty that nurtured all types of villainy that threatened to spread and engulf the rest of society. For instance, the wartime controls over the distribution of goods led to a thriving "black economy," in which local inhabitants tried to supplement their meager income and rations by evading the strict rationing laws.[65] The distribution office in Altona had to issue numerous warnings to both housewives and traders on the misuse of ration cards and on false welfare claims. By 1917 the illegal traffic in ration cards and fraudulent petty claims had reached worrying proportions.[66]

The wider the state spread its net over the consumer economy, the greater the likelihood of courtyard practices falling foul of the law. In April 1916 the masting and slaughtering of pigs came under the supervision of the municipal food distribution offices.[67] Private persons were still allowed to keep pigs but had to register these with the meat inspectorate. Strict regulations laid down when the pig could be killed (it had to be full-grown and to have reached a certain weight), and owners had first to gain the inspectorate's permission, who then supervised the slaughter. Part of the meat was then appropriated by the foods office for wider distribution. By early 1917, in the midst of severe food shortages, meat rations in Altona had been reduced to 200 grams, causing a premium to be put on the price of black market meat. As a result, secret slaughterings of young, half-weight pigs increased dramatically in the spring of 1917. And the authorities in Altona soon discovered that in subdistrict 22 of the Altstadt these slaughterings were being organized by a syndicate run by a group of widows from their courts and kitchens in Große Gärtnerstraße.[68]

The wartime *Bürgfrieden* also produced a battery of housing laws, intervening protectively on the side of weaker tenants, including those with rent arrears. Controlled rents were generally successful, remaining below other living costs, and actually declined as a proportion of the household budget during these years.[69] These protective measures remained in place after the war, continuing to protect tenants "from an intolerable rise in rents and inopportune notices to quit."[70] An amendment in March 1922 even extended rent controls to all housing built prior to July 1918 (so-called peacetime rent, or *Friedensmiete*). This invariably acted as a magnet, drawing weaker socioeconomic groups toward such housing.[71]

This protection was partially removed by the housing law of 30 June 1926, with the result that landlords took the opportunity to rid themselves of financially weak or troublesome tenants, meaning those mostly in arrears with their rents. During 1926 approximately 630 rental contracts were abrogated by landlords, and of these just over half led to evictions. The manner of the evictions provoked discomfort in some parts of the city administration. Many of those evicted were very poor tenants and included very large families, who were turned out of their homes, some just three days before Christmas, amid what were described as "unpleasant and distressing" scenes that were "downright outrageous and shameful for our social conditions."[72]

Evictions in both the private and public sector continued unabated during the Depression, when Altona's poorest were at their most vulnerable. Thus, during the first half of 1931 the local police reported a monthly average of 90 evictions, totaling 598 between 1 January and 22 July.[73] Figures for 1932 show a rise in the number of evictions between January and July, in spite of the deepening economic crisis and mass unemployment. In this period bailiffs prepared to carry out 908 evictions, though a number of them were eventually postponed. The Weimar authorities believed that many tenants scheduled for eviction were "asocial elements, unworthy of protection."[74] In fact, most were victims of unemployment or pensioners.

Rent arrears and evictions did not just affect tenants of the poor districts but extended to the better-off populations of newer housing. Indeed, most tenants of the new estates were adversely affected regardless of their occupation, as the Depression deepened. And some tenants put themselves into arrears by refusing to pay increases in rent.[75] Nor were arrears an exclusive feature of the economic climate of the early 1930s. Between 1924 and 1931 rent arrears among tenants of the model housing estate Steenkamp rose fourfold, from 10,498 reichsmark to 47,908 reichsmark. Among tenants of the new blocks arrears rose approximately 150-fold, from 1,156 reichsmark to 172,794 reichsmark. No doubt the Depression had exacerbated the problem, for by 1931 arrears from new housing accounted for 12 percent of annual rent revenue, double the level of the previous year. In the city-owned older housing the burden of arrears in 1930 was slightly less, at 10 percent of expected revenue, having also doubled over the previous year.[76]

How did the city administration, as landlord, respond to the problem of rent arrears in the new housing estates? Usually, when a tenant had got into difficulty, the housing office either made arrangements for the outstanding rent to be paid in installments until the debt was cleared or, if the tenant could no longer afford the accommodation, applied pressure (where necessary) upon the tenant to accept a transfer to cheaper (usually older accommodation).[77] Evictions seldom appear in the reports during the Depression, suggesting perhaps that some leniency was exercised. Unlike private landlords—or, indeed, the Nazi administration—the republican administration faced strong tenant organizations on the estates and appear reluctant to antagonize these groups. Eviction was kept as a last resort and as an "educative" instrument and periodically deployed against a recalcitrant tenant.[78] By 1933 tenants of municipal housing who had fallen into arrears were estimated to number 1,600, but, with their tenant associations broken, they faced imminent eviction.[79]

The gradual withdrawal of the state from its protective role in the mid-1920s led to instances of "self-help" among tenants. There was, for instance, collective opposition to bailiffs carrying out evictions in a callous manner. Neighbors rallied round when the family of W., in the Holstpassage in the heart of the Altstadt, was thrown out of their apartment in October 1926. They protested at the bailiff's callous and disrespectful way of dumping the family's meager belongings onto the street. The police had to be called to protect the bailiff from the menaces of the crowd and to prevent a "traffic hindrance." When the police filed its report of the incident, concern was expressed at the way the family was ruthlessly ejected from its lodgings, quoting a local newspaper's description of the eviction as summoning images of "mediaeval conditions."[80] This was not the only occasion when the police had to be called to the scene of an eviction. And they soon found themselves at odds with the administration's policy toward tenants in arrears.

Paul-Theodor Hoffmann recounted the case of residents of an "entire court who had not paid rent for months," partly through no fault of their own but also partly from wickedness.[81] He believed that they were incited to hold back from paying their rents by the "Müller family," and in particular by Frau Müller, described by Hoffmann as a "trouble-seeking, interfering," and "querulous woman." Under the influence of a "Frau Müller" whole neighborhoods could be led down the path of a virtual rent strike, challenging the authority of property relations. For this reason the authorities had to act ironhanded. The family was evicted, the children taken into care, and the parents separated in the asylum for the homeless. Hoffmann reported: "The whole court watched in shock. Psychologically, the effect is extremely successful."

Evictions thus allowed the city administration to reassert its control over recalcitrant neighborhoods. In a letter to the chief of police in late 1926 Senator Schöning reminded him of the indoctrinal value of the hard-line eviction:

> out of educational considerations for the head of the household to be evicted, [and] in view of the attention each eviction attracts in the neighbourhood, under no circumstances should the impact of an eviction be so weakened, thereby totally abrogating its effect. There must always be the imperative and warning to others: Avoid this, as well as and however you might.[82]

Schöning was keen to distinguish between "deserving" and "undeserving" cases, but inquiries made at the time showed that the majority of those who fell behind with their rent did so simply because they were too poor to keep up.[83] The "educative" policy of the city welfare and real estate offices came in for severe criticism from all sides, including one of their own *Bezirksvorsteher,* who described the municipal authority as one of "the most ruthless landlords," an allegation it sought to rebuff. And among the public the impression gained was that of a hard-hearted eviction policy that broke promises of social betterment and destroyed already fragile existences.[84]

Evictions did not create the problem of homelessness in Altona, though they added to it considerably. The city had an endemic problem of homelessness, due largely to the increasing numbers of unemployed migrants who flocked to it in search of work and shelter. The police processed nearly seven thousand cases of homelessness in 1923, and nearly a thousand "vagrants" were arrested.[85] In the mid-1920s the city appeared to be inundated with such people, causing an outcry in some quarters of the public. One of the reasons for coming to Altona was that a number of unscrupulous landlords were successfully attracting the unemployed homeless from the red-light and amusement district straddling the Altona-Hamburg border into makeshift and sometimes unlicensed doss houses. Once domiciled in Altona, they could apply for welfare, which then went toward paying for their primitive accommodation and for the alcohol supplied by their landlords.

In the course of a campaign against unlicensed lodging houses in late 1926 and early 1927, housing officers found examples of extreme overcrowding. One house in the Finckenstraße, in subdistrict 8 upon inspection was found to have ninety beds; another old timber-framed house in the same street had twenty-seven beds on one floor alone; another in the Kleine Bergstraße (also in subdistrict 8) had forty-one beds in sixteen rooms on two floors and in the attic; at 13 Dreierstraße (subdistrict 1) a rooming license had been granted for six beds in three rooms; the owner, however, had added an extra seven beds while only increasing the number of rooms by one.[86]

Apart from acute levels of overcrowding, the danger of fire, and risk to public health, the transient occupants of these premises were allegedly causing a public nuisance. Complaints were made to the authorities about the "shockingly raucous traffic [in people] during the evening and morning" outside the taverns where beds had been installed. Local residents of Bergstraße went in fear of the motley crowds of drunks and beggars, while local business suffered, according to reports. Forty-two local businesses from the Kleine Bergstraße, Bergstraße, Königstraße, and Rathausmarkt joined forces with Ernst Zimmermann and his fellow small entrepreneurs from the *Industrie Haus,* in the court of numbers 54–58 Kleine Freiheit, to petition the city to take action against yet another unlicensed lodging house for singles and families with children, on the third floor of their building.[87]

The majority of homeless people were deemed to be degenerate, either as the result of alcohol abuse or through an alleged choice of lifestyle, such as the irresistible urge for tramping, but "seldom because of factors beyond their control."[88] In order to combat the problem, the city opened a shelter for the homeless in early February 1925 in the Katharinenstraße in the Altstadt, and in July of the following year a workhouse at Rondenbarg in Bahrenfeld was founded.

The Katharinenstraße shelter provided temporary accommodation (up to five days) for a maximum of 300 persons in extreme need only. Women and minors under the age of eighteen had special quarters away from adult males. The shelter was open from six o'clock in the evening to six o'clock the following morning, when a warm breakfast was served. The users had to pay for their night accommodation by working at the Rondenbarg center for four hours. Conditions in the shelter were kept intentionally to a very primitive level in order to discourage all but the truly destitute. Nonetheless, in the four years between 1925 and 1928 the number of annual registrations appear to have ranged between 59,000 and 66,000, of which the overwhelming number were adult males. The two peak years were 1926 and 1928.[89] At Rondenbarg "productive work" was assigned to the daily intake of between 120 and 140 persons, according to physical or mental ability and status. Tasks were not only rigorous in order to deter the "malingering elements" but also aimed at reconstructing the lost "inner discipline" of vagabonds and delinquent youth especially, and acted thereby as a "cure," "setting [them] on the straight and narrow."[90]

For Altona's reformers toil was a useful and necessary activity; it emancipated the worker from poverty and contributed to the common good, because in their eyes work should always be "productive." It also entailed discipline and order and was thus filled with moral purpose. This ethos of work was culturally defined, however, and did not include other means of gaining an income. Traditionally, the unskilled working-class economy was a casual one. People were accustomed to having a number of marginal jobs and to drawing an income from a variety of sources. For many people welfare benefits were not so much a supplementary as a necessary source of income in an economy that provided only irregular money. During periods of crisis the poor depended primarily on handouts from the welfare office and supplemented these with income from whatever casual work that could be obtained. The most common issue over which a conflict occurred, therefore, was that related to the so-called welfare scrounger, who allegedly defrauded the city of its scarce resources by drawing benefits while also earning an income.

The background to the problem was that for much of the period Weimar's city administrations were themselves under severe financial pressures and therefore often had to seek savings wherever possible. The desire to conserve scarce resources, coupled with social prejudice against an alleged "feckless" and "work-shy" poor, meant that welfare benefits for this group came under greater scrutiny. Thus, Altona's Socialist administration drew in its welfare net, confronting the poor with a more deterrent and punitive policy of workfare and exclusion. A key strategy in this tougher welfare regime involved, for instance, regular clamp-downs on those described as welfare scroungers inhabiting the gray zones of the economy.

In 1924, for instance, the city's police were instructed to check the papers of beggars, so-called asocials, in one of a number of concerted actions with the Hamburg authorities, to see if they were also in receipt of welfare payments.[91] In early October 1929 Brauer (who was concerned about the escalating cost of welfare, which had risen from approximately 419,737 reichsmark in 1928 to 670,003 reichsmark in 1929) ordered the mass control of street traders and hawkers, "since I am of the opinion that among these people there are many who are supported by the welfare office or by the employment office."[92] If Brauer hoped that through stricter vetting savings could be made, he was to be sorely disappointed. For, of the 135 persons controlled, only 6 were found to be in receipt of some form of weekly benefit, of between nine and twenty marks. All six lived in the Altstadt.

Similar crackdowns on the "gray economy" were repeated in the early and mid-1930s.[93] In February 1931 it was the turn of poor unemployed families who had built about eighty makeshift wooden huts (*Wohnlauben*) on a piece of vacant land in Groß Flottbek. Many of these were, in fact, incomers. Brauer was irritated that the city's landscape was being spoiled by the development of what he called "crate villages" (*Kistendörfer*) inhabited by "Gypsies." He called for a draconian inquisition by officers from the city's welfare, health, and building control departments and the housing police. Such actions against what were in most respects vulnerable groups in society caused much consternation among some administrators, such as Senator Oelsner, who described the action as "administrative terror."[94]

The people of this particular crate village were not, in fact, Gypsies. Brauer's use of the term in connection to a clamp-down on welfare scroungers was based on an earlier episode in 1929, when the city's Gypsy population had been targeted. According to Senator Kirch, they were "swamping the city," and so stringent controls were called for in order to remove them from the welfare registers. The authorities, from the Social

Democrat police senator August Kirch to the liberal head of the welfare office, Dr. Baumann, agreed that the men should be made to labor in the workhouse and the women put to work as cleaners in the city's public institutions.[95]

A parallel situation arose in 1932, when large numbers of itinerant traders moved onto a piece of land on the corner of Kielerstraße and Häferweg, in subdistrict 20. The owner of the land charged a monthly rent of between ten and fifteen marks for each caravan. The traders, once they had settled, made use of their entitlement to draw small sums of welfare, up to eleven marks a week for a married couple. The caravan park was inspected on a number of occasions by municipal officers in order to check the validity of claims for support. After interrogating Frau G. and her husband, Ludwig, who proved very forthcoming, officers discovered that a number of persons on the site were allegedly making large sums of money, through house-to-house sales of fowl and personal items, such as umbrellas. The informants, who themselves were trading with little success but with a license, were clearly hoping that their benefit, which had been cut in half, would be restored as a result of their civic-mindedness. Welfare officers who went to the site on a number of occasions claimed they repeatedly found groups of "nonchalant idle loafers" enjoying a smoke in a "tobacco club" and who "in general" responded to questioning "not without irony." And, usually, the persons they really wanted to interview "had just left," thus evading control.[96]

The welfare department was worried that, since Altona presented such an easy picking, these itinerant traders would be loathe to move on. "It is really high time," wrote one official, "that one diluted the 'sweet indolence' of this type of caravan owner" through a raft of tougher measures. In order to "reduce the length of stay of dubious elements" and to deter others from following suit, he suggested that benefits be paid in kind rather than in cash; that the level of support be reduced; and that, as in the recommendation for the Gypsies in 1929, they too should be subjected to the discipline of forced labor (*Pflichtarbeit*) as a condition for receiving welfare.[97]

These recommendations were acted upon vigorously after 1933 by the Nazis, who were able to implement with greater force the draconian welfare policies begun under the republic. Thus, within ten months from January 1934 the welfare authorities in Altona had reduced the number of Gypsies dependent on public relief from 154 to 21, while a report on the handling of a group of 68 Gypsies confined to the Rondenbarg in 1934 both recalled the punitive work fare treatment meted out to Altona's "asocials" before 1933 and provided a chilling foretaste of the dehumanizing horror of the concentration camp.[98]

Being a *Hafenstadt,* Altona had its full share of taverns and drinkers. In 1932 there were 364 taverns (excluding distilleries and other licensed premises), the majority in the Altstadt and Ottensen. There was practically a tavern, sometimes more, on every corner, especially in the Altstadt.[99] The social and cultural experience of the tavern was integral to the Altstadt's everyday life (and politics, as we shall see in chap. 6). The high levels of alcohol consumption caused concern among organizations seeking the moral and physical improvement of the working class, from the church to the temperance movement to the SPD. These groups claimed that alcoholism was the root problem of crime and rootlessness, even though there was really little hard evidence to show this was the case.[100]

The numbers of men, and to a much lesser degree women, registered as having a drink problem was on the increase during the three decades from 1900. The psychiatric unit at the city's hospital, to which alcoholics were sent, treated 180 cases in 1902, 237 cases in 1906, and 262 cases in 1907. And in the first year of its founding in January 1909 the *Trinkerfürsorgestelle,* sponsored by the *Magistrat* and church organizations in Altona, dealt with 290 cases.[101] An apparent decline in cases occurred during the early years of the republic, when an annual average of 73 alcoholics were registered between 1922 and 1925. This reversed radically from the mid-1920s, however, as the municipal alcoholic welfare unit handled what appeared to be an inexorable rise in the number of cases: from 364 in 1926 to 446 in 1928, of mostly male manual workers in the "prime of their lives."[102]

Temperance charities and social workers saw a strong link between drink, domestic violence, and sexual abuse within the family. And its influence was thought to be behind the cases of habitual desertion and neglected children.[103] The journal of the welfare office in Altona, *Welfare News,* reported regularly on such cases. Typical of these was the tale of the "young, impulsive mother, with a strong disposition for flashy and extravagant things." When her violent and alcoholic common-law husband left her, she attempted suicide. Soon after she took up with another man, who also drank. He too eventually left her and her four children. Sometime later a visit to the doctor revealed that her daughter had contracted a venereal disease from the lover, who had been abusing the small girl. This particularly tragic case was apparently not unusual, though its eventual "happy ending" was.[104]

Typical also was the story of "Ernst," recounted by Hoffmann in his chronicle of Altona in the 1920s. The family, described by Hoffmann as "weak" rather than "immoral," lived in extremely cramped conditions in a two-room cellar flat. Being one of five children, Ernst shared a bed with two younger siblings. There were no bed coverings. Hoffmann expressed the typical middle-class fear that the children "see and hear too much," especially at night. The mother was unable to cope in the struggle against dirt; her smaller children crawled around on the floor in the accumulating filth. Her husband would disappear in the smoky world of the taverns, from which he often failed to return. Because the father was unable to provide for the family, Ernst took over that responsibility and sold newspapers in order to pay the rent.[105]

Some observers were prepared to deduce from the predicament of the individual the fate of society per se. The director of the municipal center for alcohol welfare, Heinrich Scholz, strongly denounced alcohol abuse. In an article published in 1929 he claimed that its degenerative influence led to a "vegetative state," eventually producing the "Untermensch" who was incapable of work or of making any useful contribution to society. Instead, this *Untermensch* imposed a heavy burden upon the community.[106] The phenomenon was applied to the incidence of property crime in particular, about which a link between alcohol abuse, poverty, and theft among children was posited. As an example of this, social workers reported the story of a sixteen-year-old boy following in the beery footsteps of his father, whose own alcoholic exploits caused his loss of work. The grinding poverty at home, coupled with an unpredictable temper, was said to have reduced his wife to a "Käthe-Köllwitz-figure" unable to cope with rearing five children. The older son also began staying out all night, would not hold down a job, and, instead of earning money, stole household items to pay for his alcohol habit.[107]

A similar story was that of the family whose father had been in regular employment as a shipbuilder but who drank heavily. He eventually deserted his wife and eight children, plunging them into dire poverty. The mother could not control the children, and the older boys soon gained the upper hand at home and also began being truant from school. During their absences from classes the boys would head for the harbor, where they hung around and stole coal. They were finally picked up by the police and placed under supervision.[108]

Alcohol-induced poverty thus brought many children into contact with a harsh and raw world. But not all poverty was brought about by alcohol abuse alone. The Children's Protection and Youth Welfare Association of Altona reported in 1920 that too many children were working on the margins of the casual economy. The association believed that this would lead to a decivilizing process.[109] This view had been underscored by the wartime spectacle of children (notably from the Altstadt) foraging for food and getting caught up in the bread and food riots of February 1917 and June 1920.[110] Youngsters, such as Ernst, were expected to contribute to the fragile household economy early in their lives, in order that the family had enough to eat and could maintain a roof over its head. Ernst therefore had to spend less time at school and more time on the streets for the family's sake. As too did twelve-year-old W. and his three siblings, who hawked fruit and vegetables on Altona's postwar streets in order to keep the family afloat. Their life on the economic brink also propelled them onto the moral margins of society, documented by the sister who gave birth at fifteen.[111]

Over the period 1923–36 petty larceny accounted overwhelmingly for the cases dealt with by the police. But apart from anecdotal evidence there is little other social data to corroborate the popular assumption regarding the link between alcohol and crime. In fact, during periods of extreme economic pressures either material need or tougher policing forced up the theft (and general crime) rate. As we shall see in chapter 6, an alleged lumpen lifestyle of petty larceny and crime in general became ever more closely synonymous with "communist low life," which threatened to break out of the slums and which, the Nazis claimed, only they could hold back.

Hans Ostwald, in his *History of Customs of the Inflation,* found that youngsters who were truant from school were often to be found hanging around on the streets looking for some means of earning a penny, usually as messengers (*Laufbürschen*). In Altona truancy accounted for between a third and half of the cases dealt with by the local police between 1923 and 1931.[112] Nearly all of them concerned young teenagers who were truant with the connivance, willing and otherwise, of their parents. While not all truants engaged in acts of petty larceny, the fact that they could roam unsupervised on the streets meant that they were already treading the terrain where such crime took place.

As we have seen, the link between a world of poverty and a culture of crime was thought to be strongest among youth. Richard Bessel, in his recent study of post-1918 German society, confirms the contemporary view that, with the removal of the "educative hand of the father" during the war, an increasingly unregulated and "unrestrained youth" emerged.[113] In Altona observers believed they had hard evidence showing a positive correlation between social degeneration, material want, political upheaval, and youth criminality. Crimes against property and antisocial behavior generally were linked to the moral neglect of youth, especially those from unskilled proletarian families in the slums. Indeed, according to Hoffmann, 60 percent of the Altona youth who appeared in court by the mid-1920s came from this milieu.[114] The city's own published crime data for 1923 (the only ones showing youth separately), however, show that youngsters accounted for barely 1.3 percent of cases processed by the criminal police. And the proportion of youth in police custody remained at around 5 percent of all of those held in the police prison in the Allee from the mid-1920s to the mid-1930s, only rising to nearly 8 percent in the crisis year of 1933, before finally falling to around 3 percent after the mid-1930s.[115]

Already by the 1920s a sizable body of sociological and publicist works purported to show a morally endangered youth in the slum quarters of the big city.[116] Living close to the red-light district that straddled the Altona-Hamburg border, youth were drawn to the bright lights and the pleasures of the forbidden Eden of commercialized leisure and sex around the Nobistor, Große Freiheit, and Finckenstraße, where they were said to congregate in droves.[117] Altona's *Bahnhofsmission* saw 5,050 new arrivals to the city in 1928, mostly working-class and young, who "daily ... can be seen gathered in the squares or at the railway station."[118] The attraction of such "Tümmelplätze" hid from youth the very real dangers of the twilight world of sexual and violent crime. The police therefore carried out regular controls and frequently raided the *Grenzlokale* and hostels, rounding up these mostly unskilled working-class youth, taking suspects of crimes into custody, and delivering the others to the city's homeless asylum and workhouse.[119]

Altona's welfare agencies painted a picture of an unregulated and unruly youth who had to be reined in. The war and revolution had not only swept away the old Wilhelmine order; it had also brought about a fundamental change in the relationship between youth and authority within the home, at the workplace, and in the public sphere. For instance, the eight-hour workday, introduced in 1918, was not only a benefit to working youth aged between fourteen and twenty years old, who accounted for about 17 and 12 percent of the work force in industry and crafts, and commerce and transport, respectively.[120] It also brought with it "much that is detrimental to youth, especially for non-organised youth," according to the head of the Office for Youth Care and Sport, Oskar Lorenzen.[121] He maintained that Altona's unskilled youth had too much time and too much money to spare. They came home from work in the afternoon and lounged around until the evening meal. By this time, bored with their domestic confinement, they went out, drifting toward the entertainment areas. Dancehalls were frequented more than before the war, and youth made up the majority of users. They appear also to have made up a large part of the clientele frequenting the dives where prostitutes could be found. Lorenzen lamented, "The high wages that youngsters have today, impels a change in life-style, that inflicts the most grievous damage to the developing young body."[122]

Unlike organized youth, who "use their free time mainly for further education" by visiting libraries, forming discussion groups, and subjecting themselves to the discipline of physical exercise, unskilled working-class youth appeared to follow only their impulses.[123] To combat their way-wardness "the office for Youth Care and Sport recognizes its duty, to deliver these youth to a better way of life."[124] In order to do so, three pro-posals were made: a recruitment drive to get youngsters off the streets and into sport clubs; a regulation making saving of earnings compulsory; col-laboration with the police to restrict dancing in public places to three days in the week and to close taverns and cafés where unlicensed dancing took place. In order to focus energies on recovering youth from the moral abyss:

> There ought to take place a rehabilitation of the whole person, start-ing from the inside. That can only happen, when the soul (*Seele*) and the body is taken care of through educative and hygienic measures and when the urge for virtuousness is awakened.[125]

This mandate to improve the quality of the city's youth was the motive for establishing a number of welfare agencies, notably the Municipal Youth Office in 1919. Three years earlier a municipal Care Office had been founded to cater for "morally endangered and spiritually *Heimatlos*" girls and women.[126] For it was recognized that the problem of delinquent behavior was not exclusive to boys. Indeed, the "moral chaos of the times," brought about by war and inflation, had thrust girls ahead of boys in the league table of offenses.[127]

Heinz Kaufmann's observation that many residents of let-rooms, in particular, were wretched one-parent families "whose mothers are not prostitutes—in terms of the law"[128] suggests how material deprivation could blur the boundaries between respectability and low life. In particu-lar, the south and east districts of the Altstadt—notably Peterstraße, Lohestraße, and Kleine Marienstraße, in subdistricts 1, 3, and 8—had gained a notorious reputation for prostitution and other criminal behavior by the end of the nineteenth century.

A home for "fallen" women and girls was opened in the Allee in 1910 by an association named "Retreat" (*Zuflucht*). This charity saw a large number of women pass through its doors each year, and four years after it opened it had to find larger premises. Between May 1915 and May 1916 ninety-two women were taken in for an average period of ten weeks. The majority were under twenty-one years old, and six were girls less than fifteen years old. In 1912 the Altona office of the Schleswig-Holstein Province Association for the Improvement of Public Morals, a church organization, estimated that around four hundred prostitutes operated from the brothels situated mainly in these neighborhoods bordering the red-light district of Hamburg St Pauli. It claimed that a further four to five thousand worked nightly as "casuals."[129] The Care Office, which took over the bulk of the work with vulnerable females picked up for "immoral behavior," was kept busy in the postwar period.

The Lutheran nurses who worked at the Care Office dealt exclusively with women who had strayed into a world of prostitution or who were at risk of doing so. Most of the fourteen thousand female new referrals to the office between 1919 and 1933 came from the Altstadt. The overwhelming majority of them were under twenty-five years old and single and came mainly from the two occupational backgrounds of domestic service and the factory. The number of shop assistants and nonworking housewives was also increasing by the later 1920s (indicating their material fragility), when there was also a rise in the overall number of cases.[130]

The route taking young women to the streets started in the home and at an early age. The following cases highlight both the problem and the disquiet among socially concerned people in positions of authority. Senta Thiemsen, a schoolteacher in a girls' primary school, possibly in subdistrict 20, carried out a study among her charges and discovered examples of emotional and physical deprivation among her pupils, who constituted a socially mixed group.[131] Thiemsen, like many social commentators at the time, was worried about the moral dangers associated with slum life and overcrowding. She noted that in some cases there was a lack of parental love, while in others, more ominously, there was little protection from exposure to adult physical passions.

Reporting on the case of Ilse, who came from an apparently economically buoyant working-class family, Thiemsen observed how "in spiritual and moral respect, however, the family is on a rather low rung which affected Ilse as a late sibling particularly badly." The problem seemed unavoidable where "the close living conditions contribute to Ilse hearing and seeing more of the adults than is advisable for her emotional development." Ilse had an illegitimate sister, which may not have surprised Thiemsen, for she noted disapprovingly that the mother frequented taverns and all-night cafés. Thiemsen was anxious that such behavior by a mother would surely be emulated by young and vulnerable children. She gave the example of Lieselotte, who at nine years old had begun to visit cinemas and operetta shows, apparently in the company of older males.[132]

We don't know if Lieselotte's case was the exception or the rule. Typical were the cases concerning slightly older girls, whose families had more or less abandoned them to their own devices and who frequently came into contact with Sister Ruth Hoffmann, who ran the municipal girls' hostel. This formidable and conservative Lutheran nurse published a description of her work in the local gazette. In the article, titled "Joy and Sorrow in the Girls Home," she gave graphic details of the experiences of a number of young women, who ended up in her care. Hoffmann established a pattern of common circumstances that pointed the moral blame on the failings of the "degenerative" family.[133]

For instance, Hoffmann cited the case of the young teenager L., who was brought to the hostel at 2 A.M. in the morning by the police after being found wandering the streets. The girl had lived with her grandmother until she was eleven, before moving back to her mother. Although her mother and stepfather had reported her missing after returning from their night-shift in a local factory, neither seemed overly concerned and did not inform the authorities where they could be found. Thus, a whole day passed before they were finally reunited with their daughter. Hoffmann was confident that the relatively early intervention by the authorities had saved L. from the unpleasant street encounters experienced by many other young women, such as that of twenty-three-year-old E.

E. was described as feeble-minded and came from a "family of welfare recipients." She had gone to live with her brother (who also had been in care as a youth) and his wife after her mother died. The two young women did not get on well, and soon E. left the household in tears. On the street she was promptly approached by a man who "comforted" her and, in doing so, passed on a venereal disease. In the contagious diseases clinic she met other young women, who gave her advice on how to get streetwise and earn money. A few days after her discharge from the hospital she was found by a social worker on the streets again and referred to the hostel, where, according to Sister Hoffmann, she received for the first time in her life an opportunity to break the cycle of deprivation and its attendant evils.

Some young women, however, were unredeemable, such as Anna Th., described by Hoffmann as a "textbook example" of those girls with a history of sexual misdemeanors "who had more or less without exception lived in those areas where a risk almost appears as given." Anna's sexual behavior made her a constant "source of infection" and therefore a danger to the public. Because she was beyond the educative hand of care and thus unsuitable material for reproductive purposes, Hoffmann recommended her mandatory incarceration in a medical clinic.[134]

The task of inculcating into the young a civic consciousness on the basis of an integrated work, home, and social life was made difficult by the adverse economic climate of the late 1920s and early 1930s. Between 1928 and January 1932 young males in receipt of regular unemployment benefits (*Arbeitslosenunterstützung,* or *ALU*) and crisis payments (*Krisenunterstützung,* or *KRU*) averaged at just under 12 percent of employable males under twenty-one years old. Young women were worse off, averaging at 18 percent of employable females (see table 6). Young people, like their elders, were experiencing longer periods of unemployment too. And even for those who had been lucky enough to find an apprenticeship or training after school there was little prospect of further work as they came to the end of it.[135]

Particularly worrying to officials was the fact that young men especially were being drawn into radical politics. Indeed, during the social and political turmoil of the Depression the number of male youths held in police custody rose to just over five hundred in 1933.[136] In order to counteract this problem the city implemented a program of "cultural unemployment welfare" and educational talks aimed at diverting youth away from the danger zone of radical politics.[137] For example, Louise Schroeder, who also lectured at Altona's welfare training school (*Wohlfahrtsschule*), took Schiller's dictum that "one should always strive to become a whole being" as the focus of a talk to students at the vocational college, Haus der Jugend, in January 1930 (and published in the city gazette one month after the shock elections that September). Schroeder exhorted her young audience to be good practitioners of republican democracy by learning to become good workers and citizens.[138]

TABLE 6.   Unemployed Youth by Gender and Type of Relief, Altona, 1928–32 (in percentages)

		Male		Female	
		Alu	Kru[a]	Alu	Kru[a]
1928	Jan.	8.7	4.6	23.1	8.4
	April	10.9	2.7	23.1	1.8
	July	13.8	1.9	12.3	5.8
	Oct.	11.6	3.0	17.3	10.3
1929	Jan.	10.0	5.1	23.0	8.0
	April	10.7	5.4	16.8	2.3
	July	11.3	5.8	17.0	3.6
	Oct.	10.2	—	15.6	—
1930	Jan.	12.5	15.5	16.9	12.0
	April	13.3	17.6	16.6	20.7
	July	15.3	20.5	10.7	14.3
1931	Jan.	16.5	36.3	21.6	23.4
	July	15.3	16.2	16.0	22.0
1932	Jan.	7.1	9.4	23.6	27.7

Source: StAH 424–27 G8, Arbeitslosen-statistik.
[a]1928/29 = 18–21-year-olds and 1930/32 = 21–25-year-olds.

The city's so-called cultural unemployment welfare programs were to take place within compulsory work clubs for fourteen- to eighteen-year-olds. The clubs were established by an edict issued by the Prussian trade minister on 7 January 1931 as part of a plan to introduce wide-ranging compulsory education for unemployed youth. At these clubs youngsters were to be kept in touch with work skills and given doses of general civic education in an attempt to provide "inner strength" for young males in particular, while a warm, filling meal was provided, no doubt to lesson their appetite for the political menus offered by "particular circles."[139] Courses and play activities for unemployed women concentrated on their feminine roles within the household. Young women who attended the job(less) club, which opened daily between 10 A.M. and 8:30 P.M. in the girls' vocational school in the Große Westerstraße, could take sewing classes, giving them the opportunity to mend their clothes and to make "cheap but tasteful articles" as well as inexpensive Christmas presents.[140] Thus, while the boys should learn to value democracy and train in the necessary skills that would integrate them into a future world of work, the girls were given insights into practical and rational housekeeping and "scientific motherhood," for "the housewife is not born. She has to be thoroughly prepared and trained."[141]

"Cleansing the Public Spirit"

Because Altona's slum quarters harbored a "naturally unruly" folk, it was logical that their clearance would restore the city to a healthy condition. In the words of local Social Democrats, "The cleansing of the slum quarters cleanses also the public spirit."[142] This goal would depend largely upon a program of new housing. Paul Hirsch, a Social Democrat and expert on municipal affairs, who became Prussia's first prime minister, told his party at its conference in 1920: "good apartments, cheap apartments, plenty of apartments, produce a good social life, a good family life, and this creates stability which makes the workers industrious and honorable."[143] Marie-Elisabeth Lüders, a DDP Reichstag deputy and a member of the National Research Association for Economic Housing, spoke on behalf of Weimar's municipal authorities when she noted:

> Germany is building because the people who are living in these crowded and insanitary hovels are deteriorating both mentally and morally; because their children must go to rack and ruin, not only physically but every other way; because such miserable living quarters are the breeding-ground for embittered revolutionaries and enemies of the state, who are daily in danger of coming into conflict with the laws of the land and of wreaking their vengeance on society.[144]

Thus, city administrations embarked upon a mission of "culture building" among the poorest in the hope of unlocking the desired "public spirit."[145] Unlike the builders of the notorious *Mietskaserne,* the barrack-like tenements of the previous century, Weimar's municipal architects sought to provide housing that was "closer to the people," which reflected the new civic impulse brought about by political change and which would lift the people to a higher consciousness.[146] To quote Frankfurt's city architect, Ernst May, one of the republic's best-known exponents of city planning: "Our new era must create new forms for both its inner and its outer life—and this new style must find its first concrete expression in city planning and in housing."[147] The arrival of democracy thus offered the opportunity to cast in stone the language of reform. In Altona, where publicly funded housing replaced the private sector as the main supplier of new homes after 1918, admirers of Brauer's policies looked back on the years between 1924 and 1929, as an era of "socialist housing culture" whereby "the proletariat had been raised from the narrow hovels and TB quarters [of the Altstadt] to the light and air" of a new civic dawn.[148]

There is little space here to describe in detail the architectural aspects of the new housing in Altona.[149] A brief outline is appropriate, however, insofar as this will throw some light on the welfare purpose of social housing in these years. The decade between 1918 and 1928 saw the construction of seventeen separate housing developments, at a cost to the city of over sixteen million reichsmark (including over five million goldmark for construction during the inflation). By 1932 another thirteen million marks had been spent on housing.[150] Much of the new housing was located in sub-districts 20, 26, 28, and 45, to the north and northwest of the old urban center. The most notable developments were the blocks along the Moltkestraße, Schützenstraße, Helmholtzstraße, Bunsenstraße, Düppelstraße and Koldingstraße, and Bahrenfelder Steindamm.

Nearly twelve hundred two- to three-roomed apartments, with an average floor space of between sixty-five and seventy-eight square meters, offered a fully rationalized, modern domestic lifestyle for the mostly young married couples who moved in. The blocks contained modern facilities, such as central heating and individual bathrooms. Day nurseries were provided for working mothers, and shops were built below the dwellings, together with communal facilities, such as dayrooms and laundries. Emphasis was placed upon natural light and spacing, with plenty of fresh air and sun. There were gardens that offered children ample room for play and which also became the focal points of residential life.[151]

"Licht," "Luft," and "Sonne" were much in evidence in the garden settlement of Steenkamp in Bahrenfeld. Together with the housing blocks, this estate formed the flagship of democratic housing policy in Altona. The underlining ethos of life in the settlement was that of healthy bodies and minds and communal harmony, away from the "bleak, dreadful stone heaps" of the slums.[152]

Steenkamp had been started in 1914 by the Mutual Aid Housing Association, in which the city had shares. The first model dwellings—incorporating seven types of houses with gardens for growing food as well as outhouses for keeping small animals or for use as workshops—were completed in time for the garden exhibition in early 1914. By the spring of 1915 there were already 53 dwellings, and more land was purchased cheaply by the city in 1916, allowing more dwellings to be erected. The estate finally passed into municipal ownership during the difficult period of the inflation, when, in July 1922, the city founded its own public housing utility, the Gemeinnützige Siedlungs AG Altona (SAGA). Construction continued at a good pace in the 1920s, so that by 1927 approximately 760 dwellings, housing around 780 families, had been built.[153]

The new housing was considerably more expensive than the city's older accommodation. The annual rent for a small prewar apartment with either two or two and a half rooms was approximately 250 reichsmark in Ottensen's Große Brunnenstraße, whereas a similar-sized unit could cost up to 480 reichsmark in the new blocks in the Helmholtzstraße and Bunsenstraße and nearly twice as much again in the Luruper Chaussee or Lunapark developments. In 1931 a three-and-a-half room flat in the Koldingstraße fetched a rent of 888 reichsmark, while an older similar size accommodation in Ottensen's Theodorstraße was more than 200 marks less. Both the Große Brunnenstraße and the Theodorstraße were, relatively speaking, "better-situated" streets.[154]

This meant that the average skilled worker earning around 181 reichsmark each month in 1929 could expect to spend as much as 40 percent of his gross income on renting a new three-and-a-half-room apartment. The proportion would have been at least 10 to 15 percent higher for an unskilled worker, for whom the average gross monthly wage was 142 reichsmark. By contrast, Altona's salaried employees were more fortunate by a wide margin. For instance, a lower- to middle-ranking public employee, from a *Stadtassistant* or *technischer Angestellte* to a *Stadtobersekretar,* earned between 285 to 325 reichsmark each month, while the director of the housing office received 605.25 reichsmark. For them the same rented accommodation would have accounted for between 22 and 12 percent of their respective incomes.[155]

Families who would have benefited most from the new housing, however, did not have the sort of incomes discussed here. Nearly 40 percent of Altona's working population (i.e., 36,314) in 1926 earned less than 1,200 reichsmark per annum, or 100 reichsmark monthly.[156] And as we have seen, in the slum districts earnings tended to be irregular. Clearly, this would have eliminated many families from the market for new housing. Moreover, tenancies tended to be regularized, fixed for longer periods and sometimes annually. High rents that had to be paid quarterly and in advance when set against a low and insecure income acted as a deterrent to the financially weaker inhabitants from Altona's "TB quarters."

Whereas Altona's manual working class made up nearly 50 percent of the local population, they accounted for just over a third of heads of household occupying a tenancy on the new estates. And, of these, skilled workers outnumbered the unskilled two to one. Conversely, white-collar employees made up a fifth of the population but accounted for around a third of the tenancies. Similarly, civil servants were overrepresented in relation to their share of the population (about 7 percent).[157] Indeed, the new housing was hugely popular among Altona's public officials, private employees, and professionals, who together made up the greater part of the population of the estates. For example, Paul Siegert, the manager of the labor exchange, Friedrich Kaestner, the director of the statistical office, Mattheus Becker, who headed the municipal press office, Paul-

TABLE 7. Occupation of Tenanted Heads of Household of Municipal Housing (in percentages)

Occupation	Steenkamp ($N = 759$)	Town ($N = 737$)
Clerical employees		
private	23.7	27.0
public	6.6	1.2
Manual workers		
skilled	19.4	21.7
unskilled	9.7	10.7
Civil servants		
Reich	13.7	15.6
municipal	7.5	4.0
Teachers	5.1	2.6
Technicians/engineers	3.2	1.9
Self-employed/traders	3.3	3.0
Media/Medical/free professionals[a]	3.2	2.4
Pensioners	2.0	1.2
Widows/unknown[b]	2.6	8.7
Total	100	100

Source: StAH 424–15 (Bauamt), Lit. L13 SAGA: 'Fünfjahre Gemeinnützige Siedlungs AG Altona' (August 1927): XV, 30.

[a]Editors = .07, 0.1; doctors = 0.4; midwives = 0.3

[b]Unknown: 7.0 of Blocks.

Theodor Hoffmann, the city archivist and author of *Neues Altona,* Hans
Berlage, another official and historian of the city, and, notably, the director of the housing office himself, Otto Fischer, were among those city
officials who enjoyed life in a model dwelling. As we can see from table 7,
Altona's new housing estates were predominantly "professional white-collar estates."[158]

The high level of capital investment meant that good care had to be
taken of the new home. Housing officials were worried that "intrinsically
valuable dwellings would become easily and rapidly changed in an ugly
way, through the inattention and tastelessness of some tenants."[159] In
order to avoid this, the city's housing office and other agencies kept files on
"social cases" and put applicants through a rigorous vetting system. Crite-
ria employed by housing officials in the early 1920s could be fairly ano-
dyne and included family size and wartime service.[160] Prospective tenants
for Steenkamp, for instance, had to demonstrate their interest in gardening and to show that "their family situation, household and lifestyle guaranteed a conscientious disposition towards creating the homestead."[161]
They also had to be prepared, however, to yield to the discipline of a collective culture, because the estate's tenants' committee cast "a wide net
that caught and ordered all of life in Steenkamp." The estate had its own
organization, the Heimatschutz, and all "healthy males between the ages
of 20 and 60" were expected to join. Leisure activities and festivities, such
as Harvest Thanksgiving, were arranged or sporting spectacles staged to
celebrate the cult of the body and children's parties and games organized.
Tenants were expected to attend educational talks and take part in the
democratic processes of tenant elections and committees.[162]

Given the culture of the estate, it is perhaps not surprising that, politically, Steenkamp remained a bastion of republican democracy, even if by
the beginning of the 1930s a polarization was apparent here also.[163]

Settlement life was highly organized, and, while some clearly revelled
in it, others found it too restrictive. For instance, frequent housing inspec-
tions ensured that guidelines were followed and that the less cultivated
household was educated on how "to avoid the undertaken refurbishments
from once again being wiped out through uncleanliness and bad living
habits."[164] "Bad living habits" covered a whole range of items, from the
choice of furnishings to how rooms were arranged or to taking in lodgers,
the latter especially frowned upon by the officials from the SAGA.[165]
Thus, for those deemed to lack the requisite skills of domestic and moral
management, no consideration was given for such accommodation. This
was the fate of the impoverished war widow, a mother of four children,
three of whom were illegitimate, and who was due to give birth to another
illegitimate child. She lived in a court dwelling and would have to remain
there until she had learned better. Similar restrictions applied to those

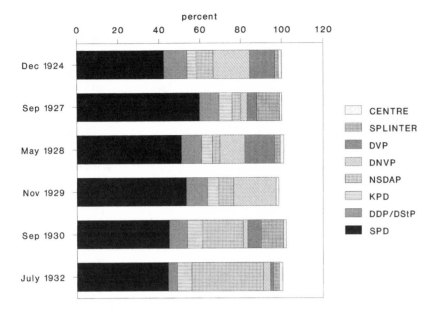

Fig. 5.   Votes by main parties in Steenkamp (electoral wards 109a–110a, percentage of valid votes)

"permanent cases which must remain under surveillance," such as one particular Altstadt family that "unfortunately cannot be brought before the law for posing a danger to the public." This family was said to be "low and dangerous in its life-style and in the way it treated its home." Such families were unlikely ever to conform to the "settlement spirit."[166] Thus, while lack of regular income and high rents were important factors preventing Altona's most impoverished families from "filtering up" the housing market, social attitudes among housing officers also played an equally important role, in spite of their ostensible role as "social architects" of the "healthy family."[167]

Yet perhaps the most significant factor militating against welfare success had to be the economy itself. Ten years after the bleak findings of the housing census were published, Max Brauer estimated that it would take another ten years to close the housing gap. But this was highly optimistic. New projects became increasingly difficult to sustain in the adverse economic climate at the turn of the decade. And by the end of 1932 the authorities had to admit that over 80 percent of the population still lived in the old dilapidated quarters of the Altstadt and other housing black spots.[168] In fact, throughout the two decades following the end of World War I the city housing office failed to keep pace with the demand for housing. And an internal report in 1937 showed that approximately 11.3 percent of households were still without their own home, compared to 9.8 percent for the other major cities of the reich.[169] The conclusions of one English housing expert, Elizabeth Denby, were that "dwellings built during the first ten years after the war were taken by the better-paid workers and the shortage of homes for the lowest income group of the population is still serious,"[170] could have been written with Altona in mind.

Paul-Theodor Hoffmann spoke for both liberal reformers and socialists when he reflected in his chronicle, *New Altona:* "It is not only important to have worked for a home of your own, but also to have time to rest and live in it. Work is important, but even more important . . . is the leisure time at home after work."[171] Max Brauer was a firm believer in social progress through individual and collective cultural activity. Upon taking office in 1924, he pledged that he was "committed to freeing the path for anyone with a thirst for knowledge and education, as far as it lies within my power to do so."[172] And by this he meant offering opportunities for after-work educational activity, theater, and music as well as improvements in the provision of primary schooling and further education. Brauer's aim was to create a strong class of workers around a positive self-image, as a counterpart to the perceived intemperate lifestyles of a degenerate working class. Thus, when the Pestalozzi School in the Kleine Freiheit was opened in November 1928 Brauer likened it to both an oasis offering to the people of the Altstadt spiritual repose and moral strength as well as being an outpost of welfare missionary zeal in the heart of the slums.[173]

His commitment to widening opportunities for popular education had been partly realized in 1919 with the founding of the Free Education Movement in Altona (Freie Bildungswesen). This initiative eventually became the municipal-run Adult Education College (Volkshochschule) in 1926.[174] Municipal-supported educational and cultural activities were brought under the jurisdiction of an Office for Culture and Continuing Education, also established in the postwar years. Eight hundred and fifty persons, the majority of them women, took part in lectures and courses in 1927. Over half were under the age of thirty, and the two largest groups were sales employees (20 percent) and manual workers (46 percent). Indeed, working-class attenders weighed evenly with those from the middle class. This changed slightly over the next couple of years. In 1929 well over half of adult males attending public lectures and workshops during 1929 on subjects ranging from natural history, psychology, and labor law to poetry and art were manual workers, compared to a participation rate of just 13 percent for female workers; the next largest group of males were employees, about a third, the same level as females clerical workers; while housewives formed the largest contingent of female attenders (36 percent).[175]

The commitment to education as a vehicle for social change was matched by an equally firm belief in the political value of popular theater and sporting activities as an educative process central to the "spiritual and cultural development of the individual and society."[176] Sport, in particular, was seen as an appropriate pursuit for teenagers. Welfare workers believed that it had an ameliorating affect on the young minds and bodies corrupted by the conditions of slum life. But there is nothing to indicate that unskilled youth were drawn to the many clubs. For, although the number of Altona's sports clubs, many of them connected to political organizations, had nearly doubled to seventy-five by the mid-1920s, actual membership did not increase significantly: from just over ten thousand in 1919 to thirteen and half thousand in 1927. Of this membership fourteen-to twenty-one-year-olds accounted for about a quarter.[177] The streets were far more attractive for youngsters.

Conclusion

Housing, educational and sports activities in Altona emphasized individual "self-improvement" and collective discipline, a philosophy common within the socialist labor movement, and of which Brauer and his party comrades were products, remained the key to "cleansing the public spirit."[178] But it is doubtful if the Altstadt "slum dweller" was reached by the city's missionizing zeal and its efforts at the social hygiene transformation of the proletarian "mass." Cultural and educational activities remained largely confined to those organized within the socialist labor movement or to the rising lower middle class of employees.

As we have seen, access to the new housing remained closed off to poor families. And everyday life and leisure in the Altstadt remained focused on neighborhood activities or commercialized pursuits. For instance, cinemagoing in the city grew steadily in importance during the 1920s, with attendance about tenfold that of theater audiences by 1928.[179] More youth remained on the streets than in the clubs. Thus, the chief target group of social policy, youth, for whom "welfare cannot commence early enough and must be as comprehensive as possible,"[180] nevertheless, managed to remain elusive to Weimar welfare, resisting efforts to discipline them. Nor did the ideal of "scientific motherhood" hold sway among many of the Altstadt's young women, for whom such a concept was crassly juxtaposed to the grim reality of the *Mietskaserne* and, in any case, stood beyond the cultural and mental horizons of the "slum" world.

If welfare failed to transform slum dwellers, nor was it any more successful at containing them. The "slum neighborhood," although oppressive in terms of life conditions, was untrammeled from the regimentation of the "new public spirit." The popular description of the Bunsen-Helmholtzstraße housing development as *Zuchthausviertel,* or "penitentiary quarter," perhaps best sums up what Altona's "unruly people" felt about welfare reforms in general.[181] Indeed, the aversion of the Altstadt's "naturally" unruly people to being "checked," "trained," and "civilized," goes a long way in explaining the particular shape of political cultures and conflict on the streets of Altona, as we shall see when we return to the slums in chapter 6.

CHAPTER 4

"Save Us from Altona!": The Battle against Incorporation, 1924–1927

> The fundamental basis of a democracy is the guarantee of protection to the
> citizens against arbitrary government and government officials.
> —*Max Brauer, "On Democracy"[1]*

On becoming lord mayor of Altona in April 1924, Max Brauer had pledged to strive for greater equality of opportunity for all citizens. This goal could only be achieved by creating a prosperous civic environment with the facilities befitting a great city. Looking to the east toward Hamburg, he stated:

> My most welcome task will be to make Altona financially strong alongside its mighty sister-city Hamburg, through promoting and establishing industry, and through the improvement of trade and transport communications. I will not rest until our city is no longer a suburb to the west of Hamburg, but is filled more and more with a communal life of its own and with its own strong independent economic foundation. I will always endeavour to provide our people with the same social and cultural level as wealthy Hamburg gives its inhabitants.[2]

Many contemporaries described Altona as a "dormitory suburb" and a "poor relation" of Hamburg.[3] In the upheaval of the postwar period there was even talk of incorporating Altona into Hamburg, as part of an overall boundary change in the Lower Elbe region. This idea, however, was shelved after fruitless negotiations between the new Prussian government and Hamburg.[4] With the prospect of a "Greater Hamburg" no longer in sight, the question of what to do with Altona was made all the more urgent. An expansion of the city's borders now fitted in with a changing mood within the new regime in Altona. For, in order to overcome Altona's image as a grimy "poor working-class suburb" of Hamburg and to create a civic vitality with the sort of life chances cherished by Brauer, the city would have to expand its municipal boundaries. The question of what should be incorporated was easily answered. To the east of Altona loomed Hamburg. Brauer thus turned his gaze to the north and west of the city where, in the bordering parish communities of the county of Pinneberg, he saw the vista of a "Greater Altona." And this project was to be one of the pillars upon which municipal policy would rest for the coming years. Therefore, the young lord mayor exhorted the members of the newly elected city council to bear in mind that "in carrying out their duties, the question of incorporation must always remain as the most important."[5]

Altona's transformation into a *Großstadt* was part of a cycle of municipal incorporations during the republican period, commencing with the creation of Greater Berlin in 1920 and ending with Breslau's expansion in 1929.[6] Urban planners believed that the city could be reconstructed according to rational and scientific principles. Their aim was a productively efficient (*Leistungsfähig*) unit that was also a "living organism," self-contained and harmonious in its provision of services, work, housing, and leisure. Unlike the incorporations of the late nineteenth century, which saw the amalgamation of mostly smaller and medium-size towns, the trend during the mid-1920s was for larger cities to encroach upon the surrounding countryside, eating up smaller parish communities and semisuburban settlements.[7]

The idea of a rational city building was congruent with Social Democratic ideas of municipal socialism based on "scientific rationalism" as well as more mundane political concerns. The larger the sphere of socialist influence locally, the more likely the success of transforming German society from below, especially after the setback of the Prussian elections in February 1921, a view reiterated at the party conference at Görlitz in September that year.[8] Thus, the creation of larger units of local administration became part of the SPD's political strategy for implementing "practical socialism."[9]

The nineteenth-century incorporations had encountered resistance, mostly because of a pervasive anti-urban sentiment, typical for the period, when small hometownsmen in outlying districts fought to halt the encroaching urban Behemoth.[10] During the 1920s the anti-urbanism of prewar territorial conflict became increasingly politicized and found articulation in the language of defense of the *vaterländische Heimat,* this time against an encroaching socialism.[11] Indeed, Brauer did little to allay middle-class fears that he was intent on creating an enlarged socialist municipal republic at their expense. He described the neighboring communities as parasites living off the cultural and educational amenities available in the city without contributing to their upkeep. And he contrasted these "comfortable tax oases" of the privileged few with the urban squalor of the disadvantaged many, declaring, "It can no longer be tolerated that the most affluent communities close themselves off—each and all must contribute to the common good."[12]

Possibly to leaven the social and political radicalism implicit in this statement, Brauer contended that Altona's plans merely represented the resumption of earlier efforts to reorganize resources and administrative life at the local level. Altona had previously expanded in the late 1880s, when it incorporated its small industrial neighbor, Ottensen-Neumühlen, the country parishes of Bahrenfeld and Othmarschen, and the small seafaring community of Oevelgönne. It had also begun negotiations with Groß Flottbek and Stellingen-Langenfelde between 1890 and 1912, but these were broken off after a change of heart on the part of those parishes. The war then interrupted any further plans to expand the city's borders. The devastation of the war also made reorganization imperative.[13]

The neighboring communities that Brauer initially had in mind were Groß Flottbek, Klein Flottbek, Nienstedten, Stellingen-Langenfelde, Lurup, Eidelstedt, Osdorf, and Lokstedt (the latter was eventually dropped from the incorporation bill). The villages and township of Sülldorf, Rissen, and Blankenese, which lay further west along the river Elbe, were subsequently included, in 1926.

The manufacturing communities of Lurup, Eidelstedt, and Stellingen-Langenfelde lay to the north of Altona and were viewed as natural sites for Altona's industrial reorganization. Concentrating mainly on food processing, notably fish meal, chemicals, stone quarrying, and wire making, industry, by the early 1920s, boasted nearly ninety factories, and workshops employed a labor force of around 1,520; (twenty years later there were fewer factories but a larger work force).[14] Land for industrial development was still relatively cheap, and the proximity to the Altona-Kiel railway, already important as a freighting artery, together with the marshaling yard in Eidelstedt, would reduce freight costs and so made these areas attractive to Altona.[15] Their incorporation would create an industrial belt 960 hectares wide and 8 kilometers long, which could comfortably accommodate all of Altona's industries and their total labor force of 20,000.[16]

Immediately to the west of Altona were the suburban communities of

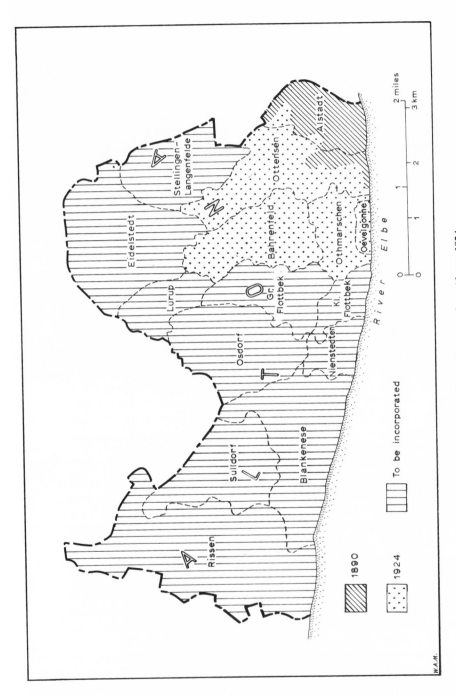

Map 7. Past and future incorporations, Altona, 1924

Groß Flottbek, Klein Flottbek, and Nienstedten. Their appeal lay in their wealth and in their location on the north bank of the river Elbe. They were comfortable financially—incomes were mostly derived from business and trade in Hamburg. In Klein Flottbek, for instance, revenue from taxation in the mid-1920s was estimated at over 130,000 reichsmark, of which nearly two-thirds was income based and a quarter from property.[17] In all three communities large country-style mansions and private parks gave these areas a grand character. Klein Flottbek and Nienstedten (together with Blankenese) were described by contemporaries as the "jewel of north Germany," while Groß Flottbek was depicted in a less flattering manner as "ostentatious" and "showy."[18] The small parishes of Osdorf, Sülldorf, and Rissen, which lay further west, were more rural in character. They had between them 1,917 hectares of moorland, arable and pastoral fields, with strong traces of an old but by no means backward farming community. For instance, Osdorf was said to have a highly developed agriculture in dairy products and market gardening. Rissen and Sülldorf also had considerable forests.[19]

Blankenese was an ancient seafaring and river community with strong local traditions, rising from the river on a hill known as the Süllberg. In 1919 it had incorporated Dockenhuden, a wealthy suburb with rail links to Altona and Hamburg, where mostly Hamburg merchants and a large number of *Bildungsbürgertum* and civil servants resided. (The latter represented 15 percent of the population.) Nonetheless, the sociocultural profile of the community was dominated by a clique of families, who formed a close-knit community clustered on the Süllberg, in an area known as the "Steps" (*Treppen*), a labyrinthine network of paths and steps connecting the homes of these families.[20] Seagoing enterprises, however, did not dominate Blankenese's economy. In 1925 the community had a working population of 7,319, of which approximately a quarter worked in industry and crafts and a third in commerce and transport; the rest of the working population was distributed unevenly across the economy: domestic service, 16.9 percent; administration and clerical, 5.5 percent; agriculture, 4 percent; health and welfare, 2.4 percent; and those without occupation details (*berufslose*) made up 10.7 percent. Out of a total of 788 businesses employing 2,734 people, over half were in commerce—mostly retail and transport. The majority of these were small-scale enterprises, making Blankenese clearly a suburb of the old *Mittelstand,* who accounted for roughly 21 percent of the economically active population by the end of the 1930s.[21]

In spite of their predominantly white-collar, upper-middle-class, and *Mittelstand* character, these suburbs also contained distinctive working-class communities. There was a small community of workers in Groß and Klein Flottbek and Nienstedten whose members mainly found employment in the local brewery, Elbschlossbrauerei, situated in Nienstedten. In Blankenese the working class formed about 43 percent of the population, with comparable levels in Osdorf, Sülldorf, and Rissen, the majority of whom worked either in Altona, Pinneberg, or Hamburg (see table 1).[22]

The taxable wealth of these communities was of obvious interest to Altona. But the city also saw in these semirural areas the potential sites for physical and mental recuperation (*Erholungsgebiet*) from the weekly stress and strain of factory work and the tempo of urban life. As suburbs of a future Greater Altona, they would not only provide parkland but also development areas for new residential settlements of small-scale, low-density housing and gardens for families.[23] An enlarged Altona would be organically harmonized through three greenbelts organized in concentric form beginning at the city center and then with two successive belts delineating the industrial, housing, and "country" zones, integrated by a new city transport system. Furthermore, the *Magistrat* claimed that the retention of the natural beauty of the north bank of the river Elbe, the maintenance of the parks and the promenade, and the prevention of excessive construction by private contracts could only be achieved under a unitary authority.[24]

In contrast to Altona, the Elbe communities were havens from socialism. They regarded themselves as small, intimate communities where an untainted prerevolutionary world of *Honoratioren* politics still held sway, led by long-serving parish leaders, such as Emil Rüss in Stellingen or Wilhelm Schumann, a retired first lieutenant, in Eidelstedt, or Otto Grotkopp in Nienstedten, or Heinrich Frahm in Blankenese. In spite of parish variations, overall, the Social Democrats in the Elbe communities represented a political minority, as table 8 shows. An incorporation into socialist, working-class Altona would destroy this comforting redoubt of the German *Heimat.*[25]

Municipal incorporations in Germany had never been conducted without a conflict of interest occurring between the concerned parties.[26] In the case of Altona the conflict clearly included issues of class coupled to traditional anti-urbanism. The incorporation conflict soon focused on the powerful symbolism of territory as *Heimat,* which took it beyond its parochial concerns. For the resistance to Altona's encroachment upon the parish communities was not just directed against Brauer and his regime but galvanized the parish middle-classes against the Weimar Republic itself. The incorporation struggle merely gave a deeper congenital dissent against the republic a clearly defined and localized focus. Yet, at the same time, the struggle and its eventual defeat revealed both the weakness of party politics and the limits of operating within the terms of Weimar

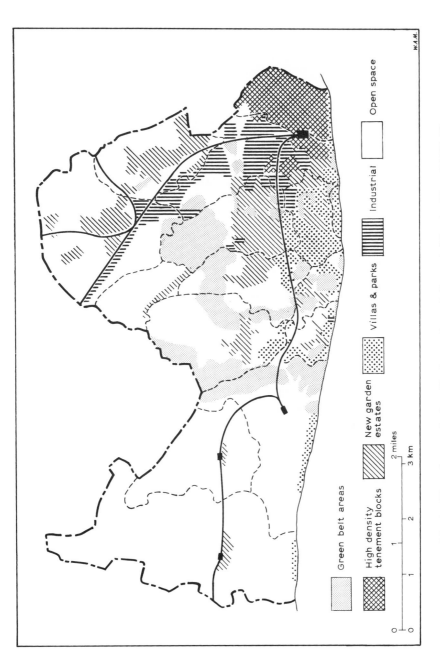

Map 8. Planned reorganization of land-use and greenbelt areas in "Greater Altona," 1924–27

Green belt areas

High density
tenement blocks

New garden
estates

Villas & parks

Industrial

Open space

W.A.M.

0   1   2 miles

0   1   2   3 km

democracy as a means to protecting local interests against a perceived arbitrary government.

"Onto the Dikes! The Heimat Is in Danger!"[27]

The campaign for a Greater Altona was inaugurated by Brauer and his new city architect, Gustav Oelsner, at a press conference in early November 1924. Brauer introduced the fifteen-man, all-party committee, chaired by a retired naval officer, Vice-Admiral Dähnhardt, and presented the petition for incorporation, submitted to the Prussian government on 21 October.[28] The committee left no doubt in the minds of its listeners that the incorporation of the communities was inevitable. The Prussian interior minister favored an expansion of Altona and had already appointed a special commissioner to speed up the process. The resulting belief that the incorporation of the suburbs would take place by ministerial decree, or a special act of parliament, sparked off one of the most ill-natured aspects in the conflict.[29]

Some in the audience were undeterred by this threat. The mobilization of resistance to Altona's plans was immediate. The campaign broadly crystallized on two levels. The first level was that of the parliamentary process: here a group of DVP and DNVP deputies spearheaded the anti-incorporation cause in the Provincial Diet in Kiel and in the Prussian parliament. At the same time, local and regional politicians came together to form a special defense committee, the *Kreis* Defense Committee (*Kreisabwehrausschuss*) based in Pinneberg (the administrative center for the

TABLE 8.   Political Configuration of the Parish Councils, 1924

	SPD	KPD	Bürgerlich	Others
Gr. Flottbek	3	1	8	—
Kl. Flottbek	3	—	6	—
Nienstedten	3	—	6	—
Stell. Langenfelde	4	3	11	—
Eidelstedt	2	—	4	6[a]
Lurup	3	—	4	—
Osdorf	3	—	3	1[b]
Blankenese	5	1	18	—

Source: StAH 424–44/11 (Gr. Flottbek), "Gemeindewahl" (4 May 1924); *Hamburger Echo* 122, 5 May 1924; 424–47/76 Heft 21; *Lokal-Anzeiger* Stellingen-Langenfelde: 143, 26 June 1926; 424–48 (Eidelstedt) bl. 117, "Gemeindewahl" (4 May 1924).

Note: No information for Sülldorf and Rissen.

[a]Beamtenliste = 3; Mieterschutz and Bodenrecht = 3

[b]Unknown

county, under whose jurisdiction the communities fell). This committee was chaired by the district administrator, Gustav Niendorf, himself a Social Democrat, and various notables from the otherwise conservative-dominated district assembly, the Kreistag.[30] The purpose of the committee was to coordinate the campaign in order to strengthen individual communal efforts at resistance.

The second level was extraparliamentary, encompassing a mass of popular associations representing either particular interest groups, such as local property owners or businessmen, or were district based, channeled through the civic associations, such as those of Nienstedten and Groß Flottbek. These various associations found a common coordinating body in the Central Committee of the Elbe Civic Associations (Zentralausschuss der kommunalen Vereine der Elbe [ZkVE]) operating from Othmarschen. Although the ZkVE was vehement in its opposition to incorporation, its leadership, like that of the political parties, was divided on the issue. The Altona members led by Heinrich Ahrendt, who we encountered in chapter 2, favored incorporation in the belief that the route to achieving a mammoth *Bürger* bloc in the city council lay through the suburbs.[31]

In the propaganda war that followed, the anti-incorporationists were well served by the local press, most notably, the *Norddeutsche Nachrichten,* owned and edited by the Kröger brothers in Blankenese. The newspaper was staunchly nationalist and unremitting in its bellicosity toward Brauer and the Prussian government. Its pages acted as an important point of collection for the anti-incorporation grievances of citizens and thus provided the individual parishes with a unity and cohesion they might otherwise have lacked. At the same time, the *Norddeutsche* radicalized public sentiment in the Elbe communities in a way that prefigured the Nazi mobilization of the early 1930s.

Soon after the pro-incorporation conference a wave of protest meetings were launched. One after the other the various local citizens' associations gathered to vent their spleen against what they saw as the audacious claims of the incorporationists from Altona. The property owners' associations of Groß and Klein Flottbek and Nienstedten formulated strongly worded resolutions, as did the small masters trade association of the Elbe communities and the local branch of the arch-conservative North West German Artisan Association. A confessional element was added by the protestant Church Association of Nienstedten after the incorporation received the backing of the Catholic Center Party.[32] In Altona itself there was disquiet among leading local manufacturers and businessmen, who feared that they would have to bear the costs of incorporation.[33]

The dominant narrative shaping the protests was the constitutional question of self-government. For instance, at their meeting on 4 November the Citizens' Association of Lokstedt invited a member of the pro-incorporation committee, August Bielfeldt, a retired headmaster and member of the DDP, to speak. Bielfeldt had written extensively in the local press on the merits of incorporation before the war and was considered a principal architect of the present claim.[34] Bielfeldt spoke for an hour, reiterating many of the points that were contained in the official document petitioning for expansion. He kept assiduously to the businesslike aspects of incorporation, mostly those dealing with the social and economic benefits to be wrung from a larger unit of local government. He did not mention the issue of local autonomy in the suburbs. His audience listened patiently until he had finished, then speaker after speaker rose to challenge Bielfeldt precisely on the question of their loss of autonomy, ignoring any other points he had made.

A Lockstedt councillor opened the attack by expressing his surprise at Berlin's decision to force Altona's lust for expansion upon the community. The councillor, a civil servant named Himmelbecker, stated that it appeared incomprehensible in an age of democratic self-determination that the Prussian government, ostensibly the bulwark of democracy, could act in this way. Another councillor referred to the appointment of a state commissioner to oversee the process as "not in accordance with the basic principles of a democratic, parliamentary-governed state," especially since it was rumored that the commissioner was not going to hear evidence from the suburbs. Another speaker compared the proposed incorporation to the "Strangulation Treaty of Versailles."[35] Those who followed him, including the leader of the council, agreed. These arguments expressing the outrage of the communities were reprinted salaciously in the *Norddeutsche.* The newspaper commented on the strange spectacle of the SPD contradicting its own principles of democracy in its hurry to lay hands on the prosperous suburbs, in what amounted to a "rape of the communities" comparable to the "injustice forced upon the nation at Versailles."[36]

Lokstedt's citizens were not the only ones concerned about the threat Altona posed to their self-government. In Groß Flottbek the Association of Property and House Owners got together to issue a declaration condemning Altona's move against its smaller and weaker neighbors and demanded that the Prussian parliament, which had been elected by the people, should heed their call and protect the weak against the strong.[37] In mid-November the Association of Tavernkeepers and Assembly Room Owners of the Elbe Communities addressed the Prussian Interior Ministry to complain that legal and democratic principles of justice were being ignored as long as local representatives were not properly consulted by Altona and Berlin. It wrote:

It is not discussed here if the advantages of the incorporation outweigh the disadvantages, and even if [one] accepted this point, it would still be a slap in the face if the petition were to be granted. The practice of our trade brings us into continuous contact with all sections of the population. So we know that it is generally expected of the government of our young republican community, in which, unlike previously, the will and only the will of the people and not that of the bureaucracy is the highest law, that it does not at any cost grant Altona's petition. If the petition is to be closely examined, then the decision should be left entirely to the affected population.[38]

The Lokstedt Association of Garden Producers, which also included horticultural clubs from Eidelstedt and Stellingen-Langenfelde, felt that it was necessary to raise the "sharpest protest against the underhanded and forceful incorporation aims of the city of Altona" in a letter to its council.[39] It resolved at an emergency meeting to resist Altona's "assault" upon the parishes' right to self-determination with "all the means in its possession."[40]

The prospect of being bypassed by those in authority precisely on a matter that so deeply affected local community life gave rise to accusations of bullying tactics and conspiratorial party politics[41] and greatly added to a deepening enmity between the people of the suburbs and the Socialist-led government of Prussia. This feeling was to some extent understandable. Altona had not bothered to open channels of communication with either the *Kreis* assembly or the individual councils, preferring instead to confer only with Berlin.[42] Brauer had insinuated that the decision would not lie locally but would be made at the highest level, namely the Prussian Council of State (of which he was a member), and with ratification by the Prussian parliament. Such a move contradicted paragraph 2 of the Prussian Rural Community Ordinance 1891 (*Landgemeindeordnung*), which required all levels of local and regional government to negotiate the grounds for an incorporation, especially where rural communities were the potential targets of towns.[43]

The campaign against Altona's annexationist claim began to acquire imagery reminiscent of the trenches. To be sure, a war mood permeated the mobilization of protest in the suburbs, recalling the fervor of August 1914. Two years earlier, during a similar mobilization against prospective plans for incorporation, the ZkVE had urged the councils to issue a "declaration of war" against Altona.[44] And this same spirit for the defense of the *Heimat* was once more invoked, even by the Social Democrat Niendorf, who spoke of the "prosecution of war" against Altona.[45] Committees for the defense of the *Heimat* were formed in each parish, along the lines suggested by the ZkVE in a letter (to each council head) that called on them to adopt "all the necessary means for collective defense."[46]

In the main, liberal pro-incorporationists avoided being drawn into a slanging match with either the *Norddeutsche* or individual opponents.[47] But the SPD press could not resist the temptation to belittle the general consternation in the Elbe communes, especially where this manifested itself in vulgar nationalism. For instance, the protests ranged in historical allusion from the mobilization fever of August 1914 to the postwar nationalist defense of the *Vaterland* during the occupation of Germany by French and Belgian troops and were laced with racist undertones. Thus, when the local Defense Committee in Stellingen convened a meeting in December, at which about fifty to sixty persons attended, Altona's behavior was likened to the "black troops in the occupied territories" [of the Ruhr], causing some bemusement in Altona.[48] And to which the *Hamburger Echo* remarked with heavy irony: "If the entire German public is not now filled with more indignation at Altona's brutality than at the refusal [of the French] to evacuate the Cologne sector, then there is no justice any more."[49] The newspaper printed a number of sarcastic articles parrying the conservative thrusts against the incorporation and Brauer's role in it.[50] The sum effect of this was to frustrate opponents and to heighten the level of antagonism between the two camps.

The dispute over the incorporation did not necessarily follow clear-cut class or political lines. For example, Eidelstedt's manufacturers supported incorporation; in the Elbe communities civil servants and sports teachers welcomed the incorporation, since they would transfer to a higher grade.[51] Nonetheless, anti-incorporationists asserted that Altona's border claim was part and parcel of partisan Socialist goals rather than serving the common interest. The anti-incorporationists, by contrast, claimed they had the interests of the German *Vaterland* at the heart of their resistance to Brauer.[52] In support of this they cited Brauer's stated intention to redistribute local resources. At one of the public meetings in the late Autumn of 1924, a manufacturer from Klein Flottbek responded to the claim by Altona that it needed new building land for both industry and housing by saying that Altona should "go it alone" with its plans for redevelopment and should not try to unload the cost of this upon the suburbs. As for the slum clearance program, the speaker, to the angry consternation of some listeners, felt there was nothing wrong in housing the families from the Altstadt in specially constructed barracks.[53]

Opponents also looked across the communal boundary line at the "socialist experiment" in Altona. Thus, the Elbe *Mittelstand,* many of whom claimed indigence, opposed an incorporation for they claimed that once in Altona they would be subjected to high local taxes, a fate worse than the inflation.[54] This argument was put by the Blankenese council in mid-1926 in its written response to Altona's proposition that it too should be incorporated. The council stated that most property owners "were persons living on small and state pensions, skippers, persons who had suffered terribly as a consequence of the inflation, and small-scale trades-people (large factories are totally absent here)."[55] Not only would the *Mittelstand* suffer expropriation through Socialist taxation, its members would be denied from carrying out their livelihood in a market subjected to the controls of the public hand. This was summed up by an anonymous letter writer to the *Norddeutsche,* addressed to the chairman of the Handicrafts Chamber for Altona and Environs, who also sat on the incorporation committee:

> Herr Neels, as chairman of the Crafts Chambers, must know that in the case of a forced incorporation the craft masters in the individual communities will be severely harmed. The complaints of the masters in Altona about the operation of the distribution of municipal contracts and supplies are really too well-known. . . . You masters can think for yourselves where you will be left in the event of incorporation.[56]

This political polarization was also manifested at the December meeting of the local Defense Committee in Stellingen.[57] Among those who attended was a small band of pro-incorporationists, led by a local SPD functionary. When he addressed the meeting, Oldenthal regretted that every discussion up to that point had been dominated by the interests of the property owners and manufacturers "and their like." It was incumbent upon him, therefore, to redress this imbalance. Oldenthal declared that the working people of Stellingen openly welcomed incorporation, since it would bring an improvement in social welfare and living standards.[58]

Oldenthal's hope that incorporation would bring with it an improvement in social welfare, was precisely one of the fears that rallied opponents to the plan. In the parish of Nienstedten, for instance, it was argued that in a city of nearly two hundred thousand inhabitants welfare provision was bound to be anonymous. The parishes, by contrast, had a more personal system in which the "plight of the individual was known more easily and more generally" and was catered for by voluntary efforts. Municipal welfare provision rendered charity obsolete, and this would undermine the structure and traditional hierarchy of life in the small community. Moreover, an extensive social welfare system catering to a large impoverished working class also meant a heavier financial burden upon the taxpayer.[59]

Renewed pressure was exerted upon the parish communities in the late spring of 1926. The Altona council had agreed in May that a fresh petition should be sent to the Prussian government.[60] This spurred Landrat Niendorf to warn the parish councils of Altona's revived efforts. In order to counter Altona's claim that the neighboring communities were already de facto tied to Altona through the provision of public utilities and cultural amenities, Niendorf urgently required information on the extent to which needs and obligations were being met locally and about local achievements. Meanwhile, independent experts were called upon to rebut Altona's claim.[61]

Predictably, the reports showed that Altona's bid had little substance. For instance, it was doubted that essential services such as gas, electricity, water, and transport-communications, would be improved upon incorporation. They asserted that most of these services were already adequately provided and at a cheaper cost to the consumer than in Altona. Indeed, according to the summary report compiled by the *Kreis* committee, incorporation would lead to a deterioration in the standard of service and in local provision.[62]

Niendorf and his colleagues also dismissed as fantasy the suggestion by Altona that it needed land for new industries and housing. They argued that there was land available within the existing borders and little indication that industry would grow once the economic downturn had passed. The *Kreis* committee was equally dismissive about the potential benefit to follow from a reappraisal of Altona's budgetary position through financial equalization (*Finanzausgleich*). It argued that any future gain from an increase in the reich income tax transfer (resulting from an increase in population), would barely cover needs. The city already had a five and a half million reichsmark deficit, which would mean an inevitable rise in local tax surcharges on property and business in order to offset costly municipal schemes. Local enterprises therefore had everything to lose by incorporation. But not only would incorporation fail to cure Altona's financial ills; the county of Pinneberg would be "finished off" too. Putting the case for a loose municipal federation based on a "general settlement plan," the *Kreis* Defense Committee argued that, otherwise, with the loss of its richest suburbs, the county's own financial position would be jeopardized. It claimed that, whereas Altona could only hope to gain at most a 5 percent increase in revenue after incorporation, Pinneberg stood to lose at least 30 percent, rising to 45 percent of its revenue if Blankenese went too.[63]

The financial burden of incorporation also began to worry some Altona industrialists, who had remained hitherto silent on the issue. In mid-1926 some members of the business community emerged in opposition to the city's incorporation plans, which they saw as another example of Socialist maladministration. At a meeting of major firms in July the president of the Chamber of Industry and Commerce, Carl Menck, expressed his doubts on a revival of Altona's economic fortunes after incorporation.[64] Local industry was already under great strain in the economic downswing of the mid-1920s, and they could ill afford any unnecessary financial burdens, least of all new land for industrial development and relocation.[65]

Indeed, the president of the chamber produced the results of a survey of 150 large firms, constituting a work force of around 11,000, that showed only 10 were in support of the proposed new industrial zone in Eidelstedt and Stellingen.[66] This result was hardly surprising. Most of Altona's industry was situated in the heart of Ottensen and in the northern districts of the Altstadt. If Brauer's proposals were to come to fruition and zoning took place, then this would mean the costly and disruptive process of transferring enterprises.

Moreover, manufacturers believed that a move to the outskirts of the city would have a knock-on effect on wage claims or on production. Because workers would have to travel at a distance, they would either have to use public transport or travel on foot, which would produce problems related to timekeeping or alertness at the workbench. Nearly half of the survey intimated that, in the event of incorporation leading to greater financial burdens, they would rather move to Hamburg, where taxation of business was nonexistent. The local business community believed that its interests were best served if Brauer put his energies into stabilizing municipal finances rather than embarking on grandiose plans.[67] For the incorporation, in Menck's view, came at a difficult time, it would incur greater burdens upon the already fragile budget, and in the last resort the city would inevitably turn to industry in order to meet the ensuing bill.[68]

After the second petition had been filed in May there was talk within the SPD that incorporation would be a matter of weeks. The liberal press was surprised, but the *Hamburger Echo* stated that a speedy conclusion to the incorporation was far from surprising, since a concession to Altona had been on the cards for weeks—in fact, ever since Brauer had been successful in lobbying the "authoritative office."[69] The office in question was that of the Prussian interior minister, Carl Severing, a close friend of the lord mayor. It was reported that Severing had fought particularly hard on Altona's behalf during a cabinet meeting to discuss the question of regional boundaries. Severing's involvement also seemed to explain the inclusion of Sülldorf, Rissen, and Blankenese, the largest and most powerful of the parishes, into the second petition.[70] Yet the expected speedy conclusion did not materialize. In contrast to the earlier phase, when Altona's position had seemed unassailable, an outcome favoring the city in the second phase appeared, for a while at least, less assured. Instead of confident action from the "authoritative office" in Berlin, there was indecision, partly resulting from its resumption of talks with Hamburg on territorial alternatives.[71] This appeared to put Brauer on the defensive. The campaign now dragged on into the summer and remained unresolved by early autumn.

The visit to the contested areas in June by the head of the provincial government administration, Regierungspräsident Dr. Adolf Johannsen, and his subsequent volte face in support of the suburbs added to an emerging perception that Brauer's ship might not make port after all. A meeting of the Special Assembly of the Schleswig-Holstein Counties in mid-September did little to speed the course of incorporation.[72] It was after this meeting that the *Norddeutsche Nachrichten* in its relentless campaign against Altona and Brauer published a rather triumphant article:

> Herr Lord Mayor Brauer, with his blue-sky optimism, which has already been ridiculed, might believe that the Prussian Landtag for the sake of his existing friendship to Herr Severing, will destroy the district of Pinneberg and incorporate 45,000 inhabitants into Altona against their definite will; against the will of the parish councils; and against the will of the county assembly. But the serious part of the population, even in Altona, do not take him seriously anymore. That's what happens when one shows-off![73]

Certainly, it seemed that the prospect of an easy ride for Altona was diminishing.

On 26 June the parish councils and the district council voted on the incorporation issue. The result was a resounding rejection from the *bürgerlichen* groups and some confusion within the local SPD. Those Social Democrats who abstained were torn between parochial sympathies and party loyalty. (It is worth noting that in the Kreistag four SPD members abstained, and the other six, including Niendorf, voted with the anti-incorporationists.)[74]

The results bolstered local morale, for they meant that the provincial diet and the Prussian parliament would now debate the claim. Thus, local interests would receive public representation at a higher political level. With Johanssen's shift toward favoring the parishes and a meeting of the conflicting parties proposed for sometime in October, it seemed to the anti-incorporationists that justice was at last at hand. The specter of communal emasculation at the hands of "red Altona," thus began to fade as the belief took hold that in the final resort incorporation would not take place after all.

But a twist in the plot unfolded during the next stage of the drama in October 1926. Things began to sour when the head of the department for municipal affairs in the Prussian interior ministry, Dr. Viktor von Leyden, visited the area. Von Leyden had the responsibility for overseeing incorporation negotiations throughout Prussia. Activists in the parishes may have been heartened by a statement he was alleged to have made in Breslau shortly before his visit to Altona. As befitting a senior civil servant, von Leyden had emphasized his strict neutrality in local discussions, stating that he would judge each case on its merits and that larger municipal units could not expect to have their borders extended by "right of might."[75] Von Leyden's words were construed as an expression of support for the smaller communities.

Von Leyden met local representatives in the dispute with Altona on 26 October. But, if there was any hope that Brauer's plans were about to founder on the rock of justice, this was quickly dispelled by events. Von Leyden's visit, instead of providing succor, produced a stream of complaints that he had handled the affair in a blatantly partisan manner, making a mockery of both the supposed impartiality of a high-ranking civil servant and of his own words.[76] During the morning a tour of the suburbs had taken place to enable von Leyden to acquaint himself with the communities in question. But this, according to opponents, had been a cruel farce:

> The comedy which the representatives of the Prussian government carried out in Altona and its environs on Monday has also been suitably commented on in the Hamburg and provincial press. Among others, the Stellinger Lokalanzeiger writes: "In the morning an inspection of the nine coveted suburbs took place. A bus of the

TABLE 9.   Parish Council Votes on Incorporation, 1926

	Against	For	Abstentions
Gr.Flottbek	8	3	1
Kl.Flottbek	6	—	3
Nienstedten	6	2	—
Lurup	4	3	—
Osdorf	4	3	1
Eidelstedt	9	2	1
Stellingen–Langenfelde	11	5	—
Blankenese	18	6	—

Source: StAH 424–47/76, Heft 21: *Lokal-Anzeiger Stellingen-Langenfelde* 143, 26 June 1926, "Ergebnis der Abstimmung der Gemeindevertretungen."

Altona Transport Company picked up a number of gentlemen at the railway station and brought them to Lokstedt from where the inspection commenced. The gentlemen disembarked in front of the Lokstedt administrative buildings, went through the meeting room, and climbed back into the bus. In Lokstedt the whole 'informing' was completed in five minutes. Then it was the turn of Stellingen and Eidelstedt where equally very short town hall visits took place. Lurup, Klein and Groß Flottbek, Nienstedten and so forth, were driven through without stopping." In view of such events it is really difficult to remain serious. The main responsibility for Monday lies with the Prussian permanent secretary, Dr. v. Leyden. . . . One cannot blame the population of the Elbe communities therefore, if it has lost its trust in the neutrality of this civil servant and will not tolerate further "informings" of this type.[77]

The morning excursion had been followed by a series of meetings in the afternoon, but neither did these hearings leave much to be hopeful about. Far from being the torchbearer of justice, von Leyden appeared in the eyes of the afflicted parishes as a creature in the service of Altona and Berlin. It was alleged that the *Ministerialdirektor* allowed Brauer and Oberpräsident Heinrich Kürbis, a party comrade and former Altona councillor, to elaborate "in epic length their pro-incorporation point of view."[78] And anyone from the suburbs who spoke out in favor of incorporation was treated similarly. The anti-incorporationists, however, were subjected to a very different handling. It was alleged that von Leyden repeatedly cut short any attempt by Landrat Niendorf to put the case against incorporation into a wider regional and national context. And each member of the local lobby was reminded to adhere strictly to matters concerning their particular community. Not surprisingly, the council leaders of Nienstedten, Klein Flottbek, and Osdorf were inclined to comment that the meeting in Altona could hardly be labeled as a "negotiation" and referred to the day as "Black Tuesday."[79]

    The belief that the proceedings were the result of a conspiracy hatched between Altona and Berlin was compounded by von Leyden's apparently dismissive attitude toward the owners of the world-famous Hagenbeck zoo and circus in Stellingen. The Hagenbeck brothers, Heinrich and Lorenz, met von Leyden in early November in order to explain why they opposed Altona's plans for enlargement. They were fearful that Stellingen had become a pawn in a boundary game between Prussia and the Hanseatic city-state, in which the interests of the parish would be sacrificed. The brothers were worried that, if Stellingen were incorporated into Altona, they would lose the benefit of Hamburg's generous provision of public transport, and this would have an adverse impact on their business. Von Leyden was not impressed with their arguments and told them not to overestimate their own importance where greater issues involving the reorganization of the *Länder* and communal borders in Prussia were concerned.

The brothers, unhappy with this meeting, appealed directly to the Prussian parliament, seeking protection from what they saw as a small self-serving clique whose decisions operated against the general good.

> It is certainly understandable that our business, which has existed for more than sixty years, which was created from our own efforts, which offers an existence to over 900 people when at full capacity, and which has paid enormous sums of tax, has the right to seek the opportunity to avoid the fate of becoming the plaything of the political schemes of a small group in the Prussian government in Berlin.[80]

The Hagenbecks pleaded for the protection of the small world of the *Heimat,* where personal achievement was synonymous with "public good" and where local notables bestowed upon the local community an element of continuity and stability in a world of change and upheaval.[81]

The disappointing experience with von Leyden led to claims of a "stab in the back" of the national-minded communities of the Elbe. Wide sections of the local population were reportedly feeling very bitter about the outcome of von Leyden's visit. The *Norddeutsche,* as usual, did not miss the opportunity to make veiled threats. With reference to the defeat and expulsion of Denmark in 1866, the editors of the newspaper commented that "the men who preside in Berlin today, would fare in the same way as the Danish King."[82] The outcome of von Leyden's visit spurred many local notables into action. At a protest meeting on the 2 November "men of business and industry" and other public figures met in order to decide on some form of popular action. One person suggested sending a mass deputation to Berlin, while another was in favor of filling hired trains with protesters in order to storm (*bestürmen*) the Prussian parliament.[83] In order to assuage the anger of the suburbs, members of the DVP in the Provincial Diet proposed that a second and "properly impartial" inspection should take place.[84]

Von Leyden's alleged behavior confirmed a widely held belief that the Socialists in Berlin and Altona would not stop short of chicanery in order to achieve their party political aim. As a member of the SPD, Brauer, according to his enemies, had a direct line of contact to Berlin and could thus draw upon "almost the whole of the Prussian administrative apparatus" in his campaign to put the suburbs under his control.[85] One opponent railed in apocalyptic language against the Socialist axis of Berlin-Altona in a letter published in the pages of the *Norddeutsche*. The writer, a man named Walther Schumann, began by blaming the government in Berlin for the outcome of the referendum in 1920, when Schleswig-Holstein lost its northern border areas to Denmark. That referendum had been contrary to the interests of the reich and was the direct result of Berlin's "unclear ideas." It had become "historically notorious" and showed "that there is absolutely no inner solidarity between the . . . predominantly sons of the soil of Schleswig-Holstein and present-day Berlin." Schumann was convinced that this time Prussia would not get its way with the province, for "the well-being of the entire Reich can be harmed through the declared methods [of Berlin]." He went on:

> And now the idea to raise from the soil a Prussian Hamburg. A Hamburg that is called "Greater Altona"! God take pity! For that one needs more than a bundle of decrees from Berlin Counsellors or Secretaries of State with such ideas. A Greater Altona is even beyond the strength of a neo-Prussian Lord Mayor.[86]

There was still a residuum of popular faith in the force of parliament. But any trust in a higher parliamentary power was dealt two blows. The first blow came in November, when the Schleswig-Holstein Provincial Diet voted 49 in favor to 9 against for a report by a special commission recommending incorporation.[87] The second blow came at the end of January, when a bill of incorporation was drafted by the Prussian Council of State, after its inspection tour of the region earlier that month.[88] The only remaining possible defense was the Prussian parliament itself. The *Norddeutsche* in a surprisingly conciliatory tone looked to the Prussian parliament to undo the mischief of the Council of State, which, "as cool as you please, had found the damned courage to disregard the wishes of the populace." Parliament represented the people, therefore:

> If justice should remain justice, and if this institution, which is supposed to represent the will of the people, does not itself wish to become a laughing-stock, then it simply cannot approve the government's draft bill. For contrary to the Council of State, parliament must take into account that the majority of the population does not want to join Altona.[89]

The editors thus differentiated between parliament as the representative body of the people and the Prussian government as the tool of a Socialist clique.

At the end of January the *Norddeutsche* published an open letter from the Citizens' Association of Blankenese-Dockenhuden to the leader of the parish council, Heinrich Frahm, who was also a member of the DVP, underlining this viewpoint. The letter was a copy of the resolution taken at an emergency meeting of the association after hearing the news of the Prussian Council of State's acceptance of the draft bill. Frahm was exhorted to join with his colleagues in sending by telegram an immediate and unequivocal protest to the Prussian parliament. The following excerpt conveys the strength of *Mittelstand* parochial and ideological sentiments:

> As representative of a considerable part of the residents in the parish administered by you, the Citizens' Association turns to you in the last, grave hour, in order to make another attempt to avert the destructive evil which threatens our locality through the incorporation into debt-sinking Altona. Enough words have been spoken! The part of the populace, which is represented by us, finally wants to see acts! This definitely greater part [of the population] does not wish to be violated in the same manner as our Fatherland was by the Allied Enemy.[90]

Yet, in the event that the Prussian parliament would not reject the draft bill, the *Norddeutsche* felt compelled to add a further note of warning: "Even if the dice should so fall, the Elbe communities would never inwardly come to terms with an incorporation, but would persist in the most bitter opposition,"[91] outside the parliamentary arena.

By early 1927 there were signs that the wider resistance was beginning to dissolve. Whereas the councils in Blankenese and Stellingen-Langenfelde had already rejected motions by their SPD councillors at the beginning of January that they should negotiate with Altona the terms of incorporation,[92] the leaders of the parishes of Nienstedten, Osdorf, Klein Flottbek, and Groß Flottbek began to prepare themselves for the inevitability of the incorporation, in spite of their continued hostility. Already in November the parish leaders of Nienstedten, Osdorf, and Klein Flottbek suggested in a letter to the *Kreis* committee that after von Leyden's visit a change in tactic was needed. Instead of outright rejection, they now thought it prudent to consider making some concessions—including sacrificing Eidelstedt, Stellingen, and Lurup—to Altona, in the hope that the beast would thus be satisfied.[93]

In order to accelerate matters a further inspection of the region took place between the 6 and 9 March by a high-powered parliamentary commission, which included the Prussian premier Otto Braun, the new interior minister, Albert Grzesinski, and Franz von Papen as secretary.[94] Brauer addressed the commission, taking the opportunity to stress the sheer importance of the incorporation (especially that of Blankenese) for the future well-being and development of the Lower Elbe region. To hearty applause he rounded off his speech by making reference to the higher interests of the democratic state, which ultimately rested upon a firm foundation of municipal independence. Brauer concluded that this independence was only possible through the creation of large municipal units. Therefore, the "small and narrow communal interests of the bordering parishes" had to be sacrificed.[95]

The progress toward creating a Greater Altona entered its final phase in the spring of 1927. A general meeting of all the parties was scheduled for the 4 April in the sumptuous hall of Altona's Kaiserhof Hotel. Also, bilateral meetings were arranged between March and June to finalize the contracts between Altona and the individual suburbs.[96] The leaders of the communities and Landrat Niendorf were unhappy about this latter arrangement because it meant there would be no collective representation. This was a tactic clearly favoring Brauer, for it had the obvious advantage that he could determine the pace of the discussions and dominate the negotiations. Thus, incorporation and the conditions upon which it was to take place would occur by "right of might" after all.

Negotiations to settle the price of incorporation proceeded during the early spring. The parish communities, especially those immediately bordering Altona, were directed by Niendorf to draw up their lists of special requirements (the so-called *Sonderwünsche*). The two Flottbeks had theirs ready by the beginning of April. Eidelstedt had its ready, having already done a U-turn the previous November after hearing that Altona would be treated generously in any future redistribution of local, regional, and federal finances (*Finanzausgleich*).[97] But the embers of resistance were not quite dead. The Nienstedten parish council decided to reject an invitation to attend a meeting with Brauer—as a means of delaying the fateful date. The middle-aged head of the parish, Otto Grotkop, made the biting comment that,

> since Altona had not found it necessary for over two and a half years to negotiate directly with the communities on the subject of incorporation, we do not consider this moment in time appropriate for us to negotiate, given the present state of the question in the legislative bodies.[98]

Stellingen proceeded more cautiously and considered an alternative plan. But Blankenese also showed signs of digging in. In a special issue of the *Norddeutsche Nachrichten* in March 1927 an appeal was made to the "Men of the Prussian House of Deputies" to help the Elbe communities to "rescue the *Heimat"* from the clutches of Altona.[99]

Ironically, it was not the "men" of the Prussian parliament who mounted the dikes to defend the *Heimat* from Altona but a female deputy from the DNVP. Frau Mehlis launched a bitter attack against Brauer, accusing him of intimidating the smaller and weaker councils of Rissen and Sülldorf. Brauer, she claimed, had issued the two councils with an ultimatum that they either come to the negotiating table immediately (on his terms) or forgo discussions altogether and so lose any prospect of extracting from Altona any future obligations to be met after incorporation.[100] Mehlis argued that a fundamental political wrong was being perpetrated by bringing the suburbs under Brauer's control. At a stroke of a ministerial pen Blankenese and the other communities, which up to that point had remained unsullied by municipal socialism, were to be thrown to the revolution of 1918. She claimed that a Socialist-led Greater Altona would mean uprooting the parish inhabitants from the soil of their *Heimat,* and, being a minority in the city, they would be virtually disenfranchised.[101]

Two further meetings in Altona were arranged: one for the end of May, when the *Regierungspräsident* was expected to attend, and the second for early June. The first meeting merely confirmed the depth of resentment felt in the suburbs toward Brauer. Nonetheless, some grudging progress was made, for on the 3 June all the representatives from the suburbs (except Blankenese) met with Brauer and his committee to finalize the special requirements. Blankenese finally agreed to a contract on the fourteenth, but the council then rejected it at a closed extraordinary meeting five days later. The SPD in Blankenese put forward another motion on the twenty-eighth, demanding that the council finally come to a decision on the matter. But this was removed from the agenda by Dr. Schramm. It was only after the Prussian parliament had passed the act making incorporation law that Blankenese's council finally accepted the contract.[102]

The last-minute tactic of causing delays was repeated in the Prussian parliament, where the deputies of the DNVP pursued the cause of the suburbs with relentless vigor. They were joined by some members of the DVP, who saw the incorporation as evidence of the "socialist hunger for power" and of "municipal megalomania."[103] These deputies continuously obstructed procedure by introducing new amendments to the bill. When the time came to vote, they either withheld their cards or absented themselves in order to deprive parliament of a quorum.[104] The most outspoken of the DVP opponents in the Prussian parliament, a deputy named Schröter, fought tooth and nail against the bill, declaiming what he felt to be a "flouting of the right to self-determination."[105] Schröter's attack upon

Altona during the final debates in parliament, while welcomed by his Pinneberg and Elbe allies in the DVP, was met with the dismay among his own party colleagues in Altona, demonstrating the power of territorial sentiments over party allegiance and discipline.[106]

With the incorporation now imminent the campaign revealed a more ugly trait. The *Norddeutsche* had already set the tone in February when it printed an article accusing Altona and Brauer of employing dirty tricks in order to gain power over the suburbs, especially Blankenese. "Our readers know the Low German saying," it wrote, "that you can't outstink a dungheap."[107] The parliamentary struggle against Altona had proven to be fruitless, and in the same article the editors noted, "we now know what Berlin thinks of the inhabitants of the Elbe communities." The positions between the suburbs, on the one hand, and the "Altona-Berlin axis," on the other, were now irreconcilable. There was talk of "bad blood" between the two, and Johannes Hammann from the Elbe Communities' Trade Association accused the Prussian parliament of a "betrayal of the Fatherland" as bad, if not worse, as in 1918. In a newspaper article Hammann spoke of the "rape of the communities" and warned the authorities in Altona, "we will stay cool and play like with like."[108]

Meanwhile, during the debate in the Prussian parliament on 26 June one of the members from the Center Party, which had continuously called for moderation and a "solution in the Christian spirit of neighborly love,"[109] revealed that Catholics in Blankenese had received an anonymous threat in the event of the Center Party supporting the bill.[110] Indeed, nationalists had revealed their sectarian antagonism against the Catholic Center Party in a number of attacks in which they concentrated on the Centre's "despicable collusion" with the Social Democrats as further evidence of a "black-red conspiracy."[111] For nationalists the ultimate act of betrayal came when the Catholic and arch-conservative von Papen voted in favor of Blankenese's incorporation during the second reading of the bill.[112]

These goings-on prompted the Catholic deputy, Grebe, to announce sarcastically during the debate in the Prussian parliament:

> I cannot suppress here a few remarks opposing the way one has resisted the inclusion of Blankenese in the bill. The honorable lady [Mehlis] who spoke previously, emphasized that this contradicts democracy etc. It has been continuously emphasized from the [*Kreis*] Defense Committee that the right of self-determination would be harmed. Well, it always leaves cause for concern when one appropriates for oneself an idea in which one does not believe.[113]

The passage of the bill had been apparently secured through a political tradeoff that, to the nationalists, was symptomatic of the corruption of the "Weimar system." The bill's triumph had not only depended on the combined support of the Democrats, Center Party, and Socialists but had also to depend on a deal with the Communists, who demanded revision of some of the paragraphs of the new *Landgemeindeordnung* as their price for supporting the bill.[114] In these circumstances the incorporation was viewed as an example of the corrupt nature of Socialist political ambition and liberal spinelessness. All along, the nationalists argued, the Altona Social Democrats led by Brauer had wheeled and dealed and bullied to achieve their goal. As far as the conservatives in the suburbs were concerned, the democratic process had been tried and found severely wanting. Indeed,

> the Prussian government adds to its colors from 1918, which had promised us freedom, peace and bread, deprivation of rights and economic strangulation. The shameful acts of the French and Poles in Germany are worthily joined by the resolutions of the Prussian government against its own people.[115]

The mobilization of the parish communities for the defense of the *Heimat* ended in defeat on 1 July, as the bill creating Greater Altona passed into law. The gulf between some quarters of the middle class and the Social Democrats was now unbridgeable. On the eve of the bill becoming law the *Hamburger Nachrichten,* closely allied with the DNVP, expressed the resentment within the nationalist camp but predicted the triumph would one day prove to be a pyrrhic victory:

> The government cannot . . . be proud of their victory. . . . To be sure, today and tomorrow the Coalition, and most of all Social Democracy, rejoices in the manner of an ecclesiastic choir. Their friends kick their legs for joy, hurrah! Now it's off to feast, yum-yum hurrah! Hurrah for Victory! For the rule of Altona, the empire of Social Democrat and Lord Mayor Brauer, has become even greater. Under Social Democratic rule Altona has received for a song the flourishing communities in the north and . . . in the west along the Elbe . . . with their taxable wealth and everything which sensible public-spiritedness has created there. What this gift really means however, will be revealed when Altona, under its Social Democratic lord and master, has to show how these thriving communities will fare in future. . . . We will come to talk again about what the Social Democrats together with the papist Center Party, not to mention the wretched Democrats, have

brought about, at some time or other in the not too distant future. For the moment, madness you win![116]

The incorporation conflict was thus added to the list of *Mittelstand* grievances, becoming another milestone on the road leading from democracy to Nazism.

Conclusion

The bitter sense of defeat was no doubt sharpened by the celebrations of the SPD in Altona. On the Friday following the incorporation the Social Democrats held a grand gala to celebrate what they described as their victory. The great hall of the Hotel Kaiserhof was decked out in red, a band played the "Internationale," and the party's local branches paraded with their banners. Important guests who had supported Altona's cause attended and gave well-received speeches of congratulations. But the biggest ovation was reserved for Brauer. He told his sixteen-hundred-strong audience that the incorporation was an integral part of the aims of the labor movement in Altona. It had been made possible because, at every level in the organization, cooperation and support had been shown. "For this reason," he told his appreciative audience, "we Social Democrats can claim the success of the incorporation campaign fully for ourselves."[117]

The incorporation was given popular acclamation in the municipal election that followed in September. The SPD fought on an "incorporation ticket" and was amply vindicated, not only in "old Altona" but in the incorporated areas too, where gains were registered. Brauer was triumphant, stating how he wished "all lord mayors in Germany the same level of support in their councils and among the general public."[118] Indeed, the election on 25 September underlined the weakness of the middle-class parties and associations, derived from their disunity over the incorporation. The DNVP suffered a humiliating defeat in every community, notably in those places where it had traditionally been the leading party. The *Gemeinschaftsliste* put on an inconsequential performance, in part underlying the contemporary observation about the "politicization" of middle-class parish pump politics.[119] On the other hand, the DVP, whose leaders in the suburbs had also opposed the incorporation, unlike their counterparts in Altona, did well, displacing the DNVP as the main bourgeois party in six of the ten communities.

Although they had been "reminded of their duty to vote" a few days before by their political leaders,[120] anti-incorporationists expressed their dissatisfaction by simply abstaining from the democratic process. There was a considerably lower voter turnout in the incorporated suburbs than there had been in either May or December 1924. In general, there was a 10 percent decrease, which was most pronounced in Blankenese, where the participation rate fell from around 84 percent in 1924 to under 67 percent. The abstentions had important consequences for of the eleven new councillors from the incorporated communities: five were socialist, one was a Democrat, three were members of the DVP, and two were from the DNVP. The *Hamburger Echo,* summed up the setback for the middle class in an undisguisedly excited commentary on the election. The paper asserted that: "It is not overstated if one describes the election result as a catastrophic defeat for the bourgeoisie." Indeed, throughout the campaign:

how they had hoped from day one for a bourgeois majority and a considerable decline in the proportion of Social Democratic votes. For with the incorporation of the suburbs, a considerable expansion of right-wing bourgeois social circles took place. How they let rip in this election campaign in order to achieve [their] victory; but we fixed the bourgeoisie to the issue of social democratic municipal work. And now?[121]

The strength of support for the Socialists in the incorporated communities may have been a vindication of their policy, but it was also due to the internal divisions and confusion within the middle-class camp.[122] For

TABLE 10. Municipal Election Results in the Incorporated Areas, 1927, Compared to 1924 (selected parties, by percentage of valid vote)

	SPD		DNVP		DVP		GL	
	1924[a]	1927	1924[a]	1927	1924[a]	1927	1924[a]	1927
Blan.	17.5	23.4	36.4	21.7	18.3	28.6	—	5.3
Eide.	25.4	41.0	15.4	10.2	15.6	12.7	31.2	7.3
GrFl.	22.4	30.0	28.6	18.4	22.6	25.8	65.1	6.5
KlFl.	21.6	27.0	28.0	22.3	25.2	31.2	—	3.5
Lur.	34.2	64.5	35.8	11.7	4.9	4.2	53.2	8.5
Nien.	25.9	34.3	31.3	17.4	18.5	23.4	—	3.3
Osd.	30.3	43.2	32.1	27.5	10.8	11.7	—	2.8
Riss.	27.7	35.6	29.8	14.7	13.5	27.1	—	4.6
Stell–Lang.	24.0	36.2	19.6	12.5	7.2	6.5	51.5	5.7
Süll.	—	45.4	—	15.1	—	13.0	—	5.0

Source: StDR 315,2, 28–29; StJü Altona (1924): 49; *Hamburger Echo* 122, May 1924; StJB Altona (1928): 101; *Amtsblatt der Stadt Altona* 39 (1 Oct. 1927).

Note: Comparable data for all suburbs is not available.

[a]Reichstag election May 1924

[b]Municipal election May 1924

instance, the "unpolitical" unity list of the *Gemeinschaftsliste* itself had been deeply divided. This group was headed by Dr. Heinrich Ahrendt, who, as we saw earlier, was one of the leaders of the Central Committee of the Elbe Civic Associations. He and the Altona-based groups had favored incorporation against the wishes of the Elbe members. Thus, while a reasonable performance was registered in Altona, the *Gemeinschaftsliste* slumped elsewhere.

Indeed, the fissures within this group were already visible before the election. Only two of the fifty *Gemeinschaftsliste* candidates lived in the suburbs, and they were placed near the bottom of the list with little chance of election. The rest came from Altona. On the other hand, Ahrendt's erstwhile colleagues from the ZkVE were either among the DNVP candidates or those of the DVP. In proportional terms the suburbs were better represented in the DVP (48 percent) than they were in the DNVP (41 percent). Though marginal, this may have helped in the former's better performance (and yet suburban representatives in the SPD accounted for only one-fifth of its 67-strong candidate list, suggesting the importance of a low turnout of voters in influencing the result).

The long struggle over the incorporation had badly split the bourgeois front and left it confused about which tactics to pursue. The middle-class *Bürger* front of 1924 was now replaced by a narrow political partisanship. Party leaders from the DVP and DNVP emphasized the need for "party professionalism" in place of "amateur politics," as the means to break the SPD's grip on municipal power. A Blankenese teacher and DNVP candidate, Johannes Jürgs, stated that the political challenge could only be mounted by "professionals [and] men of responsibility and expertise." But, while the DVP claimed the "era of the unpolitical voter is over," one of its candidates, the bank director and member of the board of the Chamber of Industry and Commerce, Karl Frahm, also paraded the years of successful cooperation with the DNVP in the "apolitical" *Bürger* bloc as a reason for supporting the DVP.[123]

Yet, as we saw in chapter 2, while both the DVP and DNVP were inveterate opponents of Brauer and the SPD, neither was capable of uniting or leading the myriad of local sectional interests or of effectively combatting the Socialists. Schramm's postelection debacle was evidence of that. The swing back to a unity list in 1929 reflected this limitation. But the desire by then was for a combination of bourgeois unity *and* hard-edged politics, rather than a simple return to the language of *Honoratioren* apoliticism.[124]

Indeed, the struggle over incorporation had raised the emotional heat in local politics by introducing both the language and sentiment of the *Heimat* as Fatherland. The anti-incorporationists saw their struggle against Altona as a continuation of the political struggles of the revolution. Germany's cities may have succumbed to the red flag, but parish communities, such as theirs, had remained true to the old national colors. Their own defeat at the hands of Brauer merely confirmed the limitations of the Weimar democratic process when it came to protecting their interests. This experience opened the door to delegitimizing Weimar politics within the incorporated suburbs and justified the politics of retribution. The *Norddeutsche* had already mapped out this terrain in a warning editorial in June:

> Government and parliament should know that the overwhelming majority of the population do not want to join Altona. That enmity will develop between Altona and the Elbe communities if one dares to force through the incorporation. It would be a blatant mockery of the spirit of democracy; an abuse of the laws of the republic, if one would incorporate without listening to the inhabitants of the Elbe communities. One has spoken a great deal about a putsch in the last few days. What the Lord Mayor of Altona is doing, to take away the right of self-determination against the will of the majority in the communities, is a putsch! Fight each government, fight each parliamentary representative, which or who would dare to abuse our people in such an outrageous way. One should take note in Altona as well as in Berlin: A compulsorily enforced incorporation would leave a wound in the hearts of the populace which would never heal. Altona would continuously and for always come up against the strongest opposition here, an opposition which would manifest itself in the bittermost fashion in every sphere of public life. One which would take on forms in the area of communal, economic and social life, which the competent authority today perhaps cannot imagine.[125]

The Kröger's were adamant that local opposition to the Weimar system would be unrelenting until Brauer was finally removed from office. What they could not know was the particular political channel into which injured sentiment would eventually flow. Nor could they predict the extent to which municipal economic policy and material grievances would also fuel middle-class opposition, as we shall see. For the moment the voices from the *Heimat* had spoken.

CHAPTER 5

Economic Struggles: The Local State and Business Interests, 1924–1932

The Visible Hand is not a Benevolent Hand.

—Altonaer Lokalanzeiger[1]

Writing on the German economy at the end of the 1920s, the American economist James Angell estimated that between 12 and 15 percent of all economic activity since the war had shifted into public control. The municipal share of this was considerable, if not the major part. Since the late nineteenth century municipal involvement in the economy had expanded dramatically, branching out from merely providing public utilities, such as gas, water, and electricity, to profit-oriented enterprise in a variety of fields.[2] World War I intensified local intervention in the economy, and this continued after the hostilities had ended. In the early postwar period the extension of the public hand into the social and economic spheres had a specific and positive role to play in the regeneration of national life. The republic's municipal leaders believed that the national economy, rather like the political structure, would have to be reconstituted from below.[3] Such a view found support among some experts in the field of public finance, who also saw in municipal public enterprise a mission of national importance.[4]

The scale of involvement at the local level, however, elicited grave misgivings from private enterprise, whose members saw in this activity a stealthy socialization of the economy through "communalization" (*Kommunalisierung*). A powerful middle-class lobby group, the Reich Council of Citizens (Reichsbürgerrat), which sought a united front of *Bürger* in the councils in order to effectively combat the Left, summed up their fear:

Ever since the Marxists had to give up the attempts to socialize our economy through Reich or state laws after the Revolution, they have attempted to achieve the gradual transformation of our economy into a public one by a detour of controlling the municipalities. . . . They declare quite openly that communal administration must become one of the most important instruments for the carrying through of socialist ideas in the spheres of economy and culture. Through the continued acquisition of new economic branches under municipal administration, through the systematic increase of the public burden upon the property and profit of the private economy, they seek to substitute the public for the private economy.[5]

For many owners, notably of small and medium-sized businesses of the sort that prevailed in Altona, Weimar's "visible hand" represented little more than systematic discrimination against them.[6] And they were clearly not reassured by the chairman of the Städtetag, Oskar Mulert, who described municipal involvement in the economy as a "moment of opportunity" for private interests, rather than as a threat.[7] James Angell's observation that "the whole question of government ownership in Germany . . . is steeped in controversy, and lies near the heart of the fundamental political and economic struggle between the socialist and non-socialist groups"[8] referred to the national level of activity. This conflict can be better charted, however, at the municipal level from the mid-1920s, when city administrations embarked on what was to become a golden era for municipal expansion.

The conflict revolved around three axes. First, that public involvement in the economy distorted the market, especially where local authorities stepped in to bail out ailing plants, usually through public monies. Commercial interests were also worried that the extension of public enterprise would squeeze their share of a diminished market and was part of an effort to socialize the economy. Second, public utilities and expansive public enterprises would result in monopolies, remove competitive pricing, and thus artificially raise costs to the consumer. Third, the private sector was concerned about the overall financial burden implicit in carrying on public enterprise, for cities often borrowed heavily in order to finance their economic activities, and private interests feared that this would result in higher taxation.[9]

Creeping Socialization of Profit or Loss?

The municipal authority in Altona came to play a major role in the local economy, both directly and indirectly. The city already owned the three main public utilities of electricity, gas, and water before World War I. The era of municipal entrepreneurial expansion only got fully under way, however, during the 1920s, under Brauer's influence. During the inflationary period the local authority extended its ownership of real estate by taking advantage of the financial difficulties experienced by property owners. By 1927 it owned 1,120 hectares of land, an increase of 77.5 percent over its 1913 level, which meant that 51 percent of Altona's total land area was under municipal ownership.[10]

In 1922 the city established the municipal housing company, the Siedlungsgemeinschaft Altona (SAGA), after acquiring the garden estate of Steenkamp, and in 1932, at the height of the Depression, it gained control of a provincial housing association. A municipal omnibus transport company, the Verkehrsaktiengesellschaft Altona (VAGA) came into being in 1924, and an air link with Magdeburg was established at around the same time. The city obtained shares in various other enterprises ranging from two regional rail lines and the Hamburg urban transport network. Shares were also obtained in the local theater company. The city owned a savings bank that had deposits in its three branches of just over two million reichsmark and had permission to establish a commercial bank; it also controlled a mortgage company. The administration had also extended its influence over a wholesale merchandizing outlet and a wood and furniture company, and it owned a quarry, sawmill, and construction works in east Prussia. These and related entrepreneurial activities represented around one and a half million reichsmark in terms of capital investment.[11]

Not surprisingly, local *Mittelstand* interests viewed the scale of activity with deep mistrust and as a prelude to a fuller emasculation of the free market economy. But, as with many municipalists, Brauer believed that the local state had a duty to provide the essential infrastructure and services of a modern industrial society, which the private sector could not. And, while he was not disinclined to stretch the parameters of the "visible hand" beyond utilities, he was not in favor of displacing the private economy entirely.[12] Broadly speaking, Brauer aligned himself with the economic doctrine elaborated by the socialist economist Rudolf Hilferding. Hilferding's interpretation of capitalist development, shared by many in the SPD leadership, was that it would become "organized" as free market competition declined in the face of private cartels and corporate organizations. Yet, as the anarchy of the untrammeled market gave way to the organized private market, it subjected the consumer to the tyranny of private monopoly. Therefore, there was a public responsibility to ensure that the individual citizen as consumer was protected by restoring the market as a positive mechanism.[13] In Brauer's words:

> Domination of the markets and of production is not a private affair. Where the positive effects of free competition have been eliminated by amalgamation, prices must be controlled and influenced by competing public companies.[14]

As a firm believer in the local state, Max Brauer was convinced that this ought to be achieved according to the "principle of the smallest means"— that is, through the municipality.[15]

Brauer's position on the role of the state in the economy was considerably more conciliatory than his opponents allowed for. Public intervention in Altona often represented merely a stepping-in by the authority wherever the private economy had failed and so did not necessarily signal permanent involvement. Therefore, while Brauer was prepared to step in and offer aid to troubled concerns, he did not intend that municipal involvement should mean the local authority playing banker to either semicorporate bodies or to private interests on any long-term basis. In Brauer's words it was "not the role of the municipality to be banker to the economy."[16]

When, for instance, a number of firms found themselves in financial difficulty during the early and mid-1920s, the city took the opportunity to assist in bailing them out. Some, like the wholesale food distributors Lebensmittelversorgung or the textile trading company Webwaren A.G. already had financial links to the city. The Webwaren had been founded during the early inflation years, when a number of unemployed clothiers formed a cooperative supported by the city. The city put up three-quarters of the company's shares, and the rest was provided by the participants. Its main function had been to distribute contracts to its individual members and to supply the city's needs (which it did to a value of around 350,000 reichsmark by the mid-1920s). The company's debt of 120,000 reichsmark was transferred to the city in the form of shares, a common practice.[17]

In order to protect its financial interest in the Webwaren, the city agreed to support the company's shareholders' plea for security on a 200,000 goldmark loan from the Hamburg Giro bank on the basis that it acquired the equivalent value in shares. Municipal intervention was thus framed in a more constructive and rational light, because, by supporting this and other companies in similar situations, "the city contributes considerably to the support of the trade outlets battling for their existence."[18] The Webwaren was virtually communalized as a result. But this was a temporary expedient. Within two years the city was winding down its interests in the company because, in improved economic circumstances, its position as major shareholder had become superfluous.[19]

Intervention was governed by a combination of pragmatism and ideology. Uppermost in many minds throughout the 1920s was the fear of unemployment and its attendant evils, especially its financial implications.[20] Short-term communalization of enterprise was used as a conjunctural measure in fighting economic downswings and, as such, was again deployed in the Depression. For instance, in the summer of 1931 the Gartmann Cocoa and Chocolate Company got into serious difficulties in the wake of the banking crisis. Its directors approached the city with a request for support in securing financial aid in the amount of 100,000 reichsmark from its creditor the Deutsche Bank und Diskonto Gesellschaft. The *Magistrat* agreed to help on condition that the city become a shareholder equivalent to the amount requested for a period of one year. It argued that not to intervene would result in the firm going bankrupt and 162 manual and 36 clerical workers joining the already swollen dole queues. In fact, intervention secured the employment of an extra fifty workers in the factory.[21] As in the case of Webwaren and other "communalized" enterprises, the city was obviously "socializing" losses rather than profit. But, instead of adding unnecessarily to the burden of the municipal purse, as alleged by opponents of intervention, this countercyclical policy was clearly intended to bring firms back onto an even keel while at the same time reducing the costs of welfare for the unemployed.

The potentially positive impact of such activities were ignored by opponents of intervention. Instead, they concentrated on what they saw as the dissipation of public finances, as the following example shows. In 1926 Julius Neumann, the managing director of a timber and furniture company, the Holsatia Works, made an application for financial help to the city, which responded favorably. Opposition groups in the city council dug their heels in, charging Brauer's administration with participating in a corrupt backroom deal.[22] The problem centered on a piece of undeveloped land on Stellinger Moor, to the north of the city, which the firm had bought at a discount from the city in 1920 and which it was now seeking to sell back in order to raise much-needed cash to cover its debts. After protracted negotiations with the municipal treasury commission, of which Neumann was also a member, the *Magistrat* agreed to buy back the land from the company. The total cost amounted to approximately 700,000 reichsmark, the equivalent to Holsatia's debt. In order to accommodate the debt the city had to borrow but, again, would obtain shares commensurate with the value of the loan and a seat on the supervisory board for the duration of the deal.[23]

The proposal went before the council and got through on a vote of twenty-nine in favor and twenty-two against. The division in the *Magistrat* was eight to two in favor.[24] The political fault line was predictable. The SPD together with the liberals and some of the DVP councillors voted for the motion. Those against ranged from the unity list to the more extreme Economic Bloc and the NSDAP. The councillors from the KPD cast their votes with the middle-class opposition on the grounds that two amendments calling for shop-floor representatives on the board of directors and for direct public ownership of Holsatia had been rejected by the SPD.[25]

The opposition was quick to capitalize on the decision to involve public money in a firm of doubtful performance and one whose owner had such close connections to the city executive. It was able to draw the affair into the public realm as yet another demonstration of political corruption, as Brauer pursued his program of socialization. The affair provided a useful platform for mobilizing opposition. Carl Bischoff, of the Unity List, saw in the measures to bail out the Holsatia a conspiracy between big finance and international Marxism. At a meeting of the civic associations on the 24 August he told a packed audience that "the Darmstädter Bank, yes indeed gentlemen, finance capital, is intimately linked with the comrades."[26] He also asserted that large corporations (alluding to the SPD cooperative, Produktion) were able to buy at below-market prices, at least at 50 percent of that charged to small firms.

His compatriot Ernst Seehase suggested to the same audience that the Holsatia should be dismantled and its various operations and labor force dispersed among the city's small joinery businesses. He believed this would be of greater benefit to the taxpayer than squandering public money in what he described as "backdoor bolshevization." According to Seehase the Holsatia's problems originated in poor management and not from a poor economic conjuncture. And, even if this were the case, "the present day economic crisis represents a great cleansing process which one should not counter by artificial and arbitrary means."[27] This view was echoed by the leading industrialist and chairman of the Chamber of Industry and Commerce, Carl Menck, who believed that "the socialization experiment in Germany has long failed and should not be allowed, as here, to be forcibly continued. One must give the economy what she is owed and refuse to contrarily maintain sick organisms of the economic body."[28] All seemed agreed that here was a clear case of throwing good money after bad. The firm allegedly had never operated fully under its own financial steam or within its means.[29]

Brauer rejected the allegations in a report to the authorities in Schleswig. By buying back the land previously sold to the Holsatia, the city would regain a valuable industrial site by designating its drainage as a public works scheme.[30] The lord mayor told councillors that the transfer of the firm's debt in the form of shares to the city was a temporary measure—here Brauer was adamant—and therefore did not represent an encroachment by the city on the domain of the private economy. Brauer refuted emphatically the allegation that the municipality was playing "banker to the economy" at the taxpayer's expense. Rather, through this action the city had prevented another thousand workers from becoming unemployed in what was already a difficult period.[31] In his report to the provincial administrator, a conservative, Brauer stressed that as soon as the company was on a firm footing the city would sell back its shares.[32]

The liberal paper *Altonaer Nachrichten* supported his action, pointing out in an editorial in early August that the imputed political dimension to the dispute—namely, the threatened socialization of the economy—was more appropriate to the revolutionary situation in 1919. This danger to property had since passed and was no longer part of the political agenda in Altona.[33] Leading liberals such as Carl Petersen and August Bielfeldt publicly endorsed intervention, providing it was limited and temporary. At a time when unemployment in the city stood at over 6,500 and was costing in the region of three million reichsmark in welfare support, they felt that to let the Holsatia go under would result in greater economic and social costs to the city. Petersen let loose a barbed arrow when he pointed out that among the critics of the city's current attempts to help the foundering Holsatia were former recipients of such aid.[34]

The Holsatia affair was thus used as an excuse to raise the vexed question of budgetary mismanagement and, to a lesser extent, the recurring tendency of the executive to bypass the consultative process in policy making in financial matters. Among the most vehement critics of wasteful expenditure were the Nazis, under Hinrich Lohse, and their sometime allies, the Economic Bloc, led by Richard Galster, a local manufacturer of men's braces and suspenders and a particularly virulent right-winger. The NSDAP, in particular, mounted a vigorous public campaign, which even reached the Provincial Diet.[35] Lohse alleged that the amount of money involved was much higher than the figure under discussion and that the difference had been transferred secretly (though he failed to produce any firm evidence). He also asserted that the firm had failed to pay any taxes for the past eighteen months and that therefore its collapse could not result in a great loss in revenue terms. This allegation was vigorously denied by Brauer, who claimed that the company's tax arrears had been halved, from 62,9895 reichsmark to 31,000 reichsmark, with further reductions imminent. Moreover, the firm, in spite of its current losses totaling around 300,000 reichsmark, had enough collateral to cover its tax debts.[36]

While Lohse concentrated his efforts on mismanagement of public money without proper supervision, Galster, as representative of the city's petty producers (he was also chairman of the Protection League of the Middle Estate of Trade, Craft and Industry), mobilized more subjective emotions. He declaimed as irresponsible and unfair Brauer's proposal for the loan of 700,000 reichsmark at a time when most of local industry was going through a difficult period but without any similar aid being made available to the city's small workshops.[37] During a particularly stormy council meeting on 2 December, Galster launched a bitter attack upon Brauer:

> Lord Mayor! Your party comrades cheer you on because you are leading private enterprise to its destruction by the excessive pursuit of communalization and thereby preparing the uprooted for Social Democracy. The sycophants who surround you are hoping for material benefits from you. . . . I cannot enjoy being a councillor in a city parliament of injustice, of untruths, of wastage and of mismanagement, in which the destruction of people's existences by taxation and communalization are pursued vigorously. The more mismanagement grows, the greater the pressure of taxation, and so existences are squeezed dry and made to perish. The arbitrariness of rule which bypasses laws and regulations and establishes new, convenient ones and enlists irresponsible accomplices, helps to complete the cruel picture; the process of communalization flourishes and marches on.[38]

The gist of this accusation is familiar to students of *Mittelstand* oppositional discourse during the Weimar Republic. But, as noted, Brauer did not believe in, nor did he pursue, the destruction of capitalism, however much he might find himself at odds with its exponents.[39] Instead, public enterprise in Altona was geared toward a social market economy operating in the interests of consumers and producers alike.[40] Indeed, Brauer stood at some distance from those on the left of the SPD in Altona, such as councillor Paul Bugdahn, who called for more local control over the economy.[41] Nevertheless, Brauer's own position notwithstanding, members of Altona's *Mittelstand* tailored their judgment according to their experience of municipal intervention.

Markets, Monopolies, and Responsibilities

When the *Magistrat* decided to install a canteen for public employees in the basement of the town hall in the mid-1920s, it is unlikely that it anticipated the wave of protest that this action provoked. The *Magistrat* had agreed that a canteen would provide employees with a cheap meal and allow them to gain the most from their half-hour lunch break, instead of having either to eat sandwiches at their desks, or to leave the premises and eat hastily elsewhere. From the city's point of view this was perfectly compatible with the practice of many modern large firms in the private sector, which sought to rationalize practices, and with that of the Prussian and reich administrations.[42] The public response was critical.

Those in Altona particularly unhappy about the canteen were the owners of restaurants, snack bars, and small lodgings in the immediate vicinity of the town hall who relied on the custom of its employees. They accused Brauer's administration of setting up a business that directly and unfairly competed with theirs. The Reich Association of Private Lunches and Boarding House Owners (Privatmittagstische und Pensionsinhaber) wrote to the *Magistrat* in October, stating that the decision to establish the canteen had caused great disquiet among its membership. Many members had little alternative means of income. Therefore, according to the association, "If the clientele is suddenly withdrawn, the [future] existence of their businesses is threatened. Some of the proprietors of the restaurants in question are older, single ladies who would find it difficult to adapt after losing their customers." The association did not fail to widen its protest to the issue of public encroachment upon private economic terrain in general and concluded, "If the municipal authorities push to one side the interests of taxpayers, that is to be deeply regretted, also [it is] absolutely undemocratic."[43]

The city authorities did not respond. The association's representative, Herr Sellner, then wrote another letter at the end of October, which also apparently remained unanswered. As a consequence of this failure to acknowledge the complaint, the association took the matter up with the *Regierungspräsident* in Schleswig. His office was also slow to respond, and, when it did, the answer was a negative one. A protest meeting of the association's members was held on 9 December, who resolved to publish an open letter to Brauer in its own organ, *Der Mittagstisch*. This was followed by a letter in January to the Prussian interior ministry.[44] The letter to the interior ministry outlined the association's grievance with the city and introduced a new dimension to the complaint that had in the meantime emerged. Sellner alleged that the canteen was to be financed from a special disposition fund, which, the association suspected, came from tax surpluses paid by the very people whose livelihoods were now threatened. This apparent injustice cut no ice with the Berlin authorities, for the ministry referred the matter back to the *Regierungspräsident* in Schleswig, who finally resolved the conflict in Brauer's favor.[45]

Conflicts over municipal encroachments upon the territory of the private economy continued throughout the republican era. They intensified during the Depression, when the competition for scarce resources was at its most acute. For instance, in the autumn of 1932 the Altona branch of the Federation of German Concrete Works (Bund der Deutschen Betonwerke e.V.) accused the administration of precipitating the city's various small cement businesses making paving stones even further into crisis after a decision was taken to set up municipal-owned cement production in the Kruppstraße. The city already owned a stone quarry in the suburb Rissen and hoped thus to integrate production vertically.[46] In a letter to the *Magistrat* the federation protested vigorously against this latest venture of the city:

> It is not comprehensible, precisely at the present time when central government is working towards a stimulation of the economy after a long and still continuing period of unemployment in the trade, that now an employment opportunity is being taken away. From an economic view-point, on no account is there a pressing need to create a municipal company.[47]

The city also came under fire for favoring nonlocal companies and cooperative organizations with political connections to the SPD when tenders for public contracts were advertised. Galster, of the Economic Bloc, accused the administration and "its SPD employees in the Municipal Building and Planning Office" of exercising a party-book network in the distribution of local contracts.[48] The following comment is typical in this respect:

> Altona's city government communalizes and socializes whatever it can, and [so] the cooperatives get the contracts for jobs and supplying. The artisanal masters have only to pay taxes, but the city never offers them the opportunity for work. . . . Whatever the city cannot provide for itself through its own public employees (*Regiebeamte*)— coffins, metal and smithying, printing and binding etc.,—it makes sure the contracts go to the cooperatives.[49]

When the city decided to install a new telephone system in the town hall a local company, the Altona-Telefon-Gesellschaft (ATG), found itself cold-shouldered as the contract went outside the city. The company chairman complained to the provincial authorities that his company had not even been invited to tender, contrary to public statements that Altona's firms would be given priority. The ATG employed a local labor force of eighty persons, who were now threatened with unemployment.[50] Here was an example of the city robbing an Altona "Peter" to pay—in this case a Hamburg—"Paul." The company wanted the authorities in Schleswig to reverse the decision and force the city to award the contract to the ATG. His demand was unsuccessful.[51]

The close study of these conflicts provide an insight into the plight of the individual citizen during the 1920s and, ultimately, into the complex process of their alienation from municipal government as the bedrock of the Weimar Republic. All too often, owners of local businesses faced what they believed to be a municipal administration impervious to their needs, which acted in a high-handed manner and without a sense of responsibility toward the city's own economically hard-pressed firms. This was the experience of Peter Brandt, who owned a small family firm that supplied and pasted notices for advertising hoardings and pillars in the town.[52] From the end of 1928 to March 1930 he fought a protracted and increasingly bitter and ultimately futile struggle with the city to keep a municipal contract dating from 1911.

His business, with the grand name Altona-Wandsbeck-Stellingen-Langenfelde Anschlagsäulen und Hamburger Plakat-Tafeln-Institut, had been established in 1869 and until 1928 had served the city without any complaint. The city decided, however, not to renew its contract with Brandt, preferring instead to employ the modern services of the Cities-Advertising Corporation (Städte-Reklame GmbH), a Frankfurt-based cartel (of which Altona was a member).[53] Brandt protested vigorously through his trade association, the Verband Deutscher Verkehrsreklame-Unternehmungen e.V., claiming that the Frankfurt firm was not able to operate on a sound financial basis because of high operating costs and therefore was not in any better position to meet the needs of the city than a small local firm. The authorities in Altona, represented by Senator Schöning, stood firm, stating that Brandt did not possess a moral right to a monopoly agreed in 1911. Brandt felt that the rejection by Brauer "was unbefitting for a firm of sixty-years standing" and was "a sign that the city does not appreciate one's merits" and was callously "indifferent to a firm going bankrupt."[54] His appeal to the authorities in Schleswig for justice fell on deaf ears.

Brandt's struggle with the city authorities apparently did not attract much public notice, but it was a familiar one during these years.[55] Other cases attracted greater attention and frequently bore political overtones, sometimes with strains of anti-Semitism added. For instance, in late 1929 protest erupted over a property deal between the city and the Jewish-owned department store chain of Karstadt. The city was accused by local business interests of selling out for "dirty lucre" by agreeing to part with an old tenement on the corner of Große Bergstraße and Große Johannisstraße at 300 reichsmark per square meter to "this deadly enemy" of the *Mittelstand*.[56] In return for permission to develop the site, Karstadt was to lend the city 100,000 reichsmark (at 7 percent interest) in order to begin the

construction of replacement dwellings elsewhere in Altona. In addition the
company would itself erect twenty dwellings over the new store, to be managed by the SAGA.[57]

Alluding to the Sklarek scandal unfolding in Berlin, *Mittelstand*
opponents to the deal accused the Altona authority equally of sleaze and
corruption in its financial dealings with "big business." In their view
Brauer's administration in concluding the deal with Karstadt had
betrayed the national community for a few pieces of silver.

> It is simply undescribable that a municipal authority is not ashamed
> to borrow the sum of 100,000 Reichsmark from the deadly enemies of
> the *Mittelstand,* from those elements who are on the verge of destroy-
> ing the independence of the respectable merchant. . . . Did it have to
> be the department store clique, Karstadt, that lent the money in order
> finally to achieve that it dictated to the authorities what and what not
> to do? Because it is fairly obvious that the creditor dictates to the
> debtor and not the debtor to the creditor.[58]

Opponents, led by Richard Galster, hoped that the negative publicity
would alienate the city administration from voters at the municipal elections scheduled for the following month and so "finally put to an end the
Bonzen by the 'grace of Bebel.'"[59]

The city authorities again came under fire for alleged corrupt practices in late 1932, when a Nazi councillor, Max Boge, himself a local tex-
tiles trader who had joined the party in January 1928,[60] made unsubstanti-
ated allegations that employees in various departments of the
administration were being circulated illicitly via the internal file trolley
with lists of wares from a local wholesale trader. Usually, this firm only
dealt in cigars and cigarettes, but it was alleged that the owner, Karl
Hilscher, who also happened to be a member of the SPD, was also selling
other items, such as cosmetics and toiletries, at great reductions (as much
as a third off) in the backroom of his business at Spritzenplatz in Ottensen.
Yet only members of the civil servants' union, the Beamtenvereinigung,
which was also close to the SPD, were eligible for these reductions.
Hilscher, it was alleged, was being actively encouraged by the city to
encroach upon the markets of local small retailers, largely chemists, and
drugstores.

The Chamber of Industry and Commerce as well as the local branch
of German Apothecaries, among whose membership "great indignation
prevailed," voiced deep concern. Inevitably, the pitch of protest grew once
the local press got hold of the story, eventually reaching the ears of the
provincial authority. But an investigation showed the allegations of a

"goods trolley racket" to be a chimera, and, although Hilscher admitted to a "backroom trade" with public employees, he denied that this had been sanctioned by city officials.[61] The city administration was exonerated of the corruption allegations, and the matter was duly closed but not without casting the city administration in a bad light.[62]

Protests against communalization centered not only around public control of firms or the issue of contracts but also on the pricing policy of municipal-owned utilities. Often complaints could be heard that the city abused its monopoly control of public utilities. Conflict thus centered on the relationship between city as provider and the individual as consumer of public services, a dimension ignored in the literature. One Altona complainant was unhappy about the introduction of a differentiated pricing mechanism for electricity based on the number of rooms rather than actual consumption.[63] Other electricity users regarded the new system as an attack upon the better-off owners of individual properties and as little more than a surrogate luxury tax. According to Erwin Horn of number 20 Schenckendorfstraße, in the villa suburb of Groß Flottbek:

First of all, I believe these [charges], coming from the municipality, to be unlawful. Secondly, the insight is becoming gradually more wide-spread among large groups of society that in the process of expropriating the middle Estate the working classes would be detrimentally affected. Without bourgeois capital the economy dies, and with it the source of employment for the worker.[64]

In this case a parochial issue became interlocked with a matter of national importance. Horn was agitated by the recent acceptance in the Reichstag of the Young Plan (12 March) and was concerned that the reduced capability to accumulate capital (as a result of higher electricity charges) would lead to an unhealthy dependence on foreign loans. In Horn's view this "would mean the same as a full enslavement of the German people" simply to satisfy the indulgence of the Altona authority in its "enthusiasm to follow particular political tendencies."[65] In time, Horn warned, the unchecked pursuit of such "political tendencies" would breed opposition to the authorities.

In many cases individuals, having failed to gain satisfaction from the city authorities, turned to the provincial authorities in Schleswig in order to find justice but frequently without success. A very irate Arthur Zöllner of Sandmoorweg in the incorporated suburb of Rissen wrote a number of letters, increasingly of an exasperated nature, between 1930 and mid-1932, protesting against his exclusion from a price discount in his electricity rates.[66] A 40 percent tariff reduction had been introduced by the municipal

utility, the Electricity Works Unterelbe (EWU), for long-standing customers whose consumption was 50 percent or less than the average level
for the previous year. Zöllner duly claimed his rebate, yet he found he did
not qualify because his electricity consumption was not low enough, and
he had only registered as a customer the previous October.

Zöllner expressed outrage at this perceived discrimination, and,
because his letters to the company soon lost their "business tone," the
EWU refused to have any further dealings with him. Zöllner persisted
nonetheless, with little success, into 1932. Early that year he wrote four
further letters to the company, the *Magistrat,* and the provincial authority
in Schleswig. He was aware that the *Magistrat* was unlikely to help him
and hoped, instead, that the *Regierungspräsident* would intervene on his
behalf. This hope was dashed. He received a letter in September explaining
that this was both a local matter and had to do with private business, for,
although the EWU was a municipal company, its legal status was private.[67]

For many members of the *Mittelstand* Brauer and the SPD (together
with their coalition partners, the liberal DDP) often appeared to be
actively conniving at undermining their economic and, therefore, social
position. The municipal authority in Altona, it seemed, had a free rein in
the marketplace to act as it wished with impunity, even after the unconsti-
tutional demise of the Socialist-led Prussian government in mid-July 1932.
Adolf Stehn, from Eichenallee in subdistrict 28, wrote to the commissarial
head of government in Prussia, Dr. Bracht, in November 1932 over a seemingly minor dispute with the city and used this to complain about economic policy per se in Altona.[68] His letter to Bracht was headed "Misuse
of the monopoly position of municipal utilities" and accused the city of
holding its customers to ransom. As in the case of Erwin Horn, he too was
agitated over electricity pricing policy, which, he believed, contravened the
Emergency Decree of 8 December 1931 stipulating a 10 percent reduction
in cartel prices.[69] According to Stehn, the situation in Socialist-controlled
Altona was such that "the public utility companies easily glide over" such
controls and "through their monopoly understand masterfully, how to
heighten the already existing dissatisfaction among the population."[70]
Stehn felt Bracht should follow von Papen's example of dismissing the
Prussian government that July and execute a coup d'état against the
Socialist authority in Altona.

On coming to power after the war, the Social Democrats introduced
a number of public holidays, not least contentious among these was that of
May Day.[71] In the mid-1920s, for instance, complaints were leveled at the
city for supporting the SPD's "class hatreds" by designating 1 May a public holiday for municipal employees. In 1925 a letter purporting to come

from a public servant was published in the *Hamburger Nachrichten* criticizing Altona's policy:

> If the Social Democratic Party wishes to celebrate the 1 May as a "world" holiday with marches and speeches full of rich phrases, and so bow to its desire to exacerbate class differences and to whip up class hatreds, well, that is more or less understandable from its internationalist standpoint. But it is an outrage when an administration, namely, the Magistrat of the city of Altona, supports this purely party event by declaring a public holiday and thereby depriving one of the right to work.[72]

The writer concluded by asking, "How did the Magistrat come to this high-handed action?" This anonymous author was not the only complainant to raise the issue of "civil liberties." The Central Committee of Altona Civic Associations added its voice, protesting bitterly how "the citizens organized in its member associations . . . see this [action] as an interference of their rights."[73]

Altona's manufacturers alleged that public holidays inflicted a "considerable financial loss" upon "large numbers," since they were affected by the reduction or even cancellation of public transport and other services indispensable to the city's economic life.[74] The president of the Chamber of Industry and Commerce, the industrialist Carl Menck, made representations to both Brauer and the provincial administration on several occasions. On 16 August 1927 he wrote to Brauer, criticizing him for the sudden closure of the local industrial rail line on Constitution Day, five days earlier. There had been no prior notification of the shutdown to local industries, other than a general notice in the press apparently referring to municipal offices only. Menck found it an "absurdity" that vital transport services should be withdrawn on these public days and requested that they run in the future. Brauer wrote a conciliatory response at the beginning of September and, without ceding ground, stated that the administration had informed local industry of the impending cancellation of services.

Not being satisfied with this, Menck took the matter further. In a letter to the *Regierungspräsident* he demanded that Brauer be censured and that public services be kept open in the future. The *Regierungspräsident*, however, had no grounds to reprimand Brauer unless there had been some irregularity in the arrangements by the city administration for the public holiday. The chamber therefore canvassed its members in a questionnaire about the impact of the holiday on their activity and sent the results to the *Regierungspräsident* in a further letter on 24 October. The answers to the questionnaire showed that a number of firms had been notified only the previous day, leaving them little time to make alternative arrangements, thus causing disruption and in some cases resulting in financial loss, especially in the fish processing industry. Industry had struck a small blow for victory, for the *Regierungspräsident* was compelled to write to Brauer, disapproving of his actions. Brauer conceded fault and promised to allow eight days notice in future.[75]

Taxation and Ruin

Weimar's *Mittelstand* needed no further proof than the burden of taxation for evidence of "bolshevization."[76] Its members believed that the realization in the municipal sphere of the republic's social agenda implied an ideologically determined budget that would have to be borne by the property-owning and producing classes.[77] Indeed, the overall level of taxation as a proportion of national income rose in this period. In 1913 it had been nearly 10 percent and by 1925 accounted for 18.1 percent, with the producing and propertied middle classes bearing a significant part.[78] According to the German economic historian Peter Christian Witt, the history of public finance in general "offers a . . . starting point for the analysis of political and social structures and power relationships and for the examination of the cause and symptoms of societal conditions and human actions."[79] Thus, the study of the individual and collective *experience* of the tax burden at the local level will help us piece together the picture of the difficult and ultimately destructive relationship between the *Mittelstand* and the Weimar polity.

As a result of Erzberger's tax reforms after World War I, local authorities found their fiscal powers restricted to adding surcharges on centrally and regionally determined taxes. In Prussia the most significant of these were the so-called *Realsteuern,* the surcharges on taxes from real estate (*Grundvermögenssteuer*) and on business turnover (*Gewerbeertragssteuer*).[80] These surcharges were, within certain constraints, elastic and offered municipal administrations a flexible means of income suited to local needs and particular social programs. Thus, the level at which they were set usually depended on the political balance of power in each council. In Altona between 1924 and 1931 the *Realsteuern* accounted for between a third and half of all tax revenue raised in the city.[81]

The major group of taxpayers in Altona, the *Mittelstand,* had been quite severely affected by the inflation. Of Altona's 13,201 self-employed, 11,273 were registered on the tax rolls, while the remainder earned so little that they did not qualify for taxation. Of those who did, the greater part (56.7 percent) earned incomes of less than 3,000 reichsmarks. In 1914 those persons liable to wealth tax (the threshold was set at 5,000 marks) had numbered 7,279. Little more than a decade later the number had fallen by over a third, to 4,702.[82] Nor did stabilization bring any particular relief. Indeed, the high cost of credit and other operating costs tightened the financial noose for many, as we shall see.

Members from Altona's *Mittelstand* therefore felt justified in their complaint that not only were they unable to carry the greater part of the local tax burden but also that its distribution was unfair and derived from the political configuration of the council, in which they were the minority. Thus, while obligated to pay up, they nonetheless had little control over how their money was being spent.

> This responsibility weighs even heavier because it is widely recognised that in large communes those parts of the population which grant taxes do not themselves pay, but to a large extent leave the payment of taxes to a powerless minority of citizens.[83]

Brauer shrugged off such complaints. The administration claimed that the *Realsteuern* in Altona were well below those for many major towns in the reich.[84] Indeed, on introducing the budget in 1930, Brauer asserted that the mid-1920s had been a period of "tax reprieve" for business and property interests in the city.[85] The onset of the Depression and central government finance policy meant that the city would come to rely even more on tax surcharges but with terrible political consequences.

By late 1930 Altona was facing a revenue shortfall of three million reichsmark, and Brauer intended to overcome this deficit by tightening the screws on tax. Naturally, this action met with opposition. As we saw in chapter 2, there had been resistance to the budget proposals in the spring. In order to avert a repeat of that event and thus delays to approving a supplementary budget, Brauer resorted to tougher measures.[86] On 4 November Brauer traveled to Schleswig to inform the *Regierungspräsident,* Dr. Waldemar Abegg, of the financial situation in Altona and of the political impasse that had emerged in the city council. He impressed upon Abegg the importance of a quick solution. Four days later, on 8 November, Brauer traveled to Berlin to attend a plenary session of the board of the Städtetag. While there he took the opportunity to see Dr. Súren in the Prussian interior ministry in order to canvass the permanent secretary's support for a state commissioner. He reported to Súren: "The critical financial condition of the city cannot be solved any longer by negotiations with the parties in the council. An intervention of the supervisory authorities is in my view imperative."[87] Brauer then sent a copy of his notes of the meeting with Súren to Dr. Wilhem Abegg, in the same ministry, who in turn sent an instruction to his brother in Schleswig, ordering the immediate appointment of a state commissioner to impose both an increase of the existing surcharges and the introduction of new levies.[88] The bombshell came on 12 November, when Brauer himself was confirmed as state commissioner.[89]

His appointment predictably unleashed a hostile reaction from his opponents. The Association of Industry and Commerce sent a telegram to the authorities in Schleswig raising the "sharpest protest" at Brauer's appointment, while the Altona House and Property Owners' Association doubted the legality of Brauer's commissarial role.[90] The Bürgerliche Gemeinschaft joined forces with the Business Party and the NSDAP, in order to protest to the authorities in Schleswig and Berlin, demanding that the provincial administration deny Brauer the satisfaction of ratifying the proposed tax increases. They denied there had been a breakdown in the workings of the council meeting on 13 November. Tax levels had been agreed by the council, though these were different to those proposed by Brauer.[91]

Altona's middle classes feared that his appointment would expose them to the merciless and dictatorial political power of the Left and phrased their protests in this vein.[92] And, indeed, they did not have long to wait for proof of this. On 13 November the council met once again to discuss the budget. The *Magistrat* brought in a new set of tax proposals, and, when these were rejected, Brauer used his power as state commissioner to impose the new taxes but omitted the new citizens' tax, thereby overriding all legal grounds for objection or delay.[93]

Richard Galster of the Economic Bloc, representing local traders, raised the "sharpest protest" in a letter to the county supervisory authority (*Bezirksausschuss*), stating that the appointment was a "mockery of local government." Echoing a commonplace view held by many from his quarter of society, Galster asserted that "the imminent bankruptcy of the city of Altona is a consequence of the *Magistrat's* corruption and wasteful economic management."[94] This sentiment was carefully exploited by Hinrich Lohse, the NSDAP *Gauleiter,* who had returned to the council in 1929. He had been in favor of a commissioner but clearly not Brauer, for he believed that Altona's finances ought to be subjected to external scrutiny.[95]

Right-wing councillors in Altona, as elsewhere, were thus not against a commissioner with special powers in principle, for they believed that a commissioner would vindicate their allegations of economic mismanagement and would impose cuts in the budget, rather than raise taxes, as Brauer proposed. Brauer's confirmation as commissioner was not what they had anticipated; it smacked of political conspiracy and infringed on their understanding of local self-government. In a local newspaper editorial critics noted that "what caused this particular indignation among the public was the fact that an absolute party politically-oriented civil servant in the person of the lord mayor was appointed to the office of state commissioner."[96]

The protests of these conservative councillors against what they alleged was Brauer's arbitrary socialist dictatorship over the *Mittelstand* were taken up by their party colleagues in the Prussian *Landtag.* The Business Party protested: "This forced tax increase represents a really draconian measure in any case, because there has not even been an attempt to find another means of covering the deficit."[97] Deputies from the DNVP headlined their protest with "Brauer appears as dictator in his own cause" and elaborated that "it seems curious that the lord mayor, whose tax proposal is 'rejected' by the council, then 'decrees' as 'state commissioner' the introduction of the rejected taxes: thus acting as a dictator in his own interest."[98]

Their case was lent weight by the fact that in a number of other cities and towns the commissioners were government officials implementing cuts in public expenditure as well as raising taxes. And it was alleged that the Prussian interior minister, Carl Severing, had misgivings about appointing local officials as commissioners.[99] The bourgeois press was also quick to revive lurid pictures of a secretive and conspiratorial politicized Prussian bureaucracy engaged in backroom maneuvers. The *Altonaer Tageblatt* commented that the city was losing its self-government at the hands of the Left, whose members were in cahoots with their friends in the Prussian government.[100] An editorial in the *Hamburger Fremdenblatt* commented on the episode and on the apparent arbitrary nature of tax increases as follows:

> State commissioners travel the country with increasing haste to put the budgets in order just before the end of the year. . . . It seems that not even enough time is left to round up the councillors so as to get to work on off-setting the deficit in cooperation with the *Magistrats.* Instead the state commissioners surprised the *Magistrats* on Monday evening with the news that the they had (with the approval of the *Regierungspräsident*) compulsorily fixed the beer tax at double its level from 1 January 1931.[101]

Brauer sought to allay fears in Altona and defuse the vehement protests in a press conference in early December. After conceding the difficulty and unpopularity of the task, he stated that the decision to resort to a state commissioner had not been taken lightly but had come about because the city council had failed to rise to the difficult task before it; the elected members might fail, but, in his view, public officers must not fail in their duty in the interests of local government. On a more combative note directed at the Right he welcomed in

> these protests a . . . declaration of faith in democratic self-govern-
> ment. If the circles who have always craved for dictatorship now base
> their protest on self-government, this proves how strong the spirit for
> democratic institutions has developed . . . that means that this storm,
> too, has not been in vain.[102]

Tax Victims: Business

As noted, the postwar years were difficult ones for middling businesses. Many of them were precariously balanced on the precipice of what must have appeared to their owners as a pit of existential destruction. Moreover, the policies pursued by Brauer's administration brought them little security. Altona's business community believed that the tax burden they faced was the bitter fruit of both financial mismanagement and founded on a political motivation to communalize the private sector and reduce independent businessmen to the status of employees.[103] As we shall see, the particular actions followed by the city council were frequently conditioned by central government policy.[104] But the local *Mittelstand* often failed to see that.

For instance, in March 1926 the authorities in Altona found they had to increase the *Realsteuern* as a result of a change in reich policy.[105] Because of this, they proposed to raise the surcharge on the property tax by 100 percent, to 300 percent, while the business surcharge would remain at 600 percent. The *Magistrat* changed its plans, however, and reduced the surcharge on the former to 250 percent but increased that on business tax to 700 percent.[106] This provoked an instant outcry from the business community. The Chamber of Industry and Commerce stated that the increase constituted an unbearably heavy burden on local firms already suffering from the midterm economic downturn.[107]

The matter had not been made any easier to digest by Dr. Ebert, the deputy mayor and city treasurer, who had earlier acknowledged the difficulties facing local business and gave an assurance that an increase in business tax would be unlikely. The chamber believed that Ebert's volte face was evidence of the disturbing power of the Socialists and Communists. In its view increased surcharges on property were more equitable because, unlike the business tax, the burden would be shared more evenly among a larger group of taxpayers. Others complained that the city was squeezing Altona's already hard-pressed businesses in order to raise the revenue needed to offset its two million reichsmark deficit. The vigorous opposition to the increases in the city council remained by and large futile.[108]

The ever active leader of the Central Committee of Altona Civic Associations, Ahrendt, repeated the view in a letter to the regional authority in Schleswig that the clasped fists of Socialists and Communists had brought about the increase and claimed an injustice had thus been perpetrated by the *Magistrat*. "Since the major part of the city's expenditure serves the public at large," he wrote, "it seems fair and just to let this be borne by the general public, exactly how the *Magistrat* in Altona had originally intended through raising the surcharge on the property tax."[109] Just how critical the tax issue was for small businesses can be gauged from the following examples.

The case of Johannes Tetens, who lived in the Friedensallee in Ottensen, provides a good illustration of the consequences awaiting those not able to pay the business tax. Until the mid-1920s Tetens had ran a small wood business from the courtyard of the building where he lived. Then, in 1926, he got into financial difficulties, could not pay the business tax in full, and eventually in March 1927 had to give up his business activities. He subsequently survived through a combination of working as a sales representative for various firms and by borrowing from friends. The same friends generously decided "in order to free him from his straitened circumstances" to employ him in November 1928 as manager of their Hamburg firm with a modest monthly remuneration of 200 reichsmark plus expenses.[110]

His tax problems with the city arose over his 1927–28 business tax dues. Even though he had given up his wood business at the end of the 1926 financial year, he had worked as a self-employed representative thereafter. He was therefore still liable for business tax from 1 April 1927 to the end of November 1928. The tax office estimated his gross earnings for the year at 7,632 reichsmark, a sum he disputed. He claimed that his taxable earnings came to 2,783 reichsmark. The Commission for Business Tax, which arbitrated the dispute, estimated his taxable earnings at 6,130 reichsmark. He stood in arrears to the tax office to the tune of 716 reichsmark 70 pfennige. But, with a high rent (170 reichsmark monthly) and a low income, he certainly could not afford to pay this.

An exchange of letters and pleas followed, but the most the tax office would concede was an arrangement whereby Tetens paid off his arrears in small monthly amounts. He was still unable to meet even this requirement. Then sometime in early April, shortly after failing to meet an installment, the city unsuccessfully attempted to seize goods in the value of the amount owed. The failure to retrieve the equivalent of the debt led the authorities in Altona to initiate bankruptcy proceedings against Tetens. For his part, as in 1925 and 1926, Tetens was once again seeking cancellation of his tax arrears.

This measure was important to Tetens and not just for financial reasons: a declaration of bankruptcy would blacken his name. For this procedure was usually reserved for "malicious debtors," a categorization he strenuously rebutted. As he wrote in his letter to Waldemar Abegg, the head of the provincial government in Schleswig, his predicament had come about through forces over which he had little control. He had tried to explain his case personally to Senator Schöning, who was the chairman of the Commission for Business Tax, but with little satisfaction, for "the gentleman appears not to find it necessary to receive citizens for reasons of high civil service status."[111] In his eyes the action on which the city was now embarked was certainly unjust and of "unnecessary harshness." He wrote:

> Swearing an oath of disclosure would destroy completely my economic existence which I wish to rebuild gradually as an employee. I would be forced to resign from the position of counselor of the commercial tribunal at the district court in Altona, a position which I have held for nine years as an honorary member. None of my private creditors, whom I owe considerably higher sums, proceeds against me in such a threatening manner because they still value me highly, despite my economic plight and because they know full well that I ended up in this predicament through no fault of my own.[112]

A cursory diagnosis of the language and structure of Tetens's letter to Abegg, in which he used his title "Counselor to the Court of Commerce" (*Handelsgerichtsrat*) and addressed Abegg, as head of the provincial administration, with the old-fashioned form "Your High Born Excellence," suggests a clash between time-honored forms of respect for status and the social leveling the postwar authorities in Altona appeared to be conducting by way of taxation.

The display of dogged bureaucratic callousness over what appeared as modest sums of money led speakers at a meeting in 1927 of the Central Committee of Altona Civic Associations to observe "how fiercely the *Magistrat* proceeds when collecting taxes; ruthlessly the bailiffs are called in if the money has not been paid within three days, and hardly a sum worthwhile mentioning is gained at the auctions of seized objects."[113]

While the mid-years were not without tax strife for some, by and large Altona's businesses got by.[114] But this changed radically during the Depression, when the administration was faced with the problem of meeting the rising cost of unemployment in a period of falling municipal revenue. In 1928 Altona had received nearly 9 million reichsmark from central government transfers. This had fallen to 6 million reichsmark by 1931 and continued to fall. In per capita terms there was a 26 percent reduction of the subsidy, from 33,70 reichsmark to 25,22 reichsmark between 1928 and 1931. This left the municipality with little choice other than to either raise existing surcharges or introduce new taxes in order to make up the shortfall. As a result, between 1928 and 1931 the per capita burden of *local* tax rose by 35 percent, from 46,24 reichsmark (1927) to 62,48 reichsmark in 1931.[115] This was high compared to the national average and triggered an avalanche of tax conflicts. The problem was that Altona's businesses were also feeling the force of the Depression. The number of insolvencies rose dramatically between 1928 and 1931, and, though a small decrease was noted in 1932, the level remained well above that of 1928.[116]

In order to avert the worst of tax increases, the representatives of local manufacturers called for stringent economies to be made in public spending, about which they believed the city had hitherto been profligate. The Chamber of Industry and Commerce and that of Handicrafts thus issued a joint communiqué calling for cuts in expenditure on what they contended as inessential services, such as the city parks, theater, vocational schools, and notably on municipal purchases of real estate; indeed, they called for publicly owned property to be sold off (see chap. 7). Furthermore, both chambers called for a halt to the payment of bonuses to members of the governing bodies of the public utilities; they estimated that a saving of 100,000 reichsmark could be made this way. The communiqué even expressed the hope that taxes might even be lowered.[117]

In addition to the charge of having a "history of economic mismanagement," the administration was now accused of exacerbating the increasingly precarious position of local firms as burdens were increased in an attempt to shore up the gaping hole in municipal finances. But this did not deflect the authorities in Altona from their stringent fiscal course. As Brauer himself admitted, "over the course of time, we have had to learn more and more to recover all tax arrears with increased vigor."[118] Indeed, in a confidential report in July 1932 Brauer acknowledged that the owners of Altona's medium and small businesses were having to bear the brunt of fiscal policies in order to save the city from financial collapse.[119] The cases that follow are typical of the condition in which Weimar's lesser businesses found themselves during this turbulent period.

The cigar box–making firm of Carl Fischer and Sons, at number 21–31 Donnerstraße in Ottensen, which employed sixty persons and had been established in the 1890s, was already suffering before 1929 as a consequence of a sectoral depression brought about by higher material costs and a curtailed market in the wake of the imposition of a tobacco tax in 1925. The firm's fragile health worsened in the Depression, and by 1932 the owner was in debt to the city tax office to the tune of eight thousand reichsmark.[120] The critical year had been 1930, when the firm nearly went bankrupt but persevered in its efforts to keep going. Nevertheless, its tax arrears mounted, and in the early summer (before the July elections) the municipal tax office decided to go ahead with a compulsory acquisition order and to hold a forced auction as a means of recouping the arrears. The owner made his appeal on 1 November 1932 to "the highest servant of the state" in Prussia, Dr. Bracht, to protect him from the "actions of the city of Altona" and a blighted future.

> One presumably cannot assume that especially His Excellency, who is the highest civil servant of the State of Prussia, tolerates the fact that a business which for nearly 40 years has striven to fulfil its obligations most meticulously, is now being condemned to bankruptcy by the actions of the city of Altona, and that as a result of this, several families will fall victim to welfare relief.[121]

For Fischer the camel's back was broken when he learned that the authorities through the treasury office had undervalued his firm for the purposes of the auction. Instead of the estimated value of 62,400 reichsmark set by the courts (though its valuation for tax purposes had been higher, 88,000 reichsmark), his firm was to be liquidated at 8,500 reichsmark, that is, at barely 14 percent of the court valuation. As a consequence, Fischer would receive only 500 reichsmark as his entitlement of the proceeds above the amount owed. He was in effect being dispossessed. He believed that the government in Berlin must certainly have some means to hand in order to protect him from arbitrary government in Altona. His arrears were not maliciously accumulated but had come about as the result of forces beyond his control. He was therefore hoping that either a total abrogation of the debt or a moratorium on it could be granted.[122]

If Fischer's experience was typical of the middle ranges of Altona's manufacturers, then the following two cases stand for the experience of small independent businesses. A Frau Möller from Blankenese had leased a cinema business that apparently did not prosper and was eventually forced to close.[123] She had outstanding arrears of leisure taxes for 1929, however, amounting to 988 reichsmark, which she could not pay. Her husband, Detlef, was jointly liable, but he could not help either. His stone-making plant, which had employed a labor force of 150, closed down in the wake of the bank crisis in the summer 1931, and Möller was declared bankrupt. The couple were now reduced to receiving charity from relatives.

The city, however, still sought to recover the arrears. To do so it began issuing orders to impound various items from the Möller household. The lawyer for the couple argued that, if this carried on, soon the Möller's would have nothing at all and would be leveled to a position of absolute destitution as a result of this locally determined action. The Möllers had learned that the city intended to furnish its planned concrete works with the equipment it would acquire from the compulsory control and forced auction of Herr Möller's business.

Alwin Schlöte, who ran a legal business from an office in the Bahnhofstraße, found he could no longer keep up with payment of his taxes after a rise in the *Realsteuern* in 1931.[124] He soon found himself the recipient of a number of distraint orders between June and September 1932, leading to various pieces of office equipment being impounded, in spite of a court decision that items such as his office typewriter could not be held in lieu of payment. The tax increases and the seizure of equipment meant that he could no longer work. He had already discharged his assistants and was now faced with the prospect of closing his office. Although he was aware that over a third of lawyers in Germany currently shared his fate as a consequence of the crisis, the causes of his immediate problems were closer to home. "There seems to be no need for me to point out that the steps taken against me by the Magistrat in Altona do not serve to boost the economy, but to destroy people's livelihoods instead."[125]

These experiences were unfortunately more common than rare and helped to create a level of resentment at a politically sensitive time. As one tax victim put it, "The [tax] office . . . wants to push me towards swearing an oath of disclosure, to take away from me the possibility of earning a living and so turn me into a recipient of welfare," and all for sixty-five reichsmark.[126]

Property Tax: Three Cases

During the Depression property taxes became a vital source of revenue for the hard-pressed municipalities. The authorities in Altona hoped to raise in the financial year 1932 somewhere in the region of twenty million reichsmark from the surcharges on the property and rent tax. This was an increase of two-and-half million marks over the level of 1931.[127] The tax squeeze was divided between extra burdens laid on property, business and trade turnover, and indirect levies on consumption. But the division appeared unfair, for the property surcharge rose the most, from just over fourteen reichsmark per capita in 1927 to nearly twenty-seven reichsmark in 1931.[128]

It is hardly surprising that Altona's property owners, who already saw themselves as "a class which has already made great sacrifices as a consequence of years of housing controls and tough tax policies in the interests of the state and the generality,"[129] now found themselves steeped in conflict over having to shoulder the burden of tax. They viewed the tightening of the local fiscal screw as tantamount to expropriation and a blatant piece of class legislation and not as the consequence of pressures from the reich authority.

Incomes from property had already begun to fall before the full impact of the Depression but had not yet developed into a general decline spread across the whole sector. From 1930 this was no longer the case. Most properties in Altona saw revenues tumble at considerable rates, some by even as much as 60 percent between 1930 and 1932. The properties worst hit were those in the older slum or slumlike quarters of the Altstadt and Ottensen.

For instance, businessman Alwin Raupert's net income for his properties at Christianstraße 20–22 (where he lived with eight tenants) and at Große Marienstraße 55 (which had four tenants), in the heart of the Altstadt, fell by just over a fifth from 4,855 reichsmark in 1931 to 3,800 reichsmark in 1932.[130] Gerhard Tolle owned three houses in the same vicinity. Over the same period the value of Tolle's rents declined by a third from 7,716 to 5,144 reichsmark.[131] For one landlord, Herr Stülken, who resided with his wife at number 9 Lohestraße, the decline in income was even more dramatic. The revenue from rents in 1930 had been 10,077 reichsmark; by 1932 this had been more than halved to 4,395 reichsmark. And, even after the Depression had begun to lift in 1934, the 1930 level on this particular property had not been regained.[132]

The problem for Altona's property owners lay in the failure of the municipal tax office to adjust tax valuations to current levels of income, instead of basing its calculations on earlier property values and rent incomes. Property owners thus felt they were paying too much tax. Not surprisingly, the Stellingen branch of the Property Owners' Association was led to comment, "town property is already bled white in tax terms, each [further] increase must lead to the ruin of many middle-class property-owners."[133] The case of seventy-year-old Fritz Irps, who owned a large five-storeyed house with fifteen tenants at number 10 Beim Grünen Jaeger, near the Hamburg border, is paradigmatic.

Irps had a history of late and irregular tax payments, allegedly due to a series of financial misfortune and to his own slackness in managing the rents from his property. In the Depression such circumstances were to close in on him. By the end of October 1932 he found himself 6,469 reichsmark in accumulated tax arrears.[134] Irps pointed out that most of his middle-class tenants were unable to pay their rent, resulting in a loss of income, although he still had to meet the costs for repairs and alterations to the house. In considering his case, however, the *Magistrat* felt that he could have shown more resolve in collecting his rents. Drawing on the city's example of financial stringency, the officials felt that "Herr Irps, to his own detriment, can barely understand that through energetic action he can force his tenants to pay up, or [he can] execute an eviction."[135]

Irps knew that, by reporting the loss of rent, he could appeal for exclusion from the rent tax.[136] In order to do so, he would have to have the precise details of his finances, and it appears he was unable to produce these in any coherent form. (He had sent bundles of papers, in no particular order, going back a number of years to the municipal tax office.) Up to this point the authorities in Altona had been prepared to show some patience with him, perhaps because he was a member of the rent arbitration committee and active in public life.[137] But this apparent leniency evaporated, for one day in the autumn of 1932, in his words, "the bailiff suddenly appeared" at his door.

The arrival of the bailiff was a blow to Irps's public esteem. He took this as a sign that the authorities believed he had lied about his finances and that this would result in public humiliation. Irps knew that he could not allow the city to proceed with impunity and fought back, not only questioning the validity of the sums calculated by the tax office but also taking exception to taxes, which had been, in his view, unjustly dictated. Irps trod a well-worn path in his letter to the *Regierungspräsident,* in which he appealed for justice against the cold hand of bureaucracy.

> It cannot possibly be the aim of legislation that taxes are calculated in this way and that one proceeds against me like this without any reason. I am 70 years old and have paid my taxes in Altona promptly for 28 years. And now I have to eke out my life . . . [in] this way. I don't want charity from the city of Altona, but only justice![138]

In some of these cases the complainants merely sought an acknowledgment and understanding from the authorities that the situation in which they found themselves was not of their making.[139] In late December 1932 Herr Dennert, the director of the mathematical instruments firm Dennert and Pape, based in the Altstadt, appealed to the authorities in Altona and in Schleswig in order to win some respite from a deadline for property tax arrears. He pleaded for greater understanding for the difficulties firms such as his were facing in the Depression. He wrote to the *Magistrat* that "we do not invoke the law in this case, we only plead for a concession which, in the present time of bad economic conditions, we can surely ask for."[140] And yet the natural justice that they expected, as in so many other cases, did not materialize.[141]

It was not only inner-city property owners who suffered, some of whom may have earned additional income through some other means. When in March 1930 a tax surcharge increase became imminent, Christoph Gehrke, chairman of the four thousand–strong Property Owners' Association, noted that "this measure will hit particularly hard the owners of villa and settlement properties who have absolutely no possibility to off-set [this]."[142] The perceived unending flow of surcharge increases coming from Brauer's office were driving them into the ground.

When Hans Holst, a homeowner from the Elbchaussee in Klein Flottbek, came to financial grief in the late 1920s as a consequence of a poor economy, he blamed "mismanagement by the *Magistrat.*" In his view his troubles began after the incorporation of Klein Flottbek, when new levels for the property tax were set by the city. A friend described in a testimonial to the city's new political masters in mid-March 1933 the process of impoverishment seemingly brought about under Brauer's regime:

> From this moment on, with an ever declining business, Herr Holst could no longer meet commitments. . . . One then refused any easing of the property tax, so that Herr Holst was forced into debts which he certainly did not want to make.[143]

He had suffered large business losses in 1931–32 and, as a result, had accumulated substantial tax arrears. Friends had then helped him out, but he still faced outstanding property tax arrears of about two thousand reichsmark. By 1932 he had lost his fifty-year-old firm, and his house was on the market. His friend's testimonial claimed that Holst had placed hope in the prospect of a Nazi government, for the NSDAP "surely had the protection of the *Mittelstand* close to its heart."[144]

Holst's case thus highlights the process of convergence between economic disaffection and political mobilization. Property owners had very little to be pleased about with the character and method of taxation under the Weimar Republic, and this dissatisfaction became magnified from 1929. They felt that they were being forced to shoulder a disproportionate part of the financial burdens of the Weimar state. They did not accept Brauer's contention in 1930 that they had done well in the past. This view not only flew in the face of their economic reality, but it was received by them as an insult and provocation. As the property owners' association wrote in response, "This comment will hardly contribute to bridging the deplorable gap which already for some time has been widening between different groups of the German people."[145]

"Pressure Begets Counter-Pressure"

Under the emergency decrees of July and October 1930 local authorities could raise the level of tax on items such as beer, drinks, entertainment, and dog licenses and were also empowered to implement a citizens' tax.[146] In Altona use of these surcharges was made from late 1930 in an attempt to remove the remaining 750,000 reichsmark of its deficit. Nonetheless, the *Magistrat* was by no means confident that increases would offset the deficit. Between 1930 and 1931 alone the citizens' tax and consumer taxes increased by more than three- and sevenfold, respectively.[147] In effect, the burden of Brüning's deflationary policy was being passed onto the municipal authorities, who in turn had little choice but to draw on what little reserves could be squeezed from the taxpayer and consumer.[148] When the taxes were introduced in late December 1930 the *Altonaer Tageblatt* noted, "In this lies . . . the cause for large groups of worthy citizens to gradually display frustration and dissatisfaction with municipal self-government."[149]

The pressure in Altona's *Rathaus* to collect any amount of tax arrears, and at any cost, thus led to a deepening rift between the administration and members of the public. The citizens' tax in particular met with vehement opposition, cutting across political divisions and provoking SPD councillors to describe it as an "unsocial burdening of the broad masses."[150] In order to introduce a measure of social justice, the tax was graduated along seven income bands, with thresholds ranging from 6 reichsmark to 1,000 reichsmark.[151] Some persons were either exempted or liable for only half of any given rate—for instance, those either exempted from income tax entirely or whose incomes were too low, including the unemployed and housewives. In some cases concerning requests for a reassessment of banding, the city could be grudgingly flexible.[152] But as a rule, because of the city's own dire financial position, applications for exemption on the grounds of hardship were usually rejected out of hand.[153]

For Erwin Schmidt, who had to support his parents, the citizens' tax was the last straw. He protested against the imposition of the tax to the *Regierungspräsident* in March 1931. "The law cannot demand something of someone when he does not have anything; and make him throw to his children dry bread."[154] Schmidt was not the only taxpayer to feel unjustly treated and even bullied. Others explicitly charted the process of social and political disintegration taking place. A city official, Herr Meier, complained to the Prussian finance ministry in Berlin that he and many others like him enjoyed a standing in the local community and had always behaved impeccably in tax matters. Meier, speaking on behalf of his fellow citizens, stated that they did not take kindly to being "ordered," rather than "requested," to meet their tax obligations. The situation in which they now found themselves was not of their making. He therefore expected the *Magistrat* to be more circumspect and not to press so hard in the collection of tax "in this period of the most acute social distress . . . in order not to further exacerbate the [social] conflicts."[155] He insisted that the minister intervene and reprimand Brauer for such roughshod behavior. Other complainants were more direct in their language and were prepared to play on general fears of political radicalization.[156]

The apparent callousness of the city authorities in dealing with those who fell behind with their taxes was of major importance in shaping the political outcome of late Weimar. Even though taxation had been contested throughout the 1920s, its imposition was never so strongly resented by the middle classes as when the threat to property and small and medium-sized businesses loomed large in those crisis-ridden years.[157] The mounting public frustration with the municipal administration fueled widespread alienation and fed into the rising tide of political disaffection from 1929. The answer to the taxpayer's problem lay, as one discontented citizen put it, in a political solution.[158]

Although much of *Mittelstand* ideology rejected party politics, it did not reject politics per se. For, when it came to looking after one's material interests and social status, the "nonpolitical German" was a very political animal indeed, as the *Mittelstand*'s shifting support for political and interest parties testify.[159] Even before the Depression *Mittelstand* protest also included support for the NSDAP. In Altona the political rhetoric employed in its attacks over issues such as the Lebensmittelversorgung, Webwaren, or Holsatia differed very little from the language employed by other extreme conservative groups during the mid-1920s. But by the beginning of the 1930s the NSDAP had distanced itself sufficiently from the failures of the conservative rainbow coalition in Altona, in order for it to appear as a feasible political option. Its breakthrough in September 1930 was certainly a product of the fiscal and material crisis among the *Mittelstand,* but it was also rooted in years of local experience of Nazi municipal politics, and this became more potent as the conservative and narrow interest parties became increasingly immobilized. Nazi success in 1930 was, therefore, not generated by "panic" alone.[160]

The close correlation between the middle reaches of business and the Nazi vote is widely accepted.[161] We saw in chapter 2 that in Altona individuals from this socio-occupational group together made up around a quarter of party membership in 1931 and that many of Altona's leading activists were petty businessmen. We also noted the degree to which there was interaction at the city level of the conservative and interest group vote and Nazi electoral performance. This interaction was most visible in those wards of the city in which the DNVP, DVP, and the DDP (and, to a lesser extent, the Business Party) had previously represented the interests of small to medium business. As much as 80 percent of the vote in these districts went to these parties. Yet, in most cases, both the DNVP and DVP collapsed after 1928, while the NSDAP went from strength to strength. The liberal party, which from 1930 had also shifted to the Right, remained remarkably stable in the *Mittelstand* wards until 1932. Notable examples of the trend are illustrated by the ward performances shown in the following set of figures and in table 11.

The socioeconomic composition of these wards was predominately *Mittelstand.*[162] Wards 8, 10, and 58 included the intersection of Bahnhofstraße, Königstraße, and Große Bergstraße, near the railway station where many small traders and office businesses were located. Wards 44 and 45*a* included the busy thoroughfare of Stresemannstraße (formerly Kleine Gärtnerstraße), where many shops and smaller assorted workshops could

TABLE 11. Nazi Votes in Altstadt, Ottensen, and Bahrenfeld, Selected Electoral Wards, 1928–32 (by percentage of valid vote)

Ward	1928	1930	1932
Altstadt			
8	4.4	30.5	55.3
10	3.5	34.8	59.7
44	6.1	34.7	57.3
45a	4.0	29.7	52.0
49	4.3	34.1	58.9
58	3.8	38.1*	61.2*
Ottensen			
74	3.2	24.7	52.5
75a	2.5	28.7	53.2
76	4.6	30.5	55.0
78	4.7*	31.9*	58.1
84	2.2	31.8	63.8*
Bahrenfeld			
107	2.2	28.0	55.3*
111	1.9	30.3	50.8
112	2.5	30.7*	52.5

Source: Compiled from electoral data published in the relevant issues of *Hamburger Echo,* Altona section.
*The highest share for the ward

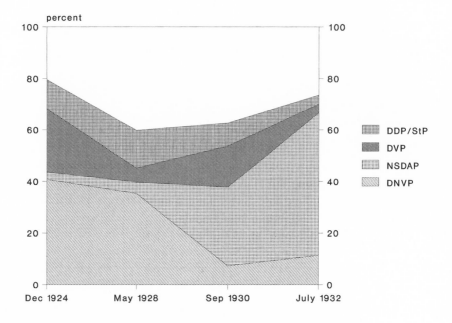

Fig. 6a–g. Change in Mittelstand votes, 1924–32.
Fig. 6a. Electoral ward 8

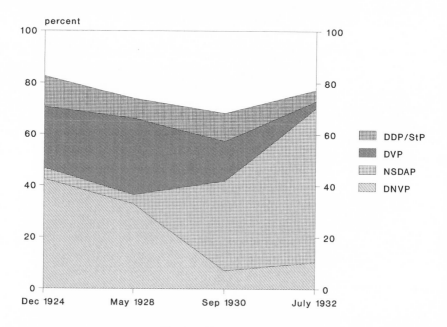

Fig. 6b. Electoral ward 10

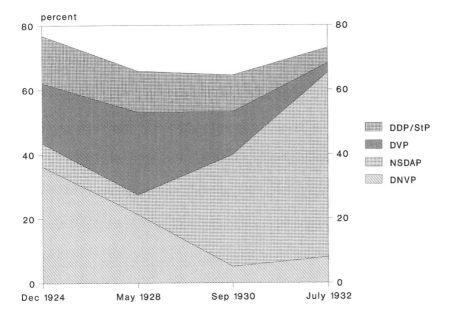

Fig. 6c.   Electoral ward 44

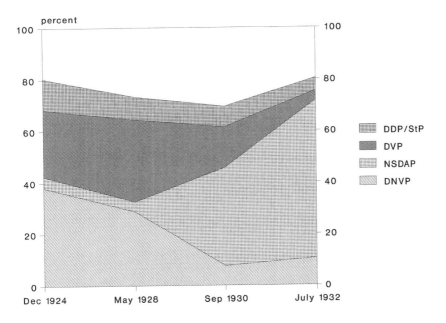

Fig 6d.   Electoral ward 58

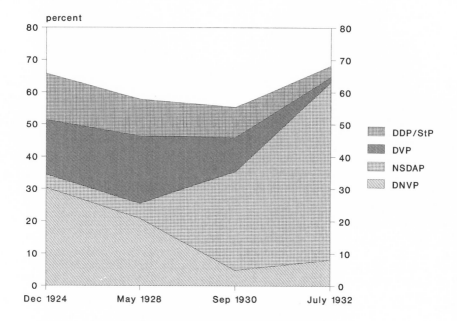

Fig. 6e.   Electoral ward 76

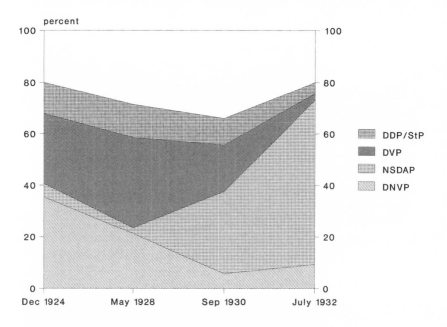

Fig. 6f.   Electoral ward 84

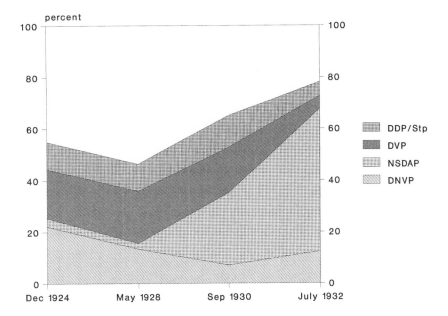

percent

100 — 100

80 — 80

60 — 60

40 — 40

20 — 20

0 — 0

Dec 1924   May 1928   Sep 1930   July 1932

DDP/Stp
DVP
NSDAP
DNVP

Fig 6g.   Electoral ward 107

be found; they also incorporated streets such as Alsenstraße or
Gefionstraße, with their largely middle-class tenants; in Ottensen wards 76,
78, and 84, in particular, were areas with a similar socioeconomic profile.
Some of these wards, particularly those in the Altstadt, were located in
areas generally understood as Socialist or Communist "territory." As such,
the turn toward the NSDAP, with its more aggressive style of politics, also
represented a resolve among the hard-pressed *Mittelstand* to do final battle
with the "Marxists" of Altona, as we shall see in the next chapter.

The ward performances shown in the table are dramatic but also typical of the Nazi vote in Altona's *Mittelstand* districts. In the equivalent
petit bourgeois wards of Blankenese levels of Nazi support were equally
high, outstripping the district average. Thus, in the petty-artisanal and
commercial neighborhoods of wards 3 and 4 in Blankenese the owners of
commercial businesses seem to have opted in considerable numbers for the
NSDAP between September 1930 and July 1932. By 1932 the Nazi share
of the vote climbed to around 64 percent in both wards. This pattern was
repeated in similar wards elsewhere in the city, albeit less starkly. There is
little doubt, therefore, that the areas with strong petty commercial and
business interests, and with many disgruntled property owners, turned to
the NSDAP for a resolution of their problems.

The final comment on the process we have been describing comes from Emmy Heinemann, who lived at number 18 Schenefelderstraße in Blankenese. His is an articulate expression of the process of alienation we have been following. The street in which he lived was in Blankenese's electoral ward 9, where the Nazi vote grew from 37.5 percent in 1930 to its peak of 55 percent in the *Landtag* election of April 1932, before falling slightly in July.

Heinemann's Hamburg-based import-export textile business with China had been precariously perched between make or bust during the 1920s, for a variety reasons, not least because of the hyperinflation and political unrest in China.[163] The Depression exacerbated his fragile position, a measure of which is gauged from the fact that he was not called upon to pay income tax for 1930, although he was still paying off in installments accumulated tax arrears. Although Heinemann had been released from the income and business taxes, he was still expected to pay the recently raised property tax surcharge, backdated to the beginning of the financial year, and the newly introduced citizens' tax. Moreover, he too was complaining about the decision to usher in electricity charges based on the number of rooms rather than on consumption. For these reasons he was convinced that his dire financial problems were brought about by the "wrong economic policies of the local authorities" and not by impersonal forces.[164]

Heinemann sought remission from these charges but did not expect to get far with the city authorities. Like many of his kind, he decided to take the matter further and write to the *Regierungspräsident,* not that he expected to find a sympathetic ear for his protest against Altona's "unjustifiable tax policy" but simply wanted to have his objection formally recorded.[165] Heinemann repeated the claim that taxes and surcharges fell more heavily on the middle classes than on the working class without any regard for individual circumstances. He prophesied that "tax and economic misery" would lead to even greater disaffection among wide sections of Altona's citizenry, whose anger would inevitably spill over into politics.[166] For "it is an old well-known saying, pressure begets counter-pressure . . . it would be a pity if representatives of the Social Democratic Party instead of working more closely together with citizens, continue to deepen the distance [between state and society]."[167] He told the *Regierungspräsident* that the situation would get out of control and end in an "explosion" because:

> after all in Germany there are, apart from the workers, businessmen who want to live and who have become impoverished through the present conditions, but have the courage to work and get back on

their feet despite their own distress. For them in particular it is made very, very difficult to remain neutral.[168]

In his view the policies pursued by municipal authorities, and Socialist Altona in particular, merely served the radical interests of the NSDAP. Heinemann was probably charting his own shifting political ground. While he claimed to know Socialist personalities such as Heinrich Kürbis, the *Oberpräsident* of Schleswig-Holstein, or to admire Max Brauer and sympathized with his efforts to transform Altona, in the end he had to admit that the revolution of 1918 and the republic it had spawned had cost him greatly in material terms but had brought him little in the way of tangible benefits. For Heinemann and his class compatriots the time had finally come to tie down Weimar's municipal visible hand.

CHAPTER 6

Street Politics in the Crisis, 1930–1933

Who conquers the streets . . . can in this way conquer the state.

—Joseph Goebbels[1]

From 1930 municipal politics began to founder upon the rocks of local budgetary crisis and an obdurate reich executive. This triggered a crisis of legitimacy in local politics, which quickly undermined the role of city councils as a site of reconciling opposing interests.[2] The effective closing down of these vents for releasing local tensions, as Brauer put it, was accompanied by a shift toward what Max Weber had earlier termed the "democracy of the streets," a process that became inevitable "in countries with either a powerless or a politically discredited parliament."[3]

The shift to the streets was part of a general political mobilization not seen since the early days of the republic, and it was a terrain that was contested mostly by the Nazis and Communists.[4] In Altona this street mobilization took place largely in the city's slum quarters. In certain parts of the Altstadt, for instance, the Communists had been able to strengthen already existing traditions of social and political radicalism. Their position came under pressure, however, as Nazis sought to wrest the city from the control of the Left. Consequently, a quasi-guerrilla warfare was conducted within the neighborhoods of the inner-city slum quarters. There is also evidence of similar violent conflicts elsewhere in Altona, notably in the suburbs of Lurup, Osdorf, and Eidelstedt among the so-called garden-shed settlers (*Laubensiedler*), made up of unemployed families,[5] but we will be concerned chiefly with the Altstadt and Ottensen.

Some have discerned in the shift to the streets a cynical and self-interested manipulation by the KPD and NSDAP of a materially beleaguered population.[6] While there may be some validity in this view, it nevertheless obscures another side to the character of late-Weimar politics. As we saw in chapter 3, the authorities in Altona and elsewhere saw the Altstadt, with its "narrow impenetrable streets . . . especially the streets near the Hamburg border . . . as particularly dangerous."[7] If it could not be reformed, it had to be tamed. Policing the slums, however, was a difficult task. In spite of the fact that five of the city's thirteen main police stations were located in the Altstadt, including the heartlands of the slum districts, the police were severely understaffed.[8] Not surprisingly, there were frequent periods when the police were overstretched.

Relations between the police and the residents of the slums were tense throughout the period. The police held the view that given the alleged Communist orientation of the local population, crime and social disorder in the slums could easily translate into a challenge to the political order. And, because the police line between law-abiding society and the revolutionary flood was attenuated, they recommended quick and ruthless action against all incidents on the streets.[9] As we shall see, the political violence and the democratic crisis of the late-Weimar period were also fueled by deeper social tensions in uneasy communities.[10]

The Communist Milieu

We saw in chapter 2 how the slums, in particular those in the Altstadt, provided the Communist Party with a level of support that remained fairly consistent over the period. In these areas the KPD was able to tap into an existing Left-Socialist tradition. Examples of these radical strongholds could be found in subdistricts 3, 9, 10, 11, 15, and 18, where, Kaufmann tells us, the "less friendly face of the lumpenproletariat" was to be found.[11] This comment is perhaps more revealing of the observer than of the observed. To be sure, for most of the period, and certainly by 1932, the typical Communist supporter and activist was unemployed and had thus fallen through the net of respectability, in some eyes.[12]

Specific examples of these pockets of support at the level of electoral wards were Pfeifers Gang and the enclosed court at number 84 Große Freiheit (ward 19), the entire odd-numbered side of Große Marienstraße (ward 20), Friedrichbaderstraße (ward 22), and Adlerstraße (ward 28). These particular neighborhoods made up Altona's own "Little Moscow." In the electoral wards 19 and 20 (in subdistrict 9) the KPD found a high and enduring level of popular support. In fact, in ward 20 the KPD vote far outweighed that of the SPD and from 1924 became the single strongest party, polling over 50 percent of valid votes. A dramatic illustration of the argument being made here can be found in the example of ward 21 (fig. 7). A similar Left stronghold was the Fischmarkt where the Communist vote

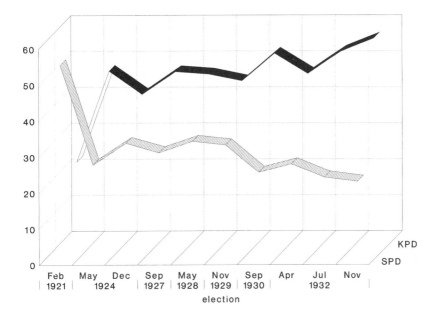

Fig. 7.   SPD/KPD vote transfers in electoral ward 21

was remarkably buoyant, bucking all trends as it grew continuously from 20 percent in 1924 to over half of the votes in 1932 (table 12).

Although the KPD never seriously threatened to displace the Social Democrats in Ottensen, its vote showed a steady increase at the expense of the SPD from 1930. This was notable in subdistricts 24 and 25 (wards 88–94). Though the KPD could never exceed the general level of Socialist support in the district, in these parts of it the raw activism of the Communists led right-wing opponents to see in some of these neighborhoods a "communist-oriented population."[13]

In particular, Erdmannstraße and Sternstraße (ward 88), or numbers 27–33 and 28–48 Taubenstraße (ward 91) and the backhouses and enclosed courts in Hohenesch in the same ward, provide vivid examples of Communist enclaves. Similarly, in the wards of subdistrict 25, especially those in the vicinity of Schulstraße and Kleine and Große Karlstraße, at least a fifth to a third of the electorate voted for the Communists. According to Kaufmann, in the tenements of the narrow backstreets and courts of Taubenstraße, Große Karlstraße, and Hohenesch one came across "bitter misery and not always the best population."[14] These streets, terraces, and courts were to a great degree homogeneous in terms of their social and political character, housing mostly unskilled workers, vulnerable to the vagaries of the labor market and who voted consistently for the communist Left.

The so-called slum area was inaccessible to the police, who readily acknowledged that their streets were impenetrable. It was not so much the physical geography that presented itself as impenetrable as the cultural world that the visitor encountered. Shared spaces and experiences produced a distinctive tradition. Indeed, the typical slum community was a world closed off to outsiders.[15]

Otto Headecke was to learn this the hard way. After the events of "Bloody Sunday" in July 1932 Haedecke, who had marched with a Hamburg contingent of SA, went to the home of Alfred Franck in the Altstadt's Friedrichbaderstraße to investigate for himself Franck's alleged part in the street battle. Franck was not at home at the time, and his mother suggested that Haedecke return that evening. Haedecke should have heeded the warning signs as he left the apartment. For he told the police, "When I stepped out of the house, several communists stood in the court, they eyed me up with piercing looks." Later that evening, he reported,

> As I neared Nr. 27, I saw that the court was full of communists. There could have been about twelve of them gathered there. Because I felt threatened by these people I did not even enter, but quickly carried on walking.[16]

Franck had been described to Haedecke as a "fanatical communist," and the area where he lived was known as little Moscow (see the election

TABLE 12.   Communist Votes in the Fischmarkt, 1924–32 (by percentage of valid votes in electoral wards 1–7)

	Wards						
Election	1	2	3	4	5	6	7
1924[a]	23.4	20.5	17.5	25.6	32.2	18.0	37.3
1928	29.1	31.6	23.0	29.3	45.4	26.0	41.0
1930	34.2	37.3	29.9	37.9	51.2	30.1	43.4
1932[b]	35.8	41.6	30.4	39.7	47.4	32.8	46.0
1932[c]	41.3	43.2	35.3	43.4	54.7	36.6	51.5

Source: compiled from electoral data published in the relevant issues of *Hamburger Echo,* Altona section.
[a]Reichstag election December
[b]Reichstag election July
[c]Reichstag election November

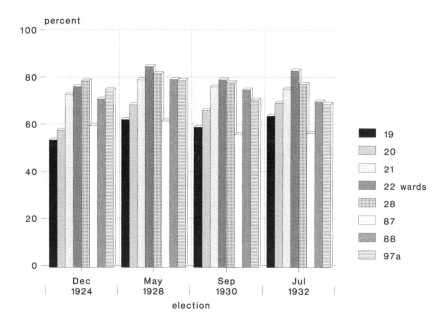

Fig. 8. Combined working-class parties' votes in "closed" neighborhoods, 1924–32 (subdistricts 9–11, 23, 26)

results in fig. 8). Haedecke finally had the wit to realize that he could not enter such territory with impunity, as he and his friends had on Sunday, 17 July. Others were to learn the hard way.

The following ordeal faced by K., a local Nazi, is a typical one.[17] After leaving the party offices in the Palmaille on 18 September 1931, he proceeded with a comrade along the Breitestraße in the direction of the fish market. They decided to part after passing three young men who swore at them. K. was followed by the three young men, who overtook him at the corner of Breitestraße and Kirchenstraße. One man stood in his path, while the other two grabbed his arms from behind. He was struck several times before freeing himself, escaping down the steps of a nearby tavern. Sanctuary was only momentary, however. The barman threw him out into the arms of his waiting aggressors, who roughed him up some more. His injuries required the services of a doctor for the following three weeks. K knew his attackers from the neighborhood, although he could not identify them by name.

By contrast, Heinrich Meissner, a local retailer, and his forty-three-year-old brother-in-law, Ernst Frank, a crane driver who lodged with him, knew their aggressors.[18] They lived at number 58 Langestraße, a property also owned by Meissner. This street was in subdistrict 7, which consisted of the explicitly Communist wards 14 and 15. The two men had been subjected to a constant stream of verbal and physical abuse before 1933. Meissner later recalled how friends of his other lodger would arrive in the street and attempt to intimidate them:

> We were . . . threatened by communists more frequently. It happened on several occasions that communists placed themselves in front of our house, drew their guns and demanded that we close our windows.[19]

The level of hostility was so intense that Frank, who was a member of a local troop of SA, felt he was a "marked man" and eventually was forced to move to Ottensen, at the beginning of August 1932.[20] A similar fate also befell a young unemployed gardener, Otto Rammelt, after he joined the SA. At the time, he lived with his father at number 162 Adolphstraße (ward 30), deep in the Altstadt's Communist territory, but after repeated attacks he went to live in relatively safe Wedel. He told the police:

> During the time I lived with my father, I was frequently pestered by my neighbours, especially those living in the terrace at the back of the house, because of my membership in the SA. On the day that the ban against the SA was lifted, and I came back from [troop] duty, . . . I was also attacked . . . I am sure that these people were put up to it by my neighbours . . . they belong partly to the communists and partly the Reichsbanner.[21]

As Rammelt's testimony suggests, allegiance to either of the normally mutually antagonistic working-class parties did not preclude a united front at the grassroots level.[22] The neighboring Adolphpassage (the terrace referred to by Rammelt) was a back terrace of eight houses containing sixty dwellings and households, many of them of long-term residences, and were members of either the SPD or KPD. They knew one another intimately, enjoyed a regular and established pattern of life, shared a broad tradition that revolved around their court or terrace, and engaged in animated debate over political differences; very often such close-knit neighborhood networks were underpinned by kinship as well as long-standing friendships.[23] The closed nature of such neighborhood communities, meant that both Nazis and, in certain circumstances, the police could expect little public sympathy or cooperation. Thus, they were helpless in counteracting even the most petty but persistent harassment, such as that meted out to Frau Carstens at number 12 Gerritstraße, not far from the

Adolphpassage, who had to "suffer badly" at the hands of her Communist neighbors.[24]

These informal neighborhood networks provided the social infrastructure for Communist organizations. The Fighting League against Fascism was established in the wake of the Nazi election victory on 14 September 1930, and the more loosely defined Anti-Fascist Action (Antifa) was founded much later, in the spring of 1932.[25] A division of the *Kampfbund* was established in Altona on 31 October in Gimpel's tavern in the Conradtstraße in subdistrict 14, with 118 men and 16 women joining. Gimpel's tavern was an ideal place to set up the league, for it lay in the Communist heartlands of the Altstadt, constituting electoral wards 26 through 28, 46, and 47.[26]

The *Kampfbund* was reportedly little more than a loose organization when it was first founded, but by 1932 it had developed a tighter organizational form. There were three main area divisions covering the Altstadt and Ottensen and two further divisions consisting of women and youth. West and East divisions covered the Altstadt, while the North division was located in Ottensen. The women and youth divisions were located in the Altstadt. Communist street activists were fewer in number than their Socialist counterparts but appear to have been a lot more effective in their work. The total membership, excluding youth members, for whom we do not have figures, stood at 872, including a division of the Red Front Fighters' League (*Roter Frontkämpferbund* [RFB]) attached to the League. Of this membership over 75 percent were thought to be active. The precise date for this figure eludes us, but it is likely that this information predates the summer of 1932. By October of that year membership appears to have declined, as it did nationally, to between 450 and 480, including 72 Red Front Fighters.[27]

Not surprisingly, the divisional meeting places were situated in Communist electoral strongholds. The East divisional headquarters was to be found at Jacobsen's tavern in the Lerchenstraße (ward 32), West division at Scheel's in the Große Prinzenstraße (ward 15) and Kirchenstraße (ward 7), North division met at the "Klausberg," a tavern on the corner of Klausstraße and Am Felde in Ottensen (ward 80), the women's group headquarters were jointly at Jacobsen's and at Gimpel's in the Conradtstraße (ward 46), while the Red Front Fighters' "400" division met in the saloons of Wiebe in the Breitestraße (ward 2) and Discher in the Bürgerstraße (ward 52).

Table 13 gives an idea of the political character of these areas.

With support at over 50 percent in some neighborhoods these areas gave the activists in the *Kampfbund* what the Chinese revolutionary leader,

Mao Zedong, was later to refer to as a "sea to swim in." Support for members was both formally and informally organized around house and street-based cells, naturally under the leadership of Communists or close sympathizers. The main requirement was that of residence in the immediate vicinity of the cell. Because of this, cells tended to be already fairly close-knit communities, enabling outsiders to be easily recognized, as we saw in the case of Haedecke, and thus provided safety from infiltration by the police and Nazis, with varying success. They also provided havens from pursuit and made the job of investigation particularly difficult for both Weimar and Nazi police and court officials.[28]

The Antifa in Altona had a total strength of around twenty-four hundred members in the late summer of 1932, organized into thirty-four divisions (*Staffeln*) and coordinated by nine committees.[29] The divisions were spread throughout the fifteen districts of Greater Altona. Their exact location remains a mystery in the majority of cases, nor are we any the wiser regarding their composition. A police report from July suggested, however, that about 70 percent of the total membership did not belong to any particular party; 10 percent was composed of Socialists (either in the SPD or the splinter Socialist Workers' Party [SAP]), and only 20 percent was made up of bona fide Communist Party members.[30]

Internal sources on individual divisions suggest a broadly similar composition. For example, in the Altstadt the Dennerstraße division in wards 50 and 51 had 109 members, of whom just over half had no party affiliation, a fifth belonged to the socialist Reichsbanner, and under a third was made up of Communists; the Annenstraße division in wards 21 and 22, which had a strength of 50 members, had a similar proportion of non-party affiliates, while the share of Socialists was higher, at 34 percent, and that of Communists at only 14 percent.[31] On the other hand, of the 200

TABLE 13.   KPD Votes in Kampfbund Divisional Areas (by percentage of valid vote)

Electoral Wards	Year			
	1928	1930	July 1932	Nov. 1932
2	31.6	37.3	41.6	43.2
7	41.0	43.4	46.0	51.5
15	45.2	49.9	50.3	55.4
32	28.4	34.1	32.8	38.1
46	42.8	46.8	54.2	57.2
52	34.0	40.7	46.0	49.6
80	18.3	23.0	23.9	25.4

Source: Compiled from electoral data published in the relevant issues of *Hamburger Echo*, Altona section.

strong Stellinger Moor division in Eidelstedt, composed of mostly unemployed youth, nearly 63 percent was unaffiliated, a third was Communist, and only 5 percent was Socialist.[32]

However political life might appear on the surface, domination of a particular area was never total. These districts were coming under growing pressure from the Nazis in their efforts to win over the petty retailers and owners of small businesses who also abounded in these neighborhoods. Thus, the KPD could not be complacent about its position here.

The "Nationalist Minded" Community

Although the Altstadt and parts of Ottensen appeared overwhelmingly proletarian, they were nevertheless moderated by pockets of the old and new middle class. Indeed, even those subdistricts often described as slums were in actual fact socially mixed areas, as we can see from table 14. The Reichstag election in 1928 and the municipal election in the following year revealed to the NSDAP that it could tap a rich seam of support in Altona and that this was not only in its middle-class suburbs but also in the socially mixed neighborhoods of the inner city.

The social and cultural community underpinning the stability of a neighborhood's political choice applied equally to the right-wing vote in

TABLE 14.   Social Structure of Selected "Slum" Subdistricts of the Altstadt and Ottensen/Bahrenfeld, 1939

Subdistrict	"Old" Middle Class[a]	"New" Middle Class[b]	Working Class
Altstadt			
3	16.4	17.7	65.9
9–10	13.4	8.8	77.8
11–14	14.4	19.9	65.7
15–16,18	13.6	20.3	66.1
Ottensen/Bahrenfeld			
21	17.7	33.7	48.6
22	14.2	22.0	63.8
23	11.5	57.1	31.4
24	14.2	22.0	63.8
25	8.8	25.1	66.1
26–27	10.2	37.7	52.1

Source: AHVW Sondernummer 6 (1 Nov. 1941): 17.
[a]Includes self-employed and home helpers.
[b]Includes Beamte and Angestellte.

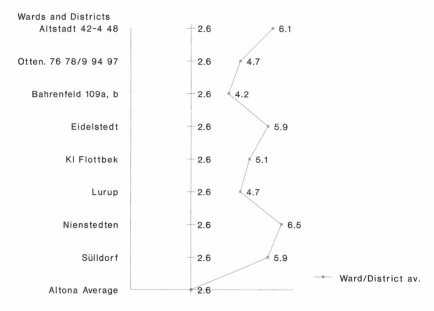

Fig. 9.   May 1928: "Nazi" electoral wards (average percentage share of wards)

Altona.[33] In May 1924, for example, the share of votes for the anti-Semitic Völkisch-Sozialer Block stood at 11 percent and nearly 13 percent in electoral wards 8 through 10, near the central station and city hall, when that for the city was 8 percent. Between 1928 and 1929 the share of the vote in these three wards more than doubled and tripled, from between 3 and 4 percent to between 10 and 12 percent. Not surprisingly, in September 1930 the party could reap a 30 percent share in wards 8 and 9 and nearly 35 percent in ward 10.

Similarly, in wards 39, 44, 45*b,* in the northeast of the Altstadt, the Nazi vote quadrupled, tripled, and more than doubled between 1928 and 1929. In 1930 the party took between a quarter and a sizable third of the vote in these three wards. Ward 58 in the heart of the central neighborhoods of the Altstadt obtained a comparable result. In Ottensen the same pattern was visible in wards 74, 75*b,* 76, 78, and 81. As figure 10 shows, in these wards above-average performances in 1928 were consolidated in 1929, offering a runway for takeoff in the 1930 elections.

These pockets of Nazi support were nurtured greatly by propaganda activity in the city.[34] While the party stepped up its activities in the countryside, it also increasingly targeted the cities of the province, most notably Altona, where attendance at meetings was usually largest. Thus, between

wards

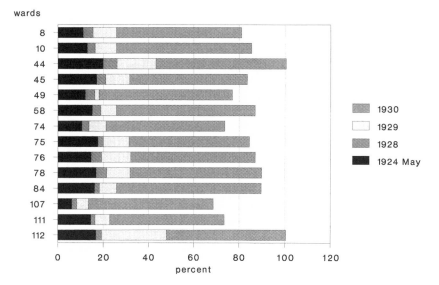

Fig. 10.   Nazi votes in selected electoral wards, 1924, 1928–30

mid-June 1929[35] and September 1930 the number of propaganda meetings and marches in Altona rose from less than a handful in the second half of 1929 and the early part of 1930 to twelve in the first half of September 1930, while attendance on average ranged from a hundred to a thousand. And as we noted in chapter 2, on special occasions speakers such as Gregor Strasser or the former kaiser's son could attract crowds up to four thousand.[36]

Underlying support for the Nazis was a whole battery of social prejudices, not dissimilar to those we charted in chapter 3. Local people who were perhaps inclined to support the Nazis emphasized the connection between "low" social standing and political radicalism. For example, fifty-three-year-old Juliane Bock, a tavern keeper from the Bürgerstraße, described to the police two families of a tenement in neighboring Schauenburgerstraße,

> I know the residents of this house quite well. . . . I knew of these [families] that they were communists. Of young Jungclaus I know that he goes together with his wife to the cigarette shop of Heinrich Hosang, at Schauenburgerstraße 30 . . . [and] . . . that this area is reputed to be a bastion of the communists. Only communists go there. Jungclaus'

outward appearance and behaviour too is totally that of a communist.[37]

The nearby Gärtnerstraße and the streets immediately surrounding it were described by Klaus Gotthardt, who lived at number 22, as "a very red neighbourhood" inhabited by "Untermenschen."[38]

Since the onset of the Depression the KPD had been intensifying its activities in the Altstadt. The party mostly addressed the material problems of the growing number of the unemployed by organizing meetings and marches, which frequently ended in scenes of public disorder. The KPD's extreme visibility fueled middle-class fears that a Communist insurrection was imminent.[39] Meanwhile, younger members took it upon themselves to harass local traders known to be Nazis or their sympathizers, mostly by plundering their shops and smashing windows. These acts affronted all property owners. The police very often failed to respond quickly enough or adequately to protect the victims.

Gustav Böhring owned a dairy goods shop in the lower part of Große Gärtnerstraße, which ran from the Conradtstraße to the Hamburg border at Beim Grünen Jaeger. In his own words, he lived "in an area where the poorest of the poor lived and where purchasing power had been most affected by the economic crisis." His experience is typical of many.[40] He was subjected to a raid in May 1932, later recounting to the authorities:

> They were 8 to 10 men, aged between 18 and 25 years, who forced their way into my shop and who, after making their haul, escaped partly through Lerchenstraße into Adolphstraße. They did not show any great hurry. Particularly since it seemed as if the looters were being shielded by passers-by.[41]

Böhring was fully aware that his was not an individual fate and underlined this fact in his letter to the *Magistrat*. He complained also about what seemed to him to be the sluggish response by police. In spite of the fact that the police station was close by, Böhring had to wait at least a full fifteen minutes before a uniformed patrol appeared, much too late to apprehend the culprits. He explained that, "because the event took only a few minutes and the police arrived after the perpetrators had gone, I could not be given sufficient protection." He reproached the *Magistrat* for abandoning traders such as he to the mercy of Communist forces in the Altstadt, whom he blamed for his ruin. At the same time he solicited "respectfully once more, that the *Magistrat* of the city of Altona show sympathy for a much affected small businessman whose existence is damaged to an even greater degree."

Böhring expected the city to compensate his loss, since his predicament was largely due to inadequate policing. Böhring's hope of compensation was guided as much by the fact that falling trade meant that he could no longer pay his taxes as it was grounded in notions of natural justice. He continued in his letter:

> I have resided in the city for a number of years and have always endeavoured to earn the satisfaction of the authorities as well as the respect of my fellow *Bürger*. Hence diligence, industry and thrift were always my prime duties.[42]

He was to be disappointed.[43] There was little sympathy from the authorities, and the perpetrators remained at large.

Not far from the Große Gärtnerstraße, at 53 Schauenburgerstraße, Marie Schröder kept a small fruit and vegetable shop. Both her husband and her son were Nazis. This put them in a difficult position, given the political allegiance of the street where they lived. In the early hours of the morning of Sunday 17 July, when a controversial election campaign march through the Altstadt was planned by the NSDAP, the windows of her shop were smashed.[44] This attack was a warning and was part of a wave of attacks against local Nazis and their sympathizers that morning to refrain from participating in the march.[45]

The damage to the shop amounted to eighty-three reichsmark, a considerable sum for a small retailer during the Depression. The couple's business insurance did not extend to glass, and they were not in a financial position to pay for the damage. As a result, the windows were boarded up, giving the impression that the shop had closed down, which it did eventually, because of the loss of trade. Marie Schröder and her husband ended up receiving local poor relief from the very state they disdained.[46]

Paul Hey took over his father's business, a dairy shop, in the Große Prinzenstraße near the old *Rathaus,* just off the Königstraße, in June 1932. Within a month his shop became a target for attack. His father, Hey senior, recounted how seven young men wielding truncheons forced their way into the shop in the early hours of the morning of 23 July. One of the youths held down the son, while the others "grabbed everything in sight and then disappeared" with around one hundred reichsmark worth of goods. Early-morning customers stood by and watched the spectacle, ignoring pleas for help.[47] Four months later, in October, the shop was again singled out for attack. At 6:30 A.M. ten youths once more forced their way into the premises, robbing Hey of sausages, bacon, and cheese, this time to the value of fifty reichsmark. Like Böhring and the Schröders, Hey was feeling the pinch of the economic downturn. These raids dealt a death blow to the family business.[48]

In Hey's view the police had failed miserably to provide the city's retailers, especially those in the Altstadt, with sufficient protection. Although there was a police post located at the old *Rathaus,* officers had been conspicuous by their absence on each occasion.[49] In such cases the Nazis not only portrayed themselves as the defenders of the small man caught between economic ruin and social chaos, but they often provided traders with legal representation at tribunal hearings.[50]

The Nazis also sought to provide protection on the streets. Very often they arrogated to themselves the policing of the city; in particular, they patrolled parts of the Altstadt, controlling the papers of passersby with apparent impunity.[51] These actions, of course, imitated the tactics of the police and increased after von Papen's coup against the government in Prussia on 20 July, climaxing during the Nazi "Seizure of Power" in early 1933.[52] As such, the SA, and the three troops of Altona's SS-Sturm, together totaling about 150 men in 1930, appeared to many citizens as a well-disciplined and orderly nationalist organization. As one Altona SS man recalled, his troop was composed "entirely of former Free Corps fighters."[53] Indeed, the leader of the Altona SS, Paul Moder, had been a captain in the Roßbach Free Corps.[54]

Other street activists stemmed from the ranks of the afflicted themselves. It would be wrong for us to view the stormtroopers as agents external to the "nationalist minded" communities in Altona's working-class districts, for the fact is that most of the leading protagonists of Nazi violence were themselves from precisely this social group: Fritz Schwennsen, who owned a coal business, led the SA in Altona; Hubert Richter, who led the most active Altstadt SA-troop, Sturm 2/31, was a master baker and owner of a *Konditorei* in the Große Bergstraße; Wilhelm Brockmann was the landlord of a tavern in Ottensen, from which he led the SS; Nico Pommerschein ran a butcher's shop in the Norderreihe and was an active SA subaltern; Max Boge, who became a councillor, owned a textile shop in the Palmaille; the master joiner Oskar Dupont owned a construction business in Schulterblatt but found time to be an active member of the local party; Detlev Gotthardt, an unemployed master joiner, was active in the SA. There were many more, too numerous to cite, but all with a similar background.[55] They all played their part in the struggle on the streets. These men from the old *Mittelstand* were certainly not waiting for others to provide them with protection. They organized it for themselves and, in so doing, attracted others.[56]

The Nazis found that the increasingly high profile of the stormtroopers and their tactics for curbing the Left through their own policing of the slum quarters gave succor to the previously faint-hearted and was an effective means of propaganda in mobilizing votes for the party.[57] For instance, subdistrict 21 in Ottensen was a socially mixed area, inhabited by mostly lower-middle-class professionals, small-scale businessmen, and skilled manual workers. The district contained the electoral wards 74 through 78, which were traditional redoubts of the DNVP. Thus, wards 76 and 78 first returned a buoyant DNVP vote and then from 1930 a strong Nazi vote. Ward 77 was a Socialist stronghold but suffered a continuing reduction of votes between 1928 and November 1932, by which date nearly half of the 20 percent deficit went to the Communists.

This shift toward the Communists might have frightened supporters of the Right, for they turned to the NSDAP in the security of the polling booth. Thus, the Nazi vote in ward 77 climbed from 3 percent in 1928 to nearly 21 percent in 1930, peaked at nearly 39 percent at the Landtag elections in April 1932, and fell slightly to 36 percent in July 1932.[58] This was still markedly less, however, than in neighboring wards 76 and 78, where the Nazi share of the vote had peaked at 52 and 59 percent, respectively.

Yet converts to Nazism considered it wise to remain anonymous until assured of absolute victory. As Walter Stolte, whose family was staunchly Social Democrat and at the time lived on the third floor at number 5 Carl-Theodorstraße in the heart of the ward, recalled the scene on the 30 January 1933:

> in our street there were admittedly not exactly masses, but quite a number of people, suddenly running around in SA-uniforms on the day, or the following day, of the "takeover" . . . people who had never risked anything before. When they went anywhere . . . they must have had a suitcase in which they kept their uniform . . . and then carried out their duties. But I had never before seen a member of the SS or SA in our street. Nonetheless, the next day when I got home I saw how a SA-man in full uniform stood at the window directly opposite.[59]

The same held true for the Altstadt, where Nazi visibility before January 1933 invited the risk of physical harm. A Nazi marcher recalled proceeding with trepidation through the narrow streets of the Altstadt's little Moscow on 17 July, and, as the marchers passed through Chemnitzstraße (subdistrict 19), "the window was opened and . . . somebody hung out a swastika . . . he had courage! This really happened! In *this* area somebody showed his swastika! . . . he had courage!"[60]

The Nazis understood well the psychological value of flying the colors as a means of mobilizing support. In the same week before the elections on the 31 July the party distributed flyers among the small traders of the Königstraße, exhorting them to show support for the NSDAP.

> Worthy fellow Germans! On the coming Sunday the miserable conditions in Germany will be put to an end. One means of propaganda of particular effectiveness is the decoration of houses with our flags. As a trader of the Königstraße you have absolutely nothing to reckon with socialist or communist customers. So you can hang out a swastika without any hindrance. It would be an act of thoughtlessness towards the nationalist clientele if their wishes were not taken into consideration because of a Jew or a socialist. For this reason we exhort you to fly our flag in the week before the election![61]

The Königstraße, like the Große Bergstraße, was a major commercial street joining Hamburg at the Nobistor, where small family enterprises tended to dominate. Both thoroughfares cut through the heart of the Altstadt and catered in large part to local residents as well as outsiders.[62] The appeal, coming in the midst of working-class violence against persons and property of the *Mittelstand*, found a resonance.

After the election the *Hamburger Echo* published a comment on the NSDAP success in the Altstadt. The writer bemoaned the fact that traders were happy to have the custom of the working class while at the same time supporting the party that was out to destroy them.[63]

The Nazi Neighborhood Offensive

Between 1930 and the summer of 1932 the Nazis were able to establish a distinctive and localized band of support through the old city (see map 9). The consolidation of the Nazi vote in these districts made imperative the provision of some sort of organizational network for supporters to feel safe and from which they could begin "to turn Marxists back into German workers," by prising them from the grip of the Left.[64] The inauguration of this process of what was to become a guerrilla war centered upon the city's taverns cannot be established with certainty. The first SA tavern in the Altstadt appears to have been "Zum Lornsenburg," run by August Flath at number 8 Lornsenplatz, in a staunchly conservative and nationalist neighborhood. Prior to establishing further Nazi bases, other locales for Nazis in the Altstadt were for "civilians," and these hardly played a role in the struggle for the streets. But sometime in 1931 the NSDAP began systematically establishing a network of local cells, using taverns that had been suffering economically from falling trade.[65] In the

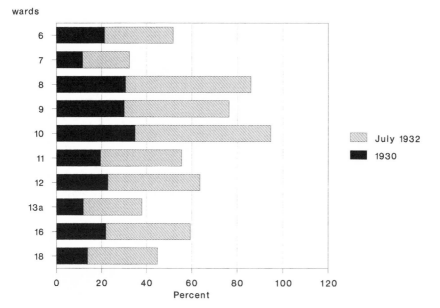

Fig. 11.   Nazi votes in the Königstraße and Große Bergstraße area, 1930 to July 1932

words of Hamburg-Altona's Nazi chronicler Hermann Okrass, these neighborhood bases

> are as important as the SA-man, the cadre and the speaker in the struggle for the city. The troops gather there, as do the sections for propaganda activities. The orders are handed out there, the election campaigns discussed and the propaganda begun.[66]

In other words, the Nazis "took the struggle to the proletariat."[67] This tactic was nothing new. As early as June 1927, the SA had provoked a brawl when it hired the *Toscasaalen* public rooms in Ottensen. Goebbels was the main speaker, and trouble was inevitable, especially when Communists in the crowd called him a "swindler" (*Gauner*).[68] The Nazis were roundly defeated, and their public meetings were subsequently banned for a period, but the purpose had been served. The fact that such a demonstration had been held at all was evidence, to the Nazis at least, that "for the first time in their history" those of the Left had been "clearly beaten in their stronghold."[69]

Although such clashes had taken place intermittently during the

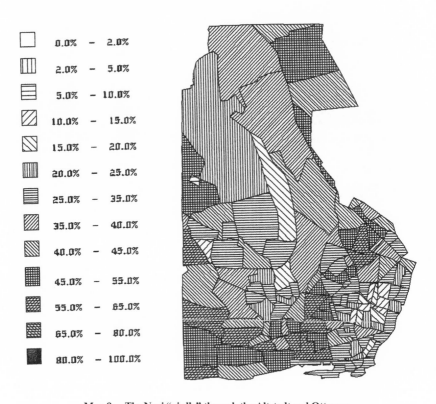

☐	0.0% – 2.0%
⊞	2.0% – 5.0%
⊟	5.0% – 10.0%
▨	10.0% – 15.0%
◪	15.0% – 20.0%
▥	20.0% – 25.0%
▤	25.0% – 35.0%
▨	35.0% – 40.0%
▧	40.0% – 45.0%
▦	45.0% – 55.0%
▩	55.0% – 65.0%
▩	65.0% – 80.0%
■	80.0% – 100.0%

Map 9.   The Nazi "girdle" through the Altstadt and Ottensen

1920s, they remained very much the exception rather than the rule. Emboldened by their electoral success in 1930, however, Nazis took the opportunity to fulfill Hitler's pledge to "eliminate the Marxist poison from our national body."[70] And, in spite of Hitler's pledge to "legality," top Nazi leaders made little effort to disguise their espousal of violence. Wilhelm Frick, who was to become the first Nazi to gain high office (in the government of Thuringia), told a demonstration in Pyritz in 1929 of the coming struggle for power:

> This fateful struggle will be fought for the time being with the ballot paper but it cannot last, for history has taught that *in battle blood flows* and iron is broken. . . . Exactly as Mussolini eliminated the marxists in Italy, so has this to be achieved in our country through *dictatorship and terror.*[71]

The response to Nazi violence was mixed. The Social Democrats, mindful of their responsibilities since 1918, complained about the increasing use of physical violence by the Nazis. They lamented that Nazis went to meetings of their opponents not to argue but to cause trouble. In Franconia SPD leaders decided to bar Nazis admission to their meetings. They accused the NSDAP of devaluing political meetings by turning them into a "playground for political rowdyism." The party leadership saw in "The *Hakenkreuzler . . .* a militaristically organised band who had turned brawling into a sport."[72] Regional leaders in Altona and Hamburg warned their members to keep clear of the Nazis and "stay at home."[73]

The Communists retaliated by drawing on their vast reserves of popular support to mobilize mass resistance to Nazi incursions and acts of violence in the slum districts. Taking seriously Heinz Neumann's slogan, they called upon working-class residents to "Strike the Fascists Wherever You Meet Them!"[74] Slogans in themselves were not enough, however, nor was spontaneous opprobrium nor, indeed, selective terror by young Communist stalwarts. Some form of cohesion through organization and leadership of a broadly based collective nature was also necessary if the Nazis were to be successfully countered. Therefore, on 4 June 1930 the Political Bureau of the Central Committee issued a resolution stating:

> The increasing bloody deeds and acts of terror of the fascists are giving rise to the strongest rage within the whole working class, going well beyond the ranks of the Communist Party, and heighten the determination among the broadest masses for the decisive battle against the fascist danger. The Communist Party must place itself at the head of this movement. The Party has at present extraordinary favorable opportunities to include large numbers of social democratic workers, *Reichsbanner, Jungbanner, SAJ* (Socialist Workers' Youth), non-party and Christian workers, in the active struggle against fascism.[75]

The chief purpose of such a broad front was to make neighborhoods impenetrable.

> No more meetings, evening discussion, nor bases of the National Socialists shall be allowed in any neighborhood; no shop shall dare to show Nazi newspapers. The street scene should be enlivened with members of the *Kampfbund.*[76]

This was to be achieved by mobilizing neighborhoods through the *Kampfbund* and the Antifa in their own defense. Communist leaders of the neighborhood defense teams were instructed:

> Everywhere where National Socialists are actively participating in the struggle against the working class, neighborhood defense teams . . . must undertake everything to achieve the removal of the person concerned from the tenement by mobilizing the workers' contempt for the National Socialists.[77]

At the peak of street violence in Altona, from mid-July 1932 to February 1933, approximately 189 public acts of political violence to either property or persons occurred. Of this number 129 are identifiable by party with certainty, either as perpetrator or victim. By far the largest number of violent acts (66) involved the Nazis. Communists were involved in 50 incidents and Socialists in only 13 cases. Close examination also reveals that the Nazis took the initiative in the greater number of incidents, though this could vary from month to month.[78]

In the second half of July until the end of August, for instance, the Communists attacked Nazis at least 12 times, whereas the Nazis attacked the Left on 9 occasions; in September the pattern repeated itself when Communists attacked 13 times, while Nazis attacked 8 times; but in October, during the run up to the election on 6 November, the Nazis attacked 22 times and the Communists only 7 times. The Socialists attacked only 8 times over the same period. Until the end of September the Nazis were the victims of attacks by the Left on 29 occasions, whereas the Socialists and the Communists together were victims in only 9 incidents. This situation reversed from October.[79]

Nazis and Communists benefited in electoral terms from this flexing of political muscle on the streets. Between 1930 and 1932 the polling areas with marked gains for both parties also happened to be in some of the most heavily contested neighborhoods in the Altstadt and Ottensen, where most of the violence had taken place. For example, in the neighborhoods located in the central part of the Altstadt—those forming districts 15, 16, and 17 and containing the eleven wards numbering 50 through 60 and those neighborhoods in Ottensen in districts 21 through 23 containing wards 77 through 80, 82 through 84, and 88 and 89—political violence became an everyday occurrence.

In a compact area of these districts of the Altstadt, for example, Nazis and Communists were responsible for the overwhelming majority of recorded cases of political street violence in the weeks leading up to the 6 November election.[80] The clashes occurred within a few neighborhoods, and so the same streets recur with regularity in the police reports. Each area had its political affiliation: Lornsenplatz was a Nazi redoubt; the lower half of Schauenburgerstraße was notorious for its "rough and ready" population and as a Communist area. Schumacherstraße, Weidenstraße, and Humboldtstraße were redoubts of social democracy.

A number of incidents frequently arose out of bravado and provocation. For instance, on the 10 September 1932 at around six o'clock in the evening an SA troop led by Helmut Stahl, who was allegedly "well-known to the courts and the police," forced their way into the tavern of Julius Eimert on the corner of Schumacherstraße and Lohmühlenstraße. This was the meetingplace for the local branch of the SPD (Altona-Nord). Eimert was not on the premises, but his barman Weber was present, together with a few customers. Stahl warned Weber that the SA would return that evening when the local Reichsbanner held its weekly meeting, "and then the place will be cleared. And for you too, you Marxist pig, we will have a few blue beans [i.e., bullets] spare."[81] Neither Weber nor his customers felt inclined to wait that long, however. They forcefully ejected Stahl and his friends from the tavern. One SA man received knife wounds during the melee that followed, and the other party comrades fled to their *Sturmlokal,* Flath's "Zum Lornsenburg" (later known as "House of the Fighter"), a few hundred feet away in Lornsenplatz.[82]

The electoral success of both Nazis and Communists directly related to their effectiveness in conducting the political struggle in the neighborhoods.[83] In fact, the KPD registered gains in 149 wards after the November elections. It thus experienced a decrease in only 10 wards, while 2 wards showed no change. This performance consolidated the party's position after its performance in July, when it gained in 156 wards against losses in 2 wards. The SPD, which had taken a passive role in the battle for the streets, suffered a continuing decline in its electoral fortunes. While it gained in 16 wards, it also registered losses in 145 wards; this was a poorer performance set against July, when it registered gains in 36 wards but losses in 124.[84] Its decline was in spite of the fact that the paramilitary organization of the SPD, the Reichsbanner, numbered around twenty-three hundred and had thus in all probability twice the number of SA and SS together.[85]

In Ottensen the Goebenstraße was the scene of five street attacks over the same period. One of the SPD's cooperative shops (*Produktion*) was located in the street (at no. 2) and had its windows continuously smashed. This street straddled a Socialist and a Nazi stronghold (wards 82–84, respectively, though at the Landtag election in April 1932 the NSDAP emerged as the strongest single party in all three wards). The area of Ottensen, where Walter Stolte lived, also served as the local headquarters of the Socialist-led Reichsbanner and Iron Front.[86] These were situated in the taverns of Johannes Brinckmann at the corner of Rothestraße and

Arnoldstraße, just around the corner from the Carl-Theodorstraße, and at Giebhardt's at number 81 Große Brunnenstraße, the latter was the SPD district headquarters in Ottensen. Stolte recounts an occasion when he was sitting in Giebhardt's, having gone there to sign up for the Iron Front, shortly after it was established in 1931:

> As I was just sitting up there, a terrible banging and clashing and screaming and so on, started behind my back. . . . Come on! . . . as I was rising and turning I just caught a sight of the landlord dashing forward and that people at the back in FAD and SA uniforms were waving their fists about . . . and all of them ran out . . . and outside they had a small, fast car, right, they all got in again and . . . away! The result of this short operation was that . . . they had slashed open a face with knuckle-dusters . . . they had smashed a glass cabinet . . . all in a split-second and then out again and off. When the police arrived there was nothing they could do.[87]

Harnessed to a doctrine of legality and discipline and clothed in a suit of social respectability, the Socialist leadership failed to develop a coherent strategy for the defense of its own political space.[88] This left a gap in the party's strategic policy that ultimately drove it to the margins of the public arena. Instead, in the critical months of 1932 repulsing the Nazis was left to individuals—with little success. On 12 July about two dozen and more SA and SS men, on returning from a local branch meeting, gathered near Robcke's tavern at number 63 Bahrenfelderstraße, a well-known Reichsbanner meetingplace. They hid behind trees in nearby side-streets and waited for their unsuspecting victims. Soon a group of Reichsbanner men appeared, easily outnumbered by six to one, and were set upon. Meanwhile, a second group consisting of Iron Front members arrived on the scene but, instead of coming to their comrades' aid, kept a safe distance and hurled nothing other than abuse at the Nazis.[89]

This lack of resolve evoked contempt for the SPD among Nazi militants and made them easy targets in the battle for the streets.[90] One by one SPD neighborhood taverns were forced to close down and, with them, the SPD's presence in the public domain.[91] Thus, not only marginal wards were lost, but, even in established strongholds such as ward 77 in Ottensen, votes drifted to the KPD *and* the NSDAP.

Electoral successes for the KPD and NSDAP merely raised the political stakes and intensified the conflict over territory—especially as the Nazis were making serious inroads into the vote in the Altstedt by 1932 and so challenging traditional left-wing hegemony. In order to sustain their electoral success in this area the Nazis had to establish a physical presence. By the same token the Communists knew that, to retain their credibility with the people of the Altstadt, they had to defend "their" territory.

As we have observed, this area stretching roughly from the Allee to the Altona fish docks was covered by a dense network of Communist cells. The party offices were located in the Große Johannisstraße; the *Korkenzieher* tavern at the corner of Schauenburgerstraße, served the party organization; the paramilitary organizations, the Rote Marine and Roter Jungsturm, met at Brandt's tavern in the Große Bergstraße; a platoon of the illegal Red Front Fighters' League was also based in the backrooms of Paul Rodegast's small bar in the Lohmühlenstraße; while Durbahn's tavern, at the corner of Schauenburgerstraße and Unzerstraße, functioned as an information bureau. Otto Kahn's bar in the Breitestraße, like that of Durbahn, was the regular haunt of Communist functionaries and local prostitutes.[92] In the crisis year of 1932 the southern district of the Altstadt proved especially troublesome to the Nazis.

In particular, Altona's state prosecutor recalled in 1933 how the area of the fish market,

> which stretches from south of Breitestraße to the Elbe, especially the streets Gr. Fischerstraße, Sandberg, Dreyerstraße and Vossensstraße, was an area of the city where members of the Communist Party or persons who sympathized with this Party had the upper hand over their political opponents. Hence one also found here strong bases of those organizations which, with a more or less close connection, supported the aims of the KPD.[93]

Trouble started in earnest in 1932 when two Communist taverns were taken over by the Nazis. These were Max Mai's tavern on the corner of Weidenstraße and Schauenburgerstraße and the tavern managed by Rosa Erdmann in the Breitestraße, another meetingplace for local Communists and the base for another local Communist sports club, barely a stone's throw from Kahn's.

Sometime in the spring of 1932 Rosa Erdmann's husband, described as an "educated and older man" with a "nationalist point of view," took over the running of the tavern at number 155 Breitestraße. Very soon he had driven out Communist customers and the members of the sports club.[94] Naturally, Erdmann's attitude and behavior did not provoke a friendly response in the neighborhood. There was widespread antipathy toward him, which the Communist leadership felt compelled to address. The metamorphosis of Erdmann's tavern from a Communist hangout into a nationalist den directly challenged Communist hegemony in the area.

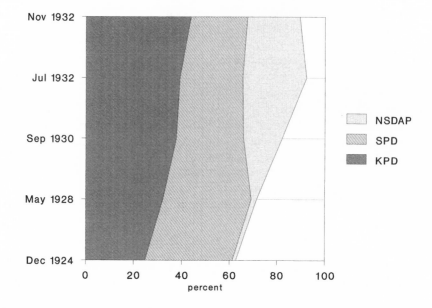

Fig. 12.   Contested Fischmarkt (electoral wards 1–7)

A relentless wave of petty harassment against Erdmann and his customers, which culminated in pistol shots being fired through the doorway,
led to the establishing of the tavern as a SS base in the summer months.
Not surprisingly,

> from the moment when the National Socialists turned up in Erd-
> mann's tavern, the attacks against it by political opponents increased.
> . . . The unconcealed efforts of the communists were obviously aimed
> either at wearing down Erdmann by constant attacks and harassment
> or at driving the SS from the tavern. The leadership of the KPD felt it
> was unbearable and dangerous for their survival in the area con-
> cerned if it came to the National Socialists remaining permanently in
> the tavern.[95]

Indeed, the headquarters of the Altstadt's illegal Red Front Fighters'
League was situated in the same area.[96] Therefore, Erdmann's tavern
posed a dangerous challenge that had to be met. The Communist leadership had little choice but to "smoke out the murderous SS-pest" from the
area.[97] The positive election results in November signaled to the KPD that

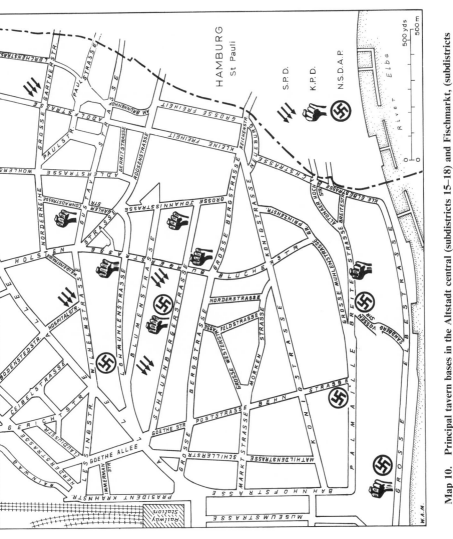

Map 10. Principal tavern bases in the Altstadt central (subdistricts 15–18) and Fischmarkt, (subdistricts 1–10), ca. 1932

it had a mandate to expel the Nazis from the Altstadt. But the party was also preoccupied with the tragic outcome of another attempt at expulsion of a Nazi base in the Weidenstraße, and it is possible that this postponed drastic action for the moment.

Yet the discovery of the corpse of a local man thought to be a Communist the following month galvanized the party into action. It was claimed that the dead man, Witt, had been shot in the back by SS men operating from Erdmann's tavern before being dumped nearby in the Kirchenstraße. An attack against the tavern was arranged for the evening of 22 December, during a regular *Sturm* social. Over the course of that day special squads of the Red Front Fighters' League, so-called Feuergruppen, from Hamburg-Eimsbüttel, were moved into the area together with units from the Red Youth Troop (Roter Jungsturm). They were placed in safehouses throughout the district to await the attack scheduled for 10 P.M. In the meantime other RFB units from Ottensen and street and house cells of the Antifa were alerted in case fighting escalated. The attack went ahead, slightly delayed due to a last-minute hitch in communications. The snipers fired over sixty rounds into the tavern, causing extensive property damage, but, fortunately for the SS men present, there was negligible physical harm.[98]

Although the Communists failed to dislodge the Nazis from Erdmann's tavern, the incident revealed the depth of local support for Communist fighters. The Nazis were, of course, incensed by the attack, as too was Dr. Diefenbach, the nationalist commissarial chief of police.[99] He recommended to the authorities in Berlin that a large reward be advertised in order to secure information and arrests of the Communists involved. The sum of money settled on was 1,000 reichsmark. The Altstadt's residents usually welcomed any opportunity to come by money, by whatever means. Yet for nearly a year, long after the Communist organizations had been effectively driven underground, police and courts came up against a solid wall of silence in the Altstadt.[100]

Mai's tavern was properly named "Zur Muhle," but, because it was the haunt of local Communists and the headquarters of the local youth sport club, *Rote Fichte,* it was widely known as "Zur *Roten* Muhle." When the "Red Mill" changed its color to brown in September it too drew the anger of the local population and Communist leaders. The Depression had taken its toll on business and on the health of seventy-year-old Max Mai. He succumbed to an offer from a certain Max Riedel, who guaranteed to fill the tavern regularly with a financially buoyant clientele under his stewardship.[101] Riedel's new clientele turned out to be Nazis. And straightaway Mai's Saloon became an active base for the SA in the central Altstadt. It was clear to local residents that the October tide of Nazi violence in the vicinity was being orchestrated from this tavern.

On becoming a SA-*Heim,* the tavern was subjected by local (mostly youthful) activists to unremitting attacks, albeit of a minor nature. Because this did not deter the Nazis, the leadership of the Red Front Fighters' League decided to close down the base permanently. The green light for a major action against the tavern came a week after the November elections. The KPD had done exceptionally well throughout the city, registering strong increases, while Nazi votes fell. In this neighborhood, however, the electoral status quo remained static, with Communists, Socialists, and Nazis maintaining more or less their July levels. It is likely that the overall good result in the Altstadt, coupled with the need to break the political impasse in this neighborhood, signaled to the local Communist leadership that the time had come to move against the tavern.

Once again the special units of the so-called Feuergruppen were mobilized from Hamburg-Eimsbüttel and the Altstadt and brought to nearby safehouses on the evening of 18 November, a Friday. The attack was set for 10 P.M. At that precise moment a disturbance was caused in some neighboring streets in order to divert the attention of the police on duty outside the tavern, whereupon shots rained into the establishment. The gun battle was brief but caused considerable damage to the interior of the premises. Neither side reported injuries, but there was a tragic consequence. A twelve-year-old boy, Hans Graack, who lived at number 50 Schauenburgerstraße, was killed in the crossfire. Each side blamed the other for the boy's death.[102]

The tragedy provoked parents and teachers from the school to call for a boycott until something was done about the tavern. A proposed strike and protest for Monday was prohibited by the police but supported by the SPD and the KPD, who jointly called for the closure of the tavern and the expulsion of the SA men from the area. In a council meeting the following Thursday, Brauer led a council motion, carried only by the majority vote of the SPD and KPD, urging Diefenbach to take action against the tavern.

> We have had a number of letters of protest from citizens, parents, teachers, from the area around Schauenburgerstraße, Weidenstraße, Bürgerstraße, etc., from which the following conclusions can be drawn: the SA-base in May's [*sic*] tavern . . . has obviously become a trouble spot of the first order for the local population. Following the appearance of the SA troops, which are based there, clashes have frequently occurred in the vicinity of the tavern. . . . Because until now . . . such unrest has never happened . . . there can be no doubt that only the accommodation of the *Stürme* in the tavern can have caused the unrest among the local population.[103]

Diefenbach refrained from taking action. He saw the problem in the presence of the KPD and not the SA, in spite of his own officers' report that the fatal shot almost certainly came from the direction of the tavern.[104] Diefenbach was not alone in his view. While Socialists and Communists were organizing their protest, a counterprotest was also being got up. Indeed, the incident illustrates the relationship between the strategy of the Nazis and the social and political needs of some sections of Altona's middle classes for protection from the Left.

The protest was organized by a group of middle-class parents from the area, some of whose children attended the same school. This group styled itself as "Unpolitical Christian Parents" and was led by Oberzollinspektor Thiele.[105] The content of their protest reveals the thoughts and mood of this mainly silent section of residents in the Altstadt. Thiele wrote to the *Regierungspräsident* in early December complaining about the joint strike protest by the SPD and KPD and expressed the view that the physical and moral danger to the children of the Altstadt was to be found in the two working-class parties, and not in the NSDAP or SA.

There was, in the group's eyes, a struggle between the forces of law and order and those of disorder for

> anyone who is privy to [local] knowledge knows that the true reason for the protest is political: namely a power struggle between the communists and the police over the closure of the SA tavern, and that the supposed danger the tavern poses to the children is only a cover for this.[106]

As far as Thiele and his friends were concerned, the real "disturbers of the peace" were the Socialists and Communists, who had to be met with firm action on the part of the authorities. As Thiele made clear, "unpolitical Christian parents could no longer be held responsible for sending their children to school in an area surrendered to communist terror."[107]

Yet the police authorities seemed to offer little protection. Indeed, to many of Altona's middle classes the police appeared either emasculated or politically partisan, from the top to the lower ranks. Altona's police chief, Otto Eggerstedt, was a prominent member of the SPD.[108] And, assuming the election results throughout the period are a useful indicator, the bulk of the police also were supporters of the SPD. In the Viktoria Barracks in electoral ward 72, where the police were billeted, the SPD took between 60 and 70 percent of the vote in 1932, and the NSDAP around 20 and 25 percent. Thus, as Altona's *Mittelstand* felt themselves increasingly exposed to Communist activity at street level, with little police protection they sought protection in the presence of the SA on the streets of the Altstadt—and looked forward to the day when the Nazis would reclaim the streets for them.

Streets and Democracy Collide

Germans experienced the last months of the Weimar Republic with a sense of deepening crisis. The country plunged further into social and economic distress, and, as we have seen, this was accompanied by a rising tide of political violence.[109] The July elections proved to be the catalyst for the worst violence on Germany's streets since the upheavals of the revolutionary period. In Prussia there were an estimated 461 incidents of violent clashes resulting in 82 deaths during June and July.[110] Many of these casualties resulted from the murderous street battles provoked by the Nazis as they staged so-called *Werbemärsche* (propaganda marches) through mainly working-class districts of towns and cities. The list of casualties grew longer as the Reichstag election of 31 July 1932 drew closer.

For example, on 8 July, a Friday, residents in Altona found themselves at the mercy of the Brownshirts when the local and regional NSDAP decided to stage a propaganda march through the city. At least a thousand stormtroopers took part, the majority of them bussed in from neighboring Hamburg and Schleswig-Holstein. The police were easily outnumbered and failed to control the marchers. Disturbances quickly broke out at a number of places as passersby, thought to be Socialists or Communists, were subjected to assault. At the main railway station, for instance, a Reichsbanner man was beaten up. The perpetrators were chased off by the police, only to regroup on the corner of Barnerstraße and Bahrenfelderstraße, outside Roos's tavern, which had been the scene of a confrontation a month earlier. As soon as they had gathered in sufficient numbers, they smashed the windows of Roos's tavern and of the Socialist cooperative shop, Produktion, opposite. Later, members of the Socialist youth organization were picked on, and that evening SA men armed with leather belts and buckles drove through the streets of Steenkamp looking for victims. Only at this late point in the day did the police manage to reassert control before any further damage was caused.[111]

That incident produced sore heads but no deaths, but the atmosphere was highly charged by events taking place elsewhere. On the following Sunday, 10 July, street battles occurred in a number of cities throughout the reich, claiming at least eleven lives. The political situation in Schleswig-Holstein was particularly brittle.[112] In Eckernförde Nazis attacked the offices of the Socialist trade union and murdered a local official.[113] Therefore, by 17 July tensions were running high. Although the context of Altona's "Bloody Sunday" was thus provided by the general political violence sweeping Germany, its quintessence is to be found in local conditions and conflicts, including the social attitudes of the police authorities toward the people of the "Abruzzenviertel."

The march on 17 July represented to the Altona SA a moment of triumph, when they would parade with impunity through the Altstadt. As one marcher later recalled, "we had marched through Red Altona without backing out."[114] But, in order to do so, Altona's Nazis needed the massed support of their comrades from neighboring Hamburg, Schleswig-Holstein, and Lower Saxony. In all they totaled around seven thousand after assembling during the course of the early afternoon at the Palmaille and Marktstraße, on the district boundary dividing Ottensen and Altstadt.[115]

Although for the greater part of those who took part in the march, the day seems to have passed without incident, throughout the afternoon reports of scuffles and minor clashes between Nazis, police, and onlookers were registered. And here and there police either cleared or closed off particular streets, such as Breitestraße and Kirchenstraße, or fired warning shots into the air, demanding that windows should be shut. Thus, before the main street battle began at 4:55 P.M. tensions were running high.[116]

The Altstadt was already in a state of high alarm in the days immediately preceding 17 July. The Communist leadership concentrated its forces here. Hundreds of local people were mobilized, mostly members of the street cells of the Antifa who were urged to be present on the streets in order to give the Nazis a hostile, though not necessarily violent, reception. Many local residents did not need prompting. A large number of Communists and sympathizers were also brought in from Hamburg, many of whom were youths.[117] Armed with staves, they gathered in the back terraces of the Christian-, Große Marien-, Große Johannis-, Denner-, Friedrichbader- and Schauenburgerstraße. Small groups of Kampfbund members and Red Front Fighters were positioned close to the Communist Party offices. Meanwhile, hardened and armed cadres from the three platoons of the Altona Red Front Fighters were also to be found in the various party taverns.[118] Communists and their sympathizers later contended that there had never been a plan actually to initiate an attack against the Nazis. Rather, the emphasis had been on defense and not attack.[119] But, even if an attack had been in the offing, in the event, unplanned, spontaneous clashes prevented the various teams of Communist fighters from carrying out a coordinated action.

The fighting that broke out at 4:55 P.M. on the crossroads of Große Marienstraße, Große Johannisstraße, and Schauenburgerstraße had been preceded by earlier attacks in the Kirchenstraße and at Grund, and they all involved the same SA *Sturm,* namely, the Altona Sturm 2/31. The Altstadt crowds singled out this troop in particular, known as the "Richter Sturm," named after its leader, the owner of a local bakery and a particularly aggressive Nazi, Hubert Richter, who believed he could "turn Marxists into German workers."[120] At that time the Richter Sturm was based in the Altstadt at Flath's tavern in Lornsenplatz and had been responsible for many acts of terror against local Communists and their sympathizers. It apparently was also successful at recruiting members from the fringes of the working class.[121] Thus, it was a threat in duplicate. The exclusive singling out of the Altstadt SA for rough treatment explains the relatively peaceful progress of the march for many of the non-Altona Nazis.

The Richter Sturm was positioned at the rear of the first section of marchers, consisting of about a thousand stormtroopers and SS, mostly from the greater Hamburg area.[122] As the troop neared the Kirchenstraße, the police reported that the waiting crowd surged against the chains dividing pavement and road in anger at the taunts coming from these Altona Nazis. Some of them showed off and called to individual residents to remove flags from the windows.[123] They sang: "We'll hang Karl Liebknecht from a tree," and made signs of throat cutting to the crowd.

The crowd responded by yelling "Red Front!" "Heil Moscow!" "Fascist horde!" and "Röhm*linge!*" This verbal exchange produced a fierce skirmish as the SA broke rank to chase off the protesters. The police were virtually powerless. Fritz Schwennsen, the Altona *Sturmbannführer,* later reported that the SA only did what the police were unable to in order to clear the streets. Similar incidents recur in the extensive records of the day's events but only in connection with Richter's *Sturm.*

As the Nazis crossed into the central districts of the Altstadt via the Große Bergstraße into Große Johannisstraße, they noticed that the number of onlookers was relatively thin on the ground. Yet, as they neared the crossroads of Große Johannisstraße and Schauenburgerstraße, the crowd thickened, pressing in on the marchers. The atmosphere was both oppressive and bewildering to the SA men. They had marched into the heart of the Communist stronghold, and, although they were many in number, there was no guarantee of safety, in spite of the police presence. Schwennsen observed:

> At first the crowd had been relatively calm. . . . When Sturm II appeared a dreadful shouting and howling started up and at the same time the crowd advanced. . . . The consequence was that from our side a counteraction was launched. . . . Our men partly took off their shoulder-straps or used their fists to force back the spectators.[124]

What Schwennsen failed to tell the police was that his men were singing, "And when Jewish blood splashes from the knife / then things will improve!"[125] and this acted as the catalyst for the crowd's anger. What followed is barely describable because of the utter confusion. The SA attempt

to again clear the streets was the signal for shooting to start; several people were fatally shot, including two SA men.[126] Eyewitnesses spoke of a
deafening noise and panic as Nazis and onlookers fled the bullets and
careening horses of the police, who cut through the crowds in an attempt
to get the marchers out of the danger zone. This clash opened the
floodgates for roughly a full half-hour's indiscriminate shooting in the
compact area between Schauenburgerstraße, Lohmühlenstraße, Schumacherstraße, and Kleine Freiheit (see map 11).

The firepower was concentrated in the hands of police detachments
from Hamburg and Altona, since the Nazis had been hurried from the
scene in the first ten minutes of trouble, and alleged Communist snipers
could not be found. Indeed, most of the eighteen victims were bystanders
and were killed *after* the ending of this incident during the pacification of
the Altstadt, which lasted into the early hours of the morning. The autopsy
reports show that nearly all were killed by weapons belonging to the police
and security forces.[127]

Nevertheless, a picture of the rule of law besieged by Altona's "unruly
Volk" was painted in official reports.[128] The police claimed that officers
had come under a barrage of sniper fire from the rooftops and upper windows of the houses lining the narrow streets through which the Nazis
marched.[129] The alleged Communist gunmen had gotten away because of
the aid they received from the largely sympathetic local population.[130] The
death toll at the end of the day was sixteen people killed, two more were to
die in the following days, and around one hundred more had suffered
wounds of one kind or another. Nearly all of them had been bystanders
and were residents of the Altstadt.[131]

The Restoration of Authority

The day also produced one other victim: democracy itself. Altona's
Bloody Sunday shook the republic to its foundations. In the public
domain politicians and the media spoke openly of a "civil war situation"
and depicted the state as endangered from the combined forces of communism and social anarchy.[132] Conservatives in the federal government took
this as an opportunity to accuse the Prussian government of failing to
guarantee the security of the nation in order to implement plans for a cen-
tralization of powers. Subsequently, on 20 July Braun's caretaker government was forcibly removed by von Papen.[133]

The idea of an insurgent working class that was both insubordinate
and contemptuous of authority, seeking to openly wage war on state and
society, was firmly planted in the mind of Diefenbach, who was appointed
commissarial chief of police in Altona for eight critical months, from 24

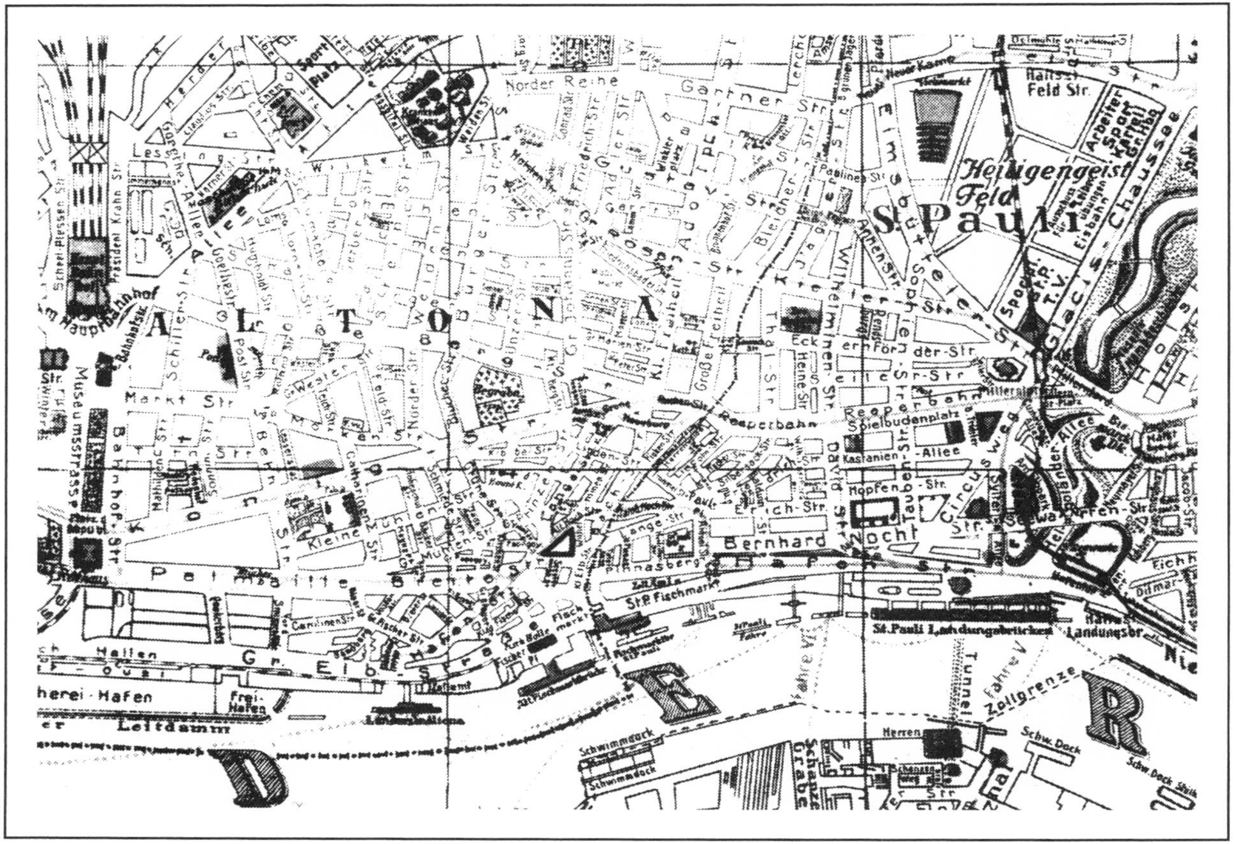

Map 11.   Area of "Bloody Sunday" street battle

July 1932 to 28 March 1933.[134] In his view the Communists and local population had not acted in self-defense but, instead, had set out deliberately
to "strike a blow at authority in order to cause the state to totter."[135]

Even though some Nazis may have felt that they had achieved their
goal on that Sunday, it was clear that their hasty retreat from the Altstadt
had shown that the area was a citadel that could not be easily taken. Both
election results from July and November revealed the extent of working-
class solidity. In July the NSDAP consolidated its primary position,
gained in the Landtag elections in April, with a third of the vote in the Altstadt. In the districts affected by Bloody Sunday, however, the Nazis
achieved well below their Altstadt average. Meanwhile, the KPD nearly
doubled their Altstadt average.

Thus, in some respects the taming of the Altstadt remained unfinished
business until after 30 January, when Hitler headed the government of
Germany, and from February, when Nazi violence was legalized after the
SA was accorded the status of ancillary police.[136] With the full weight of
the state behind them Hitler's Brownshirts were now in a stronger position
to terrorize the Left into an electoral defeat. With full support from the
police contingents of stormtroopers and SS placed the Altstadt under a
permanent state of siege.

The Reichstag and municipal elections held, respectively, on 5 and 12
March brought together for the last time in Altona the politics of the street
and the ballot box. Voter participation on 5 March remained as high as it
had been in 1932, at 86 percent. A high turnout was evident in the working-class wards of the Altstadt and of Ottensen, and as a consequence the
results were far from satisfactory for the Nazis.[137]

Nonetheless, after a demonstration outside the *Rathaus* to celebrate
the general result, Nazis and Stahlhelm staged an ostensibly spontaneous
march through the Communist heartlands of the Altstadt, this time
around the Gerritstraße area in subdistrict 11. Violence flared up after
Nazis fired warning shots into the air.[138] A week later there were minor
skirmishes as police and Nazis cordoned off streets and checked identity
papers and carried out searches of passersby. These actions were timed to
coincide with the municipal elections set for 12 March. The Nazis had not
yet taken full power locally and were particularly concerned about those
slum quarters, such as the Fischmarkt area, where neighborhood-based
resistance was not yet broken. With police and judicial backing the Nazis
swept these neighborhoods looking for known Communist activists. In the
face of this, the remnants of the Communist Party leadership went underground. Those who remained on the street were arrested and taken into
"protective custody."[139]

These tactics paid off. Generally, voter participation in Altona fell

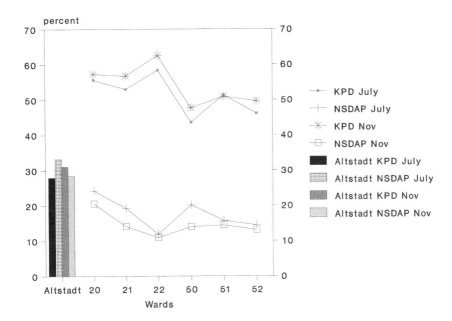

Fig. 13.   **KPD and NSDAP votes in the "Bloody Sunday" area of the Altstadt (July and Nov. 1932)**

significantly, to 73 percent. But in the Altstadt it dropped to 67 percent. From 5 March the combined Socialist and Communist vote in the Altstadt had fallen by nearly eighteen thousand votes, to fifty thousand. Meanwhile, in conservative middle-class districts of the city participation rates and votes for the Nazis soared above the city average.[140]

The night before the election, however, Altona's Nazi leaders were still uncertain about whether or not their intimidation of the Left at street level would have a successful outcome. Therefore, in order to secure power in the *Rathaus* they gave the cue for a "seizure of power" during the dawn hours of 12 March. The Altona *Rathaus* and other municipal buildings were occupied by the SS and SA under the command of the former Free Corps officer Paul Moder. Reflecting on the arduous trek to the *Rathaus* via the streets of the Altstadt, an old SS man recalled,

> One has to put oneself into our position: when one has been on the streets for so long—and the political struggle throughout Germany was partly fought on the streets—. . . and finally in one's own home town, had seized political power . . . that is to say, the city hall, then one was well-pleased . . . it was worth the effort, wasn't it?[141]

CHAPTER 7

"Under the Sign of the Swastika!": The Divided *Volksgemeinschaft,* 1933–1937

The German people have found their way back to their Fatherland, to their *Heimat,* to their ancestral home.

—*Emil Brix[1]*

On 11 March the Prussian Interior Ministry in Berlin received a telegram from the deputy leader of the NSDAP of the *Gau* Schleswig-Holstein, Emil Brix. It read:

Absolute law and order prevails. Altona breathes freely. Our actions are known to the police president, Dr. Diefenbach and the commander of the police, and are being tacitly approved.[2]

The actions Brix spoke of were the illegal occupation under force of arms of the city hall and other public buildings by SA and SS detachments under SS-Brigade leader Paul Moder and the arrests of leading public figures and political activists. Some key personalities, including Max Brauer, as well as several well-known Communist leaders, were able to escape the Nazi net, having already left the city or gone into hiding. By midnight on the day before the municipal elections, the swastika was hoisted over public buildings.[3]

Under the heading "The Reckoning: On the Putsch in the City Hall" the Kröger brothers printed an ecstatic article in their newspaper, the *Norddeutsche Nachrichten,* celebrating this local seizure of power. They cheered how "the red November betrayers of the people from the ignominious period of 1918 are now locked in the very same cells in which the young Germany had been incarcerated for years on end." The editors ranted against the internationalism of the Weimar regime, reminding their readers that "your roots as a people are grounded alone and incontrovertibly in your national traditions and in the obedience to the German nation." They concluded by cautioning their readers:

> Altona is now free. Therefore, each Altona Volksgenosse must make sure at tomorrow's election that this brave and right step of the entire people will be confirmed. Whoever, again this time, gives their vote to one of the red betrayers of the people, who until yesterday sat in the red *Rathaus,* shame themselves and their children.[4]

As with the reich elections a week before, the local elections on 12 March gave the Nazis some satisfaction (46.7 percent) but no overall majority. The combined vote of the working-class parties lay at nearly 8 percent below that of the Nazis. Polling had been low, and participation rates fell considerably in the Altstadt wards. Many voters, especially Communist sympathizers, simply kept away, either in protest or from fear of being seized by the stormtroopers.[5]

The chief task facing Hitler's government of national renewal, as it styled itself, was the restoration of stability and order in place of chaos and lawlessness—unity and pride for the *Vaterland* in place of social division and national shame. For the Nazis and conservative critics of Weimar's parliamentary system, the roots of decay, social anarchy, and financial mismanagement were to be found in the administration and political culture of the city. The devolution of power to the municipal sphere in 1918, its political democratization and corresponding internationalism, had produced a nation of *heimatlos* Germans disassociated from one another.

The Nazi mission in 1933 was to reforge the nation by first reconstructing the *Heimat,* for this was the "community in which the individual lives and from where he grows into the totality of the people."[6] The basic principle of the reconstruction of state and society, however, was different to the republican project of 1918. Society continued to be likened to the human body: the state and its various administrative apparatuses, including the municipalities, were likened to the organisms, muscles, and arteries of the body. But the Nazi party was the soul. And, because it was the soul, it was the "motor which drove the entire life of the people and thereby directs the state apparatus."[7] This was, broadly speaking, the conceptual basis of the *Volksgemeinschaft.*

This idea of the *Volksgemeinschaft,* embedded in the local community, or *Heimat,* converged with the older conservative ideal of the community as an ordered place under the aegis of an impartial and authoritarian local self-government. Altona's Nazis thus saw their mission in the city as the restoration of "the basic principles of Prussian thrift and inner cleanliness in its administration . . . and culture."[8]

Yet the return to this Prussian mode of local self-government drove a wedge fairly quickly between the self-styled representatives of the people (as the Nazis constantly referred to themselves) and the people themselves, since the administration of public affairs increasingly took place out of view. The result of this process was captured in 1944 by Carl Goerdeler, the former conservative mayor of Leipzig, who had initially favored turning the hands of the clock back to the days of *Honoratioren* local government. He noted in a tone of regret, "Communal life is dried up, self-government is dead, the citizens hardly know the name of their mayor let alone those councillors appointed by the party who thrive in secrecy."[9] This chapter sheds some light on the development and meaning of this process in the sphere of Altona's everyday life.

Politics and Administration

After the elections on 12 March Altona's council was dominated by the NSDAP, which, with thirty seats, now enjoyed an uncontested majority, especially after the ten elected Communist councillors were taken into "protective custody." In the following weeks the six councillors from the nationalist factions on the council (one National Bürgertum and five Kampffront Schwarz-Weiß-Rot) disbanded and crossed the chamber to join the Nazis, further isolating the sixteen members of the SPD faction. The level of demoralization among this group is perhaps reflected in the resignations of three of their number in April, two of whom were women, including Frau Deppe, the long-standing councillor. Their places were taken by three colleagues until the summer, when the entire faction was removed from the council chamber in the wake of the Reich Emergency Decree of 7 July and which was confirmed by a further decree of the Prussian Interior Ministry ten days later.[10]

Whereas before March 1933 the social composition of the city council had by and large reflected the social spectrum in Altona, after the purging of the council between March and July, it became predominantly *mittelständisch,* narrowly representing local property, commercial, and manufacturing interests.[11] Even the ambition in 1934 to create a *Heimat* of guild corporatism whereby each *Ratsherr* (as councillors were now called) represented one of the city's main occupational trades remained a stubborn illusion.[12]

The Nazi takeover of power in Altona saw the return to politics of men who previously had been banished to the margins of public life under

Brauer's regime. One of these was Dr. Heinrich Saß, who lived in the Friedensallee in Ottensen and who had formerly taught at the Reform Realgymnasium situated in the Königstraße. Saß had fallen victim to cutbacks in the administration when he was dismissed at the age of thirty-three on 1 May 1924, after barely two years in his post. He claimed he had been singled out for dismissal because of his *völkisch* views, which were well-known in the school. Three years later, in September 1927, he joined the NSDAP. In 1933 he received the portfolio for education and cultural affairs as well as responsibility for the Hitler Youth.[13]

Another Nazi to experience a favorable turn in his fortunes was Wilhelm Sieh, who we encountered in chapter 2. Sieh's faithful service to the movement had been first rewarded in January 1931 when he was appointed *Gau* treasurer for Schleswig-Holstein. Now in 1933 he was made *Gau* inspector, and two years later, in September 1935, he was elevated to deputy *Gau* leader. His private career also benefited from the change-over. One month after the March elections, on 11 April, he was appointed company attorney of the Hamburg Elevated Railway Company.[14] The experiences of both Saß and Sieh were typical of a number of Altona's new *Ratsherren* in 1933.[15]

If the Weimar years had represented the hegemony of the *Großstadt* and its "Marxist" politicians over the suburban *Heimat,* then arguably the advent of the Third Reich saw the triumph of the suburbs over the urban center. The removal of Brauer's regime meant that the leading men from Altona's incorporated districts now reemerged from their territorial borderlands to occupy positions of influence and power, giving them the opportunity to redefine the political center in a way previously denied them. Indeed, easily the majority of *Ratsherren* and Nazis occupying leading positions after 1933, such as the district and *Gau* speakers Dr. Hermann Schäffer from Am Klingenberg in Blankenese and Dr. Rudolph, from the Lindenallee in Groß Flottbek, lived or had lived in the suburbs and shared an aversion to the *concept* of Altona as a *Großstadt.*[16]

For example, the former parish leader of Stellingen, Emil Rüss, had joined the NSDAP on 1 December 1931, at the age of fifty-three. His move was rewarded in 1933 with an honorary senatorship, and he was appointed to sit on the district party court (Kreisgericht). A fellow traveler who joined the party in May 1932, the fifty-two-year-old former head of Nienstedten, Otto Grotkop, who had vigorously opposed incorporation in 1927, now became a full senator with responsibility for police matters. Wilhelm Schumann, the forty-year-old former army lieutenant and onetime leader of Eidelstedt, took charge of welfare in 1933 and, because of his experience as a tax clerk, was appointed to the city's finance committee. Schumann also seems to have joined the NSDAP in 1932, making a modest career in the party as well.[17]

Apart from these members of the Nazi Party, the city's new administration also included men who could be loosely described as the "unpolitical" politicals, who believed in the virtue of a strong state to protect their interests. After what appeared to them as years of turmoil, they welcomed the prospect of returning to what they understood as the ordered city. Max Harry, a prominent local baker of some substance, had spent a lifetime in the service of his hometown. He was an active local politicians who made the journey from the liberal party to the DVP and the unity lists. Finally, in 1933, as sole representative on the council of the National Citizenry (Nationales Bürgertum), he crossed the floor to join the Nazis.

Along with its reduction to a narrow social grouping and to an all-male chamber, the council ceased to function in a meaningful way, after it voted on 6 July 1933 to transfer its serious business to a three-man committee composed exclusively of Nazi financial experts.[18] This, coupled with a decline in the frequency of council meetings, brought the parliamentary procedure, in decay since the fiscal crisis of 1931–32, effectively to an end.[19] Indeed, the vote to remove the endorsement of policy decisions from the council was facilitated by the Municipal Finances Decree of 2 November 1932. According to Brix, this was a fitting end to local democratic control, "since this had no place in the Third Reich."[20]

The emasculation of local democracy continued with two further pieces of legislation, one passed at the end of 1933 and the other at the beginning of 1935, both designed to strengthen executive powers. The Prussian Municipal Ordinance passed in mid-December 1933 and came into force on 1 January; it stipulated that the lord mayor, together with a small number of *appointed* councillors, should run the daily affairs of the city. In February councillors were renamed "Ratsherren," an old-fashioned designation, and their number reduced to fifteen.[21] The Reich Municipal Ordinance of 1 January 1935 raised to twenty the number of *Ratsherren* but removed from the assembly its legal status as a legislative body. In this respect the legislation of January 1935 not only sanctioned a development fully under way since 1933 but connected to conservative ideals on the organization of state-societal relations that predated Nazi power.[22]

A new *Magistrat* of ten members was elected on 13 April and included two Social Democrats, Paul Nevermann (who, after 1945, was to become a deputy mayor of Hamburg) and Wilhelm Sievert.[23] They were both immediately relieved from their positions by Brix, using powers invested in him as commissarial mayor. Their protests were of no avail, for Brix is alleged to have exclaimed: "we (Nazis) are not here as guests of the *Mag-*

istrat, but as executors of the people. The *Magistrat* only exists *pro forma*[24]—a point underlined by the Prussian Municipal Ordinance. As a result of this law, the *Magistrat* was renamed "Gemeinderat," its size reduced to seven members, including the mayor and two honorary members. Unlike the senators of the Weimar period, the Beigeordnete, as they were now called, acted only in an advisory capacity.[25]

The city's bureaucracy was also purged of officials considered too close to Weimar republicanism. In the course of 1933 and 1934, 52 civil servants, 114 white-collar employees, and 57 manual workers were removed from municipal employment under the Law for the Restoration of the Professional Civil Service, or approximately 8, 9, and 5 percent, respectively.[26] There were obvious candidates for dismissal, such as Brauer's close party friend and senator, August Kirch, and the liberals, Deputy Mayor Ebert, Senator Schöning, and the city architect and chief planning officer, Gustav Oelsner. But the net also widened to include a number of police officers and office managers throughout the administration who were deemed politically unreliable.[27] Not only Social Democrats and their allies fell foul of the Nazis. Among those removed was also the appointee of the von Papen commissarial government in Prussia, police president Dr. Diefenbach, whose appointment had done so much to prepare the ground for the Nazi *Gleichschaltung.*[28]

Meanwhile, places were found for the Nazi party's unemployed *"alte Kämpfer,"* veterans of the years of struggle. In contrast to the overall trend showing a reduction in administrative personnel, the total number of "old fighters" in the city bureaucracy increased from 140 to 259 between March 1933 and the end of December 1935, equaling about 10 percent of all public employees by the latter date. Most of this group were accommodated in clerical posts, in which a doubling in number took place over the same period.[29]

The demands of a complex municipal system that often required an intimate knowledge of law and finance soon revealed the limitations of the new men in the *Rathaus.* The complaint by the Gauleitung of the Rheinpfalz, for example, that not a few of those willing to be pioneers in the reconstruction of a National Socialist community "continue to be mostly newcomers who have not yet sufficiently grasped the character of municipal politics"[30] was probably true for Altona too. They found themselves lost in the labyrinthine world of municipal office work as a result of poor training or lack of education.[31] And this extended to the top of the power structure in Altona.

In spite of vocational school and his qualifications as a bank clerk and a one-week training course on municipal administration in December 1933, it is doubtful if Brix had any expertise in the workings of public administration, especially where it concerned a *Großstadt* with a budget that ran into millions of reichsmark.[32] In order to avert possible financial chaos, a government counselor (*Regierungsrat*) with legal training, Dr. Hans Dehning, was seconded to Altona as deputy mayor and city treasurer. Thus, Dehning, who also lived in Blankenese, and who had been a party member since May 1932, oversaw the day-to-day management of Altona's administrative affairs. Meanwhile, Brix—who nevertheless retained final responsibility as *Oberbürgermeister*—slipped into the role of Altona's own "little Hitler," in "accordance with the penetration of National Socialism of the entire state system."[33]

Hopes

Brix had defined municipal renewal in terms of a "return to financial probity," but this was going to be a difficult task, given the scale of the financial crisis in Altona and the generally poor economic climate. During the spring and summer of 1933 Altona's debt peaked at 148 million reichsmark, or a per capita burden of 525 reichsmark. It was to take two years for it to fall to around two-thirds of that figure.[34] The debt was not helped by the acute financial burden of welfare recipients, who constituted about 67 percent of the roughly 31,000 unemployed in January 1933, costing the city over 2.5 million reichsmark in June.[35] Altona's new masters thus faced the same crippling situation as their republican predecessors.

The first problem that needed to be addressed by Brix was that of mass unemployment. At the end of the first quarter of 1933 the registered unemployed in the city stood at 30,619. Measures to get the unemployed working again had met with limited success before 1933. Hitler's proclamation "Battle for Jobs" really got under way with the two Laws for the Reduction of Unemployment on 1 June and 21 September 1933 (the so-called Reinhardt Plans) and a number of additional measures intended to stimulate public works programs at local and regional level.[36] The Nazi leadership in Altona was thus able to revive flagging existing municipal works, setting up a Work Creation and Credit Advisory Office to supervise existing programs and to encourage private industry to participate in new schemes.[37] Meanwhile, the party instigated its own special employment drives ("Sonder-Aktionen") to get the jobless (mostly party comrades) back to work and, no doubt, to make good Nazi promises of deliverance from the crisis.[38]

Encouraged by a mixture of party rhetoric on the stimulation of the economy and party action in the area of reducing unemployment, many people saw an opportunity to regain employment after years of idleness. The Nazi authorities were deluged with letters from unemployed men,

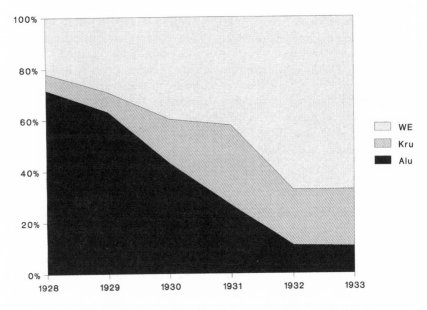

Fig. 14.   Distribution of unemployed in Altona by unemployment relief (31 Dec. 1928–31 Jan. 1933)

very often from nonmanual backgrounds, and frequently ordinary foot-soldiers of the Nazi movement, requesting intervention on their behalf in obtaining work or for small sums of money.[39] These requests, similar to the letters of complaint that besieged the Weimar authorities, reveal countless worlds of social conflicts and human misery. A forty-one-year-old waiter, Carl Rex of Wielandstraße, wrote to Kreisleiter Heinrich Piwitt in October 1933, complaining that his employer, "who claims to be a National Socialist, but who obviously does not know the meaning of the word," was trying to replace him with a much cheaper worker, an eighteen-year-old youth.[40] Rex, who had five small children, was eventually dismissed from Café Deutschland, near the railway station. He was fortunate, however, to be included in the first of many of party-instigated "special actions" to find work for the unemployed that October.[41]

The practice of dismissing older and more experienced workers in order to reduce the payroll had not been unusual in the Depression, but from 1933 it clashed terribly with the idea of a national healing and efforts to get Germany out of the crisis. The conflict of interest, as revealed by Rex's case, also showed the tension between the political rhetoric of the Nazi *Volksgemeinschaft* and the economic interests of individuals. This was clearly demonstrated to Brix and officials of the German Labor Front (Deutsche Arbeitsfront [DAF]) in the following case of the optical and precision instruments firm of Georg Butenschön in Bahrenfeld.[42]

Butenschön's business fortunes had suffered badly from the summer of 1931, since he had been forced to more or less bring his production of precision tools to a standstill. In his own words, he averted a complete collapse of his company by a mixture of personal "tenacity and sacrifice" and by branching out into the mass manufacture of glass for spectacles. He also got around the crisis by exploiting his work force. Butenschön employed two masters, four workmen (*Gesellen*), two female workers, and nineteen apprentices. Although he was manufacturing lenses, his firm was technically still part of the precision tools industry. Because of this he came into conflict with the German Metalworkers' Union (DMV) and, from 1933, with the German Labor Front over his failure to pay the rates agreed under collective bargaining. This agreement stipulated that workers receive an hourly rate of ninety-five pfennige. But Butenschön paid his four male workers half that, forty-seven pfennige, which he claimed was the going rate for unskilled work in the optical industry, and he steadfastly refused to pay more.

In order to avoid an arbitration court Butenschön dismissed the four men. The DAF approached Brix for assistance in an effort to get the men reinstated at the higher rate and to ensure that those apprentices, due to finish their training at Easter, would not be likewise dismissed. In contrast to Rex's case, Brix was prepared to enforce the Nazi's ideal of a people's community at the workplace. He wrote to Butenschön on the 23 March, politely insisting that he reinstate the four workmen at the higher rate and that measures be taken to ensure that any apprentices due to finish be retained.

For some, getting back to work was clearly the route to regaining a sense of citizenship. The fifty-year-old salesman (*Kaufmann*) Wilhelm Wenzel hoped that his appeal to the Work Creation Office in June 1934 would stem his family's declining fortunes. His three school-age children suffered for want of money, the two boys could not participate in the *Jungvolk,* and his wife had become ill due to the poor conditions of the smaller flat they had been forced to move into. He revealed in his letter how he had waited a long time for the opportunity to obtain work and now hoped that, under the job creation scheme, he would be able to get his former position back. He told the *Oberbürgermeister* that he had joined the NSDAP in July 1932 and, as a former war veteran (*Frontkämpfer*), was prepared to defend the Fatherland at any time. He was confident that his return to work would greatly facilitate his participation in the creation of the *Volksgemeinschaft.*[43]

Similarly, another man, Wolpert, solicited Brix's help in November 1934, recounting that, since being made unemployed in 1928, he had found only temporary work, mostly outdoor land schemes, under various municipal programs. He wanted a proper factory job so he could take care of his family independently instead of having to rely on the nineteen reichsmark welfare he received weekly. He was told to report to a local firm in January.[44]

Such cases, and there were many like these, reveal the great store of trust that was placed in the Nazi regime by their supporters and sympathizers among the *Mittelstand.* If Brix and his colleagues sometimes failed them, there might be disaffected voices but little likelihood of revolt.[45] The majority of unemployed was composed of the working class, however, and Brix and his party colleagues knew that one had to either reduce unemployment or face the prospect of a smoldering discontent that could ignite into Communist resistance to the regime.[46]

In the early autumn of 1934 Dr. Richard Bonne of Klein Flottbek felt moved to write to Brix on at least two occasions enclosing lists of long-term unemployed men with large families. He included brief descriptions of the ravages that enforced idleness and poverty visited upon the physical and spiritual health of husbands, wives, and children. A typical case, Bonne recounted, was that of

> Ernst Klitsch, 34 years old, Rapsweg 18. Construction worker, 3 children, 4 years unemployed. Worked for a few weeks and then became unemployed again, received an advance from the welfare [office], and through the repayments got into new debts. Upright, hard-working people. Very intelligent and able. Spirited. Developed muscular rheumatism in the trenches. He is highly recommended.[47]

Bonne also included youths in his lists, such as fifteen-year-old Ernst Sprenger, also of Rapsweg (incidentally, in one of the primitive "crate villages"—*Kistendörfer*—that had sprung up during the Depression to house poor families), who desperately wanted to learn a trade but was being pressed into signing on for clerical work. The boy had "fists like a bear and needed the physical exertion" of manual labor, according to Bonne. A common and deplorable phenomenon, Bonne complained, was the practice of doctors in the employment office who certified wives of the unemployed, who were "delicate and in poor health," as capable of working in the physically exacting fish-processing factories, "without any attention being paid to their bodily constitution."[48] Bonne reminded Brix that this was "against the will of our *Führer,*" since such factory work had a deleterious effect on the women's health (and thus indirectly attacked the procreative capacity of the reich). Instead, it should be given to their menfolk.[49]

TABLE 15.   Unemployment in Altona by Sector, Jan.–Mar. 1933

	M	F	Subtotals	% of Total
White-collar employees	2,410	965	3,375	(11.0)
Sales/office clerks	1,640	858		
Technical clerks	474	13		
Others	296	94		
Manual skilled/semiskilled	14,379	3,591	17,970	(58.7)
Forestry	600	42		
Iron/metal/engineering	5,266	175		
Machinists/stokers	154	—		
Quarrying	113	13		
Musical instruments	18	—		
Chemicals/asbestos	—	107		
Spinning	22	401		
Paper	47	187		
Leather/linoleum	157	12		
Wood/carpentry/joinery	1,453	90		
Food processing	865	1,416		
Clothing	438	313		
Construction	1,827	—		
Transport	2,495	33		
Catering/taverns	587	582		
Printing/photography	173	55		
Theater/film	—	19		
Hair	142	41		
Hygiene	22	105		
Manual unskilled	5,706	3,562	9,268	(30.3)
Domestics	—	2,275		
Quarrying	87	—		
Construction	1,013	—		
Iron/metal/engineering	322	25		
Wood/carpentry/joinery	134	39		
Food processing	232	125		
Spinning	96	40		
Others[a]	3,822	1,058		

Source: StAH 424–27 G8 Arbeitsmarktstatistik, Bestand an Arbeitslosen, n.d. I 1933, StJB Altona (1928), 123–25.

Note: Total unemployed = 30,619 (100 percent); male = 22,495 (73.5 percent); female = 8,124 (26.5 percent).

[a]Includes casual and harbor workers

Some of the cases Bonne reported included SA men and their families who, already ostracized from their neighbors because of their political beliefs, were also at risk of becoming alienated from National Socialism as a consequence of their plight. But clearly the majority of his clients came from either Communist or Socialist milieus. Bonne told Brix that he had personally corresponded with Hitler in 1931 about Communist patients who allegedly told him: "if Hitler gives us work and bread, we'll support him to a man. If he doesn't, then that'll be our chance, and we'll smash up everything." That was in 1931. Nearly four years later little appeared to have changed for many of these people. Therefore, Bonne counselled Brix:

> The power of our great *Führer* is already so secure that it cannot easily be overturned by a marxist revolt. [But] the fate of the Hohenzollerns in 1918 prove that one cannot and should not rely on the power of the bayonet.[50]

In Bonne's view the way for Brix to avert conflict and at the same time to strike a propaganda coup for the Nazi *Volksgemeinschaft* was to intercede on behalf of the unemployed, regardless of party affiliation. If work could be provided, especially among such families, then "a stream of new hope would be awakened in our people and in this way unending uncertainty and bitterness removed from wide sections of the population."[51] Brix saw the sense of this and responded positively.[52]

The degree to which Nazi efforts to reduce unemployment in Altona were generally successful is difficult to measure. In July 1935 the party in Altona instigated another special action to help place some of its unemployed comrades in a number of skilled jobs advertised by a local metal manufacturer.[53] A year later the party's district manager (*Kreisgeschäftsführer*), Eric Bannier, notified the various branches and offices of the party to inform "suitable party comrades" who were jobless that the city theater was looking for twenty stage extras (*Statisten*) at a payment of one mark per performance.[54] But these few efforts can have barely scratched the surface of unemployment and only seem to have been an attempt to placate the movement's rank and file.

And, while the numbers of the mass of unemployed did decrease statistically in the first two to three years of Nazi rule, this did not necessarily reflect their actual reintegration into the labor market. For instance, in March 1935 harbor workers were finally removed from the city's unemployment and welfare registers.[55] This sort of statistical sleight of hand repeated itself in news coverage of Altona's achievements in the "Battle for Jobs" since 1933. For example, in a short report in May 1935 praising the rapid inroads made into the columns of unemployed, the *Altonaer Nachrichten* simply excluded any mention of the welfare unemployed, who, at around 5,800, still made up the largest single group of unemployed.[56]

As we saw in chapter 3, pockets of extreme misery among unemployed families existed deep into the Third Reich and only became partially visible when highlighted by the likes of Dr. Bonne or when the miserable conditions of unemployment could be used to mobilize the idea of *Volksgemeinschaft,* as during the annual Winter Help programs, discussed later in this chapter.

Debtors and Creditors

In its annual report for 1933 the Chamber of Industry and Commerce welcomed in warm tones the "national" orientation of the new government and approvingly quoted the Nazi writer Dietrich Eckart: "Unshackled is the Reich, Fatherland, Life. And Free—is the World." For the chamber the references to "life" and "the world" related to the life and world of the economy.[57] Altona's new rulers faced not only the question of how to deal with the economic and financial crisis but, at the same time, one of how to meet the expectations of those citizens who had given their support to the Nazis. On coming to power, Brix had asserted that he would restore to public life in Altona Prussian principles of thrift and integrity in the economic sphere, in order to "build a better future." This pledge found a positive reception among Altona's *Mittelstand,* who for years felt they had been the "whipping boys" of the Socialists. A key element of the new policy was the initiation of a vigorous policy of rolling back Brauer's "dumb economic policies" (*Luderwirtschaft*).[58]

Among the areas to suffer in Brix's first budget were the republican achievements in social infrastructure, education, and culture.[59] Thus, subsidies for maintaining the theater, parks, and swimming baths were cut. The adult education classes of the Volkshochschule were to be focused on the teachings of the new state, thus transforming this Social Democratic accomplishment into the "political university of the people" staffed by members of the NSDAP, whose services were to be henceforth honorary.[60] Brix also doubted that in the current economic climate the city could afford to pay the 250,000 reichsmark subsidy for tertiary education and training for the one thousand or so ladies' companions (*Haustochter*), domestic servants, and unskilled female workers and for whom there was no legal obligation on the city to provide education. Because Altona's Nazis believed that young women "do not need to go to school," support for the city's three vocational schools was severely restricted, affecting 437 students for the sake of a saving of 61,584 reichsmark. Moreover, compulsory attendance on vocational courses for 370 unskilled male youth was lifted in April 1934, and special remedial schools, founded on "Marxist ideals," were abolished, while class sizes in the city's schools increased.[61]

There was, however, a limit to how far such encroachments upon the city's social infrastructure could go to reducing Altona's debt. But Brix was under an obligation to translate Nazi rhetoric on restoring good management to the city's finances and putting people back to work into reality. Attempts were therefore made to overcome the problem through a combination of curbing municipal involvement in the public sphere (öffentliche *Hand*), taking out new credit, and tighter fiscal and debt management.

The new administration in its early handling of the city budget acted quickly to drastically reduce its financial involvement in public services other than utilities. It also set about selling off municipal assets, such as real estate and property, shares and securities, and other movables in order to make savings. Between April and September 1933 the regime began to sell off forty urban properties and planned the sale of municipal-owned agricultural estates.[62] The combined value of Altona's shares, securities, and "other wealth" fell from around 48 million marks to 31 million marks between 1 January and 1 April 1933. Thus, the overall gross and net value of assets, which had been falling slightly since 1929, deteriorated badly after January, reaching 10 percent and less of pre-Depression values by December.[63]

Economies were most noticeable in the sphere of public-led housing, where there was a rapid reversal of policy reflected in the city's disengagement from building investment. The financial year 1930–31 had actually seen the high-water mark for completed new dwellings (1,566), of which just under two-thirds were constructed by public or semipublic bodies. Within a year of coming to power, this proportion had been reduced to 45 percent of the total number of completed dwellings, which had also fallen back to barely a third of the peak level.[64] But even these measures had their limitations. By the end of 1935 Altona's debt had been reduced to around 95 million reichsmark, or 395 reichsmark for each inhabitant. Although this was 130 reichsmark lower than the per capita burden of 1932, it was still considerably higher than the average level for major cities from the worst year of the Depression. Indeed, the unemployed continued to cost each taxpayer in Altona 23 reichsmark, about five reichsmark more than the average for the large cities and towns of the reich, well into the 1930s.[65]

Before the local seizure of power in March, Altona's worsening financial position and the political deadlock that had resulted from this, had eventually militated against any further loans being made by the Deutsche Gesellschaft für öffentliche Arbeiten (Oeffa). This agency had been set up under Brüning in order to provide funds for emergency works programs.[66] Altona owed the agency at least two and a half million marks by the autumn of 1932 but was no longer able to maintain its interest payments by early 1933. In response, the Oeffa refused to extend further loans to the city. For instance, a major program of public works totaling nearly nine million marks submitted at the beginning of January 1933 by Brauer's city planner, Oelsner, had first to be drastically revised to "essential works" only and then was refused at the end of the month. A number of similar applications in February were again refused, either by the *Regierungspräsident* in Schleswig or by the Oeffa itself.[67]

The political changes of 1933, however, brought a significant revision in the Oeffa's position. In response to a letter from Brix in June, it intimated that it was prepared to discuss with the new authorities in Altona both questions of old debt and new loans.[68] Brix was in a position, therefore, to take out a number of loans to enable work creation schemes to get off the ground and thus stimulate a revival of small business fortunes. By the end of the year he had been able to secure from the Oeffa loans amounting to three million marks as well as securing further loans from local employers.[69] These loans were the basis upon which the Nazi administration in Altona was able to hold out the promise of work to citizens.

The ability of Brix to draw on the cooperation of local employers no doubt stemmed partly from a convergence of aims between Altona's new political masters and its traditional economic leaders. But an element of menace also resided in Brix's many exhortations to public leaders on civic duty. Brix constantly spoke of the "public duty" of individuals to contribute to the national renewal. For instance, Brix was adamant that each of Altona's medium- and large-sized factories would comply with the Law for the Ordering of Labor (1934) and thus elect a shop-floor representative. When Labor Front officials reported opposition to this among at least 20 percent of Altona's manufacturers, Brix spoke of publicly denouncing these employers for obstructing the creation of the *Volksgemeinschaft.*[70] Undoubtedly, such an uncompromising stance contributed to the gulf that was to open up between many in Altona's economic circle and this man.

By the beginning of 1933 the sum of Altona's new borrowing since 1924 came to nearly 120 million reichsmark. Nearly two-thirds of this sum was made up of long-term credits, that is, borrowed for periods of not less than three years; however, around one-fifth consisted of short-term loans, which meant that they were due within twelve months of agreement. This smaller figure had been the source of much affliction to Altona, as it had been to many of Germany's cities in the Depression, primarily because it tended to be both expensive and volatile.[71] The municipal financial crisis had weakened confidence among lenders, not least because cities such as Altona were no longer able to even maintain interest payments. Sources indicate that the total sum of unpaid interest on Altona's loans stood somewhere between eight and twelve million marks by the early part of 1933, and there was little prospect that payments would be made in the foreseeable future.[72]

The city's main creditors were regional municipal credit institutes and mortgage banks, which together accounted for 60 percent of loans. Private lenders accounted for just under 10 percent, but it was their loans, totaling twelve and a half million reichsmark, that caused concern since these were largely short-term (around 62 percent of total short-term).[73] Negotiations were in progress to convert Altona's short-term loans to long-term, yet the economic climate was not conducive to conversion. And attempts in mid-March by the city treasury to get either substantial extensions on due loans or to renegotiate interest levels on existing loans met with resistance. Nevertheless, the city was able to benefit eventually from national measures allowing for the transfer of communal short-term debt to a central mortgaging body, facilitating its conversion into long-term obligations. Thus, under the *Gemeindeumschuldungsgesetz* (Municipal Debt Conversion Law, September 1933) the city was able to remove around forty-five million reichsmark of short-term liability.[74]

Through its inability or unwillingness to meet its obligations the city's Nazi administration was risking the goodwill of a natural reservoir of support. With the change-over of regime Altona's small creditors had expected a different policy to emerge from that under Brauer. They had certainly hoped for an orderly resumption of interest payments, also backdated to the point of suspension. When this did not appear, a number of creditors, large and small, sued for full retrieval of the total loan.[75]

Public statements made by Brix in an effort to try to reassure creditors fell on deaf ears.[76] Therefore, in order to fend off bankruptcy proceedings, the authorities in Altona sought to renegotiate the terms of the loans with support from the provincial authorities in Kiel and Schleswig within the framework of the *Gemeindeumschuldungsgesetz* at a meeting with its creditors on the 18 July. The result was a settlement that clearly favored the city.[77] Accordingly, creditors were to agree to a suspension of repayments for the period between 1932 and 1934; interest levels were to be reduced to a ceiling of 6.5 percent (this included unpaid interest and meant reductions of around 2 percent); a moratorium was to be declared on interest accrued up to the end of September and either converted to a capital sum or paid gradually from 1935 until 1940; normal interest payments would be resumed from October, and short-term loans could be converted to long-term. The creditors would also withdraw their notices of foreclosure. In return, the city promised among other things to consider selling off real estate in order to meet the most pressing demands. To ensure the acceptance of the deal, the city managed to get a clause inserted (clause 13) whereby the terms would become binding upon all creditors providing the combined value of loans from objectors did not exceed 20 percent of the total debt. Objections would have to be lodged within a fortnight.

The agreement was indeed opposed by at least twenty-seven creditors, ranging from small local lenders to banks with major investments, such as the Kiel Landesbank, which had lent the city six million reichsmark, and the Deutsche Girozentrale Deutsche Kommunalbank Berlin, which had lent nearly five and a half million reichsmark.[78] Together, these dissenting creditors accounted for only twenty million reichsmark, barely 14 percent of the total debt, so they found themselves faced with the prospect of having to accept terms they considered unfavorable.

Some of them, like the Norddeutsche Wollkämmerei of Bremen, resorted to the law for redress.[79] Others, usually local creditors, appealed to sentiments of natural justice. Among them were a number of individuals who relied totally on the interest payments for their livelihood and who now found it hard to reconcile themselves to the administration's apparent ease with which it acquitted itself of its responsibility toward its creditors. For some, this incomprehension eventually led them along a path of anger and disillusion with the regime locally, as the following case of Helene Gayen suggests.[80]

Gayen's husband's family had owned land in Bahrenfeld that they had sold to the city between 1920 and 1922 for nine and a half million goldmark but paid in deteriorating paper currency. Because her husband at the time was suffering from a mental disorder, the family subsequently disputed the legality of the deal and the worthless sum paid and accused the city of profiteering. Eventually, in 1929 a settlement was reached in which the city agreed to pay Herr Gayen a monthly pension of 400 marks and compensation of 100,000 marks to the family. Instead of receiving a final sum, the family agreed to convert it into a loan to the city with interest at 6 percent payable monthly. Gayen claimed that the family had little choice at the time but to accept what she later considered to be detrimental terms.

During the Depression Frau Gayen was one of the many creditors who found repayments had been suspended. This occurred first under Brauer, whose regime she blamed for her family's financial and social downward spiral, and then under the Nazis, from whom she had expected social justice and the resumption of payments, only to find that little had changed. Indeed, her situation and that of her seven children seemed to worsen as a result of Brix's attitude, making a mockery of the idea of a *Volksgemeinschaft.*

Gayen wrote to the *Oberbürgermeister* in March 1936 requesting a repayment of 15,000 marks from the remainder of the loan in order to build a house as an investment for her children. The reply she got was far from satisfactory. Otto Grotkop, the *Beigeordnete* with responsibility for financial matters, wrote to her stating that the only possible way of releasing funds was for her to accept a reduction in the level of interest by 2 percent. She was furious. Given the complicated and contentious history between the Gayen family and the city, she believed she could not be treated "just like any ordinary creditor," for "Altona owed her a moral debt." Gayen contested Grotkop's suggestion fiercely and harangued the city and Grotkop in particular and even appealed to Hitler in April 1936. The appeal failed.

Gayen's predicament with the Nazi administration in Altona was not exceptional but, instead, was typical of the Nazis' modus operandi in the conduct of business with helpless citizens. The Nazi authorities were not indisposed to exerting pressure upon individuals to postpone or cancel part or all of their loans and sometimes simply reneging on local creditors. A bitter experience was also shared by those modest owners of real estate who, having fallen behind with payment of their taxes, faced writs for foreclosure of their property.[81] SAGA tenants who had fallen behind with rent faced eviction without appeal.[82] Local tradesmen who relied on the city for contracts and licenses or who were waiting for payment were subjected to procedures and decisions that smacked of corruption.[83] A particularly striking case dating from 1935 is that of a party member, Oskar Rittner, a master carpenter from Stellingen, who apparently found himself at the center of a nasty conspiracy concocted between members of the civil administration and the party to prevent him suing for payment of a municipal contract he had already carried out.[84]

Very often those affected were the same sort of people who had contested the decisions and actions of the Weimar authorities and whose hope for a better future for themselves had been raised by the advent of a Nazi administration only to be dashed.[85] Although, ultimately, decisions affecting the financial life of the city were taken elsewhere,[86] the *Oberbürgermeister,* as local führer, had the task of interpreting and shaping the regime's policy on the ground. The market trader and SA man, Walter Brockmann, captured the growing disillusionment with the arbitrary nature of administering local life and the corrosive influence this had upon the *Volksgemeinschaft,* in a series of letters to the provincial authorities, Göring, and even Hitler. Brockmann had sought to expand his trade but constantly came up against an unsympathetic wall of civil and party officialdom that led to his business collapsing. In March 1936, after two years of frustrating battle with the city government, he wrote to the *Regierungspräsident* in Schleswig, asking: "What use are the government's laws when the departments charged with carrying them out fail to apply them, and instead behave as their fancy takes them."[87]

Brockmann's attempted defense of his personal interest was futile in the face of preserving the administration's interpretation of the *Volksge-*

meinschaft. But the apparent callousness of the authorities in Altona toward even their own supporters went deeper than merely protecting the Nazi project from the whimsy of individual interest. A hint of the underlying attitude of the Nazi leadership had been given three years earlier by Brix, when he told Altona's citizens that they shared the responsibility for the Weimar period and would have to pay whatever price was to be demanded.[88]

Scandal

Seizing power in Altona had been easy enough, but administering that power, especially where it concerned finance, was more complicated and loaded with potential conflict. Brix, as *Oberbürgermeister* and local führer, frequently felt obliged out of political considerations to interfere in the financial and administrative affairs of the city. His decisions often had a dubious legal basis, thus casting doubt on his pledge that Altona under the Nazis would return to Prussian principles of administration. The demarcation between administrative and political spheres remained as blurred as it allegedly had been under Brauer and opened the way for cavalier and sometimes corrupt practices by party functionaries and city officials.

In his early statements to the press in Altona, Brix had presented himself as a man intent on restoring order and probity to public affairs after years of what he and his compatriots portrayed as the corrupt practices of city government under the Socialists. Brix, described by the exiled SPD as a "little and self-righteous man," had often launched vitriolic attacks against the city administration for alleged excesses in the trappings of office. He had once even brought a motion before the Schleswig-Holstein Provincial Diet (of which he was a member since 1929) to abolish official cars.[89] Brix had encouraged the Nazi and rabidly nationalist press to run stories against Brauer and his executive about their having enjoyed excessively opulent lifestyles at the taxpayer's expense. The fact that attempts to initiate legal proceedings against either Brauer or his former colleagues came to nothing because of lack of evidence is not so important.[90] The allegations of corruption were a necessary instrument for legitimation during the seizure of power, which had occurred unconstitutionally. For instance, Brix claimed in public that the occupation of the *Rathaus* had been necessary to prevent incriminating evidence from being disposed of. And that the elections of 5 March had given him a popular mandate to act outside the constraints of legality in order to clean up the city's administration.[91]

It was not very long, however, before a number of the new men in the *Rathaus,* including Brix himself, faced allegations of dissolute conduct and corruption. The head of the Fischmarkt branch of the National Socialist

Factory Organisation (NSBO), a man by the name of Häusinger, was removed after he was discovered siphoning contributions from members, stealing barrels of fish intended for the unemployed, and taking bribes.[92] A section leader, Alwin Schröter, who appears to have joined the party in mid-April 1932, was accused of embezzling from the party small sums of money, which he claimed to have used in helping his unemployed colleagues.[93]

The administrators of the SA hostel for the unemployed in the Allee were caught in a racket to embezzle the welfare office. The bursar and director of the home got the men to claim higher living costs than those actually incurred and pocketed the difference.[94] Such criminal behavior among party functionaries, mostly involving petty fraud and theft, was not limited to a few isolated cases and threatened to bring the party into disrepute.[95] The district leader and head of the local political organization, Heinrich Piwitt, had to "strictly forbid" his own functionaries from trying to divert funds from the Winter Help collections by making their participation in the event conditional upon a percentage take of the proceeds.[96]

It was not long after coming to power in order to clean up the allegedly corrupt and decadent behavior of Weimar's municipal politicians that Emil Brix had repeatedly to take action to curb persistent and growing rumors concerning his own behavior. Brix strenuously countered the rumors and even called in the Nazi chief of police, Hinkel, to trace their source. But this course of action neither brought a result nor stemmed the flow of gossip. The rumors of drunkenness and venality got louder, as did those of extramarital affairs. An alleged relationship with an actress from the city theater and who, therefore, was a public employee exposed Brix to claims that he had abused his position of power in order to gain sexual gratification.[97]

Brix was a married man with two small daughters, a member of the party since 1925, and a founder of Altona's SA. He was close to the *Gauleiter* Hinrich Lohse and clearly owed his striking career to the latter's patronage.[98] But, eventually, even Lohse found Brix's position untenable. In a letter to Hess dated 20 June 1935, Lohse, who obviously had been called upon to report on affairs in Altona, wrote how Brix had been under investigation as early as the beginning of 1934. The *Gauleiter* described the Nazi mayor as a "hereditary alcoholic" who, in spite of efforts to save him from the "clutches" (*Klauen*) of alcohol, "has lapsed repeatedly during the past year."[99]

Brix had already been removed from his position as deputy *Gau* leader by Hess on 26 June 1934.[100] Presumably, this followed repeated warnings from Lohse as *Gau* leader and after the head of the civilian administration in Schleswig ordered a disciplinary investigation into Brix, "when his life-style took on such a form that to remain in office any longer appeared to damage the reputation of the state, the party and the civil service." He was suspended from the office of mayor and then forced to resign permanently at the beginning of 1936. He was replaced by Helmuth Daniels, who remained in office until Altona's incorporation into Hamburg in 1937.[101]

Even at this stage Lohse continued to protect his erstwhile protégé from any disciplinary action being initiated against him. Lohse sought in vain to find Brix a place in the private economy, but his reputation was so poor that it soon became clear that Altona's population would have nothing to do with him. Lohse eventually found Brix a position in Kiel as *Gauobmann* for the Labor Front, on condition that the discredited mayor mend his ways. But Brix, as a true reprobate, quickly abused this final demonstration of faith and within eighteen months was again in disgrace for drunken and abusive behavior as well as allegedly misappropriating funds from the DAF. A disciplinary action was brought before the party court in July 1937. Brix stood accused of dishonoring his rank through his permanent drunkenness, immoral lifestyle, and shameful and disreputable behavior within the party and in public. Yet his long and indispensable service to the *Gau,* especially his role in the conquest of Altona, was taken into account, and he was let off relatively lightly, with a suspension from holding all party offices for three years and a fine.[102]

Brix's debacle was perhaps a dramatic, if not isolated, case of Nazi bad behavior. Altona's *Kreis* leader, effectively the man in charge of the party in Altona, Heinrich Piwitt, had to struggle in order to maintain party discipline in public. Piwitt had often to remonstrate with his cadres to be moral exemplars in their everyday lives. And this seems to have been a problem nationwide. Rudolf Hess had to regularly issue circulars via the *Gau* and *Kreis* offices to party functionaries, warning them about visiting places of ill-repute, drunken rowdiness, womanizing, and generally offensive behavior in uniform. For instance, in late 1935 Sieh conveyed a warning circular from Hess against the misuse of official cars for private purposes (e.g., dating women), breaking traffic speed limits, and gratuitous use of car horns, apparently with little effect.[103] In one of many circulars to his political staff, this one dated June 1934, Piwitt enclosed a copy of instructions from Hess urging the *Gau* and *Kreis* leaders to pay more attention to the lack of probity among party officials:

> I don't want to dampen the zest for life of any National Socialist, but I demand that in the current difficult times that no *Volksgenosse* should be offended, and that the arduously won trust of the people in the National Socialist leadership will not be shaken.[104]

Therefore, political cadres were exhorted to remain close to their neighborhood roots and to ensure that they did not turn their backs on former supporters, such as simple tavern keepers, in search of the "good life" in Hamburg's clubs.

The deficient behavior we have been recounting here was not peculiar to Altona's Nazis but was a widespread phenomenon that led Hess more than once to berate political cadres.[105] The transfer of power at local level and the purges of personnel that accompanied it had been more thoroughgoing than at the national level. During the first two years of the Third Reich leading positions had been filled by party activists very often not suited for public administration. The result was that inexperienced—and, like Brix, sometimes very young—men were propelled into positions of power. Lacking the requisite degree of maturity, their behavior jarred with the concept of a *Volksgemeinschaft* and thus jeopardized the regime's authority locally.[106]

Party, Class, Race, and Control

Commenting on the *Deutsche Gemeindeordnung* at the beginning of 1940, a senior official in the party's central office for municipal affairs, Dr. Helmuth Patutschnick, declared in a lengthy memorandum:

> On the 30 January 1940, it will be five years since the DGO is in force. The meaning of this piece of legislation could already be gauged from its introduction on the anniversary of the National Socialist Revolution. It was declared a foundation of the state upon which the reconstruction of the Reich was to be completed on the soil it had prepared. The German Municipal Statute was a comprehensive result of municipal political will, which sought broad and deep-reaching solutions and a secure basis for the further development [of state and society].[107]

What this meant in practice was not only the attempt to bring municipal authorities more closely under the supervision of the ministerial bureaucracy but also an effort to give a principal role to the political organization of the party, and to Hess's apparatus in particular, over local populations.[108]

Thus, "in the interests of the complete registration of households to be supervised," the local party in Altona was reorganized in the autumn of 1936.[109] The city's 75,663 households, of a population of 242,117, were marshaled into 1,502 blocks, based on housing tenements and streets.

These were then grouped into 251 cells, which in turn were organized into thirty-two district locals (Ortsgruppen) covering the city (compared to twenty-one branches in 1934). A pyramidal structure was thus erected that led from the party leadership down to every household.[110]

While each cell consisted of around a thousand persons, each block supervised the daily behavior of about 50 households, or 160 persons. For this reason cells and blocks were unevenly distributed throughout the city. For instance, the Altstadt, which had 11 locals, had a total of 112 cells and 678 blocks. At the other extreme was Sülldorf, with 1 local, 2 cells, and 12 blocks. This system remained in place until the war, with only a slight reduction in the number of districts, to 27, after Altona's incorporation into Hamburg.

According to Dietrich Orlow, this system, from *Kreisleiter* to *Blockwart,* necessitated a sprawling army of political cadres throughout the reich. Nationally, the political organization experienced an unregulated growth of cadres, approximately 373,000 out of 1,017,000 functionaries, compared to 2.5 million actual members between 1934 and early 1935, resulting in a top-heavy party.[111] An exact figure for Altona cannot be elicited from the surviving party documentation, but it is likely that the number of "political leaders," excluding the twenty leaders of the neighborhood-based *Frauenschaften,* had doubled from about 1,000 between the end of 1933 and July 1935 to around 2,000 by the time of Altona's incorporation into Hamburg in 1937, with a caucus of between 250 and 350 more "technically able cadres" enjoying senior status (*Hoheitsträger*) at its center.[112] Even taking the larger figure of 2,000, the apparatus of control in Altona was surprisingly small when measured against both the size of the party (ca. 9,000 in 1937)[113] and the city's population of over a quarter of a million.

The return of the *Mittelstand* after 1933 as "master in its own house" cannot be underemphasized in the case of Altona and is highlighted by the social status of the leaders of the thirty-two *Ortsgruppen* that spanned the city. Almost without exception they came from the various substrata of Altona's middle class, notably from white-collar and commercial occupations, and were exclusively male.[114] This reassertion of the *Mittelstand* was most noticeable in the city's Altstadt and also in parts of Ottensen, where, as noted in earlier chapters, before 1933 either a Communist- or Socialist-inclined working class had prevailed. For instance, the *Ortsgruppen* "Altstadt" was headed by local activist Robert Hampe, a railway inspector; "General Litzmann" came under the control of William Käselau, an architect and owner of a building firm; "Holsten," which included the rougher streets of the red-light district, was put in the charge of an accountant,

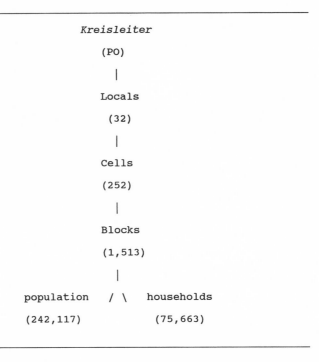

Kreisleiter

(PO)

|

Locals

(32)

|

Cells

(252)

|

Blocks

(1,513)

|

population   / \   households

(242,117)   (75,663)

Fig. 15.   Party supervisory structure in Altona, 1936

Fritz Salewski; while "Ottensen," taking in some of the few starkly Communist neighborhoods in that part of the city, became the fiefdom of Karl Kuse, a *Kaufmann*.[115]

A prime example of this return of the *Mittelstand* is that of the head of the political organization in Altona.[116] Heinrich Piwitt was born on 29 February 1892 in Minden (Westphalia) and was by profession a watchmaker, residing at one time in Ottensen's Rothestraße and in the Königstraße, both typical *Mittelstand* areas. He received his membership card on 1 July 1928 with the number 93,029. By 1930 Piwitt had become a branch leader, rising to inner-city leader in 1931 (his younger brother, Wilhelm, a middle-ranking civil servant, also became a party member in December) and finally to district political leader of Altona in 1932. He remained in this position even after the city's incorporation into Hamburg in November 1937.

Kreis leaders often wielded far-reaching power in their role as heads of the NSDAP's local political organization, especially since they techni-

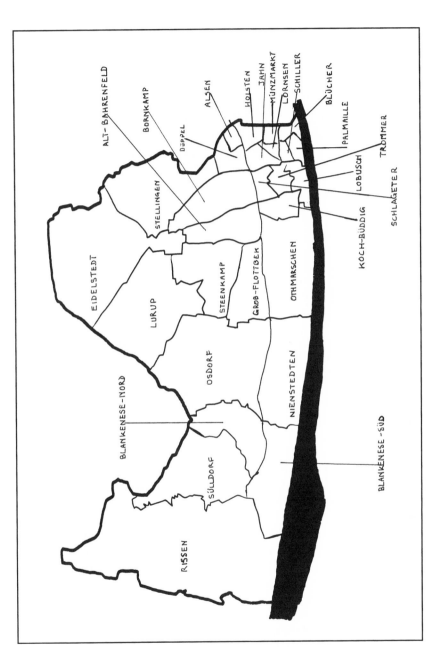

Map 12. The twenty-seven district locals of Hamburg-Altona (*Kreis* 7)

cally enjoyed Hitler's approval. In Piwitt's case the fact that he had also survived the purge of June 1934 can only have enhanced his position and is perhaps testimony to both his prim and pragmatic nature.[117] Piwitt's social profile appears to have conformed to the national stereotype of subaltern leader. Although we know little about his life before 1933, there is little to indicate that he had failed in his profession, though his career in the party may have been influenced by the adverse climate of the Depression.[118]

Were Piwitt to have experienced adverse conditions as a businessman under the republic, this was soon rectified under the Third Reich. Along with his paid position as district leader (apart from a brief interlude in 1938–39), he became a director of a municipal company, the Altonaer Kai und Lagerhaus A.G., earning an annual sum of 1,095 reichsmark together with a stipend of 316 reichsmark. If not exactly wealthy, then at least comfortable, Piwitt's career epitomizes the social opportunity offered to those who were able to ride close to the winds of political change in Germany from the 1930s. Nonetheless, unlike a large number of Altona's functionaries, Piwitt strove to lead an exemplary life free of corruption and exhorted his cadres to do the same.[119] His numerous circulars to his functionaries on the subject of public appearance and behavior convey the image of a deeply serious and pedantic man—in Peter Diehl-Thiele's words, a "Biedermann," who firmly believed that the visible virtues of discipline and order were "a reflection of an inner composure."[120]

The repressive modus operandi of the block and cell system functioned through the surveillance of the entire population of the city in their everyday habitat. But, significantly, it also required the active participation of the local population in policing their own communities. Information on all aspects of daily life was thus garnered and fed via the *Blockwart* and cell leaders to the branch leaders, who, by the fifth day of each month, in turn passed the information to the district leader's office, which had the task of compiling the local situation report for *Gau* headquarters.[121] These reports usually focused on conduct deemed hostile to the regime; they also contained information on antisocial behavior, but they could also highlight innocuous behavior, often exposing to the party authorities even the most intimate personal details and politicizing them in the process.[122] From their vantage point at the bottom rung of the party apparatus, the block, cell, and branch leaders were in a powerful position to wage a war of attrition against those perceived by local Nazis as standing either racially or ideologically outside the *Volksgemeinschaft*.

This was nowhere more in evidence than in the treatment of Altona's two thousand–strong Jewish community, whose members were not to be spared Nazism's virulent and spiteful racism.[123] As we saw in chapter 1,

Altona was a typical north German Protestant city, with a small minority of Jews. Culturally and economically, the Jewish community was mostly concentrated in the older southern and eastern districts of the Altstadt. There were two synagogues, one in the Palmaille in subdistrict 1, the other in the Kleine Papagoyenstraße in subdistrict 7. The Jewish school and community center were located in the Breitestraße, also in subdistrict 7.[124] There is little doubt that by the time of the Weimar Republic its members had been long integrated into local life, either practicing as lawyers and doctors, or heavily represented in the local economy, especially in retail; some had enjoyed prominent positions and good relations with Brauer's administration.[125]

Altona's block and cell system was used to gather information on the city's Jewish community, thereby facilitating its eventual ghettoization and actions against it. While anti-Semitic policy was passed down from the *Gau* leadership (firmly in the hands of three former Altona Nazis—the *Gau* leader, Hinrich Lohse; his deputy, the notary Wilhelm Sieh; and Wilhelm Kube as *Oberpräsident*), Piwitt, who clearly shared his *Gauleiter's* deeply rooted anti-Semitism, took an active role in translating policy into action at neighborhood level. Thus, a series of measures designed to identify and exclude Jews from the public sphere, especially from the local economy, were executed by Piwitt and his political cadres with a relentless doggedness.[126]

In August 1935, after a relaxation in the laws governing the establishment of new commercial enterprises, Sieh called upon the *Kreis* leaders to label Jews as politically unreliable, so that their applications for commercial licenses could be turned down in the first instance. In October of the same year Piwitt instructed his block and cell leaders to compile lists of all Jewish-owned enterprises in their districts. The result was a register, though by no means complete, of over two hundred names and addresses (mostly in the Altstadt) of doctors, lawyers, wholesale and retail businesses, and manufacturing workshops.[127] This action was repeated two years later, when instructions were again issued to the neighborhood political leaders to determine whether or not owners of local businesses were Jews.[128]

Piwitt also used his organization to try to ensure that the boycotting of Jewish businesses became part of an everyday *lived* culture and not just party rhetoric or an event during periods of reich initiated embargoes, such as that in April 1933 or the spring and summer of 1935.[129] Piwitt's anti-Semitic efforts were helped by the enthusiastic involvement of his political cadres in Altona. To give just one example, in December 1935 Eric Bannier's propaganda office circulated political leaders from Piwitt down to the humblest cadre of the ancillary organizations extolling a new book by the "Institute for the Study of the Jewish Question." According to Bannier, this publication "portrayed in an extraordinarily exhaustive way the disastrous influence of the Jews upon the cultural, political and economic life of Germany, so that it deserves the widest distribution."[130]

Such measures were but early steps in the administrative ghettoization of the Jews in Altona and which local leaders such as the retailer Rudolf Kessal of *Blücher,* the electrician Max Steuernagel of *Münzmarkt,* or *Kaufmann* Karl Kuse of *Ottensen,* whose jurisdiction covered neighborhoods where many Jewish businesses were located, assiduously carried out. And there can be no denying that, despite the "deep misgivings" among many of the city's citizens, even within the local party itself, after the Nazi pogrom against Altona's Jews and their property on 9 November 1938, many individuals found encouragement in the party's anti-Semitic zealousness.[131] For example, an unemployed clerk called Dennert, who after 1933 had been taken on in a local branch of the welfare office in subdistrict 14, passed onto his *Ortsgruppenleiter,* Adolf Bruhn who was also a clerk, the confidential and highly sensitive case history of an applicant, Frau Lorf, alleging that she was a Jew. Lorf strenuously denied this, but Dennert insisted the contrary, saying that he had encountered her case in the newspapers before 1933. Dennert was thus able to successfully lobby Bruhn, who as local political leader had to write a character report on Frau Lorf, into denying her assistance with her son's school fees.[132]

Dennert was not alone in his passion to identify and police the "outsiders" of the *Volksgemeinschaft.* As noted in chapter 3, Altona's Gypsy population also came in for racially determined welfare policing after 1933. Similarly, those engaged in activities on the economic margins were subjected to popular vigilance. After 1933 there was a flow of letters to the new authorities denouncing individuals said to be illegally living off the state. For instance, in April 1933 two street traders wrote to Bruno Stamer offering their services in the purging of the national body by denouncing those of their fellow street traders allegedly in receipt of welfare benefits. This newfound patriotism was also the motive for Albert Weber, from the Fighting League of the Producing Mittelstand, demanding that the eighteen persons he identified as working as "black market" traders and carriers in the Altona *Kaffeehalle* in the Kleine Freiheit should be detailed to forced labor. "It is no longer permissible that such elements, who for years under the marxist government cheated the state, should be given space in an ordered state."[133]

We saw in the previous chapter how the Nazi rise to power was facilitated by street violence. The consolidation of that power in the course of 1933 also necessitated popular violence, complementing that of the institutions of the state, notably the judiciary, in the campaign to tame the "ungovernable people" of the Altstadt.[134] By the end of 1934 the Nazis' *force majeur* against the working class was giving way to a *force douce* based on the silent terror of vigilantism.

Nazi vigilance at neighborhood level was of the utmost importance in contexts where the local population was clearly hostile to the new political masters and where social and political repression might generate popular resentment. The repertoire of oppositional behavior ranged widely. In 1933 the insurrectionary nature of political opposition to Nazism had been still in evidence, but within two years it was rarely overt and less and less politically organized.[135] But, more frequently, it manifested itself in the form of nonconformity, occasional noncompliance of Nazi rules, or, increasingly, in a general grumpiness toward the regime and its local representatives.[136] It is arguable that these types of behavior were more disconcerting to local "small" Nazis because they were more immediate and clearly represented visible evidence of a lack of enthusiasm or support for the regime.

As a result, Nazi fanatics often defined such behavior as "treasonable," a charge made all the more easy by the "Law against Malicious Attacks against State and Party and for the Protection of Party Uniforms," passed on 20 December 1934.[137] In the late spring of 1936, for example, a thirty-five-year-old man from Lurup was sentenced to six days' imprisonment and faced a fine of thirty marks for keeping his hands in his pockets instead of giving the Hitler salute during the 1 May rally at the racecourse in Bahrenfeld. He had been reported by his local cell leader and a neighbor.[138] In the same year another man was reported and sentenced to six months' imprisonment for spreading "untruths about the Führer."[139] In September 1935 the district leadership felt compelled to issue a memorandum on the contentious issue of flagging public buildings on designated occasions, such as Harvest Thanksgiving. Piwitt had been annoyed at the obduracy of some public officials who either continued to hoist the old imperial colors of red-white-black instead of the obligatory swastika or failed to even hoist a flag, thus directly challenging the public display of the Nazi-led *Volksgemeinschaft.*[140]

In the cases of more overtly hostile attitudes or behavior, those involved defined their actions for themselves. For example, forty-five-year-old Karl I. went into the city's police headquarters and drew the three arrows of the social democratic but now defunct Iron Front on the notice boards. He received a four-week prison term. Residents in some neighborhoods found an effective means of "getting back" at their Nazi *policiers* by choosing to boycott their businesses if they happened to be local traders.[141] Publican Hans Thun, who ran the Holsten Brewery tavern in Nienstedten, refused to serve beer to Nazi customers. His behavior eventually became the subject of an investigation by Piwitt, after repeated reports of his alleged abrasive manner toward Nazis among his clientele.[142]

In cases like Thun's, Piwitt's office actually preferred to avoid confrontation. Thus, Thun's premises were declared off-limits to party personnel. In fact, at least twenty-one taverns, nearly all of them in the Altstadt, were still listed in early 1937 as out of bounds for Nazi members.[143] While some of these were off-limits because of their dubious moral character, a number of them had landlords with known Communist connections who had played key roles in the pre-1933 resistance to Nazism in Altona.

A member of the party did not necessarily have to go to a Communist haunt, however, to find "resistance." For instance, Bruno R. had barely created a distance between himself and a nine-month prison term when, after a few beers in the tavern "Zur Waldschänke" in the Bahrenfelder-straße, he went up to an uniformed SS man seated at the bar and asked him what the death's head symbol meant. When the man failed to respond, R. lost all inhibitions, raised his clenched fist to the man's face, and bellowed, "Hail Moscow."[144]

The system of surveillance also operated in the workplace. One of Brix's first actions on seizing the reins of power had been to exhort public servants in Altona to send him information on individuals either thought to have supported the Weimar system actively or known to be openly hostile to Nazism.[145] Following this, a report was compiled on the headmaster of Altona's *Oberlyceum* by two of his staff, both Nazis. This formed the basis of his—and, no doubt, countless others'—dismissal in early 1933.[146] Even railway employees were encouraged to listen to the conversations of passengers and to report anything suspicious.[147]

A sense of civic duty—or malice—was possibly the reason behind the report that brought fifty-six-year-old Johannes R., a stevedore, to the attention of the Gestapo. He had been ordered to go with his workmates to the tavern next door to his works in the Blumenstraße in order to listen to the broadcast of Hitler's speech announcing the Four Year Plan. He may well have had a political axe to grind or he may just have had too many beers, for he repeatedly interrupted the broadcast and was brought before the courts for doing so, receiving eight days in prison and a forty-mark fine.[148]

Cases of certain forms of behavior at the workplace deemed as "oppositional" do not seem to have been unusual in Altona's factories. They are documented in the exclusions of non-Nazis from the Altona branch of the German Labor Front for alleged acts of "sabotage" and "anti-state" behavior. For instance, in October 1936 such alleged activities accounted for a quarter of expulsions from the organization; in February and July 1937 they accounted for nearly 70 percent of expulsions but dropped in November to just over 40 percent.[149]

As we saw earlier in the case of the Nazi Dennert and the unfortunate Frau Lorf, the delineation between the personal and the political was often lost in this system of political reporting. The system of neighborhood and workplace surveillance merely encouraged abuse by individuals caught up in petty vendettas that sometimes reached into the ranks of the *Parteigenossen* themselves.[150] For a regime that was quickly developing a sensitive ear to negative public opinion, such behavior perpetuated social conflicts and was counterproductive to establishing the *Volksgemeinschaft*. In early 1936, therefore, and not for the first time, the *Gau* leadership, in a memorandum to the district leaders, had to remind its cadres not to abuse their political position.[151] In the words of deputy *Gau* leader Sieh:

> The Party is an Order. To be allowed to belong to it, is the highest honour for a German. However, membership carries with it the heavy responsibility of serving this fellowship with all one's energy and the obligation to disseminate its aims and ideals.[152]

The reorganization of the block and cell system in 1936, with its emphasis on the constant surveillance of the minutiae of local life, reflected not only the paranoia of a regime unsure of its popular legitimacy; it also aimed to galvanize participation in the Third Reich at the party's grassroots level. Individual members and sympathizers were exhorted to take an active role in the creation of the *Volksgemeinschaft* in Altona. In lieu of democratic channels of communication they were to be not only the eyes and ears of the Nazi state, alert to shifting public attitudes and quick to report any deviation from "the foundations of the present state"[153] but also teachers of the pedagogy of *Volksgemeinschaft*. As Hitler himself told the massed ranks of political leaders at the party rally in 1935:

> Not one person alone conquered Germany, but all of us together. . . .
> One person stood at the head before the Reich, and each of you stood at the head of the struggle before a *Gau*, or a region, or a local branch. . . . Is this struggle over? The conquest of power is a deed which will never be ended. . . . The struggle goes on, and we are entering the period of the second great task: the continuation of the education of our people.[154]

"Schein" and "Sein": Mobilizing the *Volksgemeinschaft*

The spiritual reawakening of the German *Volksgemeinschaft* formed the foundation upon which Germany's economic and political renewal was to rest. The strength of the "people's community," some believed, lay in the party's ability to harness the nation's "cultural will."[155] For this reason the Nazis placed great emphasis on the educative value of cultural tasks at communal level, especially, for instance, through the "Strength through Joy" (*Kraft durch Freude* [KdF]) movement.[156] The responsibility for achieving cultural education fell to both the municipal administration and to the party's political officers on the ground.

"Cultural work" frequently meant colonizing existing collective activities or mobilizing new ones, thus giving the public sphere an unmistakably Nazi imprimatur, as a demonstration of the triumph of a dynamic *Volksgemeinschaft*. For instance, as part of the process of coordination of public life (*Gleichschaltung*), the city's various cultural bodies were brought together under one municipal roof, the Altona Office for Art and Culture; and private associations were drawn into the Reich League for *Volkstum* and *Heimat*.[157] Through the marriage of culture and municipal administration, Altona's Nazi leaders no doubt expected to achieve the

> strong educational value that constitutes its sentiment of community and in the final analysis, the people's community. Municipal cultivation of the arts is an important factor in order to keep alive permanently the connection between citizen and community.[158]

Thus, in 1934, under the aegis of these organizations, the eightieth birthday of Altona's renowned *Heimat* author, Charlotte Niese, was celebrated with much pomp. The music of Bach and old German scores dating from the High Middle Ages were popularized for the broad mass of Altona's *Volksgenosse* under the direction of Werner Schmalmack. Similarly, Shakespeare's "Measure for Measure" was adopted for Nazi racial propaganda and attracted large audiences. When the Fourth Torpedo Half Fleet visited the city at the end of May, for a "Skagerrakfeier," Brix and Piwitt ensured that this immensely popular event was turned into a lasting symbol of the *Volksgemeinschaft* in Altona. The crews of the fleet were given the freedom of the city. Nazi and local dignitaries in SA uniforms ferried ordinary sailors to various sites of interest, including the Hagenbeck zoo. And on the final evening a people's festival took place on the Elbe beach crowning a visit that "in its substance and organization presented an unforgettable model and example of a people's community that had never been seen before and whose impact would not fade so soon."[159] That same year Altona's athletic youngsters put on a mass orchestrated spectacle at the Festival of Youth on 23 June in the city stadium, apparently bringing pleasure to and gaining the enthusiastic approval of the city's older generation.[160] And barely a fortnight after the Röhm purge the Altona aerodrome was opened with great civic ceremony, "thanks to the energy of lord mayor Brix." The office for municipal affairs reported that over 25,000 spectators attended this particular event, noting that "here too, it was once again shown that aero-sports is an appropriate medium for interesting and bringing together the widest social circles."[161]

Events such as those described here could be enjoyed by the public irrespective of the attempts by the Nazis to colonize them. Evidence from elsewhere has shown only too clearly that the public grew cynical of the regime's attempts to "lead" it through staging spectacles.[162] The same could be said for the nazified calendar of public events occurring throughout the year. Thus, when in 1934 Piwitt stated that it was obligatory for the entire city to attend the "National Holiday of the German People" on 1 May, he also conceded it was "not that necessary for every people's comrade to march in the parade in order to show that he acknowledges the National Socialist state."[163]

Indeed, the relevance of public spectacle to the Nazi authorities lay, on the one hand, in creating the myth of providing a point of contact between regime and society and, on the other hand, in fostering a sense of civic purpose and disciplined activity among the lower echelons of the party. Piwitt captured both points in the same circular concerning public participation in the 1 May celebrations. Even though the entire city could not be expected to attend, he nonetheless "expected public participation to be strong so as to create a powerful general impression" of the actuality of *Volksgemeinschaft,* accomplished by the regime not by "diktat" but by "total inner joy" at "the request" and as an expression "of the desire of the entire German people." It was the task of his cadres to ensure that the population's inner joy, as far as it existed in Altona, was fully displayed. Local branch activists, therefore, had to see that every floor of every tenement exhibited a flag so that the city became "a sea of flags!"[164]

During the Weimar period the calendar of public events had been fairly modest; under the Nazis Altona experienced an explosion of public events emphasizing both joyous and solemn aspects of the *Volksgemeinschaft.* The 1 May celebrations, for instance, included the usual transmission of speeches by Hitler and Ley, from 1935 a solemn oath was taken by the massed ranks of "workers and citizens," and the Hitler Youth, in Dr. Saß's safe hands, invariably recited slogans proclaiming the existence of the German national community. After the speeches and proclamations the 1 May always ended in drinking beer, playing music, and dancing in neighborhood taverns bedecked with swastikas and other symbols of the Third Reich, demonstrating thus the joy of life of ordinary Germans in the *Volksgemeinschaft.*[165] The Harvest Thanksgiving on 6 October was celebrated in a similar way, with the day ending in an urban version of bucolic and bachanalian pleasure after the careful party orchestrations of the day.[166]

The Commemoration of the Movement's Dead on 9 November was a more sober affair intended to dignify before party and public the great sacrifice for Fatherland and the *Volksgemeinschaft* made by the soldier in field gray in the trenches or in a brown shirt on Weimar's streets. In Altona the main events took place in the municipal exhibition hall, with smaller remembrance services held in the neighborhoods or at the graves of fallen SA men, while communal tributes for all the dead took place at each of the war memorials scattered throughout the city. The remembrance days in all their careful display of solemnity and discipline, not only dignified the dead of the Nazi movement but were also conscious attempts to do the same for the living, as Piwitt's circulars show.[167]

On the occasions when Hitler's authority was tested by popular acclamation, the party rank and file was subjected to the full rigor of mobilization and the public exposed to the full paraphernalia of Nazi efforts to rally the "people's community." For example, for the plebiscite on Hitler's leadership on 19 August 1934, Altona's cell and block leaders began the day in their localities at 7 A.M. with martial music accompanying Nazi formations. As always, it was left to the local branch activists to ensure that houses and streets were transformed by green garlands (all other colors were expressly forbidden) and the public sufficiently mobilized.[168]

Under the Nazis the Winter Help, already established under the Weimar Republic, was transformed into a propaganda coup for the *Volksgemeinschaft*. Piwitt told his cadres that it "will and must be a success" for "a part of National Socialism depended on the success of the Winter Help."[169] A key instrument in gathering support for the Winter Help and for promoting the myth of communal solidarity under the Nazis was the Day of National Solidarity inaugurating the Winter Help, held in the first week of December. On this day the public was exhorted to give generously to the collectors stationed at strategic points throughout the city or, during their late-evening rounds, in the taverns and restaurants. Party members together with well-known figures from public life had to appear in solidaristic mobilization for the *Volksgemeinschaft*. According to Altona's propaganda leader, this was the day when "all leading men of the movement, from the administration, art and economy take part in this collection, because the bond to our needy people's comrades finds its most explicit expression through this personal involvement for their improvement."[170]

In order to ensure that these "leading men" did indeed appear on the streets to demonstrate their bond to Altona's *Volksgemeinschaft*, local branch leaders were instructed to provide lists of personalities residing in their districts. In any one year up to fifty collectors formed chains across a busy pavement or street, thereby giving passersby little real choice but to donate.[171] Similarly, an element of pressure existed in the door-to-door collections. Block and cell leaders had later to hand in reports on the progress of the collections, explaining in the case of low sums why this was so.[172] The names and addresses of those who did not give, and thus failed to display an identification with the people's community, would be duly noted.[173]

The reports of the *Gau* expert on municipal affairs, Dr. Sievers, by and large paint a picture of success where the contribution made by the cultural activities of Schleswig-Holstein's towns and cities in establishing the *Volksgemeinschaft* is concerned. These reports, however, were compiled from individual bulletins from the district leaders, in our case, Piwitt, who had an interest in portraying all was well in their fiefdom. Thus, in the report for March 1934 the success of collections for Winter Help in Altona's former Communist strongholds is especially commented on. The report stated that this was a sign that the promise of a people's community in Altona had won the hearts of the residents of these neighborhoods.[174] And yet the political unreliability of these same districts continued to cause concern to the Gestapo well into the Third Reich.[175] The real importance of the Winter Help collections lay not so much in what they could do for Altona's poor as in the role they played in holding up to the public eye the myth of the *Volksgemeinschaft.*

The Nazis believed that the public spectacle could be an adequate adhesive for cementing relations between state and society. This is summed up in the following excerpt taken from a civic activity report for October 1934, two months after the führer acclamation in August, which had produced alarming results in Altona.[176] Sievers reported:

> It has become usual to celebrate the swearing-in of the *Ratsherren* with special pomp. These events usually take place in the grander apartments, so that a wider circle of the population can participate. In my view, the transformation of the presentation of the *Ratsherren* and taking the oath into such a ceremony is crucially required as an opportunity for municipal self-government to manifest itself before the public, and so make visible the expression of the closeness between administration and *Volk.*[177]

Sievers had been moved to write this within a year of the *Gleichschaltung* of the municipal administrations. Increasingly, and long before Goerdeler came to pass his judgment on the decline of civic life, local Nazi leaders were having to report on public alienation from the new administration of

Ratsherren. As in Altona, where the spectacle of civic events had been honed to a fine art, the Nazi idea of the *Volksgemeinschaft* was proving to be a poor ersatz for democracy.[178]

According to Dietrich Orlow, the staged activities of the *Volksgemeinschaft* had less to do with promoting the public good than with keeping the party's rank and file occupied and enthusiastic, once everyday life in the Third Reich settled down to its mundane ordinariness.[179] How successful was the Nazi leadership in mobilizing enthusiasm for the *Volksgemeinschaft* within the ranks? In public Piwitt might have appeared complacent about the success of his cadres' efforts in establishing the *Volksgemeinschaft* in Altona. In 1936, on the occasion of the third anniversary of the city's founding of Strength through Joy, he boasted that during its three-year existence, over half the population had taken part in a KdF event.[180] This would have demanded a Herculean effort from his activists.

And yet, in the same year as he was praising the KdF, Piwitt wrote a memorandum in which he expressed his frustration, not for the first time, with his cadres for failing to give the "Hitler Gruß," or failing to ensure that the city was adequately flagged for the Harvest Thanksgiving on 6 October. The *Kreis* leader reminded his subordinates that the frequency of the "Heil Gruß" and the extent to which a part of the city was flagged were benchmarks of the success—or failure—of a neighborhood branch to provide an educative leadership to its residents.[181] The fact that Piwitt had constantly to instruct his own cadres on party discipline reflects not only his own pedantry with the rules but also the lax attitudes of the lower and middle echelons of the party. His men *had* to be reminded that the full uniform and a "raised right arm and loud crisp Heil Hitler!" were de rigueur during the campaign for the Rhineland plebiscite in 1936.[182]

While not discounting the influence of lack of training,[183] Piwitt put the poor level of discipline down to an inadequate interest in municipal affairs. Poor discipline also led Lohse himself to complain in 1936 that this was having a deleterious effect on the "cultural renewal" in the municipal sphere.[184] Inattentiveness to detail among party activists extended beyond public affirmation of the *Volksgemeinschaft,* reaching into the inner life of the party itself. Political leaders were increasingly improperly dressed, failing to observe the complex etiquette of uniform.[185] Piwitt appears to have been kept busy firing off one stern memorandum after another, barely concealing his anger at those cadres within his own command who picked and chose the events they attended according to social content and not from a sense of political and civic duty.

According to Piwitt, a leadership's duty was to lead, but, if it led by bad example, then how could one expect a simple *Blockwart* to do otherwise in his contact with the public? Piwitt was certain that the result must be an overall loss of authority of the party among the public and a corresponding weakening of the *Volksgemeinschaft.*[186] In order to combat this deficit among branch activists, the leadership in August 1935 introduced fixed evenings in the week (either Tuesdays or Thursdays), commencing in October, for compulsory meetings at which a designated party speaker would deliver a talk on a specific topic; the third Monday of the month was reserved for the *Kreis* leadership itself.[187]

To no avail. Up to the point when Altona was incorporated into Hamburg, numerous and constant efforts in the sphere of laying the cultural foundations to the much vaunted *Volksgemeinschaft* in the end proved counterproductive. As W. S. Allen found for Northeim and reports from elsewhere show, efforts to summon up the *Volksgemeinschaft* in fact led to a demobilization of interest in it, not only among the public but even within the ranks of the party itself.[188] Thus, on the eve of Altona's incorporation into Hamburg, described by Deputy Mayor Velthuysen as a "small sacrifice for the Fatherland and for the Führer,"[189] municipal life in Altona had been emptied of its raison d'être, leaving little more than the dry husk of a still divided and contested community.

CHAPTER 8

Conclusion: Local State, Central State, and Contested State

In his study of republican Prussia, Dietrich Orlow argued that the failure of its Social Democrat premier, Otto Braun, to carry through his vision of Weimar democracy upon the rock of consensus politics left not only Prussia, the largest state and the "bulwark of democracy," isolated but the republic too.[1] Orlow's thesis is equally applicable to municipal politics under the republic. For the recasting of national life after 1918 was conceived in terms of creating municipal bulwarks of democracy based on an invigorated social consensus. In this concluding chapter, therefore, we return to the first two typologies developed by Erich Becker in his model of local politics: principally the "authority relationship" and, to a lesser extent, the "integrated state organism," both introduced in chapter 1 of this study.

For the friction surrounding central-local relations constitutes one of the key underlining structural problems of the Weimar Republic, largely absent from the literature. Thus, from Karl Dietrich Bracher's seminal structuralist work on the political dissolution of the republic to the more recent interpretative histories of the republic focusing on race, youth, and gender, forty years of Weimar historiography has largely failed to ascribe any importance to central-local relations as an explanatory tool for the study of the republic and its demise. Even Allen's splendid and pathbreaking study fails to connect adequately the two levels of politics.[2] And yet, as the contents of this study bear witness, this relationship was critical in its influence on Weimar reforms, on the one hand, and in galvanizing what Robert Gellately has termed *Mittelstand* "politics of despair," on the other.[3] Its discussion, therefore, will help us to place the preceding chapters into what I believe is a useful conceptual framework for understanding the contested nature of municipal politics and the "collapse" of the republic.

After World War I supporters of democratic municipalism believed that the politically self-determined community would be a cornerstone of the nation at large. The deputy chairman of the German Association of Cities—the Deutsche Städtetag—Albert Meyer-Lülmann, claimed that municipal autonomy was the foundation of the democratic state and was therefore "an asset of the highest value." He sketched out his beliefs in a draft memorandum to the head of the association, Paul Mitzlaff, in early 1921:

> Political self-government, alongside the principle of equality for all *Volksgenossen* in the participation in public life, is also the second main buttress of the democratic people's state, since only through it can an immediate influence by the population on the process of public administration be practically achieved, which in a [centralised] bureaucratic state is excluded in reality.[4]

Article 127 of the Constitution afforded a degree of autonomy to local authorities, "within the law" and where this did not conflict with the interests of the nation. In the situation of 1918 Weimar's municipal leaders, elected by democratic franchise, believed that they were best fitted for the task of reconstituting the nation in the aftermath of war and thus redefined for themselves the nature and function of the state as a democratic and decentralized formation. As we saw in chapter 1, municipalities were to be the organic agents (Noack's "cells") of the revivified national body. From 1918 municipal authorities were busy planning—and publicizing—their roles in the transition from war to peace. And, unlike the central authorities who had plans but little impact on actual events, they were busy carrying these through.[5]

The single most important sphere in this respect was the "constitutionalization" (Peukert) of welfare through the municipality. The development of initiatives, from housing to health, from morals to social hygiene, were thought out in terms of reconfiguring the whole *Mensch* as citizen. This project called for a more proactive etatist program toward the "poor" of the slums and the intervention into the private sphere of the individual. But the venture, however grand in its vision, was limited in its ameliorative scope. It also demanded the reorganization of the regional environment—the physical locus in which the individual could be nurtured—in order to accomplish the spatial redistribution of wealth this strategy called for. Such a direct incursion onto traditional *Mittelstand* terrain fostered a sentiment of alienation that moved from the local state to the republic at large, as we have seen in the conflict over Altona's incorporation of the suburbs.

The Weimar Republic, by empowering the majority, marked a fundamental shift not only in the relationship between traditional elites and the mass at local level but also between central and local administrations within the national context. For the translation of the democratic republican vision into active policy also clashed with what we referred to in chapter 1 as the Hegelian concept of the state: hierarchically organized and administered by an unelected ministerial executive responsive only to a single locus of power that was independent of competing social forces.

For many conservatives the revolution of 1918 threatened the integrity of the state and the hierarchy of power upon which it rested. The principle of municipal autonomy only added to the challenge being mounted against the central authority by the Länder authorities over the question of the unitary state.[6] The Prussian parliament had already set up a special commission during the war to look into the question of local autonomy as part of the debate on the question of a reform of municipal codes and an eventual *Reichsreform*. This commission was headed by Bill Drews, a senior civil servant and a former Prussian interior minister.

Drews's commission reported shortly after the war and came down in favor of a top-down structure in which *depoliticized* local authorities would be subjected to firm supervisory controls from the center. Drews's essentially Hegelian conclusions were arrived at as a measure to counteract the aspirations of the larger administrations only too conscious of their powerful positions. Hence, Drews warned that not to assert the authority of the center would result in encouraging a myriad of "urban republics" at the periphery, with each pursuing its own narrow interest to the detriment of the reich.[7] The commission's findings were shelved and, with this, any prospect of resolving the relationship between central and local spheres.

By the end of the 1920s conservatives were indeed claiming that too much power had been diverted from the center to the municipalities. A leading critic of municipal autonomy, the conservative constitutional expert Ernst Forsthoff, likened this localized democratic arrangement of the republic to the Tower of Babel, blaming it for the political and constitutional turmoil by the beginnning of the 1930s.[8] To be sure, after 1918 there was not one but three identifiable sources of state authority: the reich, Länder, and municipalities, of which, in budgetary terms, the former and latter were the most important.[9] In the decade following Meyer-Lülmann's assessment, Weimar's municipalities—as the micro cells of the state—were therefore to be the sites for an unremitting war of attrition between centralizers and localists. This battle for control of the state was mostly fought over budgets, since these were the key to municipal autonomy. As a consequence, this conflict was as much conditioned by local policies as it influenced local politics, for instance, in the sphere of the public hand and local taxation, documented in chapter 5.

From the point of view of the agencies of the central state, including the Reichsbank, local budgets were ideological and inflationary and had to be curbed. Attacks on the fiscal position of the municipal authorities were, however, a thinly disguised effort to restrict their political roles. Thus, Hjalmar Schacht's attack upon municipal spending in his much publicized (and controversial) Bochum speech in November 1927 is symptomatic of the fundamental contest between the central and local spheres of the state. This conflict contributed to the growing "crisis in confidence" in the local state that led ultimately to its immobilism and to the growth in violence on the streets, which proved deadly to the republic.[10]

The process of reasserting central authority via fiscal measures was drawn out and by no means uncontested. As early as 1922, Richard Lohmann, a member of the SPD, argued that the relentless financial disempowerment of the municipalities by the central authorities was a ploy to curb "socialist local policy." Lohmann attacked what he saw as the "petty spirit of Reich (and *Länder*) unitary politics and reactionary bureaucratism" for undermining localism and for reducing local administrations to mere "organs of the state."[11] The Städtetag, in which all political parties were represented, also countered such measures as an attack upon the very foundation of Weimar democracy.[12] Thus, in a keynote speech to the Städtetag conference in Magdeburg in 1927, at which the chancellor, Dr Marx, was guest of honor, Oskar Mulert, conservative by instinct, declared that "the unshackled municipality is the cornerstone of the free state."[13] And in a radio talk in 1929 Berlin's liberal lord mayor, Gustav Böß, lectured his listeners on the paramount need to defend the principle of municipal financial autonomy vis-à-vis central authority as the bedrock of a healthy political system.[14] This was a viewpoint in which no lesser figure than Albert Grzesinski himself concurred.[15]

Nonetheless, before 1929, while the operation of ministerial policy created friction between municipal administrations and the central authorities, it did not unleash a political crisis.[16] This was to come with the onset of economic crisis in 1929. It is obvious that the budgetary constraints of the reich and Länder in the early 1930s restricted their own room for maneuver.[17] But there is also little doubt that their predicament was utilized by conservative forces in government, industry, and finance to bring what were seen as overpowerful municipal administrations to heel. The process accelerated from 1930 with the arrival of Hans Luther at the Reichsbank. Luther had always been an advocate of strong supervisory controls over municipal administrations.[18] In tandem with Brüning, and from the summer of 1932, with Chancellor von Papen and the arch-conservative Freiherr von Gayl at the reich interior ministry, the former mayor of Essen and one-time reich chancellor, set about working toward reestablishing a single and centralized authority at the expense of municipal independence.

This was done by starving local administrations of much needed cash to meet the social impact of the Depression. Luther believed that this would force upon spendthrift authorities the "healing" effect of stringent budgetary discipline.[19] This policy would not only make local administrations face up to their financial responsibilities but also, by carrying out what in effect was a harsh surrogate deflation, would undermine their popular support.[20] In the case of Altona we saw how Brauer sought to preempt this by seeking commisarial powers to force through a tough budget in 1930–31. His action was repeated in a number of towns and cities. But the situation had only worsened by early 1932, and this time it was the central authorities who employed commissioners to supplant the by now discredited local councils. Thus, by the summer of 1932 a de facto reich reform working toward a unitary and authoritarian state had come about through the emasculation of the municipal administrations. The forced demission of the Prussian government in July of that year merely hardened the process, making a return to decentralized democracy all the more unlikely. Indeed, the coup d'état was welcomed by conservatives, among them the constitutional expert Carl Schmitt and the leader of the DNVP, Alfred Hugenberg, as well as the Nazis, for reasserting the unitary authority of the central state over a fragmented polity and divided society.[21]

In spite of its far-reaching consequences von Papen's coup against Prussia represented only a partial restoration of the Hegelian authoritarian and unitary state. In spite of the climate on the Right favoring an all-out attack upon them, the Länder nevertheless remained as constitutionally autonomous bodies. And, although somewhat incapacitated, the municipal authorities still survived as elected bodies. And both remained a hurdle to the return of the fully fledged authoritarian state presiding over what von Gayl already in August 1932 called the "organically-bonded people's community," in place of the "rootless" and divided republic.[22]

This project could only be completed on the back of the Nazi accession to power. Hitler's appointment on 30 January provided the right conditions because the Nazi regime was willing to carry through the *physical* emasculation of the republic through the occupation of town halls and containment of the "red" districts of the working class—one being the symbol of Weimar democracy, the other its last bulwark. The "seizure of municipal power" by the Nazis in early March thus provided the basis for the series of constitutional changes that were to follow and not least for the two municipal ordinances of 1933 and 1935. These reforms swung the balance back in favor of the traditional elites in the central institutions of the reich and, as we saw in the previous chapter, locally.[23]

Between these dates, however, the swamping of local positions with Nazi Party faithful meant that the internal efficiency of local government remained uneven, while the pre-1933 tensions between an "unpolitical" professional bureaucracy and a "party-book" local administration remained unresolved. As the head of the municipal office in the Gau Silesia astutely observed, "The interior ministry requires the expert, while the party wants the reliable National Socialist [running local affairs]." Crash courses in municipal administration did little to alleviate the problem. And local tensions persisted wherever municipal administrators and party leaders failed to see eye to eye.[24] While one might continue to hope that the inexperience of Nazi placemen could always be overcome by training and conflicts resolved locally, the absence of a clear operative framework on the ground delimiting the spheres of party and administration remained a pressing concern.[25]

This problem was only resolved by the Reich Municipal Ordinance on 30 January 1935. This statute reconnected to the work carried out by Drews's commission but which was never acted upon under the republic. It substituted a uniform municipal code for the reich (except Berlin, which had its own code) for the different municipal ordinances that hitherto prevailed nationwide. Introduced in its preamble as the "basic law of the reich," it introduced a thoroughgoing and centrally directed reorganization of the administration of national life through the agency of the localities.[26] The law strengthened the professional executive in towns of more than ten thousand inhabitants and at the same time tightened supervision by the ministerial bureaucracy in Berlin. A number of Nazis who had assumed the mayorality in larger towns and cities in 1933 were dismissed and their places taken by career *Beamte*. This reform, therefore, represented the final stage in the "freeing" of the ministerial bureaucracy from the constraints of local and party interests.[27]

The Reich Municipal Ordinance thus settled the vexed questions of authority, responsibility, and competence of the local state in relation to the central state by establishing in law the principle: "Authority over those below, accountability to those above."[28] This maxim of bureaucratic leadership dovetailed with that of the Nazi *Führerprinzip*. By reversing the republican ideal of a nation of citizens who, through their local institutions, would be proactive in the shaping of a collective destiny, citizenship now became defined in terms of passively following national goals defined at the center, as individuals "were made to feel more pledged to the *Führer* than previously."[29] As Heinrich Heffter noted, under the *Gemeindeordnung* "the nervous system of free self-government was indeed dead; what remained was a purely decentralized administration" carrying out national tasks.[30] Thus, through Hitler the balance envisaged by Hegel in the authority relationship between the central and local state was restored.[31]

Epilogue: Brauer's Return

The resilience of local structures and the positive tradition of municipal politics under the Weimar Republic were in evidence after 1945. As in 1918, it was in the municipal arena that the nation's weakened pulse was kept beating after May 1945. In Altona, as elsewhere, the administration (stripped of its Nazi placemen) remained in situ until the summer, carrying out the necessary day-to-day tasks of food distribution and keeping civilian order, as it had done in November 1918.[1] The occupation authorities also looked to the local sphere to begin the task of rebuilding national life from below according to democratic principles. They took the Weimar experience of democratic municipal self-government as their model. This was not least because many of those involved in reconstructing civil life after the war were either admirers of the republic, like James Pollock, or had themselves been prominent exponents of municipal politics before 1933.[2]

Things were little different in Hamburg-Altona, where Max Brauer returned from exile in 1946 as part of a delegation from the American Federation of Labor in order to reestablish the cooperative movement. Brauer was promptly approached by his friends to rejoin the SPD and to stand for mayor.[3] He accepted the political challenge, gaining office after the party's majority win in the October elections.

Brauer's return in 1946 heralded a return to the old republic in more than just symbolic terms. First, a number of Altona councillors, banished in 1933, came back on the wave of the overwhelming social democratic vote to take up leading positions in the city, either in the Hamburg senate or in Altona's own devolved administration. Second, during his two terms of office, both of which were critical for shaping the city's postwar history (he was to serve as mayor until 1953 and then again from 1957 until 1960), Brauer consciously fashioned his municipal policies on his experience in Altona. He was determined to complete the work of creating a socialist and republican *Heimat,* begun in the 1920s. Addressing the first session of the postwar council on the subject of the city's budget, Brauer was confident that he would complete the project, for once again "we have the power," and the lord mayor was determined not to lose the republic a second time.[4]

Appendix

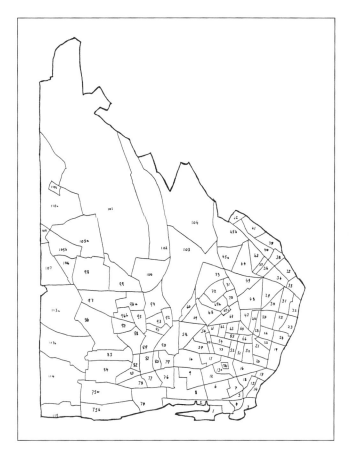

Map A1.   The Electoral wards of the city (pre-1927 borders)

TABLE A1

Subdistrict	Electoral Wards
Altstadt	
1	1 2 -3
2	-3 4
3	5 6 7
4	8 9
5	10 11
6	12 13a 13b (*Altenheim*)
7	14 15
8	16 17 18
9	19 20
10	21 22
11	23 24 25 26 27 28
12	29 30 31 32
13	33 34 35 36 37 38 39 40 41 42
14	46 47 48 49
15	50 51
16	52 53 54
17	55 56 57 58 59 60
18	61 62 63 64 65 66
19	67 68 69a 69b 70 71 72 (police HQ) 73
20	43 44 45a 45b
Ottensen	
21	74 75a 75b 76 77 78
22	79 80 81
23	82 83 84 85 86 87 88
24	89 90
25	91 92 93 94
26	95 96a 96b 97 98 99 100 101 102 103 104
Bahrenfeld	
27	105a 105b 106 107 108 109 110a 110b 111 112
Othmarschen	
28	113 114
Oevelgönne	
29	115

Source: Adapted from Statistisches Amt der Stadt Altona, *Die Straßen und Wahlbezirke in Altona* (Altona, 1932); Andreas Walther, "Die örtliche Verteilung der Wähler grösser Parteien im Städte-Komplex Hamburg auf Grund der Reichstagswahl vom 14 September 1930," *Aus Hamburgs Verwaltung und Wirtschaft. Monatsschrift des Statistischen Amts der Hansestadt Hamburg* 8, no. 6 (1931).

Note: Wards 107, 108, 110a, 113a–b, 114, and 115 are incompletely represented, and wards 109, 111, and 112 are not shown.

Abbreviations and Glossary

AHVW	Aus Hamburgs Verwaltung und Wirtschaft
BAK	Bundesarchiv Koblenz
BDC	Berlin Document Center
DDP/StP	Deutsche Demokratische Partei (from 1930 Deutsche Staatspartei)
DNVP	Deutschnationale Volkspartei
DVP	Deutsche Volkspartei
FGNH	Forschungsstelle fur die Geschichte des National-sozialismus in Hamburg
GStA	Geheimes Staatsarchiv Preussischer Kulturbesitz
HKWP	Handbuch der kommunale Wissenschaft und Praxis
IML/ZPA	Institut fur Marxismus-Leninismus beim Zentral-parteiarchiv SED (East Berlin)
IfZ	Institut für Zeitgeschichte (Munich)
JbAK	Jahrbuch der Agitations-Kommission (SPD)
KPD	Kommunistische Partei Deutschlands
LAB	Landesarchiv Berlin
LAS	Landesarchiv Schleswig-Holstein
Lexikon	Lexikon zur Parteiengeschichte
Magistrat	Upper Chamber City Council/Executive Organ of Government
MdI	Minister(ium) des Innerns
NSDAP	Nationalsozialistische Deutsche Arbeiterpartei
Oberbürgermeister	Lord mayor
Oberpräsident	Provincial governor
Regierungspräsident	Chief governmental administrator
OMGUS	Office of the Military Government, United States
SPD	Sozialdemokratische Partei Deutschlands
StABr	Staatsarchiv Bremen

StAH	Staatsarchiv Hamburg
StAK	Stadtarchiv Kiel
StDR	Statistik des Deutschen Reichs
StJB	Statistisches Jahrbuch (Altona)
StJBDS	Statistisches Jahrbuch Deutscher Städte
StJü	Statistische Jahresübersichten (Altona)
TA	Thalmann-Archiv (Hamburg)
VVN	Verein der Verfolgter des Nationalsozialismus
ZK	Zentralkomitee der KPD
ZkVE	Zentralausschuss der kommunalen Vereine der Elbgemeinden

Notes

Chapter 1

1. *Ursachen und Folgen. Vom deutschen Zusammenbruch 1918 und 1945 bis zur staatlichen Neuordnung Deutschlands in der Gegenwart* (Berlin, n.d.), vol. 3: "Der Weg in die Weimarer Republik," doc. 652, 247.

2. Jürgen Falter, Thomas Lindenberger, and Siegfried Schumann, *Wahlen und Abstimmungen in der Weimarer Republik* (Munich, 1986), 41, 44, 67–74; "Ergebnisse der Wahlen im Reich 1919–1933," in K. D. Bracher, M. Funke, and H-A. Jacobsen, eds., *Die Weimarer Republik, 1918–1933. Politik, Wirtschaft, Gesellschaft* (Düsseldorf, 1987), 630–31.

3. Among the key works are Theodor Eschenburg, *Die improvisierte Demokratie* (Munich, 1963); Gerhard Schulz, *Zwischen Demokratie und Diktatur. Verfassungspolitik und Reichsreform in der Weimarer Republik,* vol. 1 (Berlin, 1963); Wolfgang Mommsen, Dietmar Petzina, and Bernd Weisbrod, eds., *Industrielles System und politische Entwicklung in der Weimarer Republik,* 2 vols. (Düsseldorf, 1977); Michael Stürmer, ed., *Die Weimarer Republik. Belagerte Civitas* (Königstein, 1980); Karl Dietrich Erdmann and Hagen Schulze, eds., *Weimar, Selbstpreisgabe einer Demokratie* (Düsseldorf, 1980); Hagen Schulze, *Weimar. Deutschland 1917–1933* (Berlin, 1982): Karl Dietrich Bracher, *Die Auflösung der Weimarer Republik. Einer Studie zum Problem des Machtverfalls in der Demokratie,* 2d ed. (Düsseldorf, 1984); Martin Broszat, *Die Machtergreifung. Der Aufstieg der NSDAP und die Zerstörung der Weimarer Republik* (Munich, 1984); Gotthard Jasper, *Die gescheiterte Zähmung. Wege zur Machtergreifung Hitlers, 1930–1934* (Frankfurt a.M., 1986); I. Kershaw, ed., *Weimar: Why Did German Democracy Fail?* (London, 1990); Heinrich August Winkler, *Weimar 1918–1933. Die Geschichte der ersten deutschen Demokratie* (Munich, 1994). For an extensive review of recent studies of the republic, see Eberhard Kolb, "Weimarer Republik," pt. 1, *Geschichte in Wissenschaft und Unterricht* 43, no. 5 (1992): 311–21; 43, no. 10 (1992): 636–51; 43, no. 11 (1992): 699–721; 45, no. 1 (1994): 49–64; 45, no. 8 (1994): 523–43.

4. Edgar J. Feuchtwanger, "The Weimar Republic—A Failure of Representative Institutions?" *Parliaments, Estates and Representations* 14, no. 2 (Dec. 1994): 159–70.

5. But see the thoughtful essay by Rudolf Vierhaus, "Auswirkungen der Krise um 1930 im Deutschland. Beiträge zu einer historisch-psychologischen Analyse," in Werner Conze and Hans Raupach, eds., *Die Staats- und Wirtschaftskrise des deutschen Reichs, 1929–33* (Stuttgart, 1967), 155–75; and the outstanding synthesis by Detlev J. K. Peukert, *Die Weimarer Republik. Krisenjahre der klassischen Moderne* (Frankfurt a.M., 1987).

6. William Sheridan Allen, *The Nazi Seizure of Power: The Experience of a Single German Town, 1922–1945,* 2d rev. ed. (New York, London, Toronto, and Sydney, 1984). Apart from Allen's pioneering study, see the excellent local studies by Rudy Koshar, *Social Life, Local Politics, and Nazism. Marburg, 1880–1935* (Chapel Hill and London, 1986); Lawrence D. Stokes, *Kleinstadt und Nationalsozialismus. Ausgewählte Dokumente zur Geschichte von Eutin, 1918–1945* (Neumünster, 1984); Ursula Büttner, *Hamburg in der Staats- und Wirtschaftskrise 1928–1931* (Hamburg, 1982).

7. Eike Hennig, "Regionale Unterschiede bei der Entstehung des deutschen Faschismus: Ein Plädoyer für 'mikroanalytische Studien' zur Erforschung der NSDAP," *Politische Vierteljahresschrift* 21 (1980): 152–73; J. H. Grill, "Local and Regional Studies on National Socialism: A Review," *Journal of Contemporary History* 21 (1986): 253–94. The most important regional studies for Schleswig-Holstein are Rudolf Heberle, *Landbevölkerung und Nationalsozialismus. Eine soziologische Untersuchung zur politischen Willensbildung in Schleswig-Holstein 1918–1932* (Stuttgart, 1963); Gerhard Stoltenberg, *Politische Strömungen im schleswig-holsteinischen Landvolk, 1918–1933* (Düsseldorf, 1962); Rudolf Rietzler, *"Kampf in der Nordmark." Das Aufkommen des Nationalsozialismus in Schleswig-Holstein (1919–1928)* (Neumünster, 1982). See also Jeremy Noakes, *The Nazi Party in Lower Saxony, 1921–1933* (London, 1971); G. Pridham, *Hitler's Rise to Power: The Nazi Movement in Bavaria, 1923–1933* (London, 1973); Rainer Hambrecht, *Der Aufstieg der NSDAP in Mittel- und Oberfranken (1925–1933)* (Nuremberg, 1976); Wilfried Bohnke, *Die NSDAP im Ruhrgebiet, 1920–1933* (Bonn-Bad Godesberg 1974); Johnpeter Horst Grill, *The Nazi Movement in Baden, 1920–1945* (Chapel Hill, 1983).

8. Keith Nield and Geoff Eley, "Why Does Social History Ignore Politics?" *Social History* 5, no. 2 (1980): 249–71. Critics include Dieter Langewiesche, "Politik—Gesellschaft—Kultur. Zur Problematik von Arbeiterkultur und kulturellen Arbeiterorganisationen in Deutschland nach dem 1. Weltkrieg," *Archiv für Sozialgeschichte* 22 (1982): 359–402; Hans-Ulrich Wehler, "Neuromantik und Pseudorealismus in der 'neuen' Alltagsgeschichte," in idem, *Preußen ist wieder chic* (Frankfurt a.M., 1983), 99–106; Klaus Tenfelde, "Schwierigkeiten mit dem Alltag," *Geschichte und Gesellschaft* 10 (1984): 376–94. Critical defenders include Alf Lüdtke, "Rekonstruktion von Alltagswirklichkeit—Entpolitisierung der Sozialgeschichte?" in R. Berdahl, A. Lüdtke, H. Medick, et al., *Klassen und Kultur. Sozialanthropologische Perspektiven in der Geschichtsschreibung* (Frankfurt a.M., 1982), 321–53; K. Bergmann and R. Schörken, eds., *Geschichte im Alltag—Alltag in der Geschichte* (Düsseldorf, 1982); Detlev Peukert, "Alltagsgeschichte—Mode oder Methode," in Heiko Haumann, ed., *Arbeiteralltag in Stadt und Land. Neue Wege der Geschichtsschreibung,* vol. 94, Das Argument (Berlin, 1982), 8–39 (special

issue); Geoff Eley, "Labour History, Social History, *Alltagsgeschichte:* Experience, Culture, and the Politics of the Everyday—a New Direction for German Social History?" *Journal of Modern History* 61, no. 2 (June 1989): 297–343.

9. StAH 424–88, Nachlaß Max Brauer, box 6, Miscellaneous notes for speeches in the United States in the 1930s (n.d.); LAB 142, StB 270 II, Der Städtetag, *Mitteilungen des deutschen Städtetages* 21, 28 Oct. 1927 (special issue: "Reichspolitik und Städte"). LAB 142, StB 1181, Gustav Boß, notes for radio talk, "City and Self-Government" (1932). Lewis Mumford, *The City in History: Its Origins, Its Transformations, and Its Prospects* (Harmondsworth, 1966), 656.

10. Hans Herzfeld, *Demokratie und Selbstverwaltung in der Weimarer Epoche* (Stuttgart, 1957); Wolfgang Hofmann, *Zwischen Rathaus und Reichskanzlei. Die Oberbürgermeister in der Kommunal- und Staatspolitik des Deutschen Reiches von 1890–1933* (Stuttgart, 1974); Otto Büsch, *Geschichte der Berliner Kommunalwirtschaft in der Weimarer Epoche* (Berlin, 1960); idem., ed., *Beiträge zur Geschichte der Berliner Demokratie, 1919–1933 / 1945–1985* (Berlin, 1988). On the nineteenth century, see Heinrich Heffter, *Die deutsche Selbstverwaltung im 19.Jahrhundert* (Stuttgart, 1950, 1969); Dieter Langewiesche, "'Staat' und 'Kommune': Zum Wandel der Staatsaufgaben im Deutschland im 19. Jahrhundert," *Historische Zeitschrift* 248 (1989): 621–35.

11. But see the important contributions from Wolfgang Ribhegge, "Die Systemfunktion der Gemeinden. Zur deutsche Kommunalgeschichte seit 1918," in *Aus Parlament und Zeitgeschichte. Beilage zur Wochenzeitung Das Parlament* B.47 (Nov. 1973); Beatrix Herlemann, *Kommunalpolitik der KPD im Ruhrgebiet, 1924–1933* (Wuppertal, 1977); Volker Wunderich, *Arbeiterbewegung und Selbstverwaltung. KPD und Kommunalpolitik in der Weimarer Republik. Mit dem Beispiel Solingen* (Wuppertal, 1980); Heinz-Jürgen Priamus, ed., *Deutschlandwahn und Wirtschaftskrise. Gelsenkirchen auf dem Weg in den Nationalsozialismus* (Essen, 1994); and Uwe Rennspieß, *Aufstieg des Nationalsozialismus. Eine vergleichende Lokalstudie der Bergbaustädte Ahlen und Kamen i.W.* (Essen, 1993) are important recent case studies. See also the unpublished theses from James Wickham, "The Working Class Movement in Frankfurt a.M. during the Weimar Republic" (Ph.D. diss., University of Sussex, 1979); Timothy Moss, "Cities in the Inflation: Municipal Government in Berlin, Cologne and Frankfurt Am Main during the early years of the Weimar Republic" (Ph.D. diss., Oxford, 1991).

12. P.Th. Hoffmann, "Politik und Geistesleben in Altona vom 17. bis 19.Jahrhundert," *Zeitschrift des Vereins für Hamburgische Geschichte* 39 (1940): 39–80; Hans Berlage, *Altona. Ein Stadtschicksal. Von den Anfängen bis zur Vereinigung mit Hamburg* (Hamburg, 1937); Martin Ewald, ed., *300 Jahre Altona. Beiträge zu seiner Geschichte* (Hamburg, n.d); Franklin Kopitzsch, *Grundzüge einer Sozialgeschichte der Aufklärung in Hamburg und Altona,* 2d ed. (Hamburg, 1990); Anthony McElligott, "Municipal Politics and the Rise of Nazism. The Case of Altona" (Ph.D. diss., University of Manchester, 1990), chap. 2.

13. LAS 309/11333: Eingemeindung Ottensens mit Altona.

14. The Jewish community had declined from 2,650 to 2,006 between 1925 and 1933, StDR 451, no. 3 (1933), 32–33, 41. Jens-Peter Finkenhäuser, and Evelyn Iwersen, "Die Juden in Altona sind längst vergessen . . . ," in Stadtteilarchiv

Ottensen, ed., *"Ohne uns hätten sie das gar nicht machen können."* *Nazi-Zeit und Nachkrieg in Altona und Ottensen* (Hamburg, 1985), 126–57.

15. GStA, Rep. 87, 6410: Die Groß Hamburg Frage 1922–1937. The two cities had been cooperating on administrative matters since the 1920s, *Amtsblatt der Stadt Altona* 52, no. 29 (Dec. 1928) (hereafter: *Amtsblatt*): "Das Abkommen des 'als ob' zwischen Hamburg und Preußen." Jost Dülffer, "NS-Herrschaftssystem und Stadtgestaltung: Das Gesetz zur Neugestaltung deutscher Städte vom 4. Oktober 1937," *German Studies Review* 12 (1989): 69–89.

16. Paul Marquardt, "Das Problem der wirtschaftliche Stellung Altonas im Städtekomplex Hamburg-Altonas seit seiner Einverleibung in Preussen. Ein Beitrag zur Gross-Hamburg-Frage" (Ph.D. diss., University Hamburg, 1924).

17. Heinz Kaufmann, *Die Soziale Gliederung der Altonaer Bevölkerung und ihre Auswirkungen auf das Wohlfahrtsamt* (Altona, 1928), 27.

18. H-K. Möller, "Die Ottenser Metallindustrie," in Ausstellungsgruppe Ottensen—Altonaer Museum, eds., *Ottensen. Zur Geschichte eines Stadtteils* (Hamburg, 1982), 109–31.

19. Paul-Theodor Hoffmann, *Neues Altona,* 2 vols. (Altona, 1929), 1:525–28; Günther Marwedel, "Die Industrie," in Matthias Becker, ed., *Die Stadt Altona. Monographien deutscher Städte,* vol. 27 (Berlin, 1928), 211–13. M. Voigt, *Das Werk Altona-Bahrenfeld der Reemtsma Cigarettenfabriken. Musterbetriebe Deutscher Wirtschaft 2* (Berlin, 1928). Cf. StAH 122–23 Arbeiterrat Groß-Hamburg: Sozialpolitik: Arbeitsrecht, nos. 54–56, 63, 65 (for sweated trades); StDR 416, 6a, 22; Kaufmann, *Soziale,* 33–34. "Gesund und frisch durch Fisch," in *Ottensen,* 133–43.

20. Th. Geiger, *Die soziale Schichtung des deutschen Volkes* (Stuttgart, 1932), 95; McElligott, "Municipal Politics," 112.

21. StAH 421–5 Kc 1a I, and Kb 3IV (Wiese/Schmidt) and Kb 3V (Eckart). Cf. Erich Carl Roßbach, *Betrachtungen zur wirtschaftlichen Lagen der technischen Privatangestellten in Deutschland* (Karlsruhe in B., 1916), 31; Der Deutschnationale Handlungsgehilfen-Verband, *Rechenschaftsbericht des DHV für 1929* (Hamburg, 1930), 106; Siegfried Kracauer, *Die Angestellten. Aus dem neuesten Deutschland* (1929) (Frankfurt a.M., 1930); Erich Fromm, *Arbeiter und Angestellte am Vorabend des Dritten Reiches. Eine sozialpsychologische Untersuchung* (Munich, 1980); Sandra Coyner, "Class Consciousness and Consumption: The New Middle Class During the Weimar Republic," *Journal of Social History* 3 (1977): 310–31; Burkhart Lauterbach, ed., *Großstadtmenschen: Die Welt der Angestellten* (Frankfurt a.M., 1995).

22. Kaufmann, *Gliederung,* 44.

23. StDR 416 (1925), 6a, 22.

24. Geiger described parts of the *Mittelstand* as *proletariode, Schichtung,* 90–91 and pt. 3. Cf. Heinz-Gerhard Haupt, "Kleinhandler und Arbeiter in Bremen zwischen 1890 und 1914," *Archiv für Sozialgeschichte* 22 (1982): 95–132; Karlheinz Jasper, "Die Lage des Lebensmitteldetailhandels zur Zeit der industriellen Urbanisierung (1870–1914) unter besonderer Berücksichtigung der kleinen Nachbargeschäfte, dargestellt am Beispiel der Stadt Köln," *Scripta Mercaturae* (1977): 57–76; Konrad H. Jarausch, "The Crisis of German Professions 1918–1933," *Jour-*

nal of Contemporary History 20 (1985): 379–98; Charles McClelland, *The German Experience of Professionalization. Modern Learned Professions and their Organizations from the Early Nineteenth Century to the Hitler Era* (Cambridge, 1991).

25. StJB Altona (1928): 174–75. Leonhard Fritsching, "Der Mittelstand als Klasse. Zur Wirtschaft des nichtkapitalistischen Unternehmers," *Schmöllers Jahrbuch* 4 (1930): 109–30.

26. E. Becker, "Gemeinde," *Staatslexikon* 3 (Freiburg im Breisgau, 1959), col. 689. See also the influential work of Georg Simmel, *Conflict and the Web of Group Affiliations,* trans. Kurt H. Wolff (Glencoe, Ill., 1955).

27. Georg Wilhelm Hegel (1770–1831), "The German Constitution: Concept of the State"; and "Philosophy of Right and Law," para. 291; both in C. J. Friedrich, ed., *The Philosophy of Hegel* (New York, 1953), 532ff. (references are to this edition); J. E. Erdmann, "Die preussische Aklamation oder der Staat als höchster, sittlicher Organismus," in H. Ottmann, ed., *Individuum und Gemeinschaft bei Hegel,* vol. 1 (Berlin and New York, 1977), pt. 3, pp. 126–35, 149–81.

28. "Philosophy of Right and Law," paras. 272, 275, 281, 291; Cf. "German Constitution," 543.

29. See in general, Albert Shaw, *Municipal Government in Continental Europe* (London, 1895), 289–322.

30. Hans Luther, "Die Stadt als Teil des neuen Staates," in Paul Mitzlaff and Erwin Stein, eds., *Zukunftsaufgaben der deutschen Städte* (Berlin-Friedenau, 1922), 23–25.

31. Wolfgang Hofmann, *Bielefelder Stadtverordneten. Ein Beitrag zu bürgerlichen Selbstverwaltung und sozialen Wandel 1850 bis 1914* (Lubeck and Hamburg, 1964), 135–46; idem, *Zwischen,* 34; Richard J. Evans, *Death in Hamburg: Society and Politics in the Cholera Years 1830–1910* (Oxford, 1987), 1–49; Heffter, *Selbstverwaltung,* 101; Mack Walker, *German Home Towns: Community State and General Estate* (London, 1971), 264.

32. *Rechtstaat* (1870), quoted in James Sheehan, *German Liberalism in the Nineteenth Century* (London, 1978), 156; Heffter, *Selbstverwaltung,* 372.

33. LAB 142/1 StB 4747 subfiles a–u; Hugo Lindemann, "Aufgaben und Tätigkeit der Gemeinden im Kriege," *Archiv für Sozialwissenschaft und Sozialpolitik* 40 (1915): 196–266.

34. *Ursachen und Folgen,* vol. 3, doc. 526, 4.

35. Ibid., doc. 572, 86–87; Erich Koch-Weser, "Die Stadt im Rahmen des Staates," in Mitzlaff and Stein, *Zukunftsaufgaben,* 8.

36. Hugo Heimann, "Zur Demokratisierung des Gemeindewahlrechts in Preußen," *Die Neue Zeit* 1, no. 22 (1918): 507; Koch-Weser, "Die Stadt," 17.

37. LAB 142, StB 270 I: Oskar Mulert, "Reichsaufbau und Selbstverwaltung in der Verfassungsreform" (lecture at the Verwaltungsakademie, Berlin, 11 Feb. 1929), 11ff.

38. Max Quarck, "Die Demokratisierung der Gemeindeverfassung," *Die Neue Zeit* 40 Jg. 1, no. 14 (30 Dec. 1921): 313–18, 343–47, here: 315; idem, "Selbstverwaltung und preussische Regierung," *Die Gesellschaft* 1, no. 1 (1924): 145–52. Quarck had been a member of the constitutional working group chaired by Hugo Preuss.

39. For Preuss's views on self-government, see Schulz, *Zwischen Demokratie,* 1:126–34; H. Pohl, "Weimarer Reichsverfassung und kommunale Ebene—der Ansatz von Hugo Preuss als Bestandsgarantie der gemeindlichen Selbstverwaltung," *Das alte Stadt* 13 (1986): 185; Wolfgang Hardtwig, "Großstadt und Bürgerlichkeit in der politischen Ordnung des Kaiserreichs," in Lothar Gall, ed., *Stadt und Bürgertum im 19. Jahrhundert* (Munich, 1990), 19–64, here: 62; Moss, "Cities," 22–23. But see Priamus, *Deutschlandwahn,* 11–12, on the "fiction" of local authorities as carriers of democracy.

40. Koch-Weser, loc. cit.

41. Viktor Noack, ed., *Taschenbuch für Kommunalpolitiker* (Berlin, 1922), 7.

42. Luther, "Die Stadt als Teil," 33–37; Ernst Forsthoff, *Lehrbuch des Verwaltungrechts,* vol. 1, Allgemeiner Teil, 9th ed. (Munich, 1966), 492–94; Wolfgang Hofmann, "Plebiszitäre Demokratie und kommunale Selbstverwaltung in der Weimarer Republik," *Archiv für Kommunalwissenschaften* 4 (1965): 264–81; McElligott, "Municipal Politics," chap. 1.

43. Günter Püttner, ed., *Handbuch der kommunalen Wissenschaft und Praxis* (Berlin, 1981), 1:77–90; Heffter, *Selbstverwaltung,* chap. 3 in particular; Georg-Christoph von Unruh, "Die Entwicklung der Kommunalverfassung in Deutschland im Zeitalter des Konstitutionalismus," in Helmut Naunin, ed., *Städteordnungen des 19. Jahrhunderts. Beiträge zur Kommunalgeschichte Mittel- und Westeuropas* (Cologne and Vienna 1984), 1–18. Ernst Rudolf Huber, *Die Verfassungsgeschichte in Deutschland seit 1789,* vol. 4, *Struktur und Krisen des Kaiserreichs* (Stuttgart, 1969), 361–62.

44. LAB 142, StB 2934. Unruh, "Entwicklung," 3–9.

45. Forsthoff, *Lehrbuch* , 492; E. M. Hucko, ed., *The Democratic Tradition: Four German Constitutions* (Oxford, New York, and Hamburg, 1987), 153, 177.

46. Ernst Rudolf Huber, *Die Verfassungsgeschichte in Deutschland seit 1789,* vol. 7, *Ausbau, Schutz und Untergang der Weimarer Republik* (Stuttgart, 1984), 864–65; Dietrich Orlow, *Weimar Prussia, 1925–1933: The Illusion of Strength* (Pittsburgh, 1991), chap. 9; McElligott, "Municipal Politics," 55–82.

47. LAB 142, StB 2934, see correspondence between the Geschäftsführer des Preußischen Städtetages (Mitzlaff), and mayors of Cologne (Konrad Adenauer), 17 Sept. 1920; and of Essen (Hans Luther), 18 Sept. 1920; cf. Moss, "Cities," chaps. 5–6.

48. Schleswig-Holstein's ordinance was introduced in 1869. See Hans Ohlen, "Albert Hänel und die Schleswig-Holsteinische Städteordnung vom 14 April 1869" (Ph.D. diss., Faculty of Law, University of Heidelberg, 1929); Christoph Engeli and Wolfgang Haus, *Quellen zum Modernen Gemeindeverfassungsrecht in Deutschland* (Stuttgart, 1975), 422–52; Frederick C. Howe, *European Cities at Work* (London and Leipzig, 1913), 244–45; William Harbutt Dawson, *Municipal Life in Germany* (London and New York, 1914), 84–87.

49. For the background, see Hardtwig, "Großstadt"; Sheehan, *German Liberalism,* 230; Aldelheid von Saldern, "Sozialdemokratische Kommunalpolitik in Wilhelminischer Zeit," in Karl-Heinz Naßmacher, ed., *Kommunalpolitik und Sozialdemokratie: der Beitrag der demokratischen Sozialismus zur kommunalen*

Selbstverwaltung (Bonn-Bad Godesberg, 1977), 18–62, here: 25ff., which refers to "crisis."

50. Wolfgang Hofmann, "Preußische Stadtverordnetenversammlungen als Repräsentativ-Organe," in Jürgen Reulecke, ed., *Die deutsche Stadt im Industriezeitalter. Beiträge zur Modernen deutschen Stadtgeschichte* (Wuppertal, 1978), 31–56, here: 49; Heffter, *Selbstverwaltung*, 615. Hardtwig, "Großstadt," 49, argues that the wealthy elites were actually withdrawing from their *Honoratioren* roles by this period. For popular responses, see Richard J. Evans, "'Red Wednesday' in Hamburg: Social Democrats, Police and Lumpenproletariat in the Suffrage Disturbances of 17 January 1906," *Social History* 4, no. 1 (1979): 1–31.

51. In Offenbach Social Democrats gained control of the council between 1901 and 1904, and again in 1910, but its local ordinance, the *Bürgermeisterverfassung,* ensured that the party did not control the administration. See Helmuth Croon, "Das Vordringen der Parteien im Bereich der kommunalen Selbstverwaltung," in Helmuth Croon, Wolfgang Hofmann, and Georg Christoph von Unruh, eds., *Kommunale Selbstverwaltung im Zeitalter der Industrialisierung* (Stuttgart, 1971), 15–58, here: 52. Adelheid von Saldern, "Sozialdemokratische Kommunalpolitik," 29, gives the slightly higher number of 11,999 councillors by 1913; Sozial Demokratische Partei Deutschlands, *Protokoll sozialdemokratischer Parteitages* 1909 (Berlin, 1909), 38; and *Protokoll* (1913), 27. Cf. Adelheid von Saldern, "Die Gemeinde in Theorie und Praxis der deutsche Arbeiterorganisationen 1863–1920. Ein Überblick," *Internationale Wissenschaftliche Korrespondenz* 12 (1976): 295–352; Dieter Rebentisch, "Die deutsche Sozialdemokratie und die kommunale Selbstverwaltung. Ein Überblick über Programmdiskussion und Organisationsproblematik 1890–1975," *Archiv für Sozialgeschichte* 25 (1985): 1–78, here: 20; this special issue of the *Archiv* has a number of useful contributions on municipal politics spanning the period.

52. "Aufruf der Preußischen Regierung, 13 Nov. 1918," in *Preußisches Gesetzsammlung 1918,* 187. Cf. "Das Reichstagswahlgesetz, 30. Nov. 1918," RGBl. 1918, 1345.

53. *Mitteilungen der Zentralstelle des Deutschen Städtetages* 7, no. 21 (1920): 448–52; ibid., 11, no. 9 (1924): 124–32; LAB 142/1 StB 992/I, "Zusammensetzung der Stadträte in 212 Städten Bayerns nach dem Stande vom 1. Januar 1925"; *Statistische Vierteljahresberichte des Deutschen Städtetages* 2 Jg., no. 4 (Dec. 1929): 196–99: "Kommunalwahlen 1929"; Deutscher Städtetag (6 Dec. 1929): "Die Bürgerschaftswahl in Lübeck am 10. November 1929"; see the relevant volumes of SPD, *Protokoll,* and Georg Fülberth, *Konzeption und Praxis sozialdemokratischer Kommunalpolitik 1918–1933. Ein Anfang* (Marburg, 1984), 124ff.

54. StJBDS 23 (1928), pt. 9: "Städtische Kollegien und die letzten städtischen Wahlen," 217 (table 2), 282–89; StJBDS 28 (1933): pt. 25, "Ergebnis der Gemeindewahlen 1933 in Preussen," 550–56. Hofmann, *Zwischen,* 57ff.

55. Fritz Terhalle, *Die Finanzwirtschaft des Staates und der Gemeinden. Eine Einführung in die Staatsfinanzwirtschaft* (Berlin, 1948), 298–99. Werner Abelshauser, "Die Weimarer Republik—ein Wohlfahrtsstaat?" in Werner Abelshauser, *Die Weimarer Republik als Wohlfahrtsstaat. Zum Verhältnis von*

Wirtschafts- und Sozialpolitik in der Industriegesellschaft, Vierteljahresschrift für Wirtschaftsgeschichte Beiheft 87 [Stuttgart, 1987], 9–31, here: 17.

56. StAH 424–88, Nachlaß Brauer, box 6, "Notes on City Government: (The Modern City and Its Administration)," 7.

57. Artur Molkenbuhr, "Das Beispiel Altona," *Die Gemeinde* 7 (1929): 315–18.

Chapter 2

1. Cited in JbAK, 1907–8, 34.

2. IML/ZPA St 18/217 bl. 51–52: Der Minister des Innern II (Diels) 1272 OP Schleswig-Holstein/65, Berlin, 17 Aug. 1932, "Entwurf," 4.

3. On this aspect, see Erhard Lucas, *Arbeiterradikalismus. Zwei Formen von Radikalismus in der deutschen Arbeiterbewegung* (Frankfurt a.M., 1976); Dirk Hänisch, *Sozialstrukturelle Bestimmungsgründe des Wahlverhaltens in der Weimarer Republik. Eine Aggregatdatenanalyse der Ergebnisse der Reichstagswahlen 1924 bis 1933* (Duisburg, 1983), 166, 183.

4. Geiger, *Schichtung,* 25ff. 106–38, for definition.

5. AHVW Sondernummer 6 (1 Nov. 1941), 17: Schaubild 2.

6. *Bericht über die Gemeinde-Verwaltung Altona in den Jahren 1863 bis 1888, 1863 bis 1900,* 3 vols. (Altona, 1889–1906), Zweiter Teil, 368 (hereafter *Bericht,* 1, 2, and 3).

7. *Bericht,* 2:362.

8. *Bericht,* 1:410–11; *Bericht,* 2:363–64; StDR 291/2, 23; StDR 315/2, 29; StJBDS 18 (1923): 629, table V1a; StJü Altona (1923), 53–54 and (1924), 49–50; *Amtsblatt* 12, 31 Mar. 1933.

9. *Das Deutsche Reich von 1918 bis Heute* [I], ed., Cuno Horkenbach (Berlin, 1930), vol. 2: "Politische und Verwaltungsstruktur des Deutschen Reiches," 383ff.

10. In Schleswig-Holstein the qualification (*Zensus*), was raised to 1,200 marks, SPD *Protokoll* 1909, 35. *Bericht,* 1:403–5; *Bericht,* 2:364.

11. *Altonaer Stadtkalendar* 1919 (Altona, 1919), 80; Anthony McElligott, "Altona vor dem Ersten Weltkrieg. Zur wirtschaftlichen und politischen Entwicklung," in Arnold Sywottek, ed., *Das andere Altona, Beiträge zur Alltagsgeschichte* (Hamburg, 1984), 22–38, here: 32.

12. Egbert Baumann, *Kriegsfamilienunterstützung in Altona. Grundsätze und Aufwendungen der Kommission für Familienunterstützung in drei Kriegsjahren* (Altona, 1917), 66; Hoffmann, *Neues Altona,* 1:4.

13. StAH 424–29 (Lebensmittelamt), IB/2a 1: Niederschriften über die Sitzungen der Lebensmittel-Kommission v. 8. Feb. 1917 bis 14. Aug. 1918, bl. 99: 4 July 1917.

14. StAH 424–2 IVe 34 (1918), Sitzung 1 Aug. 1918, 81; Sitzung 1 Oct. 1918. *Altonaer Tageblatt,* 16 Aug. 1918 and ibid., 1 Oct. 1918; *Hamburger Echo,* 4th, 5th and 18 July 1918; Hoffmann, *Neues Altona,* 1:41, 48–49. StJü Altona (1923), 52.

15. Hoffmann, *Neues Altona,* 1:4–10; Thomas Krause, "Revolution in Altona," in Sywottek, *Das andere Altona,* 39–59, here: 40–59.

16. StAH 424–2 IVe (Städtische Kollegien) 34 (1918) Sitzung 12, 14 Oct. 1918.

See Walther Lamp'l, *Die Revolution in Groß-Hamburg* (Hamburg, 1921); Fred Baumann, *Um den Staat—Ein Beitrag zur Geschichte der Revolution in Hamburg 1918–19* (Hamburg, 1924). Völker Ullrich, *Die Hamburger Arbeiterbewegung vom Vorabend des ersten Weltkrieges bis zur Revolution 1918/19,* 2 vols. (Hamburg, 1976).

17. StABr. 4,65 IV 4d 1, 10 Mar.–31 July 1919; Hoffmann, *Neues Altona,* 1:6, 8.

18. Hoffmann, *Neues Altona,* 1:41.

19. StAH 97 (Handschriftsammlung), sig. 22 CMXXII: "Aufzeichnungen über Altoner Vorgänge 1918–1923" (P-Th. Hoffmann and Josef Gierlinger); StAH 97, sig. 23 CMXXIII: (Curt Weiß). For Hamburg: Richard Comfort, *Revolutionary Hamburg. Labor Politics in the Early Weimar Republic* (Stanford, California, 1966), chap. 3; F-W. Witt, *Die Hamburger Sozialdemokratie in der Weimarer Republik. Unter besonderer Berücksichtigung der Jahre 1929/30–1933* (Hannover, 1971), 19–35; Jutta Stehling, "Der Hamburger Arbeiter- und Soldatenrat in der Revolution 1918–19," in Herzig et al., *Arbeiter in Hamburg,* 419–28.

20. *Altonaer Tageblatt,* 2 Oct. 1918.

21. Hoffmann, *Neues Altona,* 1:7; Comfort, *Revolutionary Hamburg,* 64–67; Suzanne Miller, "Die Sozialdemokratie in der Spannung zwischen Oppositionstradition und Regierungsverantwortung in den Anfängen der Weimarer Republik," in Hans Mommsen, ed., *Sozialdemokratie zwischen Klassenbewegung und Volkspartei* (Frankfurt a.M., 1974), 84–105.

22. StAH 424–2 IVe 35 (1919), Sitzung 15 May 1919. Ernst Rudolf Huber, *Deutsche Verfassungsgeschichte seit 1789,* vol. 5: *Weltkrieg, Revolution und Reichserneuerung 1914–1919* (Stuttgart, Berlin, Cologne, and Mainz, 1978), 1164.

23. Krause, "Revolution," 46, 49. Hofmann, *Zwischen,* 57–68; Moss, "Cities," 39–58.

24. StAH 424–2 IVe 34 (1918), Sitzung 1 Oct. 1918, "Anfrage SPD-Fraktion (Kürbis and Sievert)," 110. Sitzung 15 Nov. 1918, 145. Hoffmann, *Neues Altona,* 1:7–8, 39. Heimann, "Zur Demokratisierung," 507.

25. StAH 424–2 IVe (1919) 35, Sitzung 12, 31 July 1919; Hoffmann, *Neues Altona,* 1:42.

26. StAH 424–88, Nachlaß Harbeck; Hoffmann, *Neues Altona,* 1:41.

27. StJü Altona (1924), 52–53; StAH 424–2 IVe 34 (1918) Sitzung 9 (1 Aug. 1918): 81; Sitzung 11 (1 Oct. 1918), 109; IVe 35 (1919) Sitzung 15 (23 Oct. 1919); Hoffmann, *Neues Altona,* 1:39ff., for biographical notes.

28. Herzfeld, *Demokratie,* 20.

29. StAH 424–2 IVe 40 (1924), bl. 389: Sitzung 18 Sept. 1924. They both left the *Magistrat* within the year (Hoffmann, *Neues Altona,* 1:6, 50, nn. 50–51).

30. StAH 424–2 IVe 34 (1918), Sitzung 14, 145. *Altonaer Stadtkalender* 13 (1925): "Zum Geleit"; Leo Lippmann, *Mein Leben und Meine Ämtliche Tätigkeit. Erinnerungen und ein Beitrag zur Finanzgeschichte Hamburgs,* ed., Werner Jochmann (Hamburg, 1964), 207, 222–23; Witt, *Hamburger Sozialdemokratie,* 31.

31. Hoffmann, *Neues Altona,* 1:50.

32. StJü Altona (1923), 53.

33. StAH 424–10 (Stadtausschuss), Der Oberburgermeister, memorandum to heads of administrative departments, 8 Apr. 1922; *Amtsblatt* 7, 18 Feb. 1928. The number of committees had been reduced to forty-eight by the latter date.

34. StAH 424–2 IVe 35 (1919), Sitzung 5 (13 Mar. 1919).

35. LAB 142 StB 992/II, *Mitteilungen des Deutschen Städtetages* 11, no. 9 (1924): cols. 123–32.

36. LAB 142, StB 2138 (Hausfrauverein). Cf. on bourgeois activism, Roger Chickering, "'Casting Their Gaze More Broadly': Women's Patriotic Activities in Imperial Germany," *Past and Present* 118 (Feb. 1988): 156–85; R. J. Evans, *The Feminist Movement in Germany, 1894–1933* (London and Beverly Hills, 1976).

37. LAB 142 StB 3774, *Mitteilungen des Deutschen Städtetages,* no. 1 (1926): 14–18; and: "Die Frau in Gemeindevorstand und Gemeindevertretung" (Beilage zum Nachrichtenblatt des Bundes Deutscher Frauenvereine vom 15. April 1926). StJBDS 23 (1928): 266. Anni Staudinger (KPD), interview, 2 Feb. 1983. There is not, as far as I know, an up-to-date study of women in municipal politics for this period, cf. Gabriele Bremme, *Die politische Rolle der Frau in Deutschland. Eine Untersuchung über den Einfluß der Frauen bei Wahlen ud ihre Teilnahme in Partei und Parlament* (Göttingen, 1956); Karen Hagemann, *Frauenalltag und Männerpolitik: Alltagsleben und gesellschaftliches Handeln von Arbeiterfrauen in der Weimarer Republik* (Bonn, 1990); Claudia Koonz, *Mothers in the Fatherland* (London, 1988), 30 (n. 19 in particular).

38. Dr. Emilie Kiep-Altenloh, 29 Jan. 1983; Martin Schumacher, ed., *M.d.R. Die Reichstagsabgeordneten der Weimarer Republik in der Zeit des Nationalsozialismus, Politische Verfolgung, Emigration und Ausbürgerung 1933–1945. Eine biographische Dokumentation,* 3d rev. ed. (Düsseldorf, 1994), 1400.

39. *Amtsblatt* 7, 18 Feb. 1928; StJB Altona (1928), 124–25; LAB 142 StB 3774, Deutscher Städtetag: Zulassung von Frauen für den mittleren Verwaltungsbeamtendienst (Ergebnis einer Rundfrage v. 25. März 1927); and in the same file: Zentralstelle f. Gemeindeämter der Frau, Frankfurt a.M., Sonderdruck aus "Die Frau" (Aug. 1923), Marguerite Wolf "Entwicklungstendenzen in der kommunalen Frauenarbeit"; Susanne Zeller, *Volksmütter—mit staatlicher Anerkennung—Frauen im Wohlfahrtswesen der zwanziger Jahre* (Düsseldorf, 1987). In this respect, Renate Bridenthal and Claudia Koonz, "Beyond *Kinder, Küche, Kirche:* Weimar Women in Politics and Work," in Renate Bridenthal, Atina Grossmann, and Marion Kaplan, eds., *When Biology became Destiny. Women in Weimar and Nazi Germany* (New York, 1984), 54–55, rightly speak of a male cross-party "tokenism" regarding women's equality.

40. LAS 309/8317, "Polizeiamt Altona to Regierungspräsident Schleswig, Tgb. 4/14, betr. Sozialdemokratische Bewegung, 7 Feb. 1914; *Hamburger Echo* 118, 11 Mar. 1921; JbAK 1911/12, 12ff. On the regional SPD in this period, see Holger Rüdel, "Die Bedeutung der Sozialdemokratie im Hamburger Raum für die Entwicklung der deutschen Arbeiterbewegung unter dem Sozialistengesetz. Das Beispiel Schleswig-Holstein," in Herzig et al., *Arbeiter in Hamburg,* 193–202. According to data complied by the *Forschungsstelle für die Geschichte des Nationalsozialismus in Hamburg,* "Liste der Altonaer Stadtverordneten 1921–1933," of

the 48 Social Democrats (out of 51) who were councillors at one time or other between 1921 and 1933, the age cohorts in 1927 would have been: 20–29 years: 3; 30–39: 17; 40–49: 18; 50–59: 7; 60ff.: 3; unknown: 3. I am grateful to Karl Ditt, who kindly drew my attention to this unpublished material.

41. JbAK 1910/11, 10–19 ("Berufs-Statistik"); *Jahresbericht des königlichen Commerz Collegien zu Altona* (1889): 28, and (1890): 20. Cf. Robert Michels, "Die deutsche Sozialdemokratie: Parteimitgliedschaft und soziale Zusammensetzung," *Archiv für Sozialwissenschaft und Sozialpolitik* 23 (1906): 471–556; Richard N. Hunt, *German Social Democracy, 1918–1933* (Yale, 1964), chap. 3.

42. For biographical details, Hoffmann, *Neues Altona,* 1:44, 46–47; *Forschungsstelle, "*Liste." McElligott, "Altona," 35; On "respectable" and "rough" workers in the Hamburg-Altona area, see Michael Grüttner, "Arbeiterkultur versus Arbeiterbewegungskultur," in Albrecht Lehmann, ed., *Studien zur Arbeiterkultur* (Münster, 1984), 244–46.

43. *Amtsblatt* 17, 26 Apr. 1924, "Wahlvorschläge für die Stadtverordnetenwahl in Altona."

44. Its vote rose to nearly 51 percent in May 1928 (McElligott, "Municipal Politics," 200–203, 457). Hans-Georg Bluhm, "Steenkamp: Zur Entstehungsgeschichte einer Grossstädtischen Vorortssiedlung in Hamburg-Altona" (M.A. Diss. University of Hamburg, 1987), 155. See also chap. 3, fig. 5.

45. StABr 4,65 IV 4 2 (Zentralpolizeistelle Hamburg), weekly reports: 11 Sept. 1919; and no. 168, 24 Sept. 1919; and report no. 7, 12 Mar. 1921. StABr 4,65 IV 4d 3, weekly report no. 197, 2 Dec. 1919; StAH Außerordentliches Gericht: C240/23 Bd.1/2; C267/23; C2188/23; D1266/23.

46. The authorities estimated the AUU to number around 10,000, distributed among 80 factories, while the German Communist Workers' Party (KAPD) in Altona stood at around 800 at this time, though the majority rejoined the KPD: StABr 4,65 IV 4e 2, weekly report 2 Sept. 1919; ibid., 4,65 IV 4e 3, report 85, 11 Oct. 1921. The Altona branch of the KPD was incorporated into the Greater Hamburg organization in the late spring of 1924 amid much acrimony, StABr 4,65 IV 4e 3, reports: no. 83, 6 Oct. 1921; no. 90, 24 Oct. 1921; ibid., 4,65 IV 4e 4, report no. 3, 9 May 1924. Cf. Frits Kool, ed., *Die Linke gegen die Partei-Herrschaft* (Olten and Freiburg im Breisgau, 1970), for oppositional groups.

47. StABr 4,65 IV 4e 6, situation report: 16 June 1928. The party leader from 1925, Ernst ("Teddy") Thälmann, was himself an unskilled dockworker from Hamburg, Hannes Heer, *Thälmann* (Reinbek, 1975). See Hartmut Wunderer, "Materialien zur Soziologie der Mitgliedschaft und Wahlerschaft der KPD zur Zeit der Weimarer Republik," *Gesellschaft. Beiträge zur Marxschen Theorie 5* (Frankfurt a.M., 1975), 257–77, here: 261–63, 278; Siegfried Bahne, "Die kommunistische Partei Deutschlands," in Erich Matthias and Rudolf Morsey, eds., *Das Ende der Parteien 1933. Darstellungen und Dokumente* (Düsseldorf, 1979), 655–739, here: 660ff.; Ossip K. Flechtheim, *Die KPD in der Weimarer Republik* (Frankfurt a.M., 1969), 240–41; Aviva Aviv, "The SPD and the KPD at the End of the Weimar Republic: Similarity within Contrast," *Internationale wissenschaftliche Korrespondenz zur Geschichte der deutschen Arbeiterbewegung* 14 Jg. (1978): 171–86, here: 179–80; Klaus-Michael Mullmann, *Kommunisten in der*

Weimarer Republik: Sozialgeschichte einer revolutionären Bewegung (Darmstadt, 1996); Eric D. Weitz, *Creating German Communism 1890–1990: From Popular Protest to Socialist State* (Princeton, NJ, 1997).

48. *Amtsblatt* 17, 26 Apr. 1924; no. 37, 17 Sept. 1927; no. 45, 9 Nov. 1929; *Forschungsstelle,* "Liste." Silvia Kontos, *Die Partei Kämpft wie ein Mann* (Basel and Frankfurt a.M., 1979).

49. Hoffmann, *Neues Altona,* 1:50 n. 48.

50. Bezirksleitung der KPD, "Bericht der Bezirksleitung der KPD der Wasserkante (1928–29)," 79.

51. IML/ZPA 54/7776, ZK KPD Abteilung Kommunalpolitik, *Kommunistische Gemeindepolitik. Beschlüsse und Erläuterungen* (Berlin, n.d.), 6. LAS 309/ 22572, *Instruktion für die neugewählten kommunistischen Gemeindevertreter* (Berlin, 1924), 4 (a copy of this document is also in IML/ZPA 54/12985); IML/ZPA 60/5433, Zentralkomitee der KPD, Abt. Kommunalpolitik, *Kommunistische Parlamentstaktik gegen die Faschisierung. Ausserparlamentarische Massenkampf in den Kommunen* (Berlin, 1932); See StABr. 4,65 IV 4e 5, situation report no. 6 -14-, 15 June 1926, for the creation of an office for municipal work. Hermann Weber, *Die Generallinie. Rundschreiben des Zentralkomitees der KPD an die Bezirke 1929–1933. Quellen zur geschichte des Parlamentarismus und der politischen Parteien. Dritte Reihe: Die Weimarer Republik,* vol. 6 (Düsseldorf, 1981), doc. 15c, "Anweisungen zur Kommunalarbeit 3: Verbindung mit der Massenarbeit: Kommunalfraktion" (1930): 107–9. Herlemann, *Kommunalpolitik,* 13–14.

52. *Instruktion,* 3.

53. *Altonaer Nachrichten* 32, 9 Aug. 1924, for quote. StABr. 4,65 IV 4e 5, situation report no. 9, 14 Oct. 1926; 4,65 IV 4e 6, situation report no. 8, 21 Dec. 1927. *Forschungsstelle,* "Liste." Hermann Weber, *Die Wandlung des deutschen Kommunismus. Die Stalinisierung der KPD in der Weimarer Republik,* abr. ed. (Frankfurt a.M., 1969), 270–71; idem, "Zur Politik der KPD 1929–1933," in Manfred Scharrer, ed., *Kampflose Kapitulation. Arbeiterbewegung 1933* (Reinbek, 1984), 121–61, here: 161.

54. StABr 4,65 IV 4d 1, report no. 80, 28 June 1919; ibid., 4,65 IV 4d 2, weekly reports: 25 Aug. 1919, and no. 172, 29 Sept. 1919. Anthony McElligott, "Mobilising the Unemployed: The KPD and the Unemployed Workers' Movement in Hamburg-Altona during the Weimar Republic," in Richard J. Evans and Dick Geary, eds., *The German Unemployed. Experiences and Consequences of Mass Unemployment from the Weimar Republic to the Third Reich* (London, 1987), 228–60; Angelika Voß, Ursula Büttner, Hermann Weber, *Vom Hamburger Aufstand zur politischen Isolierung. Kommunistische Politik, 1923–1933 in Hamburg und im Dritten Reich* (Hamburg, 1983); Eric D. Weitz, "State Power, Class Fragmentation, and the Shaping of German Communist Politics, 1890–1933," *Journal of Modern History* 62 (1990): 253–97.

55. StJü Altona (1923), 52–53; StJü Altona (1924), 48.

56. Voß et al., *Hamburger Aufstand,* 82–103; Büttner, *Hamburg,* 430–41.

57. For instance, 13.5 percent of the 1924 list lived in the same Ottensen wards in which the Communist vote was conspicuously high; and the remaining 6 percent in Bahrenfeld and Othmarschen *(Amtsblatt* 39, 1 Oct. 1927. Antonio Gramsci,

Selections from Political Writings 1910–1920, ed. Quentin Hoare [London, 1977], 167–78; James Wickham, "Working-Class Movement and Working-Class Life: Frankfurt am Main during the Weimar Republic," *Social History* 8 [1983]: 315–43).

58. Bezirksleitung der KPD, "Bericht 1932," 98; see Christoph Timm, "'Eine Art Wildwest.' Die Altonaer Erwerbslosensiedlungen in Lurup und Osdorf von 1932," in Sywottek, *Das andere Altona,* 159–75.

59. L. Elm, "Freisinnige Volkspartei 1893–1910," *Lexikon* 2, 694–707; W. Fritsch, "Deutsche Demokratische Partei (DDP) 1918–1933," *Lexikon* 1, 574–622; Sigmund Neumann, *Die Parteien der Weimarer Republik,* 2d ed. (Stuttgart, Berlin, Cologne, and Mainz, 1965), 48–54; Martin Vogt, "Parteien in der Weimarer Republik," in Bracher et al., *Die Weimarer Republik,* 134–57, here: 142. Ursula Büttner, "Vereinigte Liberale und Deutsche Demokraten in Hamburg, 1906–1933," *Zeitschrift des Vereins für Hamburgische Geschichte* 63 (1977): 1–34.

60. City comparisons can be gleaned from StDR 315,2 (May 1924); StDR 372,2 (1928); StDR 382.2 (1930); StDR 434 (1932, 1933). Falter et al., *Wahlen,* 67–75.

61. *Hamburger Nachrichten* 299, 30 June 1927; *Altonaer Nachrichten* 239, 12 Oct. 1929. Cf. Georg Decker, "Zur Soziologie der Reichstagswahlen," *Die Gesellschaft* 5, no. 2 (1928): 1–12, here: 8; Larry E. Jones, "Sammlung oder Zersplitterung? Die Bestrebungen zur Bildung einer neuen Mittelpartei in der Endphase der Weimarer Republik," *Vierteljahreshefte für Zeitgeschichte* 25 (1977): 265–304, here: 271; idem., *German Liberalism and the Dissolution of the Weimar Party System, 1918–1933* (Chapel Hill, 1988).

62. *Sozialdemokratische Partei-Korrespondenz,* no. 7, July 1930, 470–78. McElligott, "Municipal Politics," 457; Bluhm, "Steenkamp," op. cit. Jürgen C. Hess, "Wandlungen im Staatsverständnis des Linksliberalismus der Weimarer Republik 1930–1933," in Karl Holl, ed., *Wirtschaftskrise und liberalen Demokratie. Das Ende der Weimarer Republik und die gegenwärtige Situation* (Göttingen, 1978), 46–88.

63. Neumann, *Parteien,* 57; W. Ruge, "Die Deutsche Volkspartei (DVP) 1918–1933," *Lexikon* 2, 413–46.

64. Wolfgang Treue, ed., *Deutsche Parteiprogramme seit 1861* (Göttingen, 1968), 113, 115.

65. *Altonaer Nachrichten* 224, 24 July 1927. See the analysis in *Sozialdemokratische Partei-Korrespondez,* nos. 8–9 (Aug.–Sept. 1930): 519–23.

66. *Altonaer Nachrichten* 224, op. cit. Henry Ashby Turner, *Stresemann and the Politics of the Weimar Republic* (Princeton, NJ, 1963), 266; Larry E. Jones, "The Dissolution of the Bourgeois Party System in the Weimar Republic," in Richard Bessel and E. J. Feuchtwanger, eds., *Social Change and Political Development in Weimar Germany* (London, 1981), 268–88. For Hegel on personalities: "Concerning the English Reform Bill," in Friedrich, *Philosophy of Hegel,* 543.

67. Peter Fritzsche, *Rehearsals for Fascism: Populism and Political Mobilization in Weimar Germany* (New York and Oxford, 1990), 197–98; Thomas Childers, "The Social Language of Politics in Germany: The Sociology of Political Dis-

course in the Weimar Republic," *American Historical Review* 95, no. 2 (Apr. 1990): 331–58.

68. Neumann, *Parteien,* 55; Ruge, "Deutsche Volkspartei," 413ff.

69. *Amtsblatt* 37, 17 Sept. 1927. Ernst Hamburger, "Parteienbewegung und Gesellschaftliche Umschichtung in Deutschland," *Die Gesellschaft* 11, no. 1 (1925): 346, 348; Georg Decker, "Der Tod einer Partei," *Die Gesellschaft* 5, no. 1 (1928): 385–99, here: 385; Neumann, *Parteien,* 61; Fritzsche, *Rehearsals,* 196; Lewis Hertzmann, "The Founding of the German National People's Party (DNVP), November 1918–January 1919," *Journal of Modern History* 30, no. 1 (1958): 24–36, here: 25; W. Ruge, "Die Deutschnationale Volkspartei (DNVP), 1918–1933," *Lexikon* 2, 476–528.

70. Usually in districts with an existing anti-Semitic vote, *Bericht* 2:357–64. LAS 309/12561 (Versammlungen), Polizeipräsident Altona, Abt.VIIa130/2/23, 16 Mar. 1923, "Betr. Ruhrkundgebung"; and: komm. Polizeipräsident to Regierungspräsident VIIa 162/III/23, 5 Apr. 1923, "Ruhrkundgebung"; and 309/22918, bl. 190; *Altonaer Nachrichten* 17 Mar. 1923 and *Altonaer Nachrichten* 203, 3 May 1923; *Hamburger Nachrichten* 494, 20 Oct. 1928; Decker, "Tod," 395; Falter et al., *Wahlen,* 189.

71. *Amtsblatt* 39, 1 Oct. 1927.

72. See the candidates lists published in *Amtsblatt* 17, 26 Apr. 1924; ibid., no. 37, 17 Sept. 1927; ibid., no. 45, 9 Nov. 1929; *Altonaer Adreßbuch* 1929, part V, 3. Cf. Koshar, *Social Life;* Celia Applegate, *A Nation of Provincials: The German Idea of Heimat* (Berkeley, Los Angeles, and Oxford, 1990).

73. Hamburger, "Parteienbewegung," 341; Günther Hollenberg, "Bürgerliche Sammlung oder Sozialliberale Koalition? Sozialstruktur, Interessenlage und politisches Verhalten der bürgerlichen Schichten 1918/19 am Beispiel der Stadt Frankfurt am Main," *Vierteljahreshefte für Zeitgeschichte* 27 (1979): 392–430.

74. StAH 424–44 (Groß Flottbek) 7, report on the meeting of the communal associations, 17 Feb. 1924.

75. StAH 122–3, Arbeiterrat 1, Band 1, Teil 1, Protokolle: 13. Sitzung des Arbeiter- und Soldatenrats (Groß Hamburg), 21 Nov. 1918, 4–7; for a different interpretation, Krause, "Revolution," 50–51.

76. StABr 4,65 4d 4, situation report no. 202, 17 Dec. 1919; 4,65 4e 3, situation report no. 55, 22 July 1921; and the reports in *Bremer Nachrichten* 148, 5 June 1919; ibid., 20 Dec. 1919.

77. *Hamburger Echo* 47, 16 Feb. 1924: "Zu den Magistratswahlen."

78. Christoph Timm, *Gustav Oelsner und das Neue Altona. Kommunale Architektur und Stadtplanung in der Weimarer Republik* (Hamburg, 1984).

79. StJü (1924), 47–48.

80. StJü (1923), 52–53.

81. Ohlen, "Albert Hänel," 23–48.

82. StAH 424–2 IVe 40/5 16 Apr. 1924: Vorlage 13, Türck et al. to Herrn Bürgermeister der Stadt Altona, "Betrifft Einwendungen gegen die am 30. März 1924 erfolgte Wahl des Bürgermeisters Brauer zum Ersten Bürgermeister."

83. Ibid.

84. Cited in Hoffmann, *Neues Altona,* 1:42–43.

85. Türck et al., op. cit.

86. *Hamburger Fremdenblatt* 2, 2 Jan. 1925: "Altona im Jahre 1924."

87. *Hamburger Nachrichten* 517, 4 Nov. 1927: "Der Mißtrauensantrag gegen den Oberbürgermeister Brauer."

88. *Hamburger Echo* 302, 1 Nov. 1927. Hermann Bauermeister was a local manufacturer and member of the *Gemeinschaftsliste;* Karl Frahm was a bank director and member of the DVP.

89. Dörr was branch secretary of the white-collar union, *Zentralverband deutscher Angestellten;* see entry in *Altonaer Adreßbuch* 1927.

90. "Der Mißtrauensantrag gegen den Oberbürgermeister Brauer," op. cit. StAH 421–5 Kb 3 bd. 3, *Norddeutsche Nachrichten* 266, 12 Nov. 1927.

91. *Hamburger Echo* 329, 8 Nov. 1927: "Regierungspräsident hilf!"

92. Ibid.

93. "Der Mißtrauensantrag," op. cit.

94. *Altonaer Nachrichten* 268, 15 Nov. 1929.

95. Wirtschaftspartei e.V., *10 Jahre Reichspartei des deutschen Mittelstandes* (Berlin, ca. 1930). Martin Schumacher, *Mittelstandsfront und Republik: Die Wirtschaftspartei-Reichspartei des deutschen Mittelstandes 1919–1933* (Düsseldorf, 1972).

96. *Altonaer Nachrichten* 270, 18 Nov. 1929; Schumacher, *Mittelstandsfront,* 115; Rietzler, *Kampf,* 418; Lewis Hertzmann, "Gustav Stresemann: The Problem of Political Leadership in the Weimar Republic," *International Review of Social History* 5 (1960): 361–77, here: 374.

97. *Altonaer Nachrichten* 270, 18 Nov. 1929; Schumacher, *Mittelstandsfront,* 117ff.

98. *Altonaer Tageblatt* 127, 3 June 1930.

99. Hertzmann, "Gustav Stresemann," 364; Neumann, *Parteien,* 60.

100. *Altonaer Tageblatt* 300, 22 Dec. 1932: "Zur Senatorenwahl"; and no. 301, 23 Dec. 1932: "Nochmals zur Senatorenwahl"; *Hamburger Tageblatt* 291, 22 Dec. 1932: "Wer wird in Altona Senator?"

101. *Altonaer Nachrichten* 117, 21 May 1928. National leaders believed the "catastrophic defeat" was "payment for four years of double-play" that had plunged the party into bitter factionalism, H. Weiß and P. Höser, eds., *Die Deutschnationalen und die Zerstörung der Weimarer Republik. Aus dem Tagebuch von Reinhold Quaatz 1928–1933* (Munich, 1989), 39, 71, 89, entries 21 May 1928, and 18 Nov. 1929; Attila Chanady, "The Disintegration of the DNVP, 1924–1930," *Journal of Modern History* 39 (1967): 65–90, 80, 82–90. Anneliese Thimme, *Flucht in den Mythos. Die Deutschnationale Volkspartei und die Niederlage von 1918* (Göttingen, 1969), 20.

102. Literally, "Drang nach Sammlung," Decker, "Soziologie," 11; Jones, "Sammlung," 267; Fritzsche, *Rehearsals,* 204.

103. LAB 162/1 StB 992/11: "Betrachtungen über die Kommunalwahlen 1929", hrsg. v. Geschäftsführenden Präsidium des Reichsbürgerrats (31 May 1931), 3, 12–13.

104. Jones, "Dissolution," 270–75; idem, "Sammlung," 263.

105. StABr. 4,65 II A.9.a. and, 4,65 II H 4 a II; and in, LAS 309/22990

(Heimatschutz); 309/22855 (Bewegungen im März 1920/Kapp); LAS 309/22927 (Rechtsorganisationen 1923–24).

106. LAS 309/22923, Gesamtverband Nationaler Berufsverbände: Deutsche Arbeiterbund (1922); LAS 309/22695 (1923), Deutsche-Völkische Arbeitsgemeinschaft; *Amtsblatt* 17, 26 Apr. 1924. Werner Dietz, *Deutschland Erwache. Dokumente aus der Hitler-Partei* (n.p., 1932); Rietzler, *Kampf,* chap. 2. Cf. Martin Broszat, "Die Anfänge der Berliner NSDAP 1926/27. Dokumentation," *Vierteljahreshefte für Zeitgeschichte* 8 (1960): 85–118.

107. LAS 399/65 file 6, Hinrich Lohse, "Die Revolution der NSDAP," 41–48, 67; LAS 309/22750 (Stadtring der Vaterländischen Verbände). Geoff Eley, "Conservatives and radical nationalists in Germany: the production of fascist potentials 1912–1928," in Martin Blinkhorn, ed., *Fascists and Conservatives. The radical right and the establishment in twentieth-century Europe* (London, 1990), 50–70.

108. Dietz, *Deutschland Erwache,* 1–6.

109. BDC: Personal File v. Allwörden, SA-Personal-Fragebogen: born 1 June 1892 in Altona, membership no. 7476 (13 June 1925).

110. StAH 421–5 Kc1a II, Deposition: "Lebenslauf," born 19 May 1892 in Groß Wisch (Kreis Steinburg), membership no. 7540 (13 June 1925). Cf. BDC: Personal File Sieh, SA-Personal-Fragebogen.

111. BDC: Personal File Brix, SA-Führer-Fragebogen: born 4 Nov. 1902 in Husum, membership no. 7486 (13 June 1925); ibid., Personal File Schmalmack, SA-Personal-Fragebogen: born 4 Aug. 1897, membership no. 7543 (13 June 1925).

112. Rietzler, *Kampf,* 387. Hermann Okrass, *"Hamburg bleibt Rot" Das Ende einer Parole* (Hamburg, 1934), 123ff. Fritzsche, *Rehearsals,* 202. Martin Broszat, "Die Struktur der NS-Massenbewegung," *Vierteljahreshefte für Zeitgeschichte* 31 (1983): 52–76.

113. StJü Altona (1924), 52; StJBDS 23 (1928), 277, 280; C. Mierendorff, "Gesicht und Charakter der Nationalsozialistischen Bewegung," *Die Gesellschaft* 7, no. 1 (1930): 489–504, here: 489, wrongly gives 1.8 percent as the result in Altona; in Nuremberg the VSB received 11.8 percent of the vote, and in Elbing received 11.6 percent.

114. It also changed its name to *Nationalsozialistische Deutsche Arbeiterpartei* in Apr. StAH 424–2 IVe 41 (1925), bl. 182: Sitzung 16 Apr. 1925; Hoffmann, *Neues Altona,* 1:627 n. 49.

115. BAK Slg. Schumacher 208 I/2, bl. 154–55: letter to Esser (Munich) 11 May 1925; Jeremy Noakes, "Conflict and Development in the NSDAP 1924–27," *Journal of Contemporary History* 1 (1966): 3–36; Dietrich Orlow, *A History of the Nazi Party, 1918–1933,* vol. 1 (Newton Abbot, 1969), chaps. 3–4.

116. See the scathing observation of Nazi council politics in *Hamburger Echo* 266, 26 Sept. 1927. StAH 424–2 IVe 40 (1924), bl. 224: Sitzung 19 June 1924, Drucksache 44 (Brauer's income); 424–2 IVe 42 (1926), 26 Mar. 1926, Drucksache 418/469/448/488 (Webwaren A.G.); 424–2 IVe 45 (1929), 7 Dec. 1929 Drucksache 1256; LAS 301/5038 (Kommunalangelegenheiten der Stadt Altona), and LAS 309/22804 (Republikschutzgesetz). for examples of various smear campaigns against Brauer. Cf. Rietzler, *Kampf,* 390–91.

117. *Altonaer Nachrichten* 67, 19 Sept. 1924. StAH 424–2 IVe 46 (1930), 5 Feb.

Drucksache 1276 (attack on Senator August Kirch). H-J. Zimmermann, *Wählerverhalten und Sozialstruktur im Kreisherzogtum Lauenburg 1918–1933. Ein Kreis Zwischen Obrigkeitsstaat und Demokratie* (Neumünster, 1978), 443–75; Stoltenberg, *Politische Strömungen,* 151; Peter Wulf, "Ernst Oberfohren und die DNVP am Ende der Weimarer Republik," in E. Erdmann, P. Wulf, eds., *"Wir bauen das Reich." Aufstieg und erste Herrschaftsjahre des Nationalsozialismus in Schleswig-Holstein* (Neumünster, 1983), 165–87, here: 172. Stokes, *Kleinstadt,* doc.I 16A III, 83–84, reveals the acrimony between the NSDAP and DNVP; and Volker Franke, *Der Aufstieg der NSDAP in Düsseldorf. Die nationalsozialistische Basis in einer katholischen Großstadt* (Essen, 1987), 80, shows its violent nature.

118. BAK Slg.Schumacher 208 I/2 (Gau Schleswig-Holstein), bl. 140–45: Lohse to Hitler, 3 Mar. 1925. Werner Stephan, "Zur Soziologie der Nationalsozialistischen Deutschen Arbeiterpartei," *Zeitschrift für Politik* 20 (1931): 793–800; Michael H. Kater, "Zur Soziographie der frühen NSDAP," *Vierteljahreshefte für Zeitgeschichte* 19 (1971): 124–59; Thomas Childers, "National Socialism and the New Middle Class," in Reinhard Mann, ed., *Die Nationalsozialisten. Analysen faschistischer Bewegung* (Stuttgart, 1980), 19–33.

119. As well as drawing on the candidates lists published regularly in the *Amtsblatt,* this account is based on records in: StAH 421–25 Kc1a II, Deposition (curriculum vitae); BDC: Personal File Stamer, membership no. 7546, Personal-Fragebogen; and *Führerlexikon* ("Unsere Führer" [1931]), 70.

120. BAK Slg.Schumacher 208 I/2, bl. 253: notification of change of address, 25 Aug. 1928; StAH 424–2 IVe 44 (1928), 28 June 1928, "Vorlage," 8.

121. BDC: Personal File Böge, membership no. 73670, 1 Jan. 1928, Personal-Fragebogen. See also the substantial file on personal conflicts in the Nienstedten branch: BDC: Personal File John Wohlers, sub-file: Akten des Obersten Parteigerichts, III. Kammer.

122. These data are based mainly on information in police and court reports, newspapers, and party correspondence, in BAK Slg.Schumacher 208 I/2, bl. 139–351: Gau Schleswig-Holstein; StAH 614, 2/5 A5a NSDAP; LAS 352/1240–1250, files of the Sondergericht. Cf. Jürgen Genuneit, "Methodische probleme der quantitativen Analyse früher NSDAP-Mitgliederlisten," in Mann, *Die Nationalsozialisten,* 34–66; Herbert Andrews, "The Social Composition of the NSDAP: Problems and Possible Solutions," *German Studies Review* 9 (1986): 293–317.

123. William Sheridan Allen, "Farewell to Class Analysis in the Rise of Nazism: Comment," *Central European History* 17, no. 1 (1984): 55–62; Jürgen Falter and Dirk Hänisch, "Die Anfälligkeit von Arbeitern gegenuber der NSDAP bei den Reichstagswahlen 1928–1933," *Archiv für Sozialgeschichte* 26 (1986): 179–216; Conan Fischer, *The Rise of the Nazis* (Manchester and New York, 1995). Cf. Michael Kater, "Sozialer Wandel in der NSDAP im Zuge der nationalsozialistischen Machtergreifung," in Wolfgang Schieder, ed., *Faschismus als soziale Bewegung. Deutschland und Italien im Vergleich* (Göttingen, 1983), 25–67, here: 30, 32, and table 3; idem, *The Nazi Party: A Social Profile of Members and Leaders, 1919–1945* (Oxford, 1983), 52–55.

124. BAK Slg.Schumacher 208 I/2, bl. 333–38: Gaupropagandaleitung, "Tätigkeitsbericht für Januar 1931," 2, which noted difficulties in Kiel too.
125. BAK Slg.Schumacher 208 I/2, bl. 177–80: correspondence between Lohse and Hess. *Schleswig-Holsteinische Tageszeitung* 25, 31 Jan. 1929. See Orlow, *History,* vol. 1, chap. 4; and Peter Stachura, "Der kritische Wendepunkt? Die NSDAP und die Reichstagswahlen vom 20.Mai 1928," *Vierteljahreshefte für Zeitgeschichte* 26, no. 1 (1978): 66–99.
126. LAS 309/22998, Polizeipräsident Altona, Abt.IA, 24 June 1929, Geheim! Betr. Stärkenachweisung ü.d. NSDAP; ibid., Übersicht über die nationalsozialistische Bewegung in Reg.bez. Schleswig (report for Sept.); ibid., Der Pol.präs. Landeskriminalpolizeistelle Ob I4 1, 25 Jan. 1930.
127. LAS 309/22918, bl. 325: Preuß. Pol.präs. Abt. IA 2 July 1929, Betr. Annäherung zwischen NSDAP und Stahlhelm. LAS 309/22634 (Wahlbewegung and Krawalle); 309/22918 (Stahlhelm 1925–1930); Werner Jochmann, ed., *Nationalsozialismus und Revolution: Dokumente* (Frankfurt, 1963), doc. 100, 315; Rietzler, *Kampf,* 416; Fritzsche, *Rehearsals,* 200.
128. LAS 301/4690, OP 30A62, 17 Dec. 1929, Oberpräsident to Interior Ministry: Nachweisung, reports for Oct. and Nov. Cf. LAS 309/226669 (Versammlungstätigkeiten), Abt. Polizeipräsident Altona, Nachweisungen.
129. *Altonaer Nachrichten* 117, 21 May 1928; ibid., no. 270, 18 Nov. 1929; *Hamburger Echo* 319, 18 Nov. 1929.
130. *Sozialdemokratische Partei-Korrespondenz,* no. 11, Nov. 1929: "Gegen Rowdys und Verbrecher," 592.
131. LAS 301/4690, report of Landrat Pinneberg, 4 Feb. 1930: Nachweisung (Jan. 1930); LAS 301/4691, OP 30A62 (Oberpräsident to MdI), reports for June, July, and Sept. See Heinrich Bennecke, *Wirtschaftliche Depression und politischer Radikalismus 1918–1938* (Munich and Vienna, 1970), 351–69.
132. It gained 27 percent in Schleswig-Holstein; the other two main manufacturing centers, Kiel and Neumünster, also showed slightly higher levels of support, namely, 22.7 percent and 23 percent, respectively: StDR 382.II, 27.
133. *Altonaer Nachrichten* 215, 15 Sept. 1930.
134. Ibid.; *Hamburger Echo* 255, 15 Sept. 1930.
135. James Pollock, "The German Reichstag Elections of 1930," *American Political Science Review* 24 (1930): 989–95, here: 993.
136. *Hamburger Echo* 255, 15 Sept. 1930. Rudolf Hilferding, "In der Gefahrenzone," *Die Gesellschaft* 7, no. 2 (1930): 289–97, here: 290. Hans Neisser, "Sozialstatistische Analyse des Wahlergebnisses," *Die Arbeit* 7, no. 10 (1930): 654–59; Jürgen Bergmann, Klaus Megerle, "Wer unterstützte die Nationalsozialisten? Das Verhältnis der gesellschaftlichen Gruppen zur nationalsozialistischen Bewegung," in Klaus Megerle, ed., *Warum gerade die Nationalsozialisten?* (Berlin, 1983), 146–95.
137. *Hamburger Echo* 6 May 1928; Jochmann, *Nationalsozialismus,* doc. 97, 300–306.
138. *Hamburger Echo* 101, 25 Apr. 1932, 1 Beilage. Harold L. Childs, "Recent Elections in Prussia and other German *Länder,*" *American Political Science Review* 26 (1932): 698–705, here: 698. For two recent reviews of whether or not the

NSDAP was exclusively a party of the "lower middle class" or a "people's party": Thomas Schnabel, "'Wer wählte Hitler.' Bemerkungen zu einigen Neuerscheinungen über die Endphase der Weimarer Republik," *Geschichte und Gesellschaft* 8, no. 1 (1982): 116–31; F. Lenger, "Mittelstand und Nationalsozialismus? Zur politischen Orientierung von Handwerkern und Angestellten in der Endphase der Weimarer Republik," *Archiv für Sozialgeschichte* 29 (1989): 173–98. For a forceful view of the longer trajectory of middle-class political realignments, Geoff Eley, "What Produces Fascism: Pre-industrial Tradition or a Crisis of the Capitalist State?" *Politics and Society* 12 (1983): 53–82.

Chapter 3

1. *Amtsblatt* 14, 7 Apr. 1928.

2. Paul-Theodor Hoffmann, *Mit dem Zeiger der Weltenuhr* (Hamburg, 1949), 244–45.

3. LAS 309/11333 (Eingemeindung Ottensens), Magistrat Ottensen, Denkschrift: "Die Vereinigung der Städte Altona und Ottensen und der Ortschaften Bahrenfeld, Othmarschen und Oevelgönne zu einer Gesamt-Gemeinde (November 1882)," 7. Heinrich Bleicher, "Franz Adickes als Kommunalpolitiker," in *Franz Adickes, Leben und Werk. Frankfurter Lebensbilder XI* (Frankfurt, 1929).

4. Hoffmann, *Neues Altona*, 1:218.

5. Molkenbuhr, "Das Beispiel Altona," 315.

6. Reprinted in: *Hamburger Echo*, 20 Dec. 1960, 10: "Hamburg hat Max Brauer viel zu danken." Hoffmann, *Neues Altona*, 1:42–43.

7. J. N. Tarn, "Housing reform and the emergence of town planning in Britain before 1914," in Anthony Sutcliffe, ed., *The Rise of Modern Urban Planning, 1800–1914* (London, 1980), 71–98, here: 84; Rüdiger vom Bruch, ed., *Weder Kommunismus noch Kapitalismus. Bürgerliche Sozialreform in Deutschland vom Vormärz bis zur Ära Adenauer* (Munich, 1985); Brian Ladd, *Urban Planning and Civic Order in Germany, 1860–1914* (Cambridge, Mass., and London, 1990).

8. Peukert, *Weimarer Republik*, 133–34. Juan Rodriguez-Lores, "Stadthygiene und Städtebau. Am Beispiel der Debatten im Deutschen Verein für öffentliche Gesundheitsplege 1869–1911," in Jürgen Reulecke and Adelheid Gräfin zu Castell Rüdenhausen, eds., *Stadt und Gesundheit. Zum Wandel von "Volksgesundheit" und kommunaler Gesundheitspolitik im 19. und frühen 20. Jahrhundert* (Stuttgart, 1991), 63–75; Evans, *Death in Hamburg*, chap. 2.

9. Jürgen Habermas, *Theorie des kommunikativen Handelns* (Frankfurt a.M., 1981), 2:522ff. Michel Foucault, *History of Sexuality*, vol. 1 (London, 1979).

10. Charles Tilly, *From Mobilization to Revolution* (Reading Mass., 1978) 172. Michel Foucault, *Discipline and Punish: The Birth of the Prison* (London, 1978).

11. *Bericht* 2:13, 19, 21; StAH 424–27 I/14 Statistik, Correspondence [to Dr. Hundt] 15 Aug. 1918; StJB Altona (1928), 20; Der Stadt Altona: Amt für Wirtschaft und Statistik, *Tatsachen in Wort, Zahl und Bild* (hereafter *Tatsachen*), no. 8 (10 Sept. 1936): 2.

12. StAH 424–27 (Statistik) B I3, Bevölkerungsbewegung—Allgemeines—

Tabelle II, Stand der Bevölkerung 1910–27; StJü Altona (1909), Anhang A, 1 (table 1). Berlage, *Altona,* 171, 180.

13. StJü Altona (1924), 51.

14. StAH 424–27 I3 (Häuserzählung): "Wohnstätten Altonas am 16 Juni 1925," for a list of the factories and workshops in the Altstadt; AHWV 16, no. 1 (1939): 4; Günther Marwedel, "Die Industrie," in Matthias Becker, ed., *Die Stadt Altona. Monographien deutscher Städte* (Berlin, 1928), 27:211; Hoffmann, *Neues Altona* 1:526; Kaufmann, *Gliederung,* 62–63. Cf. Walter Jackstein, *Liebe alte Stadt* (Hamburg-Altona, 1940).

15. Hoffmann, *Neues Altona,* 1:82–83.

16. *Amtsblatt* 9, 6 Mar. 1927: "Die Überbevölkerung der Stadt Altona"; StJB Altona (1928), 314–16. Gustav Oelsner, "Altona" in *Proceedings of the XIII International Housing and Town Planning Congress,* 3 vols. (Berlin, 1931), 3:45–46; Harold Jenner, *". . . man muß in die Hinterhöfe, Keller und Dachwohnungen gehen." Kirche und Stadt in Altona* (Hamburg, 1993), 112–17. McElligott, "Municipal Politics," 401.

17. Kaufmann, *Gliederung,* 71.

18. "Wohnstätten Altonas am 16 Juni 1925," op. cit.

19. StJü Altona (1904–9). There were still 2,618 inhabited attic dwellings by the mid-1920s, "Die Überbevölkerung der Stadt Altona," op. cit.

20. StAH 424–18 I 14 (Statistik), Dr. Hundt to Sen. Schöning, 23 May 1918; *Amtsblatt* 17, 30 Apr. 1927: "Die Wohnstätten und Wohnungen in Altona"; StJB Altona (1928), 324.

21. "Wohnstätten Altonas am 16.Juni 1925," op. cit.

22. Dr. Hundt to Sen. Schöning, 23 May 1918, op. cit. Cf. StAH 424–18 I/12 Wohnungsamt: "Dritter Bericht" (15 Nov. 1918–15 Nov. 1919), 40, "Vierter Bericht" (15 Oct. 1919–1 Apr. 1921), 26–27.

23. Ibid., 28; StDR 362:I, 94.

24. McElligott, "Municipal Politics," 398. See Lutz Niethammer and Franz Bruggemeier, "Wie Wohnten die Arbeiter im Kaiserreich?" *Archiv für Sozialgeschichte* 16 (1976): 61–134.

25. StAH 626–27 BI 23, Magistrat, Das Statistisches Amt (18 Feb. 1888), "Jahresbericht über die Veränderungen im Stande der Bevölkerung während des Jahres 1887: Die Sterbefälle nach den Todesursachen"; StJB Altona (1928), 13, 24–25.

26. Wohnungsamt, "Dritter Bericht," 48–49.

27. StAH 424–24 (Wohlfahrtsamt) IV 3.2 (Soziale Fürsorge Allg.), Amt für Wirtschaft und Statistik (7 Dec. 1937) to Herrn Bürgermeister Velthuysen: betr. "Notlage in der Altstadt."

28. "Notlage," 2, 4; StAH 424–27 I, Wohnungsmarkt in Altona 1931–1936: report by K[aestner ?] to Stadtrat Grotkop, 9 Nov. 1934, betr. "künftiger Wohnungsbedarf in Altona."

29. StJü Altona (1923), 8.

30. Ibid. (1923), 2–3, 10; StJü Altona (1924), 2–3, 10; StJB Altona (1928), 8, 11, 13. Kaufmann, *Gliederung,* 68–69; StAH 424–27, no. BI 18: "Gestorbene Kinder christlicher Eltern unter 5 Jahren nach Stadtteilen (1929–1933)"; ibid., no. BI 20:

Statistik über die Säuglingssterblichkeit (1890) 1929–34: "Der Stadtmedizinalrat an die Oberbürgermeister mit der Bitte um Weitergabe, Amt für Statistik, 9 Mai 1934"; ibid., no. BI 22: "Sterbefälle nach Stadtbezirken und Stadtteilen" (1934, 1935, 1936).

31. StJB Altona (1928), 275; Hoffmann, *Neues Altona,* 1:218.

32. Egbert Baumann, *Kriegs-Familienunterstützung in Altona. Grundsätze und Aufwendungen der Kommission für Familienunterstützung in vier Kriegsjahren* (Altona, 1919), 241–42, 246–47. StAH 424–1 I 15 IX, Betr. Unterstützungen der städtischen Verwaltung (Sonderleistungen auf dem Gebiet des Wohlfahrtsamtes); StAH 424–24, Aktz. I 10.6 (Wohlfahrtskommission), Kinderschutz und Jugendwohlfahrt (e.V.) Altona, *Jahresbericht 1920* (Altona, n.d.).

33. LAB 142/2 StK 717, Chef des Feldeisenbahnwesens Gruppe A no. 1574 Generalstab Mappe 10: Massenspeisungen, 20 Oct. 1916; StAH 424–29 (Lebensmittelamt), I E III/5, Aufstellung der Monatlichen Portionszahl sämtlicher Kriegsküchen für die Zeit vom November 1916–April 1917; ibid., 142/2 StK 1051 (Kriegsküchen), various reports; StJbDR 39 (1918): 158–62, ibid., 40 (1919): 348–52. By comparison, the corresponding percentages for Hamburg, Frankfurt and Hannover were: 25, 20, and 12, respectively, LAB 142/2 StK 1051, Altona Berichte an das stellv. königliche Generalkommando des IX Armeekorps Abt. V. Altona, n.d. (1917).

34. StAH 424–24 Aktz. I 10.6, bl. 4, minutes of the Wohlfahrtskommission, item 3: "Massnahmen zur Mittelstandsfürsorge," 23 Feb. 1920.

35. StAH 424–24 42, Auszug aus dem Protokoll der Sitzung der Armenkommission am Dienstag 13. Sept. 1921; StAH 424–24 BIV 3 Bd.2 (altes Signatur), Probleme der Stadt Altona, II Sachausgaben (1924–25).

36. StAH 424–24 Aktz. I 12.1 Unterstütztungsamt vol. 1: Die in den einzelnen Bezirken Januar bis März 1923 verausgabten Barunterstützungen und Suppenzeichen; an undated memo from the *Magistrat* to the *Bezirksvorsteher* in the same file puts the amount distributed in cash at 21.6 million marks.

37. StAH 424–24, Aktz.I 12.1, Unterstützungsamt, Abt.: Vorübergehende Fürsorge, 14 Feb. 1923.

38. StAH 424–24 42, Bericht des Vereins von 1830 (Rudolphi, 1927); ibid: Erhebung über die durchführung von Volksspeisungen in deutschen Großstädten, shows 106,273 litres were distributed in 1925 and 161,512 in 1926.

39. StAH 424–24 32:2, Unterakte Erwerbslosenselbsthilfe eV. 1 Mai 1933: "An unsere verehrten fordernden Mitglieder!"

40. StAH 424–24 32:2, Unterakte: Schulkinder und Schulentlassene 1932–1933: Wohlfahrtamt 300, report: 12 Sept. 1932. Cf. League of Nations, Health Section, memorandum: "The Economic Depression and Public Health" (Document A II.I.1932), summarized in: *International Labor Review* 26, no. 6 (Dec. 1932): 841–46.

41. StAH 424–29 II 226: Acta betreffend die im Armenhause bei Osdorf aufgenommen und von dort entlaßenen Kinder, 1884/85 bis 1908.

42. "Notlage," 2.

43. StAH 424–32:2, Wohlfahrtsamt: Familienfürsorge to Hauptstelle Wohlfahrtsamt, 23 Mai 1933, Betr. Besondere Sachleistungen aus Anlass der

Schulentlassung, zur Verfügung 20 Feb. 1933; StAH 424–24 56:3, NSDAP Gau Schleswig-Holstein Amt für Volkswohlfahrt St.Kr. Altona, 27 Mar. 1935, Konfirmandenaufstellung.

44. Baumann, *Kriegs-Familienunterstützung* (1919), 161–65; StAH 421–5 Kb3 IV (camp Trischen).

45. StAH 424–24 Aktz. IV 40:14 (altes Signatur) Arbeiterwohlfahrt, annual reports for 1925–31.

46. *Wolhfahrtsnachrichten der Stadt Altona* 4 Jg., nos. 11–12 (Aug.–Sept. 1928): 171.

47. StAH 424–24 56:3, NSDAP Gau Schleswig-Holstein Amt für Volkswohlfahrt to Oberbürgermeister Hauptstelle Wohlfahrt, 14 Aug. 1934, "Liste für Mütterverschickung" (Hilfswerk Sommer 1934): 53 cases of mothers and children; and letter 26 Apr. 1935, for list of 113 children for Sept. 1934–Mar. 1935.

48. StAH 424–24 56:3, NSDAP Gau Hamburg Kreis Altona, Kreiskassenverwalter to Oberbürgermeister Altona 18 Mar. 1938, for list of 659 welfare unemployed family heads. StAH 424–24 32:3, Der Oberbürgermeister Wohlfahrtsamt 300, 24 Mar. 1934, and ibid., 301/E, 17 May 1934, for impoverished, mostly elderly property-owners.

49. Dr. Walter Cimbal, "Das psychologische Beratungsamt," in W. Jackstein, ed., *Deutschlands Städtebau: Altona* (Berlin-Hallensee, 1922), 37–42.

50. *Amtsblatt* 2, 14 Jan. 1928: "Wohnungsnot."

51. Jürgen Brandt, "Die Beseitigung verwahrlöster Wohnviertel in Deutschland," in *Proceedings,* 1:72. Kaufmann referred to them as *Abschaum der Großstadt,* approximating *Lumpenproletariat* (*Gliederung,* 62). See Robert Warnecke, "Razzia Grenzlokale," in *Altonaer Tageblatt* 98, 25 Oct. 1924.

52. StAH 424–18 I/14, Baupflegeamt to Senator Schöning, 9 Feb. 1918, "Bericht über den Befund der Altonaer Leerstehenden Wohnungen."

53. StAH 424–1 I 15 IX, Senator Schöning to Prussian Interior Minister and Regierunspräsident Schleswig, 2 Nov. 1925, "Betrifft Unterstützungen für Einzelaufgaben der städtischen Verwaltung: (6) Betrifft Sonderleistungen auf dem Gebiet des Wohlfahrtsamtes, 66b: Magistrat Wohlfahrtsamt, A.Nr.D.100 Bn/M (Abschrift)."

54. Lothar Danner, *Betrachtungen zur Geschichte der Ordnungspolizei 1918–1933* (Hamburg, 1958), 264.

55. StAH 424–24 56:3, Deutsche Forschungsgemeinschaft wissenschaftliche Akademikerhilfe: Notarbeit 51, Stellv. wiss. Leiter Dr. Hans Kinder to Wohlfahrtsamt Goethealle, "Betr. Feststellungen gemeinschädlicher Regionen in der Stadtgemeinde Altona durch die Notarbeit," 29 Aug. 1935; *Dokumentation Faschistischer Sanierungspolitik: Notarbeit 51 der Notgemeinschaft der Deutschen Wissenschaft Gemeinschädigende Regionen des niederelbischen Städtegebietes 1934/35* (repr., Hamburg, 1984), 19; Michael Grüttner, "Soziale Hygiene und Soziale Kontrolle. Die Sanierung der Hamburger Gängeviertel 1892–1936," in Herzig et al., *Arbeiter in Hamburg,* 359–72; Richard J. Evans, ed., *The German Underworld* (London, 1988); Michael Schwartz, "'Proletarier' und 'Lumpen'

Sozialistische Ursprünge eugenischen Denkens," *Vierteljahreshefte für Zeitgeschichte* 42, no. 4 (1994): 537–70.

56. *Amtsblatt* 15, 17 Apr. 1931.

57. "Aufgaben, Wesen und Bedeutung der Wohlfahrtspflege in Altona," in *Wohlfahrtsnachrichten der Stadt Altona* (hereafter: *Wohlfahrtsnachrichten*), 4 Jg., no. 1 (Oct. 1927): 2–5; *Wohlfahrtsnachrichten* 4 Jg., no. 2 (Nov. 1927): 18–19; see chap. 7, map 12.

58. StAH 424–29 I H I/1, Beschwerde (1917); Anthony McElligott, "Petty Complaints, Plunder and Police in Altona 1917–1920. Towards an Interpretation of Community and Conflict," in Peter Assion, ed., *Transformationen der Arbeiterkultur* (Marburg, 1986), 110–25. See Volker Ullrich, *Kriegsalltag. Hamburg im ersten Weltkrieg* (Cologne, 1982); Ute Daniel, *Arbeiterfrauen in der Kriegsgesellschaft: Beruf, Familie und Politik im Ersten Weltkrieg* (Göttingen, 1989); Anne Roerkohl, *Hungerblockade und Heimatfront. Die kommunale Lebensmittelversorgung in Westfalen während des Ersten Weltkrieges* (Stuttgart, 1991); Belinda Joy Davis, "Home Fires Burning: Politics, Identity and Food in World War I Berlin" (Ph.D. diss., University of Michigan, 1992); idem, "Food Scarcity and the Empowerment of the Female Consumer in World War I Berlin," in Victoria de Grazia and Ellen Furlough, eds., *The Sex of Things: Gender and Consumption in Historical Perspective* (Berkeley, Calif., 1996), 287–310.

59. McElligott, "Petty Complaints," 115–16; StAH 424–29 1B 1/2a Bd.1: Niederschriften der LA-Kommission, reports of 25 Feb. and 1 Mar., bl. 17: 20–25; StAH 424–16 (städt. Polizeibehörde: ungeordnetes Material), Entscheidungen anläßlich der Lebensmittelunruhen (1917): Zusammenstellung der . . . entstandenen Schäden (23–24 Feb.), 12 June 1917; and "Zusammenstellung" together with two lists of participants in the rioting in same file.

60. StAH 424–16, Polizei Revier Bahrenfeld, Betrifft: Plünderungen von Brotläden, 25 Feb. 1917; ibid., letter from Richard Galster to Oberbürgermeister Schnackenburg, 25 Feb. 1917; ibid., Entscheidungen: nos. 13, 21, 35, 46/76, 48/68, 61, 65 and that of Mathilde Strauß.

61. StAH 424–16 Belege 45/68 (Schlüter). Bread losses came to 66 marks, while that of his property came to 82 marks and 60 pfennige.

62. McElligott, "Petty Complaints," 117–18; StAH 424–12/1: Polizeirevier 4, Bericht über die Unruhen am 26 Juni 1920, in particular.

63. Ibid., 12/11, no. 85; and 12/6, vol. 2, no. 45.

64. LAS 309/22855, Polizeiamt Altona, 29 June 1920: Betr. Unruhen am 26, 27 und 28 Juni 1920 (Tolgreve and Co.); StAH 424–12/11: no. 57 (Sellhorn).

65. McElligott, "Petty Complaints," 110–15.

66. StAH 424–29 (Lebensmittelamt) 1.B I/1, Mitteilung über das Lebensmittelamt, no. 51 (June 1917); 424–29 I.G V/4, bl. 14: report from Meldestelle Rev. III 10 Feb. 1917; and StAH 424–29 1.H.I/1, and 424–29 1C.II/4, contain a number of cases of ration card fraud. Baumann, *Kriegs-Familienunterstützung* (1917), 46, 68.

67. StAH 424–29 1G V/2 Magistratsverordnung, 30 Sept. 1916; Lippmann, *Mein Leben*, 218.

68. StAH 424–29 1G V/2: königl. Provinzial Fleischstelle der Provinz Schleswig-Holstein Altona, an sämtl. Herren Landräte und Herren Oberbürger-

meister, Tgb. 683/17, 22 May 1917; ibid., Magistrat JNr. LA IV 619/17, Verzeichnis der Geheimschlachtungen, 18 Aug. 1917.

69. International Labour Office (ILO), *European Housing Problems since the War* (Geneva, 1924), 20, 28, 324ff.; Ludwig Preller, *Sozialpolitik in der Weimarer Republik* (1949; repr., Düsseldorf, 1978), 67–70.

70. ILO, *European Housing,* 18.

71. Hoffmann, *Neues Altona,* 1:108, 204.

72. StAH 424–24 56: Preuss.Pol.präs. Abt.III, 2980/26 to Magistrat, 14 Jan. 1927 (Barth); StAH 424–24 52 Städtisches Wohnungsamt, Oelsner to Senator Lamp'l, 14 Feb. 1927; and Städtisches Wohnungsamt, Fischer to Senator Lamp'l, 14 Feb. 1927.

73. StAH 424 52: Abschrift, Städtische Polizeibehörde 170 zur sofortige Stellungnahme, Lamp'l to Senator Kirch and Dr. Baumann, 22 July 1931.

74. StAH 424–24 52 report, "Zur Obdachlosenfrage in Altona" (Lund), 1 Aug. 1932.

75. StAH 424–15 Lit. L 13 SAGA "Geschäftsbericht" annual reports for 1927–33, for references to this.

76. Arrears for pre-1918 municipal-controlled housing were 101,654 RM; in 1930 the combined level of arrears for all new housing stood at 95,376 RM, "Geschäftsbericht," report 1930, 1, 7. Cf. StAH 424–18 (Wohnungsamt), 14/2, "Ausstellung ü.d. Stand der Einnahmen und Ausgaben des W.A., 1 April–30 Sept. 1930," 5 Nov. 1930.

77. "Geschäftsbericht," reports 1924 and 1931.

78. "Geschäftsbericht," reports 1925; 1927, 2; 1928, 7ff.

79. "Geschäftsbericht," report 1933, 4; *Altonaer Nachrichten* 128, 1 June 1933; *Norddeutsche Nachrichten* 126, 1 June 1933.

80. StAH 424–24 52, (Abschrift) Polizeipräsident, Abt.III to Magistrat der Stadt Altona, 9 Oct. 1926.

81. Hoffmann, *Neues Altona,* 1:34. The following is based on Hoffmann's account.

82. StAH 424–24 52, Schöning to Polizeipräsident, 15 Oct. 1926, and copy with correction, 15 Nov. 1926.

83. StAH 424 24 52, Schöning to Bezirksvorsteher and Kommissionsmitglieder, 16 Aug. 1926; Ibid. (Abschrift) Städtische Polizeibehörde -170- zur sofortigen Stellungnahme. dez. Lamp'l, 21 July 1931; ibid., Report, "Zur Obdachlosenfrage in Altona." Fischer's letter to Lamp'l, op. cit., 14 Feb. 1927.

84. StAH 424–24 52, Auszug aus dem Protokoll der Sitzung des Unterstützungsausschusses am Dienstag, 15 July 1924 (Bezirksvorsteher Wöhnert). Grundvermögensamt (Oelsner) to Wohlfahrtsamt, 29 July 1924. StAH 424–24 Unterstützungsamt 1/2, Letter from Pieron, Nov. 1931.

85. StJü Altona (1923), 25–26.

86. StAH 424–16, Az. Sp.XII 76, Herbergen im Altona.

87. Ibid., Ernst Zimmermann and others, letters to the municipal police, health board and housing department, 23 Dec. 1926, 11 Jan. 1927, 18 Jan. 1927, 28 Jan. 1927, 21 Apr. 1927; and reports of Städtische Polizeibehörde Abt.III to the municipal and the regional supervisory body (Bezirksausschuss): 21 Jan. 1927, 2

Feb. 1927, and 15 Feb. 1927, in the same file. StAH 424–24 G8 (Bekämpfung der Bettelei 1924–1938): Städtische Wohlfahrtsamt, 12 Mar. 1924.

88. *Wohlfahrtsnachrichten* 4 Jg., no. 2 (Nov. 1927): "Ueber die Gemeinnützige Arbeitsstätte in Altona."

89. StJB Altona (1928), 71; Hoffmann, *Neues Altona,* 1:28.

90. "Ueber die Gemeinnützige Arbeitsstätte in Altona," op. cit.; *Wohlfahrts-nachrichten* 4 Jg., no. 3 (Dec. 1927): 69; *Amtsblatt* 45, 9 Nov. 1929: "Die öffentliche Wohlfahrtspflege in Altona in den letzten Jahren." See Künstlerhaus Bethanien, ed., *Wohnsitz: Nirgendwo. Vom Leben und vom Überleben auf der Strasse* (Berlin, 1982).

91. StAH 424–24 48: Bekämpfung der Bettelei 1924–1934, 1938, Wohlfahrt-samt Hamburg to Wohlfahrtsamt Altona, 9 Feb. 1924; ibid., Städt. Wohlfahrtsamt (Altona), Betr. Einführung v. Wohlfahrtschecks, 12 Mar. 1924.

92. StAH 424–24 32:2, Unterakte: Strassenhändler, Der Oberbürgermeister Z.I.B. to Wohlfahrtsamt, 26 Oct. 1929; StAH 424–24 32:2, "Unterakte: Her-anziehung Unterhaltungpflichtigen zu Unterstützungskosten (1931) 1933. StAH 424–27 BIV 3, vol. 1, Soziale Fürsorge—Allgemeines: 1928–1933, "Personenkreis der öffentliche Fürsorge und Fürsorgekosten im Berichtvierteljahr: Januar-März 1929," for the cost of unemployment welfare relief. The 1928 figure has been extrapolated from the amount given for 1929 and calculated to the number of recipients.

93. StAH 424–24 32:2, Städt. Polizeibehörde, Betr. Aufstellung von Wohnwa-gen der Dombezw. Marktbezieher, 6 Jan. 1930; StAH 424–24 32:3, Arbeitsamt Hamburg III/4 Ermittlung: An das Wohlfahrtsamt Altona, 24 Jan. 1934.

94. StAH 424–24 32:2, Schriftwechsel, Brauer to Oelsner, 25 June 1931 (origi-nal report, Wohlfahrtsamt, 16 Feb. 1931); and ibid., Magistrat 40, Oelsner to Wohlfahrtsamt, 8 July 1931, for his complaint.

95. StAH 424–24 32:2, Polizeiamt Abt.III, Betrifft Zigeunerlage, 9 Sept. 1929; ibid., Unterstützungsamt, Schriftverkehr, 17 Sept. 1929; ibid., Wohlfahrtsamt, 10 Sept. 1929; and inquiry by Deutscher Städtetag, Rundfrage III 521/29 "Bekämp-fung des Zigeunerwesens," 18 Nov. 1929, in the same file. Hoffmann, *Neues Altona,* 1:84.

96. StAH 424–24 32:2, unmarked report, 11 Nov. 1932.

97. StAH 424–24 32:2, report by Wohlfahrtsamt (Dorn), 21 Dec. 1932.

98. The Gypsies were forcedly disinfected, had their heads shaven, and given a daily bread ration of 200 grams, StAH 424–24 32:2, Unterakte: Zigeunerangele-genheiten—Markreisende—Schausteller; cf. StAH 424–24 48, Arbeitslager Rick-ling. Detlev J. K. Peukert, *Inside Nazi Germany: Conformity, Opposition, and Racism in Everyday Life* (New York, 1987), 210–14; Michael Burleigh and Wolf-gang Wippermann, *The Racial State: Germany 1933–1945* (Cambridge, 1991), chap. 5.

99. *Altonaer Adreßbuch* 1932, 3:285–86.

100. *Jahresbericht des öffentlichen Trinkerfürsorgestelle in Altona, 1911–12* (Altona, 1912), 9. More generally, James S. Roberts, *Drink, Temperance and the Working Class in Nineteenth-Century Germany* (Boston, London, and Sydney, 1984); Michael Grüttner, "Alkoholkonsum in der Arbeiterschaft 1971–1939," in

Toni Pierenkemper, ed., *Haushalt und verbrauch in Historischer Perspektive. Zum Wandel des privaten Verbrauchs in Deutschland im 19. und 20.Jahrhundert* (St. Katharinen 1987), 229–73.

101. StAH 424–9 II 194 (Trinksüchtige), report by Dr. Cimbal, 26 Apr. 1908; *1 Jahresbericht der Öffentlichen Trinkerfürsorgestelle Altona* (Altona, 1910); Jenner, *Kirche und Stadt,* 98.

102. *Wohlfahrtsnachrichten* 4 Jg., nos. 9–10 (June–July 1928): 146; ibid., 5 Jg., no. 6 (Mar. 1929): 89–91; ibid., 6 Jg., no. 1 (Oct. 1929): 5. StJB Altona (1928), 32. For data on the increase in alcohol-related deaths: StJB Altona (1928), 14.

103. *Jahresbericht der öffentlichen Trinkerfürsorgestelle,* 12, 17; Hoffmann, *Neues Altona,* 1:36.

104. *Wohlfahrtsnachrichten* 5 Jg., no. 1 (Oct. 1928): 8–9.

105. Hoffmann, *Neues Altona,* 1:33.

106. *Wohlfahrtsnachrichten* 5 Jg., no. 6 (Mar. 1929): 89; ibid., 6 Jg., no. 1 (Oct. 1929): 3, 10. In general, see Peter Weingart, Jürgen Kroll, Kurt Bayertz, *Rasse, Blut und Gene. Geschichte der Eugenik und Rassenhygiene in Deutschland* (Frankfurt, 1988), 254–59.

107. *Wohlfahrtsnachrichten* 6 Jg., no. 1 (Oct. 1929): 11.

108. *Wohlfahrtsnachrichten* 5 Jg., no. 4 (Jan. 1929): 63–64.

109. Kinderschutz und Jugendwohlfahrt (e.V) Altona, *Jahresbericht,* 1, col 2.

110. E.g., StAH 424–12 11 (Aufruhr-Tumultschäden), no. 61; StAH 424–29 (Lebensmittelamt), 2.A. VIII/1, u.a. Bewachung von Getreideanlagen und Mühlen; LAS 352/1245, files 344, 350.

111. *Wohlfahrtsnachrichten* 5 Jg., no. 2 (Nov. 1928): 26–27. StAH 424–16, Verwaltungsbericht für die Zeit 1. Jan. 1927 bis 31. Mar. 1929.

112. Ibid., 1. Apr. 1929 bis 31. Mar. 1930; ibid., 1. Apr. 1930 bis 31. Mar. 1931; ibid., 1. Apr. 1931 bis 31. Mar. 1932. StAH 424–27 B V1, Statistik über die Tätigkeit der städtischen Polizeibehörde (1924–27), 1928–36. Hoffmann, *Neues Altona,* 1:372–73. Hans Ostwald, *Sittengeschichte der Inflation: Ein Kulturdokument aus den Jahren des Marksturzes* (Berlin, 1931).

113. Hoffmann, *Neues Altona,* 1:266, for quotes; Richard Bessel, *Germany after the First World War* (Oxford, 1993), 242–51; Elizabeth R. Harvey, *Youth and the Welfare State in Weimar Germany* (Oxford, 1993).

114. Hoffmann, *Neues Altona,* 1:269; StAH 424–29 2 A VIII/1 Hagen/Inselmann to *Magistrat,* 31 Mar. 1919; *Wohlfahrtsnachrichten* 4 Jg., no. 4 (Jan. 1928), 70ff.; *Wohlfahrtsnachrichten* 4 Jg., nos. 9–10 (June–July 1928): 146–48; *Wohlfahrtsnachrichten* 5 Jg., no. 7 (Apr. 1929): 103; Cimbal, "Beratungsamt," 41; StAH 421–5 Kb 3 IV, Brauer to Regierungspräsident, 14 July 1932, on child vandalism in the Altstadt.

115. StJü Altona (1923), 25; StJb Altona (1928), 77; StAH 424–27, no. B VI, Polizeigefängnis Altona: "Zahl der Häftlinge" (tables for 1930–35), and: "Die Häftlinge im Altonaer Polizeigefängnis 1936–193."

116. Summarized in, Detlev J. K. Peukert, *Jugend zwischen Krieg und Krise: Lebenswelten von Arbeiterjungen in der Weimarer Republik* (Cologne, 1987); cf. Harvey, *Youth,* chap. 6; Eric A. Johnson, *Urbanization and Crime. Germany 1971–1914* (Cambridge, 1995), 191–98.

117. Hoffmann, *Neues Altona,* 1:265.
118. *Wohlfahrtsnachrichten* 4 Jg., nos. 11–12 (Aug.–Sept. 1928): 169–71; *Wohlfahrtsnachrichten* 4 Jg., nos. 9–10 (June–July 1928): 149–50; Rolf Lindner, "Straße-Straßenjunge-Straßenbände. Ein zivilisationstheoretischer Streifzug," *Zeitschrift für Volkskunde* (1983): 192–208.
119. Warnecke, "Razzia."
120. StDR 406, 194–96; and no. 455/13 (1933), 36–37.
121. StAH 424–24 40, reports: Amt für Jugendplege und Sport (Lorenzen), 14 Jan. 1922, and 31 July 1922.
122. Report by Lorenzen, 14 Jan. 1922, op cit. Lynn Abrams, *Workers' Culture in Imperial Germany. Leisure and Recreation in the Rhineland and Westphalia* (London, 1992); Mark Roseman, ed., *Generations in Conflict: Youth Revolt and Generation Formation in Germany, 1770–1968* (Cambridge and New York, 1995).
123. A survey of the public library, municipalized in early 1921, revealed that three-quarters of its 35,000 borrowers were working-class; as were half of the 37,924 users of the reading room, and one-fifth were under twenty-one years old (*Volksbücherei,* no. 4, Altonaer Museum, 5 Jan.1922, copy in StAH 424–24 40).
124. StAH 424–24 40, Städtische Wohlfahrtsamt an das Gewerbeaufsichtsamt, 20 Oct. 1922.
125. Hoffmann, *Neues Altona,* 1:395.
126. Ibid., 397; StAH 424–24 37, Bericht über die Tätigkeit des Pflegeamtes Altona in dem Jahre 1919. Cf. Ursula Nienhaus, Einsatz für die 'Sittlichkeit': Die Anfänge der weiblichen Polizei im Wilhelminischen Kaiserreich und in der Weimarer Republik," in Alf Lüdtke, ed., *'Sicherheit' und 'Wohlfahrt' Polizei, Gesellschaft und Herrschaft im 19. und 20. Jahrhundert* (Frankfurt a.M., 1992), 243–66, here: 247–48.
127. According to Hoffmann, *Neues Altona* 1:266, delinquent girls outnumbered boys 4 to 1 between 1918 and 1920.
128. Kaufmann, *Gliederung,* 66.
129. Jenner, *Kirche und Stadt,* 96, 98.
130. StAH 424–24 37, Städtisches Pflegeamt, for details; *Wohlfahrtsnachtrichten* 6 Jg., nos. 9–10 (June–July 1930): 94–97.
131. StAH 97, Handschriftsammlung sig 41 CMXLI, Senta Thiemsen, "Der Einfluß des Milieus auf das Grundschulkind" (Ms. Altona, 1931).
132. Ibid., 34, 47.
133. *Amtsblatt* 13, 29 Mar. 1930: "'Freud' und Leid im städtischen Mädchenheim."
134. 424–24 37, Städtisches Pflegeamt to Magistrat, Wohlfahrtsamt, Herrn Dr. Baumann, 4 Feb. 1928. Cornelia Usborne, *The Politics of the Body in Weimar Germany: Women's Reproductive Rights and Duties* (London, 1992). Cf. Robert G. Moeller, "The State of Women's Welfare in European Welfare States," *Social History* 19, no. 3 (Oct. 1994): 385–93, for a critical review.
135. StAH 424–27, G7/G8, Arbeitsmarkt Altona: Statistik 1916–36; *Wohlfahrtsnachrichten* 5 Jg., no. 1 (Oct. 1928): 6.
136. "Zahl der Häftlinge," op. cit.
137. Dr. Walter Jackstein, "Kulturelle Erwerbslosenfürsorge in Altona," *Amts-*

blatt 14, 8 Apr. 1932. Jackstein coined the phrase, "culture of the unemployed" (*Kultur der Arbeitslose*), ibid., no 51, 23 Dec. 1932.

138. Louise Schroeder, "Die Bedeutung der staatsbürgerlichen Erziehung unserer Jugend," in *Amtsblatt* 41, 11 Oct. 1930. On the importance of democratic civics, see K. G. Fischer, ed., *Politische Bildung in der Weimarer Republik: Grundsatzreferate der "Staatsburgerlichen Woche," 1923* (Frankfurt a.M., 1970).

139. *Wohlfahrtsnachrichten* 7 Jg., no. 2 (Mar. 1931), 14–21. Joachim Bartz and Dagmar Mor, "Der Weg in die Jugendzwangsarbeit. Maßnahmen gegen Jugendarbeitslosigkeit zwischen 1925 und 1935," in Gero Lenhardt, ed., *Der Hilfslose Sozialstaat Jugendarbeitslosigkeit und Politik* (Frankfurt a.M., 1979), 28–93, here: 38–49. Harvey, *Youth,* 126–31.

140. *Amtsblatt* 48, 4 Dec. 1931; and no. 7, 19 Feb. 1932.

141. *Amtsblatt* 3, 3 Feb. 1933. This view entirely ignored a shift in girls' expectations of their career choices, "Die Arbeit der Berufsberatung," *Wohlfahrstnachrichten* 4 Jg. 2 (Nov. 1927): 9–11; "Die berufswünsche der Mädchen und ihre Erfüllungsmöglichkeiten," ibid., 6 Jg., nos. 9–10 (June–July 1930): 98–100; Bridenthal and Koonz, "Beyond Kinder," 43.

142. *Hamburger Echo* 266, 26 Sept. 1927.

143. SPD, *Protokoll* 1920, 225. Cf. Adelheid von Saldern, "Sozialdemokratie und kommunale Wohnungsbaupolitik in den 20er Jahren—am Beispiel von Hamburg und Wien," *Archiv für Sozialgeschichte* 25 (1985): 183–237.

144. Marie-Elisabeth Lüders, "Why, and How, Is Germany Building? The Motives and Methods of Germany's Extensive Building Program," in *Passing through Germany* (Berlin, 1930), 92–98.

145. Manfredo Tafuri, *The Sphere and Labrynth, Avant-Gardes and Architecture from Piranesi to the 1970s* (Cambridge Mass., and London, 1990), chap. 7, for a useful discussion.

146. StAH 424–15, Lit.A 21, Magistrat Oelsner, 1d.345/27, to Nordische Industriebank Ütermann, Pflüger and Co., Hamburg, 29 Mar. 1927.

147. Quoted in Barbara Miller Lane, *Architecture and Politics in Germany, 1918–1945,* 2d ed. (Cambridge Mass., and London, 1985), 90, 41–45, 129. John Robert Mullin, "City Planning in Frankfurt, Germany, 1925–1932: A Study in Practical Utopianism," *Journal of Urban History* 4, no. 1 (Nov. 1977): 3–28; Nicholas Bullock, "Housing in Frankfurt 1925 to 1931 and the new Wohnkultur," *Architectural Review* 163, no. 976 (June 1978): 335–42; Peukert, *Weimarer Republik,* 183.

148. Molkenbuhr, "Das Beispiel Altona," 317. StAH 424–27 A I 4d, Statistik über die Bautätigkeit in Altona, Band 4: 1893–1928; "Die Wohnstätten und Wohnungen in Altona"; StJü Altona (1909), Anhang A, 2. Cf. von Saldern, "Sozialdemokratie," 209.

149. McElligott, "Municipal Politics," chap. 5, for full details. Cf. Timm, *Oelsner.*

150. StAH 421–25, Kb 8b, Wirtschaftsberatung deutscher Städte A.G., Bericht no. 229, Teil I, Verwendung der seit 1924 aufgenommenen Schulden, 48; Hoffmann, *Neues Altona,* 1:630, n. 135, for a financial breakdown of the individual developments consructed between 1918 and 1927. More generally: Dan Silverman,

"A Pledge Unredeemed: The Housing Crisis in Weimar Germany," *Central European History* 3 (1970): 112–39; Michael Ruck, "Der Wohnungsbau—Schnittpunkt von Sozial- und Wirtschaftspolitik. Problemen der öffentliche Wohnungspolitik in der Hauszinssteuerera 1924/25–1930/31," in Abelshauser, *Die Weimarer Republik als Wohlfahrtsstaat,* 91–123.

151. StAH 424–15 Lit. L.13, SAGA, "Fünf Jahre Gemeinnützige Siedlungs AG Altona" (1927), 30; Hoffmann, *Neues Altona,* 1:113–19; Timm, *Oelsner,* 201–9. Cf. Nicholas Bullock, "First the Kitchen—then the Facade," *Journal of Design History* 1, nos. 3–4 (1988): 177–92; Mary Nolan, "'Housework Made Easy': The Taylorized Housewife in Weimar Germany's Rationalized Economy," *Feminist Studies* 16, no. 3 (Fall 1990): 549–77.

152. Der Heimstätter-Vereinigung Steenkamp e.V, "Zehn Jahre Steenkamp 1920–1930. Festschrift zur Zehnjahr-Feier der Siedlung Steenkamp" (Altona, 1930), 3, 14; H. Frank, "Charakteristisches von der Emmichstraße," in *Altonaer Stadtkalendar* 5 (1916): 105–7; StAH A450/6, "Geschichtlicher Überblick über die Leistungen der Stadt Altona vom Kriegsende bis zur Eingemeindung (Groß-Altona) 1918–1927," 15; Hoffmann, *Neues Altona,* 1:121–38.

153. "Fünf Jahre," op. cit.

154. *Amtsblatt* 51, 20 Dec. 1930; ibid., no. 15, 17 Apr. 1931, ibid., no. 41, 16 Oct. 1931; Timm, *Oelsner,* 138, 185 and n.459; Hermann Hipp, *Wohnstadt Hamburg. Mietshäuser der 20er Jahre Zwischen Inflation und Weltwirtschaftskrise* (Hamburg, 1982), 33–34. Preller, *Sozialpolitik,* 333, 384–86. Peter-Christian Witt, "Inflation, Wohnungswirtschaft und Hauszinssteuer. Zur Regelung von Wohnungsbau und Wohnungsmarkt in der Weimarer Republik," in Lutz Niethammer, ed., *Wohnen im Wandel. Beiträge zur Geschichte des Alltags in der bürgerlichen Gesellschaft* (Wuppertal, 1979), 397.

155. StAH 424–18 AIII/2 Haushaltsvoranschlag für 1927, a) "Persönliche Ausgaben"; McElligott, "Municipal Politics," 386–89. Cf. Rainer Skiba, Hermann Adam, *Das Westdeutsche Lohnniveau zwischen den Beiden Weltkriegen und nach der Wahrungsreform* (Cologne, 1974), 191, 193; "The German Family Budget Enquiry of 1927–1928, *International Labour Review* 22 (1930): 524–32; Hans Speier, *Die Angestellten vor dem Nationalsozialismus. Zur deutschen Sozialstruktur 1918–1933* (Frankfurt a.M., 1989), 78.

156. *Wirtschaft und Statistik* 1929, no. 1, 20, cited in: Hoffmann, *Neues Altona,* 1:219.

157. StJB Altona (1928), 104; StJBDS 30 (1935), 370.

158. McElligott, "Municipal Politics," 378–81. Adelheid von Saldern, "Die Neubausiedlungen der Zwanziger Jahre," in Ulfert Herlyn, Adelheid von Saldern, Wulf Tessin, eds., *Neubausiedlungen der 20er und 60er Jahre. Ein historisch-soziologischer Vergleich* (Frankfurt a.M., and New York, 1987), 29–74.

159. Hoffmann, *Neues Altona,* 1:111.

160. StAH 424–18 I/10, Der Staatskommissar für das Wohnungswesen, St.Z.736 (Berlin) 5 June 1919; Kommission für Siedlungs- und Wohnungswesen, Auszug aus dem Protokoll der Kommission, 5 Jan. 1920, 34, and Vfg. 14 Jan. 1920.

161. StAH 424–18 I/10, Bericht der Anmeldestelle für Heimstätte (12 June 1919), and report on applicants for Steenkamp, 14 Jan. 1920. Ibid., I/14 (Statistik),

Baupflegeamt, 9 Feb. 1918. Hoffmann, *Neues Altona,* 1:133–38. Adelheid von Saldern, "'Daheim an meinem Herd . . .' Die Kultur des Wohnens," in A. Nitschke, G. A. Ritter, D. J. K. Peukert, R. vom Bruch, eds., *Jahrhundertwende. Der Aufbruch in der Moderne 1880–1930,* 2 vols. (Reinbek, 1990), 2:34–60.

162. On social disciplining, see Adelheid von Saldern, "Neues Wohnen, Wohn-verhältnisse und Wohnverhalten in Großanlagen der 20er Jahre," in Axel Schildt and Arnold Sywottek, eds., *Massenwohnung und Eigenheim. Wohnungsbau und Wohnen in der Großstadt seit dem Ersten Weltkrieg* (Frankfurt a.M. and New York, 1988), 201–21, here: 206–11.

163. "Zehn Jahre Steenkamp," 5–6, 15, 16–17, 22. Cf. Adelheid von Saldern, "The Workers' Movement and Cultural Patterns on Urban Housing Estates and in Rural Settlements in Germany and Austria during the 1920s," *Social History* 15, no. 3 (Oct. 1990): 333–54; Anthony McElligott, "Workers' Culture and Workers' Politics on Weimar's New Housing Estates: A Response to Adelheid von Saldern," *Social History* 17, no. 3 (Jan. 1992): 101–13.

164. Hoffmann, *Neues Altona,* 1:84; von Saldern, "Neues Wohnen," 208.

165. Sub-tenancies accounted for 8 percent of all new housing tenancies, com-pared to the city average of 14 percent, StDR 362.I, 82–105.

166. Wohnungsamt, "Dritter Bericht," 45, 49–50.

167. See Stefan Bajohr, "Illegitimacy and the Working Class: Illegitimate Moth-ers in Brunswick, 1900–1933," in Richard J. Evans, *The German Working Class, 1888–1933* (London, 1982), 142–73; David Crew, "German Socialism, The State and Family Policy 1918–1933," *Continuity and Change* 1, no. 2 (1986): 235–63; idem, "'Eine Elternschaft zu Dritt'—staatliche Eltern? Jugendwohlfahrt und Kon-trolle der Familie in der Weimarer Republik 1919–1933," in Lüdtke, *"Sicherheit" und "Wohlfahrt,"* 267–94.

168. *Amtsblatt* 14, 7 Apr. 1928. There were 250 individual projects in progress at this point; StAH 424–2 IVe 44 (1928), bl. 184: minutes of council meeting, 3 Apr. 1928; 424–15 Lit A, no. 21 SPD Eidelstedt. *Amtsblatt* 44, 4 Nov. 1932; ibid., no. 7, 4 Jan. 1933, "Die Bautätigkeit."

169. StAH 424–18 I 38/21, Office circular, 7 Jan. 1921; StAH 424–27, AI/4d, table: "Reinzugang an Wohnungen auf 1000 der Bevölkerung"; *Amtsblatt* 2, 14 Jan. 1928: "Die Wohnungsnot in Altona"; StAH 424–27, I1 (Wohnungsmarkt in Altona 1931–1936): K[aestner] to Stadtrat Grotkop, 9 Nov. 1934, Betrifft: Künf-tiger Wohnungsbedarf in Altona, Z.Vfg.v., 19 Oct. 1934; *Tatsachen* 9, 10 Oct. 1936: "Der Wohnungsbau in Altona. Früher und jetzt," 3; StAH 424–27, I2: An das I/Flakregiment 6, Altona-Osdorf I Va Az 63 f 23(v), 7 Apr. 1937, Betrifft: Wohnungsmangel in Altona; StDR 362.II, 141.

170. Denby, *Europe Re-housed* (London, 1938), 143–44.

171. Hoffmann, *Neues Altona,* 1:76, 544.

172. "Hamburg hat Max Brauer viel zu danken," op. cit.

173. *Amtsblatt* 45, 10 Nov. 1928: "Zur Eroffnung der Pestalozzi-Schule" *Amts-blatt* 22, 11 June 1929: "Montessori Kinderheim"; "Notlage," 3. Crew, "German Socialism," 258. Hoffmann, *Neues Altona* 1:84.

174. StAH A752: 71C, Press cuttings (Brauer).

175. StJB Altona (1928), 94. *Amtsblatt* 21, 25 May 1930: "Aus der Kulturarbeit der Altonaer Stadtverwaltung."
176. *Amtsblatt* 23, 7 June 1924.
177. StAH 424–27 B II 10/1, Statistik über das Turn- und Sportwesen in Altona, 1925–1928; StJB Altona (1928), 43–48; "Aus der Altonaer Jugendpflege," pts. 1–2, *Amtsblatt* 21, 25 May 1929; and no. 22, 1 June 1929; Heinrich Lüdtke and Oskar Lorenzen, *Die Turn- und Sportstadt Altona* (Altona, 1927); Patricia Arnold and Dagmar Niewerth, "'Heraus Genossen! Am Freitag hängt jeder Genosse seine Radiohörer an den Nagel!' Die Arbeitersportbewegung in Altona in der Weimarer Republik," in Sywottek, ed., *Das andere Altona*, 60–76.
178. LAS 309/22587 (Sozialistische Kulturpolitik), *Hamburger Echo* 238, 27 Nov. 1927: "Für eine sozialistische Kulturkartell" (on Altona).
179. StJB Altona (1928), 96.
180. Altonaer Wohlfahrtsamt (Dr. E. Baumann), *Wohlfahrtspflege in Altona, 1918–1924* (Altona, 1924), 94.
181. Hoffmann, *Neues Altona*, 1:117; von Saldern, "Sozialdemokratie," 208–23; Anthony P. McElligott, "Das "Abruzzenviertel." Arbeiter in Altona 1918–1933," in Herzig et al., *Arbeiter in Hamburg*, 493–507.

Chapter 4

The quotation, "Save Us from Altona!" is from *Norddeutsche Nachrichten* 55, 7 Mar. 1927.
1. StAH 424–88, Nachlaß Brauer, box 6, notes: "On Democracy."
2. Reprinted in: *Amtsblatt* 21, 24 May 1924; Erich Lüth, *Max Brauer, Glasbläser, Bürgermeister, Staatsmann* (Hamburg, 1972), 95–96.
3. *Bericht*, 2:595; StAH 424–1 16 (Urkunden und Rechtsätzen), Oberbürgermeister Bernhard Schnackenburg, "Denkschrift betreffend die Notlage der Stadt" (1910), 34–35; A. Bielfeldt, "Vom Eigenleben Altonas," *Altonaer Nachrichten*, 18 June 1927; Berlage, *Altona*, 172; P-Th. Hoffmann, *Die Elbe: Strom Deutschen Schicksals und Deutschen Kultur* (Hamburg, 1939), 255.
4. StAH 424–1 1 15 (Regierungserlässe und Erklärungen, Denkschriften etc. betreffend: die Sonderstellung Altonas mit Rücksicht auf die Nachbarschaft Hamburgs), Der Oberbürgermeister: Betrifft den Antrag von Hamburg auf Hafen- und Gebietserweiterung (3 July 1917); StAH 424–3 (Magistrat) II, Fritz Schumacher, "Das Gebiet Unterelbe Hamburg im Rahmen einer Neugliederung des Reiches" (Hamburg, 1922). Werner Johe, "Territorialer Expansionsdrang oder Wirtschaftliche Notwendigkeit? Die Groß-Hamburg-Frage," *Zeitschrift des Vereins für Hamburgische Geschichte* 64 (1978): 149–80. Christoph Timm, "Der Preussische Generalsiedlungsplan für Gross-Hamburg von 1923," *Zeitschrift des Vereins für Hamburgische Geschichte* 71 (1985): 75–125.
5. *Amtsblatt* 23, 7 June 1924.
6. LAB 142, StB 5201, Eingemeindungs- und Enteignungsfragen 1918–1930; Horst Matzerath, "Städtewachstum und Eingemeindungen im 19.Jahrhundert" in: Reulecke, ed., *Die deutsche Stadt*, 67–89, here: 78–79; Jürgen Reulecke, *Geschichte der Urbanisierung in Deutschland* (Frankfurt a.M., 1985), 148–49.

7. StAH 424–44 (Gr.Flottbek) 7, minutes of the Städtebaukongress Amsterdam 1924; StJbDS 24 Jg. (1929): 233; and 25 Jg. (1930): 239; J. R. Mullin, "Ideology, Planning Theory and the German City in the Inter-War Years," pts. 1–2, *Town Planning Review* 53, nos. 1–2 (Apr.–July 1982): 115–30, 257–72.

8. *Kommentar zu den kommunalpolitischen Richtlinien der SPD* (Berlin, 1929), 20–24. Richard Breitman, *German Socialism and Weimar Democracy* (Chapel Hill, 1981), 132–34. Franz Osterroth and Dieter Schuster, *Chronik der deutschen Sozialdemokratie,* vol. 2: *Vom Beginn der Weimarer Republik bis zum Ende des Zweiten Weltkrieges* (Berlin, Bonn-Bad Godesberg, 1975), 81–82, 88.

9. StAH 424–1 15, Entschliessung der SPD-Fraktion (Altona), 22 Mar. 1922, point 1. StAH Arbeiterrat Groß-Hamburg 312, Groß-Altona-Frage, 2–9; SPD *Protokoll* (1921), 37; idem, *Die kommunalpolitischen Richtlinien der SPD beschlossen in der gemeinsamen Sitzungen des kommunalpolitischen Beirats und des Reichsausschusses für Kommunalpolitik am 29 September 1928* (Berlin, n.d.), pts. 1–2: "Das Aktionsprogramm," 12–16; *Kommentar,* 3, 62; Karl-Heinz Naßmacher, "Kommunaler Sozialismus oder Kommunalisierung der Sozialdemokratie?," in idem, ed., *Kommunalpolitik und Sozialdemokratie,* ll; Helmut Arndt, "Zu einigen Aspekten sozialdemokratischer Kommunalpolitik in der Weimarer Republik," *Jahrbuch für Regionalgeschichte* 9 (1982): 105–19, here: 108; Rebentisch, "Die deutsche Sozialdemokratie und die kommunale Selbstverwaltung," 13, 27–35.

10. Wolfgang Krabbe, "Eingemeindungsprobleme vor dem Ersten Weltkrieg: Motive, Widerstände und Verfahrensweise," *Das alte Stadt* 7 (1980): 368–87.

11. Material on this in: LAB 142, StB 444 and 447; LAB 142, StB 1325 I and II. W. Forst, *Robert Lehr als Oberbürgermeister. Ein Kapital Deutscher Kommunalpolitik* (Düsseldorf and Vienna, 1962), chap. 7; Herlemann, *Kommunalpolitik,* 128–35; Wunderich, *Arbeiterbewegung,* 48–54; Herzfeld, *Demokratie,* 2.

12. *Hamburger Nachrichten* 542, 18 Nov. 1924; *Schleswiger Nachrichten* 271, 17 Nov. 1924; *Hamburger Echo* 343, 13 Dec. 1924.

13. LAS 309/11333 (Eingemeindung Ottensens zur Altona); *Bericht,* 2:595; Berlage, *Altona,* 176; StAH 424–47 75 (Stellingen-Langenfelde); StAH 424–1 15, Die Städtischen Kollegien der Stadt Altona: An die Deutsche Nationalversammlung Weimar; An die Preußische Landesversammlung Berlin, Denkschrift, Feb. 1919.

14. *Amtsblatt* 6, 7 Feb. 1925; J. Brix and P. Fischer, "Das Industriegebiet von Altona" (Nov. 1925), in StAH D/515, and in the same file: A. Bielfeldt, "Die Notwendigkeit der Eingemeindung" (newspaper clipping, *Altonaer Nachrichten* n.d.); AHVW *Sondernummer* 6 (1 Nov. 1941): 17. J. Hinsch, *Die Eidelstedter Chronik* (Stellingen-Langenfelde, 1926), 118–25, 244; O. Hintze, *Geschichte von Eidelstedt* (Hamburg-Eidelstedt, 1965), 95, 100–106, 115–19; U. Krell, *Lurup von der holsteinischen Landgemeinde zum Hamburger Stadtteil* (Hamburg, 1978), 106.

15. StAH 424–1 I 15 XI, betr. Eingemeindung: Abschrift, Magistrat, Antrag auf Herbeiführung der Eingemeindung der Landgemeinden, 21 Oct. 1924, 7–8; Brix and Fischer, "Industriegebiet," 7.

16. Ibid., 1, 4; *Amtsblatt* 2, 12 Jan. 1924, article by city engineer Hans Berlage.

17. StAH 424–44/8 (1924–27), Fragebogen des Kreisausschusses, Jnr.KA 5392/92, 5 Dec. 1925; StAH 424–45/5, Fragebogen des Kreisausschusses KA

5392/93 n.d. (1925); StAH 424–45 15 (Kl. Flottbek), Gemeindevertretung Tgb.1798/26 to Landrat, Pinneberg, 22 June 1926.

18. *Hamburger Nachrichten* 16 July 1925: "Großstadtgrenzen"; *Norddeutsche Nachrichten* 55, 7 Mar. 1927 (special issue on the Elbe communities).

19. StJB Altona (1928), 3, 117, 119; cf. StAH 424–44 75, 76 (Stellingen-Langenfelde, Eidelstedt); Berlage, *Altona,* 185.

20. *Norddeutsche Nachrichten* 55, op. cit., for a romanticized image of the "Blankenese *Lotsen.*"

21. StDR 416/1 6a, 34–37; ibid., 404/13, 68–71, 73; see StDR 408, 32: *Berufszählung.*

22. AHVW 16, no. 1 (1939): 4.

23. StAH 424–3 II Bibl. Gruppe D, J. Brix, and P. Fischer, "Gutachtliche Äusserung über den Zusammenhang zwischen Eingemeindungs- und Grünflächenfrage der Stadt Altona." Timm, *Oelsner,* 85, 108–9.

24. Magistrat, Abschrift, 21 Oct. 1924, 4; StAH 424–43 IIA3 Band II, Abschrift: Magistrat to Regierungspräsidenten, Betrifft: Finanzausgleich und Eingemeindung der Stadt Altona, 9 June 1926, 8.

25. On *Heimat* culture, see the excellent study by Celia Applegate, *A Nation of Provincials,* chap. 6; Benedict Anderson, *Imagined Communities,* rev. ed. (London, 1991), chap. 8. Cf. Harold Poor, "Anti-Urbanism in the Weimar Republic," *Societas* 6 (1976): 177–92.

26. Hofmann, *Zwischen,* 160–69.

27. StAH 424–43 II, *Norddeutsche Nachrichten* 49, 28 Feb. 1927.

28. StAH 424–3, Magistrat II (Eingemeindung ZAS), *Lokstedter Zeitung* 261, 5 Nov. 1924; StAH 424–3 II A3 2, Abschrift: Antrag auf Herbeiführung der Eingemeindung der Landgemeinden, 21 Oct. 1924. Hoffmann, *Neues Altona,* 1:629 n. 96, has a list of the committee. For Oelsner, see Timm, *Oelsner,* 102–9; E. Lüth and J. Matthei, *Der Baumeister Gustav Oelsner* (Schriften der Freien Akademie der Kunste, Hamburg, 1984).

29. Stadt Altona (Werbeausschuss), *Stimmen zur Frage eines grösseren Altona. Zusammengestellt vom Werbeausschuss für ein grösseren Altona* (Altona, 1925); *Lokstedter Zeitung* 261, op. cit. StAH 424–43 Bd II, letter from Kreisausschuss (Landrat Niendorf) to the Gemeindevorsteher, 18 June 1926.

30. GStA Rep.77 5696, (Übersicht ü.d. Ergebnis der Neuwahlen zu den Kreistagen [1925]); and Rep.77 5697 (Ergebnis der Kreistagswahlen v. 29 Nov. 1925, Nachweisung ü.d. parteipolitische Zusammensetzung der Kreistag, Regierung Schleswig), 51. The composition was as follows: DNVP = 19, DDP = 2, SPD = 10, KPD = 2. For Landrat Niendorf, see Rietzler, *Kampf,* 87; Stoltenberg, *Politische Stromungen,* 47.

31. StAH 424–44 (Groß Flottbek) 7, Bericht über die am Dienstag, den 17. Februar . . . ausserordentliche Mitgliederversammlung des Kommunalvereins für Altona-Othmarschen, 7.

32. See the various resolutions drawn up and printed on a flysheet in: StAH 424–43 AII I; on the role of the Nienstedten Church Council, *Norddeutsche Nachrichten,* 9 Mar. 1927; *Nachrichten des Werbeausschusses* 45, 25 Mar. 1925, for the Altona Branch of the Center Party support for the incorporation. For the

Altona and regional NWGAA, see Peter Wulf, *Die politische Haltung des schleswig-holsteinischen Handwerks 1928–1932* (Kiel, 1967).

33. StAH 424–3 II, Verein für Industrie und Gross-Handel, Bericht, undated (1926), claiming to represent a labor force of 11,000; and in the same file: Gruppe D, "Verhandlung des verstärkten 27 Ausschüsses des preussischen Landtages am 27 März 1927 . . . ," 20–21; *Hamburger Echo* 184, 6 July 1926.

34. The sum of Bielfeldt's views can be found in two long articles published in special issues of the (liberal) newspaper *Altonaer Nachrichten,* in StAH 424–3 Mag II: "Eingemeindung" (newspaper clippings).

35. *Lokstedter Zeitung* 261, 5 Nov. 1924, for the report of the meeting on which the foregoing is based.

36. StAH 421–5 Kb5a I, *Norddeutsche Nachrichten* 330, 22 Dec. 1924: "Aus der Heimat."

37. *Lokstedter Zeitung* 261, 5 Nov. 1924; *Norddeutsche Nachrichten* 268, 13 Nov. 1924.

38. StAH 424–44 8, letter from the *Vorstand des Gastwirts- und Saalbesitzer-Vereins der Elbgemeinden* to the Prussian interior ministry, 18 Nov. 1924.

39. StAH 424–47 76, bl. 27, letter to Gemeindevorsteher, Tg.I 1708, 19 Nov. 1924.

40. StAH 421–5 Kb5a I, report of protest meeting in Blankenese to which 300 to 400 persons came (*Hamburger Echo* 150, 2 June 1926).

41. *Hamburger Nachrichten,* 4 Mar. 1925, Sonderdruck: "Die Eingemeindungsfrage eine sozialdemokratische Parteiangelegenheit."

42. StAH 424–3 II, Bittschrift: Pinneberg 1924; StAH 424–43 IIA3 II, Schreiben: Der Landrat und Vorsitzende des Kreisausschusses, 18 June 1926.

43. StAH 424–43 IIA3 II, *Landrat* to individual council leaders, 18 June 1926; Krabbe, "Eingemeindungsprobleme," 372–75; cf. Matzerath, "Städtewachstum," 83; Reulecke, *Urbanisierung,* 78–86.

44. StAH 424–43 IIA3 I, Letter 5 Apr. 1922 to the *Gemeindevorsteher* (in Blankenese etc.); several other letters conveying the belligerent mood in the suburbs can also be found in this file.

45. StAH 424–47 76, bl. 32: letter from the KDC to Gemeindevorsteher Rüss in Stellingen-Langenfelde, 24 Aug. 1925.

46. StAH 424–44 8 (Groß Flottbek), letter from ZkVE to heads of Groß Flottbek, Klein Flottbek, Nienstedten, Lurup and Osdorf, 13 Oct. 1924.

47. A point well observed by the Center-Right (*Schleswiger Nachrichten* 271, 17 Nov. 1924).

48. *Nachrichten des Werbeausschusses* 10, 3 Dec. 1924.

49. StAH 421–5 Kb5a I, *Hamburger Echo* 359, 30 Dec. 1924; the quote is taken from an article titled: "Die Verschärfung der diplomatischen Beziehungen. Bemühungen um die Entspannung der Lage," referring to tensions surrounding the postwar treaty negotiations.

50. E.g., *Hamburger Echo* 7, 7 Jan. 1925; and no. 14, 14 Jan. 1925.

51. See the reports in: *Nachrichten des Werbeaussschusses* 19, 22 Dec. 1924; no. 25, 19 Jan. 1925; no. 38, 21 Feb. 1925; no. 29, 24 Jan. 1925; no. 36, 12 Feb. 1925.

Altonaer Nachrichten 141, 21 June 1926: "Die Eidelstedter Beamten für die Einge-meindung."

52. *Hamburger Echo* 7, 7 Jan. 1925: "Reichspräsidentenwahl und Altonaer Eingemeindungsfrage."

53. *Hamburger Nachrichten* 542, 18 Nov. 1924.

54. *Norddeutsche Nachrichten* 268, 13 Nov. 1924.

55. StAH 424–3 Magistrat II (Eingemeindung), Stellungnahme der Gemeinde Blankenese zu dem Eingemeindungsantrag der Stadt Altona, 17 June 1926, 5.

56. *Norddeutsche Nachrichten* 268, 13 Nov. 1924; *Nachrichten des Werbeauss-chusses* 49, 25 Apr. 1925.

57. *Nachrichten des Werbeausschusses* 10, 3 Dec. 1924.

58. StAH 421–5 Kb5a I, *Lokal Anzeiger für Stellingen-Langenfelde* 299, 20 Dec. 1924 (Sunday ed.); *Nachrichten des Werbeausschusses* 19, 22 Dec. 1924.

59. StAH 424–44 7, "Referat des Herrn Gemeindevorsteher Grotkop, Nien-stedten" (n.d.); *Hamburger Nachrichten,* 16 July 1925: "Großstadtgrenzen."

60. Report of this meeting (21 May 1926) in *Hamburger Echo* 140, 22 May 1926, and *Hamburger Nachrichten* 233, 22 May 1925: "Städtische Kollegien"; a copy of the petition can be found in StAH 424–43 IIAs II. *Hamburger Echo* 150, 2 June 1926, for the individual political parties.

61. StAH 424–43 II A3 II, Der Landrat und Vorsitzende des Kreisausschusses Pinneberg KA 2176, 31 May 1926; idem, to Herrn Gemeindevorsteher Blankenese 16 June 1926, and 18 June 1926. StAH 421–5 Kb5a II (ZAS), "Gegen die Einge-meindung nach Altona," report of meeting, probably in Oct. 1926. For the experts' reports: StAH 424–43 IIA3 I (KDC Pinnebrg, Dr.rer.pol. Köser); StAH 424–44 7 (Herr Dahlgrün); StAH 421–5 Kb 5a I–III, for responses.

62. StAH 424–44 8, Kreisabwehrausschuss Pinneberg, "Der Landkreis Pin-neberg und die Eingemeindungsbestrebungen der Stadt Altona," n.d.; and "Die Altonaer Eingemeindungsbestrebungen und der Landkreis Pinneberg," 27 May 1926; StAH 424–3 II, Kreisabwehrausschuss Pinneberg, "Bittschrift an den Preussischen Staatsrat," n.d. (probably end of 1926).

63. "Die Altonaer Eingemeindungsbestrebungen," 2. Timm, "Preussische Generalsiedlungsplan," op. cit.

64. StAH 421–5 Kb 5a I, *Hamburger Nachrichten* (Abendausgabe), 19 July 1926.

65. LAS 301/5038, Verein der Industrie und des Großhandels v. Altona-Ottensen and the Industrie- und Handelskammer Altona, report, 6 Jan.1926; and report to Chamber of Industry and Commerce, 2 Apr. 1926.

66. StAH 424–3 II, *Altonaer Tageblatt* 153 (1 Beilage: *Ottensener Nachrichten*), 5 July 1926.

67. StAH 421–5 Kb 5a I, *Norddeutsche Nachrichten* 143, 23 June 1926, and no. 152, 3 July 1926; *Rendsburger Tageblatt* 58, 10 Mar. 1927; cf. *Hamburger Echo* 199, 21 July 1926: "Arbeitgeberinteressen und Kommunalpolitik."

68. *Altonaer Nachrichten* 197, 19 July 1926; *Norddeutsche Nachrichten* 165, 19 July 1926.

69. *Hamburger Echo* 147, 30 May 1926.

70. StAH 421–5 Kb 5a I, *Hamburger Fremdenblatt* 148, 31 May 1926; StAH

421–5 Kb 5a II, *Norddeutsche Nachrichten* 224, 25 Sept. 1926: "Der unverbesserliche Optimismus des Altonaer Oberbürgermeisters."

71. Hans-Peter Ehni, *Bollwerk Preussen? Preussen-Regierung, Reich-Länder-Problem und der Sozialdemokratie 1928–1932* (Bonn-Bad Godesberg, 1975), 105.

72. *Hamburger Nachrichten* 435, 18 Sept. 1926: "Die Schleswig-Holsteinischen Landkreise und die Eingemeindungsfrage."

73. "Der unverbesserliche Optimismus," op. cit.

74. StAH 424–47 76, Heft 21: *Lokal-Anzeiger Stellingen-Langenfelde* 143, 26 June 1926: "Ergebnis der Abstimmung der Gemeindevertretungen (June 1926)."

75. *Norddeutsche Nachrichten* 252, 28 Oct. 1926: "Das Komödienspiel im Altonaer Ratshaus."

76. StAH 421–5 Kb 5a II, *Flensburger Nachrichten* 263, 9 Nov. 1926: "Kleine Anfrage" (Mehlis, DNVP), for a report of the discussion in the *Landtag.*

77. *Norddeutsche Nachrichten* 253, 29 Oct. 1926: "Wie die Regierung sich informiert." The inspection took place on Tuesday, not Monday.

78. "Kleine Anfrage," op. cit.

79. StAH 424–45 5, copy of letter to *Kreisausschuss* Pinneberg, 3 Nov. 1926.

80. *Hamburger Correspondent* 538, 18 Nov. 1926.

81. *Norddeutsche Nachrichten* 55, 7 Mar. 1927. StAH 421–5 Kb 3 IV, unidentified newspaper cutting: "Altona's Ehrenschuld gegen Hagenbecks Tierpark." Cf. Thimme, *Flucht in den Mythos,* 115; Valentin Lupescu, "Zur Soziologie der deutschen Kleinstadt," *Die Gesellschaft* 8 (1931): 464–71; Stokes, *Kleinstadt,* doc., I/18c.

82. "Das Komödienspiel," op. cit. The reference is to the defeat of the Danish monarch at the hands of Prussian and Austrian troops in 1866.

83. StAH 424–3 Mag.II, 75/1954, pamphlet, "Die von Preußen beabsichtigte Teillösung Groß-Altona des Niederelbe-Problems und die Stellungnahme der betroffenen preuß. Gemeinden des Kreises Pinneberg." This file contains also a copy of a hostile lecture by councillor and *Kreistag* member, Dr. Schramm. For counter-arguments: StAH 421–5 Kb5a II: unidentified newspaper cutting "Gegen die Eingemeindung nach Altona"; StAH 122–3, Arbeiterrat 312 (Groß-Altona-Frage), 5–6, with cutting from *Freie Gewerkschaft* 3, 19 Jan. 1927.

84. "Kleine Anfrage," op. cit.

85. *Norddeutsche Nachrichten* 39, 16 Feb. 1927: "Alle Mittel sind ihnen Recht"; *Altonaer Nachrichten* 258, 4 Nov. 1926: "Der erböste Monopolist—Despotentum an der Unterelbe—Privilegien und ihre Grenzen."

86. *Norddeutsche Nachrichten* 259, 5 Nov. 1926: "Berlin-Altona bringt das Wohl des Reiches in Gefahr: Zur Zwangseingemeindung."

87. StAH 421–5 Kb5a II, *Hamburger Fremdenblatt* 328, 27 Nov. 1926; *Kieler Zeitung* 538, 27 Nov. 1926. Zimmermann, *Wählerverhalten,* 307, 526, and n. 848.

88. StAH 424–43 IIA II, Schreiben des Landrats Pinneberg KA 5383, 5 Jan. 1927; the inspection by the "Haupt Gemeinde-Ausschusses des preussischen Staatsrates" took place on 10 Jan.

89. StAH 421–5 Kb5a II, newspaper clipping from *Norddeutsche Nachrichten,* Feb. 1927: "Verfrühter Jubel in Altona."

90. *Norddeutsche Nachrichten* 25, 31 Jan. 1927.

91. "Verfrühter Jubel"; Thimme, *Flucht,* 150–53.

92. StAH 424–43 IIA3 II (Auszug): Sitzungsprotokoll der Gemeindevertretung Blankenese, 9 Jan. 1927; StAH 424–47 66, bl. 9: Antrag der SPD (signed, Borchers), 8 Jan. 1927.

93. StAH 424–45 5, Die Gemeindevorsteher (Nienstedten, Klein Flottbek and Osdorf) an den Kreisausschusses in Pinneberg, 3 Nov. 1926.

94. Preußischer Landtag no. 0302 2 Wahlperiode, 1 Tagung 1925–27, "Bericht über die Reise des verstärkten 27. Ausschusses zur Begutachtung der Neuregelung der Kommunalen Grenzen im preußischen Unterelbegebiet: 6–9 März 1927, Berichterstatter v. Papen."

95. *Amtsblatt* 10, 12 Mar. 1927. Paul Hirsch, "Staat und Gemeinde," in Noack, ed., *Taschenbuch,* 7–11.

96. StAH 424–43 IIA3 BL.11, letter from the Magistrat Z.I.(Bürgermeister Ebert), 14 Apr. 1927.

97. StAH 424–44 8: Der Gemeindevorsteher Groß-Flottbek to Landrat Niendorf, Tgb. no..1124, 29 Mar. 1927 (report of council decision); StAH 424–45 5, Der Gemeindvorsteher Klein-Flottbek to Landrat Niendorf, 2 Apr. 1927; StAH 424–45, Landrat, memorandum, 4 Apr. 1927; *Lokal Anzeiger* (Eidelstedt) 264, 11 Nov. 1926. On the *Finanzausgleich* (financial equalization): Preußischer Landtag no. 5335 2 Wahlperiode, 1 Tagung 1925–27, "Entwurf eines Gesetzes über einen Sonderfinanzausgleich zugunsten preußischer Randgemeinden (= Kreise) in der Nachbarschaft von Stadtstaaten." Bruno Asch, "Finanzausgleich und Gemeinde," *Die Gesellschaft* (1930); Ehni, *Bollwerk,* 106–8; Karl-Heinrich Hansmeyer, ed., *Kommunale Finanzpolitik in der Weimarer Republik* (Stuttgart 1973), chap. 4.

98. StAH 424–45 (Kl.Flottbek), letter from Grotkop to Magistrat Altona, Tgb.1237, 22 Apr. 1927.

99. StAH 424–47 66, bl. 13: "Beschluß," 4 Jan. 1927; bl. 14: Gemeindevorsteher Niendorf to Gemeindevorsteher Stellingen, 17 Jan. 1927; *Norddeutsche Nachrichten* 55, 7 Mar. 1927: "Rettet uns vor Altona!"

100. Minutes of debate: Preußisher Landtag Sitzung 293–95, 21 June 1927, cols. 20972–21040, here: Preußischer Landtag Sitzung 293, 21 June 1927, col. 20982, DNVP deputy, Frau Mehlis; minutes of the *Handelsverein* of the Elbe communes printed in, *Norddeutsche Nachrichten* 118, 21 May 1927. For examples of obligations defined by the smaller communities, StAH 424–44 8, (Groß Flottbek) Der Gemeindevorsteher Tgb.1124, to Landrat in Pinneberg (Wünsche) 29 Mar. 1927; StAH 424–45 5 (Klein Flottbek), Der Gemeindevorsteher 2 Apr. 1927, Sonderwünsche.

101. Preußischer Landtag, Sitzung 293, cols. 20980–81.

102. StAH 424–43 IIA3 II, Städtische Kollegien Altona Drucksache no. 716 (Anlagen), 14 June 1927, and Auszug aus dem Sitzungsprotokoll der Gemeindevertretung, 28 June 1927; letter, Landrat Pinneberg, 25 May 1927, to the heads of parish councils; StAH 424–2 IVe, DS 716, Anlage, Besprechung der Sonderwünsche, die die Vororte für den Fall der Eingemeindung erhoben; StAH 421–5 Kb5a III, for the list of signatories, 29 June and 30 June 1927.

103. Preußischer Landtag, Sitzung 293, col. 20979.

104. StAH 421–5 Kb 5a III, newspaper clipping from *Hamburger Echo* 170, 22 June 1927.

105. StAH 421–5 Kb 5a II, newspaper clipping from *Hamburger Nachrichten* (Morgenausgabe), 12 Dec. 1926.

106. StAH 421–5 Kb 5a III, newspaper clipping from *Hamburger Correspondent* 220, 12 May 1927.

107. *Norddeutsche Nachrichten* 39, 16 Feb. 1927.

108. *Norddeutsche Nachrichten* 118, 21 May 1927: "Die Vergewaltigung." The same references and imagery appear in issue no. 55, 7 Mar. 1927.

109. *Nachrichten des Werbeausschusses* 45, 25 Mar. 1925.

110. Preußischer Landtag, Sitzung 293, col. 20989, Center Party Deputy Grebe.

111. *Hamburger Nachrichten* 299, 30 June 1927: "Das Unterelbegebiet Opfer der Preußenkoalition."

112. StAH 421–5 Kb5a III, *Norddeutsche Nachrichten* 118, 21 May 1927, excerpt of a letter from a DNVP member of parliament.

113. Preußischer Landtag, col. 20988, Grebe.

114. Preußischer Landtag, Sitzung 293, cols. 20999–21001.

115. "Die Vergewaltigung," op. cit.

116. "Das Unterelbe-Gebiet Opfer der Preußenkoalition."

117. StAH 421–5 Kb5a III, *Hamburger Echo* 187, 9 July 1927: "Vereinigungsfeier der Altonaer Sozialdemokratie."

118. *Hamburger Echo* 302, 1 Nov. 1927: "Oberbürgermeister Brauer antwortet."

119. *Amtsblatt* 39, 1 Oct. 1927: "Zur Stadtverordnetenwahl v. 25 September 1927," the author of the article noted that Blankenese, Eidelstedt and Klein Flottbek were exceptions.

120. *Altonaer Nachrichten* 222, 22 Sept. 1927: "In letzter Stunde"; and 224, 24 Sept. 1927.

121. *Hamburger Echo* 266, 26 Sept. 1927: "Altona und Umgegend: Der sozialdemokratische Sieg."

122. *Altonaer Nachrichten* 225, 26 Sept. 1927.

123. *Altonaer Nachrichten* 224 24 July 1927, and no. 215, 14 Sept. 1927. *Schleswig Holsteinische Wähler Zeitung* (DNVP), 9 May 1928, for Jürgs. Cf. D. P. Walker, "The German Nationalist People's Party: The Conservative Dilemma in the Weimar Republic," *Journal of Contemporary History* 14 (1979): 627–47, here: 628–29.

124. Childers, "The Social Language of Politics in Germany," 331–58.

125. Cited in *Hamburger Echo* 150, 2 June 1927.

Chapter 5

1. *Altonaer Lokalanzeiger* 260, 6 Nov. 1930.

2. James Angell, *The Recovery of Germany* (Yale, 1929), 245; Carl Herz, "Die Organisation der Gemeindewirtschaft," *Die Gesellschaft* 4, no. 2 (1927): 465–72; Gerold Ambrosius, *Der Staat als Unternehmer. Öffentliche Wirtschaft und Kapitalismus seit dem 19.Jahrhundert* (Göttingen 1984), 68; Wolfgang R. Krabbe,

"Munizipalsozialismus und Interventionsstaat," *Geschichte in Wissenschaft und Unterricht* 30 (1979): 265–83; idem, *Kommunalpolitik und Industrialisierung. Die Entfaltung der städtischen Leistungsverwaltung im 19. und frühen 20. Jahrhundert. Fallstudien zu Dortmund und Münster* (Stuttgart, 1985).

3. LAB StB 270 II, Oskar Mulert, "Aktuelle Probleme der deutschen Kommunalpolitik," 3; idem, "Wirtschaft und Gemeinden," *Wirtschaftsblatt Niedersachsen* 7 Jg., nos. 23–24 (1927): 403; Lindemann, "Aufgaben und Tätigkeit," 196–266; Statistisches Reichsamt, *Deutsche Wirtschaftskunde. Ein Abriß der deutschen Reichsstatistik* (Berlin, 1933), 313.

4. Fritz Terhalle, *Finanzwirtschaft* (Jena, 1930), 92. See Ben Lieberman, "Luxury or Public Investment? Productivity and Planning for Weimar Recovery," *Central European History* 26, no. 2 (1993): 195–213.

5. Reichsbürgerrat, "Betrachtungen über die Kommunalwahlen 1929," 1.

6. StJB Altona (1928), 132. *AHVW* (1939): 1, 4. Details in: McElligott, "Municipal Politics," 111–19. *Deutsche Wirtschaftskunde*, 101; Henry Ashby Turner, *German Big Business and The Rise of Hitler* (New York and Oxford, 1987), xvff., 191; H. A. Winkler, "Vom Protest zur Panik: Der gewerbliche Mittelstand in der Weimarer Republik," in Mommsen et al., eds., *Industrielles System*, 778–91, here: 789; T. Childers, *The Nazi Voter. The Social Foundations of Fascism in Germany, 1919–1933* (Chapel Hill and London, 1983), 64, 66, 143, 151–52.

7. Mulert, "Wirtschaft und Gemeinden," 405.

8. Angell, *Recovery*, 245.

9. Dr. Paul Jostock, "Die Schulden der öffentlichen Verwaltung," *Magazin der Wirtschaft*, 6 Jg., no. 50 (12 Dec. 1930) 2291–95, copy in: LAB 142 StB 2846. The liberal economist Fritz Terhalle thought that the problem was grossly exaggerated (*Finanzwirtschaft*, 88; Angell, *Recovery*, 243ff.).

10. See the minutes of the council for details: StAH 424–22 IVe 35–40 (1919–24). Kurt Tybusch, "Die kommunale Bodenpolitik der Stadt Altona in den letzten 40 Jahren" (Diss.Jur. Univ. Hamburg, 1926); StJB Altona (1928), 4.

11. StAH 421–25 (Regierung Schleswig) Kb 8b, Wirtschaftsberatung Deutscher Städte, "Bericht no. 240," pt. 2: 149–50, 152–53; StAH 421–25 BA 2b 2, bl. 17; *Amtsblatt* 21, 27 May 1932: "Übernahme der Gewobau-Grundstücke durch die Stadt"; StAH 424–88, Nachlaß Brauer, box 6, "Notes on city government," 11. *Amtsblatt* 50, 18 Dec. 1931: "Unsere VAGA." McElligott, "Municipal Politics," 59–69, 141, 145–47; Richard Lutz, "Der Öffentliche Nahverkehr in Altona und die Städtische Verkehrspolitik 1918–1933," in Sywottek, *Das andere Altona*, 141–57. H. Lindemann, O. Most, and A. Südekum, *Kommunales Jahrbuch* (Jena, 1927), 13–17.

12. Max Brauer, "Öffentliche und Private Wirtschaft," *Der Städtetag* 10 (1931): 457.

13. Rudolf Hilferding, "Die Aufgaben der Sozialdemokratie in der Republik," *Protokoll Sozialdemokratischer Parteitag Kiel 1927* (Berlin, 1927). See Harold James, "Rudolf Hilferding and the Application of the political economy of the Second International," *Historical Journal* 24, no. 4 (1981), 847–69; H-A. Winkler, ed., *Organisierter Kapitalismus. Voraussetzungen und Anfänge* (Göttingen, 1974). Cora Stephan, "Wirtschaftsdemokratie und Umbau der Wirtschaft," in Wolfgang

Luthardt, ed., *Sozialdemokratische Arbeiterbewegung und Weimarer Republik. Materialien zur gesellschaftlichen Entwicklung 1927–1933,* 2 vols. (Frankfurt a.M., 1978), 1:281–352.

14. Brauer, "Öffentliche und Private Wirtschaft," 456.

15. Max Brauer, "Die Heutige Lage der Öffentliche Wirtschaft" (1951), 6, cited in F. Zeiß, "Kommunales Wirtschaft und Wirtschaftspolitik," in Hans Peters, ed., *Handbuch der kommunalen Wissenschaft und Praxis* (Berlin, 1956), 3:620.

16. *Hamburger Fremdenblatt* 243, 2 Sept. 1926.

17. StAH 424–2 IVe 40, Magistrat, Drucksache 59, Vorlage 25, Kämmerei Kommission, 24 June 1924 (Webwaren); StAH 424–2 IVe 41, Magistrat, Drucksache 247, Vorlage 19, 17 Apr. 1925 (Lebensmittelversorgung); *Ämtliche Mitteilungen* 36, 14 Oct. 1926.

18. Magistrat, Kämmerei Kommission, 24 June 1924.

19. StAH 424–2 IVe 42, reply to Antrag 2 (NSDAP), Drucksache 488, 15 May 1926.

20. StAH 424–2 IVe 40, letter: Verein Altonaer Manufakturisten, representing 150 textile traders, 23 June 1924.

21. StAH 424–2 IVe 48 Magistrat, Drucksache 1657, 21 Nov. 1932.

22. StAH 421–5 Kb 8a, Städtische Kollegien, Anlage zur Geheim-Vorlage der Verkehrkommission vom 14 Mai 1926 (NS.434), and 19 May 1926, "Bericht über die Holsatia-Werke-Neumanns" (report by city accountant, Dr. Trimpop); McElligott, "Municipal Politics," 497.

23. StAH 421–5 BA a 2b I, Städtische Kollegien: Drucksache 485a, 27 Aug. 1926; Drucksache 671, 12 Apr. 1927. There were sixteen members: 3 from the Magistrat, 11 elected members of the council, and 2 public members. There was also one ex officio member. Its political configuration was: 7 SPD, 2 KPD, 1 DDP, 1 DVP, 1 DNVP, 2 Bürger Bloc, 2 nonparty (*Amtsblatt* 7, 18 Feb. 1928).

24. StAH 424–2 IVe 42 (1926), Sitzung 6, 21 May 1926, Drucksache 454, Vorlage 11, 4 June 1926 (Kämmerei-Kommission and Verkehrskommission); minutes of meeting 2 Sept. 1926, Drucksache 485a Vorlage 23 (27 Aug. 1926).

25. StAH 424–2, IVe 42, Städtische Kollegien, Drucksache 485a, Vorlage 23, 27 Aug. 1926; and Drucksache 485b, Vorlage 24, 1 Aug. 1926.

26. *Altonaer Nachrichten* 197, 25 Aug. 1926: "Um das Schicksal der Holsatia-Werke." Carl Bohret, *Aktionen gegen die "kalte Sozialisierung" 1926–1930* (Berlin, 1966), 59–82; Winkler, "Vom Protest zur Panik."

27. "Um das Schicksal der Holsatia-Werke."

28. *Hamburger Nachrichten* 407, 2 Sept. 1926; *Altonaer Nachrichten* 203, 1 Sept. 1926.

29. *Hamburger Correspondent* 394, 25 Aug. 1926.

30. LAS 301/5038, sub-file Holsatiawerke; StAH 421–5 Y b (Produktive Erwerbslosenfürsorge) files 34–7: Notstandsarbeiten Stellinger-Moor 1926–1933.

31. *Amtsblatt* 36, 4 Sept. 1926 (Special issue "B"); and the report in *Hamburger Fremdenblatt* 243, 3 Sept. 1926: "Die Holsatia-Werke vor den Städtischen Kollegien in Altona." The DANAT was to adopt about a third of the 3,200,000 reichsmark value of shares.

32. StAH 421–25 Kb 8a, Magistrat to Regierungspräsident in Schleswig, Betrifft: Sanierung der Holsatia-Werke AG (zur Verfügung 22 Sept. 1926), 14 Oct. 1926.

33. *Altonaer Nachrichten* 202 (30 Aug. 1926).

34. Petersen also stressed the implications of the tax fallout which would result from bankruptcy, "Um das Schicksal der Holsatia-Werke," op. cit.; *Hamburger Echo* 212 (30 Aug. 1926): "Die Treibereien gegen die Holsatia"; StJB Altona (1928), 279, 293.

35. LAS 301/5038, Der Regierungspräsident, JNr.IAI 2160 4a to Magistrat Altona, 5 June 1925; StAH 421–5 Kb 8a, Fraktion NSDAP to Regierungspräsident, 23 Sept. 1926; *Hamburger Nachrichten* 481, 19 Oct. 1926.

36. StAH 421–5 Kb 8a, Brauer to Regierungspräsident (Verf.: IA I 3499.12.13, 6 Oct. 1926) 16 Oct. 1926, and 16 Nov. 1926, Betrifft: Sanierung der Holsatia-Werke.

37. *Hamburger Correspondenzblatt* 406, 1 Sept. 1926.

38. StAH 421–5 Kb 8a, *Die Hochwacht* 17/1, Jan./Feb.1927. See *Altonaer Nachrichten* 282, 3 Dec. 1926.

39. StAH, 424–88, Nachlaß Brauer, box 6, notes: "Socialism, War, Private Property."

40. Brauer, "Öffentliche und Private Wirtschaft," 457.

41. StAH 424–2 IVe 45 24 Jan. 1929, Städtische Kollegien, Drucksache 1086 (Antrag SPD-Fraktion) 16 Jan. 1929; see the articles by Bugdahn and others in, *Hamburger Echo* 403, 31 Aug. 1926; *Hamburger Fremdenblatt* 243, 3 Sept. 1926.

42. StAH 421–5 Kb 3 III, Magistrat z.III, letter, 11 Feb. 1927. Cf. Hoffmann, *Neues Altona,* 1:55–70.

43. StAH 421–5 Kb 3 III, Reichsverband der Privatmittagstisch- und Pensionsinhaber, Sitz Hamburg, letter to Magistrat Altona, 13 Oct. 1926.

44. StAH 421–5 Kb 3 III, letter to Prussian Interior Ministry, 22 Jan. 1927.

45. StAH 421–5 Kb 3 III, Regierungspräsident to Sellner, 16 Feb. 1927.

46. StAH 421–5 Kb 3 V, Magistrat 40, to Regierungspräsident, 1 Oct. 1932.

47. StAH 421–5 Kb 3 V, Bund to Magistrat, 12 Sept. 1932, and copied to Regierungspräsident.

48. *Hamburger Nachrichten* 33, 21 Jan. 1927, for report of council meeting. StAH 421–5 Yb 1–11, 18, for individual cases.

49. *Norddeutsche Nachrichten* 268, 13 Nov. 1924: "Eine Anfrage an den Vorsitzenden der Altonaer Handwerkskammer."

50. StAH 421–5 Kb 3 II, Altona-Telefon-Gesellschaft GmbH, Banhofstraße 58, letter to Regierungspräsident 24 Apr. 1925.

51. Ibid. (marginalia by an anonymous civil servant for a reply to his letter). On this issue of contracts, see the complaint by the Altona-Ottensen Association of Industry and Wholesale Trade against Hamburg's policy of nonreciprocity, LAS 301/5038, letter to Industrie- und Handelskammer, 2 Apr. 1926, 5.

52. StAH 421–5 Kb 3 IV, Stockmann/Brandt, "Memorandum ü.d. Behandlung des Reklamewesens der Stadt Altona" (C Stockmann), 28 Aug. 1929. Details in: McElligott, "Municipal Politics," 516–22.

53. StAH 421–5 Kb 3 IV, Stockmann/Brandt, Magistrat (Heuer) to

Regierungspräsident, 14 and 28 Jan. 1930. On the development of the Städtereklame, see LAB 142 StB 4879, StB 4042, StB 3443.

54. StAH 421–5 Kb 3 IV, Brandt to Magistrat, "Betrifft Anschlagsäulen," 15 Apr. 1929, and letter to council, 27 June 1929; see his letters to the Regierungspräsident 4 Feb. 1930, and 17 Feb. 1930.

55. StAH 421–5 Kb 3 V, the case of Franz Eckart, who unsuccessfully tried to run a haulage business.

56. *Grösse Glocke* 44, Oct. 1929: "Altona's Pump bei Karstadt."

57. StAH 421 Kb 3 IV (Karstadt) Grundvermögensamt to Regierungspräsident Schleswig, 26 Oct. 1929. The Real Estate Office also saw in this plan an opportunity to widen a notoriously narrow part of the street thus facilitating easier traffic flows.

58. *Grösse Glocke* 44, Oct. 1929: "Karstadt, der Machthaber in Altona."

59. *Grösse Glocke,* loc. cit.

60. BDC: Personal File, Böge, membership no. 73670 (1 Jan. 1928, Personal-Fragebogen).

61. StAH 421–5 Kb 3 V, Magistrat 10, 14 Jan. 1933.

62. *Altonaer Nachrichten* 12, 14 Jan. 1933.

63. LAS 301/5038, letter to Reichsministerium des Innern, 22 May 1930. StAH 424–88, Nachlaß Brauer, box 6, notes: "A Few Problems of Municipal Power Policy."

64. LAS 301/5038, Horn to Elektrizitätswerk Unterelbe A-G, 21 May 1930. See P-C. Witt, ed., *Wealth and Taxation in Central Europe. The History and Sociology of Public Finance* (Leamington Spa, 1987), 17.

65. LAS 301/5038, Horn to Interior Minister, 22 May 1930.

66. StAH 421–5 Kb 3 V 2, case of Arthur Zöllner.

67. Ibid., letter to Regierungspräsident, 16 Sept. 1932. His other letters to the Magistrat were dated, 7 Apr. 1932, 7 June 1932, 15 July 1932, 5 Aug. 1932.

68. StAH 421–5 Kb 3 V 2, case of Adolf Stehn; McElligott, "Municipal Politics," 524–25, for details.

69. Preller, *Sozialpolitik,* 397.

70. StAH 421–5 Kb 3 V, Stehn to Bracht, 23 Nov. 1932; and Brauer to Regierungspräsident, 3 Jan. 1933.

71. StAH 424–2 IVe 35 (1919), 14 Apr. 1919, Vorlage Z1c 5825, 72.

72. *Hamburger Nachrichten* 199, 30 Apr. 1925.

73. StAH 421–5 Kb 3 II, Zentralausschuß der Kommunalen Vereine zu Altona to Regierungspräsident in Schleswig, 30 June 1925.

74. StAH 421–5 Kb 3 III, correspondence between Menck and Brauer (16 Aug. 1927, 2 Sept. 1927), and Menck to Regierungspräsident (17 Sept. 1927, 24 Oct. 1927).

75. StAH 421–5 Kb3 III, for copies of the correspondence to Brauer and the questionnaire.

76. See Harold James, *The German Slump. Politics and Economics, 1924–1936* (Oxford, 1986), 42.

77. LAB StA 751 (Städtetag), Niederschrift, 23 Jan. 1928 and StA 752, Niederschrift, 29 Apr. 1929, 24 June 1929, 26 Sept. 1929, 31 Oct. 1929; C. L. Holtfrerich,

"The Modernization of the Tax System," in Witt, *Wealth,* 125–35, here: 127. Cf. Terhalle, *Finanzwirtschaft,* 57.

78. Angell, *Recovery,* 240ff., 314ff., 322; Holtfrerich, "Modernization," 135.

79. Witt, *Wealth,* 9ff, 13, 17.

80. On public and municipal finance, Fritz Terhalle, *Die Finanzwirtschaft des Staates und der Gemeinden. Eine Einführung in die Staatsfinanzwirtschaft* (Berlin, 1948); idem, "Geschichte der deutschen öffentlichen Finanzwirtschaft vom Beginn des 19.Jahrhunderts bis zum Schlüsse des Zweiten Weltkrieges," in W. Gerloff, F. Neumark, eds., *Handbuch der Finanzwissenschaft,* 2d ed. (Tübingen, 1951), 273–326; Josef Wysocki, "Die Kommunalfinanzen in Erzbergers Reformkonzept: Finanzzuweisungen statt eigener Steuern," in Hansmeyer, ed., *Kommunale Finanzpolitik,* 35–59; Klaus Epstein, *Matthias Erzberger und das Dilemna der deutschen Demokratie* (Frankfurt a.M., Berlin, and Vienna, 1976), chap. 13.

81. StAH 421–5 BA 2a, Magistrat 610 Steueramt, 23 July 1931; StJB Altona (1928), 274; StJBDS 25 (1930), 441. *Norddeutsche Nachrichten* 87, 14 Apr. 1933.

82. StJB Altona (1928), 275; Hoffmann, *Neues Altona,* 1:219; Robert Kirchhoff, *Die Entwicklung Altonas in den Jahren 1923 und 1924. Erläuterungen zu den statistischen Jahres-Übersichten der Stadt Altona* (Altona, 1925). On the inflation: Gerald D. Feldmann, Carl Ludwig Holtfrerich, Gerhard A. Ritter, Peter-Christian Witt, eds., *The German Inflation/Die Deutsche Inflation. Eine Zwischenbilanz* (Berlin and New York, 1982).

83. *Amtsblatt* 11, 15 Mar. 1930.

84. *Amtsblatt* 10, 8 Mar. 1930: "Die Gewerbesteuer 1925–1929 in Altona im Vergleich zu anderen Städten, insbesondere zu Hamburg"; *Amtsblatt* 5, 3 Feb. 1933: "Staats- und Gemeindesteuern in Altona" I, and *Amtsblatt* 6, 10 Feb. 1933: "Staats- und Gemeindesteuern in Altona" II. Cf. Mulert, "Wirtschaft und Gemeinden," 406.

85. *Amtsblatt* 13, 29 Mar. 1930: "Oberbürgermeister Brauer Zum Haushaltsplan 1930"; StAH 421–5 BAa 2a, Der Magistrat to the chairman of the Bezirksausschuss and Regierungspräsident, 22 May 1930, 5.

86. *Amtsblatt* 49, 6 Dec. 1930: "Zu den Steuerfestsetzungen des Staatskommissars."

87. StAH 421–5 Kb 41 1, Copy of report from Brauer to Súren, 8 Nov. 1930.

88. StAH 421–5 Kb 41 1, Prussian M.d.I. W.St. Altona 18 to Regierungspräsident Schleswig, 11 Nov. 1930.

89. StAH 421–5 Kb 41 1, Regierungspräsident IG 12 to Brauer, 12 Nov. 1930. See LAB StB 435, Rundfrage I606/30 Dt. Städtetag, 11 Dec. 1930. Commissioners were sent into at least 541 Prussian towns and cities, Wolfgang Haus, "Staatskommissare und Selbstverwaltung 1930–1933. Fragwürdige Überlieferungen zum "Versagen" der demokratische Kommunalverwaltung," *Der Städtetag* (1956): 96–97; James, *German Slump,* 77–79.

90. StAH 421–5 Kb 41 1, Telegram 054/056, 14 Nov. 1930; and letter from Altonaer Haus-und Grundeigentümer Verein (Chr. Gehrke) to Bezirksausschuss, 13 Dec. 1930.

91. StAH 421–5 Kb 41 1, Fraktion Bürgerliche Gemeinschaft to Bezirksausschuss, Betr. Staatskommissar, 27 Nov. 1930; and copy of protest to the Regier-

ungspräsident, Schleswig; see also, Telegram to Preuss. Staatsministerium, 15 Nov. 1930; and letter with resolution to Bezirksausschuss, Betr. Festsetzung von Kommunalsteuern, 6 Dec. 1930.

92. StAH 421–5 BA d I, Letter Buccerius/Sanwer to Bezirksausschuss, 12 Mar. 1931, Betr. Klage im Verwaltungsstreitverfahren der Norddeutschen Oelmühlenwerke Karl Marxstraße 158/160, 2; Bezirksausschuss, Bescheid, AB 132/31.62, 5 Nov. 1931, in same file.

93. StaH 421–5 BAa 2a, copy of council minutes of 13 Nov. 1930. StAH 421–5 Kb 41 1, Regierungspräsident IG 3010 Altona 12, 21 Nov. 1930 to Prussian M.d.I, Betr. Steuerfestsetzung in Altona, report by Regierungsrat Dr. Schifferer.

94. StaH 421–5 BAa 2a, Richard Galster, letter to Bezirksausschuss, 21 Nov. 1930. Jostock, "Die Schulden."

95. StAH 421–5 Kb 41 1, Letter to Regierungspräsident Schleswig, 18 Nov. 1930; *Hamburger Nachrichten* 125, 6 May 1931.

96. *Altonaer Tageblatt* 301, 27 Dec. 1930. Cf. Horst Matzerath, *Nationalsozialismus und kommunale Selbstverwaltung* (Stuttgart, 1970), 54ff.; Grill, *Nazi Movement*, 239, 345–47; Bohnke, *NSDAP im Ruhrgebiet,* 176.

97. LAB StB 435, Preußischer Landtag, Wahlperiode I 1928/30, cols. 2279/80, Wirtschaftspartei: kleine Anfrage 1911 and 1929, 9 Dec. 1930.

98. Ibid., col. 2207, DNVP (Mehlis u. Gen.): kleine Anfrage 1847, 16 Nov. 1930.

99. *Altonaer Tageblatt* 301, 27 Dec. 1930: "Selbst Severing Missbilligt." For Severings's enthusiastic approval of tax commissioners, Heinrich Brüning, *Memoiren 1918–1934* (Stuttgart, 1970), 208.

100. *Altonaer Tageblatt* 304, 31 Dec. 1930: "Altonas entzückende Silvester-Überraschung."

101. *Hamburger Fremdenblatt* 362, 31 Dec. 1930: "Neues Steuerdiktat für Altona."

102. "Zu den Steuerfestsetzungen."

103. See the numerous cases in: StAH 421–5, ser. K (Kommunalaufsichtenssachen) secs: Kb 3 vols. ii–vi, Kb 41, vols. i–iii, Kc 1 vol. v and 1a vols. i–iii.

104. StAH 421–5 BAa, Brauer to Provinzialrat, 23 Aug. 1932.

105. Reinhold's Tax Reduction Law (31 Mar. 1926) had forced local authorities to increase surcharges and backdate them in order to maintain levels of revenue, Peter Reinhold, *The Economic, Financial and Political State of Germany Since the War* (Yale, 1928), 60–66. See James, *German Slump,* 43–44.

106. StAH 421–5 BAa 2a, Beschluss der Städtische Kollegien in der gemeinschaftlichen Sitzung vom 30 March 1926 (copy); ibid., Städtische Kollegien, Drucksache 404, 12 Mar. 1926: Magistrat betrifft Gewerbesteuer Umlagebeschlüsse über den Steuerbedarf der Stadt Altona für das Haushaltsjahr 1926.

107. StAH 421–5 BAa 2a, Industrie- und Handelskammer to Regierungspräsident, 23 Apr. 1926.

108. *Amtsblatt* 10, 8 Mar. 1930: "Die Gewerbesteuer"; StJB Altona (1928), 274, 277; StAH 421–5 Kb 5a I, for reports of council meeting on the 21 May 1926, in

Hamburger Echo 140, 22 May 1926; *Hamburger Nachrichten* 233 (Morgenausgabe), 22 May 1926.

109. StAH 421–5 BAa 2a, Zentralausschuss der kommunalen Vereine zu Altona, Ahrendt, Bahnhofstraße 6, to Bezirksausschuss Schleswig, 1 Apr. 1926.

110. StAH 421–5 Kb 41 I (Tetens), Der Magistrat/Str.Vii Zg.85 381/28 to Regierungspräsident in Schleswig, 4 May 1929; and letter from D. and H. Möller, Massivdeckenbau GmbH to Vorsitzenden des Gewerbesteuerausschusses für den Stadtkreis Altona, 14 Mar. 1929.

111. Ibid., letter to Dr. Abegg, 26 Apr. 1929.

112. Ibid., 2.

113. StAH 421–5 Kb 5a II, report of meeting of the Altonaer Hafenverein at Otto Grimm Restaurant, Blankenese.

114. StAH 421–5 BAa 2a, Ersuch des Magistrats, 13 Mar. 1928, "Festretzung der Realsteuerzuschläge 1928/29." Cf. Städtische Kollegien: Drucksache 850, 14 Mar. 1928, in the same file.

115. StJBDS 25 (1930), 441, 447, 453; StJBDS 27 (1932), 139, 142, 145, 148; StJBDS 28 (1933), 142.

116. McElligott, "Municipal Politics," 137, table 2.8: "Bankruptcies and Liquidation in Altona, 1913–1933."

117. StAH 421–5 BAa 2a, Joint communiqué: Industrie-und Handelskammer and Handwerkskammer to Magistrat, 1 Apr. 1930; ibid., letter to Bezirksausschuss, 6 May 1930; "Haushaltsplan 1930: Begleitbericht, Anlage 7: Bilanz der Stadt Altona" (31 Mar. 1929).

118. StAH 421–5 BAa 2a, Der Magistrat to Bezirksausschuss and Regierungspräsident, 22 May 1930, 13 page report from Brauer.

119. StAH 421–5 Kb 41 II, Magistrat 61 (Brauer) to Provinzialrat Schleswig-Holstein/Kiel durch den Bezirksausschuss Schleswig, Geschäftsnummer BAa 248/3263, 23 Aug. 1932, 2, 4.

120. StAH 421–5 Kb 41 II, Magistrat to Regierungspräsident, 611/22510/32, 16 Feb. 1933; ibid., Der Vorsitzende des Grundsteuerberufungsausschusses (Schleswig), Tgb. Nr. Le 3/37/1932, 31 Dec. 1932.

121. StAH 421–5 Kb 41 II, letter to Dr. Bracht, 1 Nov. 1932.

122. Ibid.

123. StAH 421–5 Kb 3 V (Möller), Magistrat 1200 to Regierungspräsident, 11 Aug. 1933, "Beschwerde . . . ," Dr. Walter Buchholz to Regierungspräsident, 20 July 1933; and ditto, J.Nr.IG 2031, 18 Sept. 1933.

124. StAH 421–5 Kb 41 II, Magistrat (Steueramt/Beschwerdestelle) 6103 to Regierungspräsident, 24 Mar. 1933.

125. StAH 421–5 Kb 41 II, Alwin Schlöte to Regierungspräsident, 22 Dec. 1932. On the situation among self-employed lawyers, see, in general, McClelland, *German Experience*, 154–59, 193–205.

126. StAH 421–5 Kb 41 II, Wilhelm Jentsch Jr. to Bezirksausschuss, 11 Feb. 1933.

127. StAH 421–5 BA 2a Magistrat 610 (Steueramt), 23 July 1931. Cf. "Staats-und Gemeindesteuern in Altona," 1, op. cit.

128. StJBDS 25 (1930), 447; StJBDS 28 (1933), 138. The exact figures were 14,24, and 26,70 reichsmark.

129. StAH 421–5 Kb 41a I, "Zu den Steuerfestsetzungen des Staatskommissars. Eine Erwiderung des Altonaer Haus- und Grundeigentümervereins e.V.," 4. Martin Schumacher, "Hausbesitz, Mittelstand und Wirtschaftspartei in der Weimarer Republik," in Mommsen et. al., eds., *Industrielles System*, 836–46.

130. StAK 28643/25, Deposition, 7 Dec. 1932.

131. StAK 28648/12, Deposition, 23 Nov. 1932.

132. StAH 421–5 Kb 3V, Stolken, letter to Regierungspräsident, 5 July 1935.

133. StAH 421–5 BAa 2a, Grundeigentümer Verein Stellingen-Langenfelde to Magistrat, 8 Mar. 1930, minutes of members meeting. Cf. Peter-Christian Witt, "Tax Policies, Tax Assessment and Inflation: Towards a Sociology of Public Finances in the German Inflation, 1914–1923," in idem, *Wealth*, 137–60, here: 149–50.

134. StAH 421–5 Kb 41 II (Irps). This figure broke down as follows: 1931–32: 1,959.11 reichsmark, Apr.–Oct. 1932–33: 4,510.74 reichsmark, Irps letter to Regierungspräsident, 25 Oct. 1932.

135. Ibid., Magistrat to Regierungspräsident 611/40090/32, 11 Nov. 1932.

136. On the background to this: Witt, "Inflation, Wohnungswirtschaft und Hauszinssteuer"; Michael Ruck, "Der öffentliche Wohnungsbaufinanzierung in der Weimarer Republik," in Schildt and Sywottek, eds., *Massenwohnung und Eigenheim*, 150–200.

137. He had previously run for office as a member of the Gemeinschaftsliste (*Amtsblatt* 37, 17 Sept. 1927).

138. StAH 421–5 Kb 41 II, Irps to Regierungspräsident, 25 Oct. 1932; and his letter of 29 Nov. 1932.

139. StAH 421–5 Kb 3 IV (Reif, Größe Fischerstr.).

140. StAH 421–5 Kb 41 II (Dennert), Dennert and Pape had been established in 1848 in the Friedenstraße (Altstadt subdistrict 13). Letter to Magistrat Altona, Stundungsstelle, Abt.FM G/T. 28 Dec. 1932; see also their appeal to the Oberpräsident, 28 Dec. 1932.

141. Ibid., Regierungspräsident IG 3010 Altona, 30 Mar. 1933. Cf. StAH 421–5 Kb 41 II (Krömer).

142. StAH 421–5 BAa 2a, Altonaer Haus und Grundeigentümer-Verein to Magistrat, 28 Mar. 1930 (Zum Schreiben v. 19 Mar. 1930 Str.IX. Städtische Kollegien Drucksache 1303, 29 Mar. 1930, Betrifft: Gemeindesteuerumlagebeschlüsse über den Steuerbedarf der Stadt Altona f.d. Haushaltsjahr 1930; see other related protests in the same file: Verein Altonaer Anwälte (VAA) to Bezirksausschuss, Betrifft Antrag des Magistrats Altona auf Erteilung der Genehmigung gemäss Para 44 der Gewerbesteuerverordnung. StAH 421–5 Kb 41 I, for notices of further tax increases (13 Nov. 1930).

143. StAH 421–5 Kb 41 II, Holst to Magistrat, 17 Mar. 1933; letter from W. Elers, C. Schnitler to the Prussian finance minister, 3 May 1933.

144. Ibid., 2. But see the disapointment in store for tax-payers after Mar. 1933, StAH 421–5 Kb 41 II.

145. "Zu den Steuerfestsetzungen des Staatskommissars. Eine Erwiderung."

146. Preller, *Sozialpolitik,* 396.

147. StAH 421–5 Kb 41 I, Städtische Kollegien Drucksache 1432 (Magistrat: Ebert/Brauer), Betrifft: Einführung der Bürgersteuer (Gemeinde-Bürgersteuer-Ordnung) 12 Dec. 1930; StJBDS 28 (1933): 138.

148. Werner Jochmann, "Brünings Deflationspolitik und der Untergang der Weimarer Republik," in D. Stegmann, B-J. Wendt, P-C. Witt, eds., *Industrielle Gesellschaft und politische System. Beiträge zur politischen Sozialgeschichte. Festschrift für Fritz Fischer zum siebzigsten Geburtstag* (Bonn-Bad Godesberg, 1978), 97–112; Peter-Christian Witt, "Finanzpolitik als Verfassungs- und Gesellschaftspolitik. Überlegungen zur Finanzpolitik des deutschen Reiches in den Jahren 1930 bis 1932," *Geschichte und Gesellschaft* 8, no. 3 (1982): 386–414; Knut Borchardt, "Zwangslagen und Handlungsspielräume in der großen Wirtschafts-krise der frühen dreißiger Jahre: Zur Revision des überlieferten Geschichtsbildes," in Stürmer, *Belagerte Civitas,* 318–39; Carl-Ludwig Holtfrerich, "Alternativen zu Brünings Wirtschaftspolik in der Weltwirtschaftskrise?" *Historische Zeitschrift* 235 (1982): 605–31.

149. *Altonaer Tageblatt* 301, 27 Dec. 1930.

150. StAH 421–5 Kb 3 IV, Diercks, letter to Regierungspräsident, 17 Feb. 1930, and 3 Sept. 1932. StAH 421–5 Kb 41 a I, Elbe Housing Association to Magistrat, 22 May 1931; StAH 421–5 BAa, Mieterverein Altona u. preußische Umgebung e.V. to Magistrat Str.IX, 31 Mar. 1930; StAH 421–5 Kb 41 II, SPD Resolution 2 Dec. 1932; Magistrat 610 to Regierungspräsident, 17 Jan. 1933.

151. Städtische Kollegien Drucksache 1632, (Magistrat: Ebert/Brauer), Bet-rifft: Einführung der Bürgersteuer (Gemeinde-Bürgersteuer-Ordnung) 12 Dec. 1930. *Economist,* 2 Aug. 1930: "Economic Report," 231.

152. StAH 421–5 Kb 41 I, Ceaser Brokan, letter to Regierungspräsident, 1 May 1931; Magistrat Steueramt 6136/I/3651, 8 May 1931.

153. StAH 421–5 Kb 41 II, letter from Magistrat 617/4/06008, to Regierungs-präsident, 6 Mar. 1933 (Charlotte Müller).

154. StAH 421–5 Kb 41 I, Schmidt to Regierungspräsident, 13 Mar. 1931, and Magistrat to Regierungspräsident, 25 Mar. 1931.

155. StAH 421–5 Kb 41 II, Meier, Groß Flottbek, to Prussian finance minister, 26 July 1932.

156. StAH 421–5 Kb 41 I (Bethien); StAH 421–5 Kb 41 II, cases of Plambeck, Geert, König, Kuratorium der höheren Schulen, bank official Preu, all in the same file.

157. Vierhaus, "Auswirkungen der Krise," 155–75; Bennecke, *Wirtschaftliche Depression,* chaps. 4–5.

158. Letter in *Altonaer Tageblatt* 301, 27 Dec. 1930.

159. *Nordwestdeutsche Handwerkszeitung,* 22 Mar. 1919, "Handwerk und Sozialisierung," in Heinz-Gerhard Haupt, ed., *Die Radikale Mitte. Lebensweise und Politik von Handwerkern und Kleinhändlern in Deutschland seit 1848* (Munich, 1985), doc. 35d, 182; Frank Domurad, "The Politics of Corporatism: Hamburg Handicrafts in the Late Weimar Republic, 1927–1933," in Bessel and Feucht-wanger, eds., *Social Change,* 174–206; Geoff Eley, "The German Right,

1860–1945: How It Changed," in idem, *From Unification to Nazism: Reinterpreting the German Past* (London and Sydney, 1986), 231–53, here: 235–36.
160. Theodor Geiger, "Panik im Mittelstand," *Die Arbeit* 7, no. 10 (1930): 637–54. Winkler, "Vom Protest zur Panik," and idem, "From Social Protectionism to National Socialism: The German Small Business Movement in Comparative Perspective," *Journal of Modern History* 48 (1976): 1–18; Peter Wulf , "Die Mittelschichten in der Krise der Weimarer Republik 1930–1933," in Holl, *Wirtschaftskrise,* 89–102, here: 96. See the incisive critique by Alfred Braunthal, "Die Ökonomischen Würzeln des Nationalsozialistischen Wirtschaftsprogrammes," *Die Gesellschaft* 9, no. 1 (1932): 486–99.
161. Dirk Stegmann, Claus-Dieter Krohn, "Kleingewerbe und Nationalsozialismus in einer agrarisch-mittelständischen Region. Das Beispiel Lüneburg 1930–1039," *Archiv für Sozialgeschichte* 17 (1977): 41–98; D. Stegmann, "Bürgertum und Politik in der Weltwirtschaftskrise" and "Kleinstadtgesellschaft und Nationalsozialismus," in Lüneburger Arbeitskreis "Machtergreifung," ed., *Heimat, Heide, Hakenkreuz. Lüneburgs Weg ins Dritten Reich* (Hamburg, 1984), 16–27, 82–166; Turner, *German Big Business,* 203. Horst Matzerath and Henry A Turner, "Die Selbstfinanzierung der NSDAP 1930–1932," *Geschichte und Gesellschaft* 3 (1977): 59–92.
162. *Alphabetisches Straßen-Verzeichnis der Stadt Altona* (Altona, 1931), 37–38.
163. StAH 421–5 Kb 41 II, Heinemann to Regierungspräsident, 12 Jan. 1931.
164. Heinemann to Regierungspräsident, 7 Feb. 1931.
165. Heinemann to Regierungspräsident, 12 Jan. 1931.
166. Heinemann to Magistrat, 13 Jan. 1931.
167. Heinemann to Regierungspräsident, 12 Jan. 1931.
168. Heinemann to Magistrat, 7 Feb. 1931.

Chapter 6

1. Joseph Goebbels, *Kampf um Berlin.* vol. 1: *Der Anfang (1926–1927)* (Berlin, 1939), 86.
2. LAB 142 StA 752, Sitzung des Vorstandes, Niederschrift 17 Jan. 1930, 2–3; *Politik und Wirtschaft in der Krise 1930–1932. Quellen Zur Ära Brüning,* doc. 41: "Denkschrift des Reichskommissars Oberbürgermeister Goerdeler für Reichskanzler Brüning" (3 Feb. 1932), 1255–60. Ernst Forsthoff, "Um die kommunale Selbstverwaltung," *Zeitschrift für Politik* 21 (1930); Arnold Köttgen, *Die Krise der kommunalen Selbstverwaltung* (Tübingen, 1931). Simmel, *Conflict,* 18.
3. Max Weber, "Parliament and Government in Germany," in Max Weber, *Economy and Society. An Outline of Interpretative Sociology,* ed. Günther Roth and Claus Wittich, 2 vols. (Berkeley, Los Angeles, and London, 1978), 1460. Brüning, *Memoiren,* 372; Bracher, *Auflösung,* 63–64; idem, "Democracy and the Power Vacuum: The Problem of the Party State during the Disintegration of the Weimar Republic," in Volker Berghahn and Martin Kitchen, eds., *Germany in an Age of Total War* (London, 1981), 189–202; Jasper, *Die gescheiterte Zähmung,* 41, 53; Manfred Funke, "Republik im Untergang. Die Zerstörung des Parlamentarismus

als Vorbereitung der Diktatur," in Bracher et al., *Die Weimarer Republik,* 505–31, here: 514.

4. Eve Rosenhaft, *Beating the Fascists? The German Communists and Political Violence, 1929–1933* (Cambridge, 1983); Conan Fischer, "Unemployment and Left-Wing Radicalism in Weimar Germany, 1930–1933," in Peter D. Stachura, ed., *Unemployment and the Great Depression in Weimar Germany* (London, 1986), 221; Richard Bessel, "Political Violence and the Nazi Seizure of Power," in idem, ed., *Life in the Third Reich* (Oxford, 1987), 4–5, 14–15; Bernd Weisbrod, "Gewalt in der Politik. Zur politischen Kultur in Deutschland zwischen den beiden Weltkriegen," *Geschichte in Wissenschaft und Unterricht* 43 Jg., no. 7 (1992): 391–404.

5. Bezirksleitung KPD, "Bericht 1932," 92–99. The KPD had strong support in wards ten and eleven in Blankenese, where they had a share of the vote five to six times higher than the district average. For Osdorf and Eidelstedt, see ibid., 94; Heinz Karl Kücklich and Erika Kücklich, *Die Antifaschistische Aktion. Dokumentation und Chronik Mai 1932 bis Januar 1933* (East Berlin, 1965), 11, 259.

6. Hermann Weber, "Die KPD im Kampf gegen SPD and NSDAP," in Wolfgang Michalka, ed., *Die nationalsozialistische Machtergreifung* (Paderborn, Munich, Vienna, and Zurich, 1984), 85; idem, "Zur politik der KPD," 127; idem, ed., *Die Generallinie,* ix; Flechtheim, *Die KPD,* 258–59, 263–69.

7. IML/ZPA St 18/217, bl. 51–52, Der Minister des Innern II (report prepared by Diels) 1272 OP Schleswig-Holstein/65, Berlin, 17 Aug. 1932, Entwurf, 4; *Hamburg Echo* 172, 19 July 1932, for the view of police president, Otto Eggerstedt (SPD).

8. StAH 424–16, Polizeiamt 1900–1926, part 3, sec. b, "Die Polizeireviere"; ibid., "Verwaltungsbericht," 1 Jan. 1927–31 Mar. 1929; Cf. Polizeipräsidium Hamburg, "Chroniken der Hamburger Polizei" (typed mss. n.d.), pt. 6: 11–12, 15; StJB Altona (1928), 6. Gerd Stolz, "Die Schutzpolizei in Altona und Wandsbek 1869–1937," *Zeitschrift des Vereins für Hamburgische Geschichte* 63 (1977): 35–68.

9. StABr. 4,65 II Z 11, 1528/249, "Denkschrift über Kampfvorbereitungen radikaler Organisationen," 1 Nov. 1932–1 Dec. 1933, 39–56, here: 40, 44; StAH 424–16, Das Polizeiamt, Der Oberpol.Inspekt.I 127, 11 Feb. 1919; 424–29 IG V/1 LA 1385/18, 20 July 1918; "Chroniken," pt. 6: 9–12; Hoffmann, *Neues Altona* I, 364, 366; Warnecke, "Razzia." Polizei-Oberstleutnant K. Schröder, "Straßen- und Häuserkampf," *Die Polizei* 24, no. 20 (20 Oct. 1927): 489–91; ibid., no. 21 (5 Nov. 1927): 518–50; ibid., no. 22 (20 Nov. 1927): 548–51.

10. Hans-Gerd Jaschke and Martin Loiperdinger, "Gewalt and NSDAP vor 1933: Ästhetische Okkupation und Physische Terror," in Reiner Steinweg, ed., *Faszination der Gewalt. Politische Strategie und Alltagserfahrung* (Frankfurt a.M., 1983), 123–55, here: 140–42. Cf. E. J. Gumbel, *Vier Jahre Politischer Mord* (Berlin, 1922); Helmut Heins, interview, 17 Dec. 1982; idem, "Das Geschehen um den "Blutsonntag" in Altona. Hintergründe, Erlebnisse, Zusammenhänge, Entwicklungen," MS (Hamburg, 1982), 5.

11. Kaufmann, *Gliederung,* 60, 66–67; McElligott, "Municipal Politics," 413–14.

12. LAS 352/1242/141 (Tessnow, Gr.Gärtnerstraße: ward 31); 352/1244/260

(Kehl, Gerritstraße: ward 26); 352/1242/116 (Meyer, Kl.Freiheit: ward 21); 352/1244/104 (Riemann, Grund: ward 16). By Oct. 1932 just over 69 percent of new members were unemployed (Bezirksleitung, "Bericht," 68; McElligott, "Mobilising the Unemployed," 241–42). See also, Eve Rosenhaft, "The Unemployed in the Neighbourhood: Social Dislocation and Political Mobilisation in Germany 1929–33," in Evans and Geary, eds., *German Unemployed,* 194–227; Siegfried Bahne, "Die Erwerbslosenpolitik der KPD in der Weimarer Republik," in H. Mommsen, H. Schulze, eds., *Vom Elend der Handarbeit. Probleme historischer Unterschichtsforschung* (Stuttgart, 1981), 477–96.

13. VVN Hamburg, copy: Anwaltschaft Altona, Helmreich 109/35 Geschäftsnummer 11.J.370/34 11 Ks.1/35, 7/35, "Im Namen des . . . Volkes," (Aschberg und gen.), 60.

14. Kaufmann, *Gliederung,* 71. Cf. AHVW 16, no. 1 (1939): 4. See *Altonaer Adreßbuch* volumes for 1929 and 1932, for the socio-occupational structure. Klara von Eyll, "Stadtadreßbücher als Quelle für die Wirtschafts- und Sozialhhistorische Forschung—das Beispiel Köln," *Zeitschrift für Unterricht* 24, no. 3 (1979): 12–26.

15. Warnecke, "Razzia." Cf. Robert Roberts, *The Classic Slum* (Manchester, 1971); Jerry White, *The Worst Street in North London: Campbell Bunk, Islington between the Wars* (London, 1986).

16. LAS 352/1242/117, Strafsache . . . Alfred Franck, bl. 10ff: minutes of evidence, 9 Dec. 1932.

17. LAS 352/1242/90, bl. 14: Strafsache . . . Peter Wolter, Deposition, n.d.

18. Ibid., bl. 29–34, statement by Ernst Frank.

19. Ibid., bl. 145d: statement by Meissner, 29 Dec. 1932, 1.

20. LAS 352/1242/119, Strafsache . . . Hermann Baatz, bl. 6: testimony of Ernst Frank. His enemies eventually shot and wounded him, StAK 29641/37, Aufruhrschaden: Frank, Ernst Frank, letter to the municipal legal office requesting compensation, and letter to Cllr. Max Boge (NSDAP), 30 July 1932. On the Tumult Compensation Law: *Amtsblatt* 46, 18 Nov. 1932: "Ersatz von Tumultschaden."

21. LAS 352/1245/301, Strafsache . . . Otto Rammelt, bl. 12–15: statement to the police, 1 Jan. 1933,

22. Anthony McElligott, "'. . . und so kam es zu einer schweren Schlägerei': Sraßenschlachten in Altona und Hamburg," in Maike Bruhns, Thomas Krause, Anthony McElligott, Claudia Preuschoft, Werner Skrentny, *"Hier war doch alles nicht so schlimm." Wie die Nazis in Hamburg den Alltag eroberten* (Hamburg, 1984), 58–85, here: 70. Robert Morrison MacIver, *Community: A Sociological Study Being an Attempt to Set Out the Nature and Fundamental Laws of Social Life* (London, 1928), 144; Anthony P. Cohen, *The Symbolic Construction of Community* (London, 1989), 20, 108.

23. LAS 352/1244/254, evidence of Emil Kniesel, 23 Aug. 1932; LAS 352/1244/284, evidence of Jakob Pasternak; 352/1245/301, bl. 3: evidence of sixty-eight-year-old Adolf Kiel, 1 Sept. 1932; and bl. 1: evidence of Friedrich Rauchstadt, 3 Aug. 1932, in the same file; 352/1245/328, bl. 2ff.: evidence of Elsa Grothkopp, 28 Sept. 1932; Max Weber, "Political Communities," *Economy,* 902.

24. VVN Hamburg, Copy of Anklageschrift Sondergericht Altona, Son.KS.1/35 6/35, trial report of Aschberg und Gen. 9–18 Apr. 1935, 80. LAS 352/1244/272, Meyer u. Gen., bl. 4f., statement to the police, 22 Aug. 1932.

25. Weber, *Wandlung,* 364–65 for the *Kampfbund;* Kücklich, *Antifaschistische Aktion;* StABr 4,65 IV 4e vol. 7, situation report 29 Nov. 1930, 10–12, Altona.

26. The tavern was located in ward 46, where, in 1930 the KPD's share of the vote was 46 percent, rising to 54 and 57 percent in July and Nov. 1932.

27. IML/ZA St3/622, copies of two police situation reports: 11 Oct. 1932, and one undated; StABr. 4,65 IV 4e vol. 7, situation report 2, 28 Nov. 1931, 14; Franz Feuchtwanger, "Der Militarische Apparat der KPD in den Jahren 1928–1935," *Internationale Wissenschaftliche Korrespondenz* 17, no. 4 (1981): 485–533.

28. IML ZPA St.3/129, bl.16–30, Abschrift: Pr. MdI II D.7067, 27 July 1933; LAS 352/1244/278 (Alex Kuhlmann), bl. 27–38: interrogation 17 Nov. 1932, on the Dennerstraße neighbourhood *Staffel.*

29. The Altona *Antifa* constituted 40 percent of the Hamburg/Altona/Wandsbek regional membership (Kücklich, *Antifaschistische Aktion,* 260).

30. LAS 309/22813, Polizeipräsident (Altona) Abt. IA, 29 July 1932; Regierungspräsident Schleswig IPP 961 II/6, to Min.d.I., Betr. Vorbereitungen der KPD zu einem bewaffneten Aufstand, 10 Aug. 1932.

31. StABr. 4,65 IV 4e, vol. 7, situation report 2, 28 Nov. 1931; IML ZPA St 3/622, Der Polizeipräsident Altona, situation report 11 Oct. 1932; LAS 352/1244/278, bl. 39–51: interrogation 18 Nov. and 19 Nov. 1932; bl. 56–59 testimony of Heinrich O., Holstpassage, 22 Nov. 1932; Kücklich, *Antifaschistische Aktion,* 258.

32. Ibid., 259. Stellinger Moor was in actual fact the Voluntary Labor Duty (FAD) camp.

33. Max Weber "The Neighbourhood: An Unsentimental Economic Brotherhood," *Economy,* 361, 363.

34. LAS 301/4690 (Versammlungstätigkeit), Polizei Altona Abt.IA (Reg.Rat Schabbahard) to Oberpräsident, 1 July 1929; LAS 309/22996 (Versammlungstätigkeit), Pol.präs. Altona IA 861/31 to Regierungspräsident, 11 Apr. 1931.

35. LAS 309/22669, Oberpräsident Nr.OP.1514, Vfg. Erlaß 16 Mar. 1929, to Regierungspräsident, 5 June 1929. Statistics appear to have been systematically compiled only from this year.

36. LAS 301/4690, culled from monthly reports compiled by the office of the Oberpräsident.

37. LAS 352/1244/282, Meyer u. Gen., Polizei Abt.IA 3949/32, 19 Oct. 1932.

38. STAK 28646/68, Aufruhrschaden: Gotthardt, Gotthardt, statement n.d. (attached to letter to the Chairman of the Investigations Committee for Tumult, 26 Sept. 1932. LAS 352/1242/124, Strafsache . . . Meyer u. Gen., bl. 4: statement by Emil Fühler, a retired policeman who was shot by the police on the 17 July 1932 but who was convinced that only Communists could have been responsible. He later died of his wounds.

39. LAS 309/22813, Polizeipräsident Altona IA 646/32, 10 May 1932; Polizeipräsident to Regierungspräsident IA Betr. KPD-Bewegung, 4 Nov. 1932; see ibid., Polizeipräsident IA 2855/32, 11 Nov. 1932, evidence of Ewald Morrell

(NSDAP) Händler, Lornsenplatz 3. See report of 7th Polizei Revier, Pol.Sekr. Emil Ross, 3 Nov. 1932, for receipt of letter from Hubert Richter (Sturmbann-führer SA 2,6 8/31), in same file.

40. StAK 28643/29, Aufruhrschaden: Böhring.

41. Ibid., bl. 17: letter to Magistrat, 24 May 1932; and for the following quotes.

42. Ibid., bl. 19–20: letter to Rechtsamt, 10 June 1932.

43. Ibid., bl. 21: Decision of the municipal Rechtsamt 1200, 15 June 1932. StAH 424–16, Städtische Polizeibehörde, letter to Böhring, 24 Sept. 1931.

44. StAK 28646/60, Aufruhrschaden: Schröder, Rechtsamt 1200/E 29 Nov. 1932: two reports of 7th Polizei Revier to Rechtsamt: Tg. 1174/32 16(17) July 1932, and 9 Dec. 1932.

45. Ibid., Rechtsanwalt Voß to the Tumult Commission, 27 Sept. 1932.

46. Voß to Tumult Commission, 12 Sept. 1932.

47. StAK 28645/77, Aufruhrschaden: Hey, Jakob Hey, statement to Recht-samt 25 July 1932; Paul Hey, deposition to the Tumult Commission, 8 Sept. 1932. Cf. 5th Polizei Revier Abt.I, report, 26 Sept. 1932.

48. Ibid., Ortspolizei Abt.II (u.a. Gewerbe), 21 Sept. 1932.

49. Hey to Tumult Commission, 30 Oct. 1932.

50. StAK 28642/114 and 125; StAK 28645/78 and 81, Aufruhrschaden: Burmeister and Danielsen (Kiel).

51. Jaschke and Loiperdinger, "Gewalt," correctly observe that first the Nazis had to undermine the legal forces of the state, 145; Anthony McElligott, "Street Politics in Hamburg, 1932–33," *History Workshop Journal* 16 (1983): 83.

52. LAS 309/22721, Zusammenstoss 15 Mar. 1933, the shooting of Helmuth Witzel; McElligott, "Straßenschlachten," 84.

53. Albert Stenwedel, interview, 19 Mar. 1984, tape 1; LAS 309/22998 (NSDAP), Zusammenstellungen, Polizeipräsident Altona IA 43 01/3, 1 Mar. 1930; StABr. 4,65 IV 4e, vol. 6, situation report 2, 16 June 1928, 24; Okrass, *"Hamburg bleibt rot,"* 179, 227.

54. Okrass, *"Hamburg bleibt rot,"* 124.

55. According to police sources party membership had reached approximately 450 in early 1930; Nazi sources suggest a doubling of this membership by 1931. See chap. 2, table 5. Both Mathilde Jamin, *Zwischen den Klassen. Zur Sozialstruktur der SA-Führerschaft* (Wuppertal 1984), chap. 4; and Richard Bessel, *Political Violence and the Rise of Nazism: The Storm Troopers in Eastern Germany, 1925–1934* (London and New Haven, 1984), chap. 3:1, acknowledge a working-class presence in the SA but place greater emphasis on the lower-middle-class composition of subaltern leadership. For a stronger emphasis upon working-class members: Conan Fischer, *Stormtroopers: A Social, Economic and Ideological Analysis, 1929–35* (London, 1983).

56. See Domurad, "Politics of Corporatism," 174–206; Eve Rosenhaft, "Working-Class Life and Working-Class Politics: Communists, Nazis and the State in the Battle for the Streets, 1928–1932," in Bessel and Feuchtwanger, *Social Change,* 207–40; Richard Bessel, "Violence as Propaganda: The Role of the Storm Troopers in the Rise of National Socialism," in Thomas Childers, ed., *The Formation of the Nazi Constituency, 1919–1933* (London, 1986), 131–46.

57. Idem, "The Rise of the NSDAP and the Myth of Nazi Propaganda," *Wiener Library Bulletin* 33, nos. 51–52 (1980): 20–29.

58. In this ward, the Nazi vote had been just under 8 percent in May 1924.

59. Walter Stolte, interview, 24 Mar. 1982, tape 2.

60. Stenwedel, loc. cit.

61. Cited in *Hamburger Echo,* 3 Aug. 1932.

62. *Amtsblatt* 39, 29 Sept. 1928: "Die nächste Zukunft der Königstraße," also *Amtsblatt* 47, 29 Nov. 1928: "Die Königstraße bei Tage."

63. *Hamburger Echo,* 3 Aug. 1932.

64. *Hamburger Nachrichten* 19 July 1932: "Der Reigen des Todes," quoting the leader of the SA Troop 2/31, Hubert Richter. Cf. Okrass, *"Hamburg bleibt rot,"* 124–25, 261.

65. Stenwedel, interview, tape 2; Heins, interview, loc. cit.

66. Okrass, *"Hamburg bleibt rot,"* 252–53.

67. Stenwedel, interview, tape 1.

68. StABr. 4,65 IV 4e vol. 6, Police situation report 5, June 1927, 18–19.

69. W. Recken and Julius Krafft, *Hamburg unterm Hakenkreuz* (Hamburg, 1933), 78; Okrass, *"Hamburg bleibt rot,"* 140. In physical terms the Communists were the victors.

70. Adolf Hitler, *Mein Kampf,* Eng. trans. Ralph Mannheim, intro. D. C. Watt (London, 1969), 621.

71. Wilhelm Frick, 18 Oct. 1929, cited in: Robert Kempner, ed., *Der Verpaßte Nazi-Stopp. Die NSDAP als Staats- und Republikfeindliche hochverräterische Verbindung. "Preussische Denkschrift von 1930,"* reprint. (Frankfurt a.M., Berlin, and Vienna, 1983), 61.

72. *Sozialdemokratische Partei-Korrespondenz,* no. 11 (Nov. 1929): 592.

73. *Hamburger Echo* 169, 16 July 1932: "Laßt Euch nicht provozieren!" However, younger Reichsbanner members might sometimes engage in street politics. McElligott, "Straßenschlachten," 64. For a critical review of the SPD's response to Nazism, Karl Ditt, *Sozialdemokraten im Widerstand. Hamburg in der Anfangsphase des Dritten Reiches* (Hamburg, 1982).

74. St.ABr. 4,65 IV 4e vol. 7, situation report 4, 31 Dec. 1929, 3, report on Wasserkante/Altona. Cf. James Ward, "'Smash the Fascists . . .' German Communist Efforts to Counter the Nazis, 1930–31," *Central European History* 14 (1981): 30–62; Rosenhaft, *Beating,* chap. 4, and, in particular, 91–106.

75. "Resolution des Polbüros des ZK der KPD," 4 June 1930, cited in, *Faschismusanalyse und Antifaschistischer Kampf der Kommunistischen Internationale und der KPD 1923–1945* (Heidelberg, 1974), 153.

76. StABr. 4,65 IV 4e vol. 7, situation report 28 Apr. 1931, 8.

77. LAS 309/22813, KPD Organisationen 1924–1933, Bezirksleitung Wasserkante, Sekretariat H(am)b(ur)g, 5 Aug. 1932: "Was sind die Schwächen der Antifaschistischen Aktion?" 2; ibid., "Welche Aufgaben haben die Schutzstaffeln der Antifa für die nächste Zeit?" 1.

78. LAS 309/22721, Übersicht über politische Ausschreitungen im Polizeibezirk Altona-Wandsbek (für die Zeit vom . . .), Rg.Vfg.v. 16 Sept. 1932, -IPP 1239/6. These appear to be the only monthly reports to have survived and include

a total of 217 incidents over this period, the majority (i.e., 189) in Altona. They represent the total number of *reported* or *known* acts. Wolfgang Kopitzsch, "Politische Gewalttaten in Schleswig-Holstein in der Endphase der Weimarer Republik," in Hoffmann and Wulf, *"Wir bauen das Reich,"* 19–39, gives a surprisingly selective account of political violence based on this source.

79. Übersicht, 20 July–31 Aug. 1932; 1–25 Sept. 1932; 1–31 Oct. 1932.

80. Übersicht, 1–30 Nov. 1932.

81. *Hamburger Echo* 219, 12 Sept. 1932: "SA Terror Wächst Wieder"; cf. *Hamburg Echo* 143, 15 June 1932.

82. *Hamburger Echo* 188, 6 Aug. 1932, for attacks on local SPD by SA men operating from Flath's tavern, and *Hamburger Echo* 228, 22 Sept 1932, for retaliatory attacks on the tavern.

83. *Hamburger Echo* 183, 1 Aug. 1932.

84. *Amtsblatt* 31, 5 Aug. 1932; *Amtsblatt* 45, 11 Nov. 1932.

85. IML/ZPA, St 3/622, bl. 331, undated report on *Gau* strength of Reichsbanner; Altona formed the 8th District of the Reichsbanner in Schleswig-Holstein. Karl Rohe, *Das Reichsbanner Schwarz Rot Gold. Ein Beitrag zur Geschichte und Struktur der politischen Kampfverbände der Weimarer Republik* (Düsseldorf, 1966).

86. Stolte, interview, tape 2.

87. Ibid. FAD (Freie Arbeitsdienst [Voluntary Labor Service]).

88. See Ditt, *Sozialdemokraten;* Hans Mommsen, "Die Sozialdemokratie in der Defensiv: Der Immobilismus der SPD und der Aufstieg des Nationalsozialismus," in idem, ed., *Sozialdemokratie,* 106–33; Hagen Schulze, "Die SPD und der Staat von Weimar," in Stürmer, *Belagerte Civitas,* 272–86, esp. 280; and the relevant documents in: Luthardt, ed., *Sozialdemokratische Arbeiterbewegung,* 2:219–58. On the question of working-class "respectability," Richard J. Evans, ed., *The German Working Class* (London, 1982).

89. *Hamburger Echo* 166, 12 July 1932: "Erneutes SA-Wühlen in Altona."

90. Stenwedel, interview, tape 2:2; and from the Communist side: Harder v. Bargen, interview, 16 Feb. 1984.

91. STAK 28646/69, Aufruhrschaden: Roos: Antrag des Gastwirt Roos auf Schadenersatz auf Grund des Tumultschadensgesetz, 29 June 1932; Reviervorsteher, 8th Polizei Revier to Magistrat Altona, 28 Oct. 1932.

92. Heins, interview, loc. cit.; StAH 614–2/5 A5a NSDAP Altona, Der Kreisleiter, Rundschreiben no. 10/1937, 1 Feb. 1937, Betrifft: Lokalverbote.

93. IML/ZPA St3/129 Reichssicherheitshauptamt Abt. IV, bl. 1–59: Staatsanwaltschaft, Abschrift 11 Son.L. 22/33 Sdg. 388/33, here bl. 32ff.: "Im Namen des Volkes! Strafsache gegen Reschke, Retslag und gen." (18–19 Dec. 1933), 3.

94. LAS 309/22721, Polizeipräsident Altona, Abt.IA to Regierungspräsident Schleswig, 23 Dec. 1932, and 2 May 1933; *Schleswig-Holsteinische Tageszeitung* 300, 22 Dec. 1932: "Moskau wird aktiv."

95. IML/ZPA St. 3/129, Reichssicherheitshauptamt Abt.IV, 3–4; LAS 301/4709, Polizeipräsident Altona, 19 Nov. 1932.

96. Its leaders were: Walter Reschke (political), Heinrich Heins (technical),

Paul Mehnert (organization), IML/ZPA St. 3/622 Reichsicherheitshauptamt IV, bl. 2, 59–60: Aus dem Lagebericht des Polizeipräsident 48/32, 10 Oct. 1932; LAS 309/22721, Polizeipräsident IAd to Regierungspräsident, 2 May 1933.

97. "Moskau wird Aktiv."

98. LAS 309/22721, Polizeipräsident (Dr. Diefenbach) to Regierungspräsident, 23 Dec. 1932, "Feuerüberfall in der Breitestraße, 21 Dec. 1932," and Polizeifunkdienst-Kiel, 21 Dec. 1932.

99. Diefenbach was Oberregierungsrat in Hannover, and replaced Otto Eggerstedt after the latter was suspended in the wake of von Papen's coup against Prussia. He had been commissarial police president in Altona from 30 Nov. 1922 to 1 Mar. 1923 (Stolz, "Schutzpolizei," 46–47, 68).

100. LAS 309/22721, "Feuerüberfall"; ibid., Polizeipräsident Altona to Regierungspräsident, 2 May 1933.

101. StAK 28645/73/Mai, Max Mai, statement to Rechtsamt 22 July 1932. Riedel later absconded, owing Mai money.

102. The trajectory of the bullet led the police to conclude that it had come from the tavern, LAS 309/22721, Polizeipräsident Altona to Regierungspräsident, Schleswig, Betr. Einen politischen Terrorakt, 19 Nov. 1932.

103. LAS 309/22721, Der Oberbürgermeister to Polizeiprasident, 16 Dec. 1932: "Entschliessung der städtischen Kollegien, 24 Nov. 1932"; Magisrat to the Polizeipräsident, 1 Dec. 1932.

104. LAS 309/22721, "Feuerüberfall"; ibid., Polizeipräsident to Regierungspräsident, 22 Dec. 1932, Antrag der städtischen Kollegien.

105. The group included parent representatives from the Girls' II Elementary School, Wilhelmstraße, and the Boys' I Elementary School, Weidenstraße. Some information on the social background of this group can be found in: StAH 424/24 (Wohlfahrtskommission) Aktz.I 10.6, Schuldeputation, Schreiben, 20 Dec. 1929.

106. LAS 309/22721, Oberzollinspektor Thiele to Regierungspräsident, n.d. (2 Dec. 1932)

107. Ibid.

108. After 1933, Eggerstedt was held in Esterwegen concentration camp, where, on the 12 Oct. 1933, he was murdered. Biographical notes on Eggerstedt can be found in, *Der Sozialist. Mitteilungsblatt der SPD Landesorganisation Hamburg,* 4 Jg., no. 13 (1 Dec. 1949): "Erinnerungen an Otto Eggerstedt"); Schumacher, *M.d.R.,* 308–20.

109. *Akten der Reichskanzlei Weimarer Republik: Das Kabinett von Papen 1. Juni bis 3. Dezember 1932,* vol. 1: *Juni bis September 1932,* ed. Karl-Heinz Minuth (Boppard am Rhein, 1989), doc. 53, "Niederschrift des Staatssekretärs Planck über eine Unterredung mit den deutschnationalen Abgeordneten des preußischen Landtages v. Winterfeld und Borck am 8. Juli 1932," 190–91; Gotthard Jasper, "Zur Innerpolitischen Lage in Deutschland im Herbst 1929," *Vierteljahreshefte für Zeitgeschichte* 8 (1960): 281.

110. See *Akten der Reichskanzlei:* Kabinett von Papen, 249 n. 1. *Preussen contra Reich vor dem Staatsgerichtshof: Stenogrammbericht der Verhandlungen vor dem*

Staatsgerichtshof in Leipzig vom 10. bis 14. und vom 17. Oktober 1932, intro. Arnold Brecht (Berlin, 1933), 14–17.

111. *Hamburger Echo* 164, 9 July 1932; LAS 301/4709 Zusammenstöße, Polizieprasident Altona IA 1254/32, 4 Apr. 1932, for a similar incident on the 3 Apr.

112. Kopitzsch, "Politische Gewalttaten," 23–28.

113. Ibid., 30; Bessel, *Political Violence,* 85–89.

114. Stenwedel, interview, tape 1.

115. LAS 352/1244/249, copy of the original police report by Polizeioberleutnant Kosa; LAS 309/4709, Regierungspräsident Schleswig to Prussian M.d.I. I PP 6, 19 July 1932, Betr. Blütige Ausschreitungen der Kommunisten in Altona (socalled Abegg Report), and reprinted in: *Akten der Reichskanzlei:* Kabinett von Papen, doc. 67, 248–56; Stenwedel, interview, op. cit., tape 3.

116. LAS 301/4709, Altona Police, 27-page report of a public meeting on the 14 Sept. 1932 of the "Bloody Sunday Non-Party Inquiry" (Abt. IA, 15 Sept. 1932). Wolfgang Kopitzsch, "Der "Altonaer" Blutsonntag," in Herzig et al., *Arbeiter in Hamburg,* 509–16; Bessel, *Political Violence,* 86–87.

117. Thus, of 87 persons from Hamburg who were arrested on 17 July about a quarter were under eighteen years of age ("Abegg Report," op. cit., 8).

118. These were 1 (Elbegebiet), 2 (Zentrum/Munzmarkt), 3 (Ottensen); overall command appears to have been in the hands of August Lütgens, later condemned and executed for his alleged part in the battle, Anthony McElligott, "Authority, Control, and Class Justice: The Role of the Sondergerichte in the Transition from Weimar to the Third Reich," *Criminal Justice History* 15 (1995): 209–33.

119. "Bloody Sunday Non-Party Inquiry," evidence of Stanislaus Switalla (Polleiter, i.e., political leader, and party secretary in Altona), 13. Rote Hilfe Deutschlands, *Die Wahrheit über den Blutsonntag in Altona. Tatsachenschilderungen von Augenzeugen und Verwundeten* (Berlin, n.d), 4–5.

120. "Reigen des Todes."

121. See the list of Nazi witnesses from this *Sturm,* in LAS 352/1246, "Zeugen."

122. Stenwedel, interview, tape 1.

123. "Bloody Sunday Non-Party Inquiry," witness Frau Horowitz (from Mörkenstraße 72[II]), 17.

124. LAS 352/1245/320, Fritz Schwennsen, 6-page statement to the public prosecutor, 21 Sept. 1932, 4. Schwennsen was the *Sturmbannführer* of Sturm 1/31.

125. LAS 352/1246, Strafsache . . . Reese und gen, bl. 13: evidence of an elderly couple Richter, Große Marienstraße 55, 30 July 1932, 17 Dec. 1932.

126. Léon Schirmann, *Altonaer Blutsonntag 17. Juli 1932. Dichtungen und Wahrheit* (Hamburg, 1994), 111–15.

127. LAS 352/1243 (for autopsy reports). Cf. Schirmann, *Altonaer Blutsonntag,* 116–23.

128. IML/ZPA St. 3/622 Reichsicherheitshauptamt IV, bl. 87–100: Der Pr.Min. des Inn. II 1272 O.P. Schleho, Berlin, 18 Nov. 1932 (final report). In this final report from the Prussian Interior Ministry, the authorities claimed that at least ten armed five-man groups had fired upon the police. This version of events has carried over into the literature, for example, as well as Kopitzsch, cited above, Huber, *Ver-*

fassungsgeschichte, 7:1052–3. Ursula Büttner, Werner Jochmann, *Hamburg auf dem Weg ins Dritte Reich. Entwicklungsjahre 1931–1933* (Hamburg, 1983), 30–31.

129. LAS 352/1244/249 and 252: reports by Pol.Maj. Wendt; LAS 352/1242/102: report by Pol.Lt. Schieritz, responsible for clearing Gr.Marienstraße 62 and the surrounding area.

130. IML, ZPA, IV 3/2/1078, St. 18/217, bl. 63ff.: Der Pol.präs. A/W IA 3557/32, 17 Sept. 1932, Betr. politische Ausschreitungen und Strassenunruhen v. 17.7.32.

131. LAS 352/1241, Der Oberstaatsanwalt als Leiter der Anklagebehörde. Altona. 11 Son. J. 3/32. Namenverzeichnis zur Strafsache gegen Meyer u. Gen. wegen Aufruhrs: Getötete und verletzte Personen; Schirmann, *Altonaer Blutsonntag,* 152–53.

132. "Minister Besprechung vom 11. Juli 1932, 16.30 Uhr," *Akten der Reichskanzlei:* Kabinett von Papen, doc. 57, 204–8.

133. Thomas Trumpp, "Franz von Papen, der preußisch-deutschen Dualismus und die NSDAP in Preußen. Ein Beitrag zur Vorgeschichte des 20 Juli 1932" (Ph.D. diss., University of Tübingen, 1963); *Akten der Reichskanzlei:* Regierung v. Papen, doc. 73, 267–72; Harry graf Kessler, *Tagebücher, 1918–1937. Politik, Kunst und Gesellschaft der zwanziger Jahre* (Frankfurt a.M., 1961), entry 21 Sept. 1932, 691.

134. *Akten der Reichskanzlei:* Regierung v. Papen, doc. 72: "Ministerbesprechung vom 20. Juli 1932, 18 Uhr," 265–66; ibid., doc. 76: "Sitzung des Preußischen Staatsministeriums vom 21. Juli 1932," 281–82. Diefenbach soon found himself in conflict with Max Brauer, LAS 309/22721, Der Polizeipräsident Altona-Wandsbek in Altona an den Herrn Regierungspräsident in Schleswig, 22 Dec. 1932. In an interview after the war, Brauer described Diefenbach as a "Nazi," Landesbildstelle, HTB 480, no. 161, "Bürgermeister Brauer erzählt u.a. von der Machtergreifung 1933."

135. "Politische Ausschreitungen und Strassenunruhen v. 17.7.1932," op. cit.

136. Karl Dietrich Bracher, Gerhard Schulz, Wolfgang Sauer, *Die nationalsozialistische Machtergreifung. Studien zur Errichtung des totalitären Herrschaftssystems in Deutschland 1933/34* (Frankfurt a.M., 1962), vol. 3: Wolfgang Sauer, "Die Mobilmachung der Gewalt," 239–40. Stolz, "Schutzpolizei," 62.

137. *Amtsblatt* 12, 31 Mar. 1933: "Die Wahlen am 5. und 12. März 1933."

138. IML/ZPA, StA3/622, Polizei Oberst Munzenburg, "Bericht über die Ereignisse aus Anlass des Fackelzüges der NSDAP am 6.3.1933," 7 Mar. 1933.

139. Annie Staudinger, interview, 2 Feb. 1983. The number of "criminal" arrests rose dramatically from 2,006 in 1932 to 2,674 in 1933. Male youths were predominantly among those arrested, Polizeigefängnis Altona: "Zall der Häfthaje." On the role of the judiciary in Altona, McElligott, "Conservative Authority."

140. *Amtsblatt* 12, 31 Mar. 1933.

141. Stenwedel, loc. cit. Bessel in his numerous works on Nazi violence, relegates it to secondary significance in Hitler coming to power. Thomas Childers and Eugene Weiss, "Voters and Violence: Political Violence and the Limits of National Socialist Mass Mobilization," *German Studies Review* 13, no. 3 (1990): 481–98.

Chapter 7

"Under the Sign of the Swastika!" is quoted from the district political leader of the NSDAP, Heinrich Piwitt, in *Amtsblatt* 10, 8 Mar. 1933.

1. *Norddeutsche Nachrichten* 283, 4 Dec. 1933.

2. BDC: Personal File Emil Brix, Der kommissarische Oberbürgermeister Emil Brix to Preussische Ministerium des Innern z.Hd. des Herrn Kommissar Daluge [*sic*], M.d.L., Anlage 1, 11 Mar. 1933

3. StAH 421–5 Kb 3a, Der Regierungspräsident Schleswig, 10 Mar. 1933 I.B.P. -8-; ibid., Polizeifunkdienst, SSd no. 4, 56 11 0308. StAH 421–5 Kb 3a, Der Regierungspräsident (Wallroth) IG2050 to Brix, 14 Mar. 1933, and Regierungspräsident IG 2031, 22 Mar. 1933, in same file; *Norddeutsche Nachrichten* 60, 11 Mar. 1933: "Altonas Rumpfmagistrat verhaftet"; *Kieler Zeitung* 71, 12 Mar. 1933: "Die große Säuberungsaktion: Die Neuordnung in Altona."

4. *Norddeutsche Nachrichten* 60, 11 Mar. 1933: "Abrechnung. Zum Umsturz auf dem Rathaus." The preceding quotes are from this source.

5. Anni Staudinger, interview, 2 Feb. 1983. The Nazis took nearly 49 percent of seats for towns and cities with populations over 20,000, at the Prussian local elections, StJBDS 28 (1933): chap. 25: "Ergebnis der Gemeindewahlen 1933 in Preußen." Matzerath, *Nationalsozialismus,* 61–68; Schulz, *Zwischen Demokratie und Diktatur,* 442–59.

6. BAK NS22/572, Nachlaß Prof. Dr. Wolfgang Schultz, Reichshauptstellenleiter Dienstelle Rosenbergs, Kulturmappe. *Völkische Beobachter,* 24 Aug. 1939: "Grundgedanken nationalsozialistische Kulturpolitik."

7. BAK NS25/568, Schriftwechsel mit der Schriftleitung "NS-Gemeinde," bl. 119–32: Amtsleiter Schön, "Nationalsozialismus und Gemeindepolitik," 8.

8. Emil Brix, interview: *Altonaer Tageblatt* 67, 20 Mar. 1933; *Schleswig-Holsteinische Tageblatt* 67, 19 Mar. 1933; *Norddeutsche Nachrichten* 64, 16 Mar. 1933: "Die Neuordnung in der Altonaer Verwaltung."

9. Gerhard Ritter, *Carl Goerdeler und die deutsche Widerstandsbewegung* (Munich, 1964), cited in, Ribhegge, "Systemfunktion," 18.

10. StAH 421–5 Kb 3a, Der Staatskommissar mit der Führung der Geschäfte des Oberbürgermeister und des Magistrats beauftragt, Betrifft: Geschäftsverteilung, 14 Mar. 1933; *Verwaltungsbericht der Stadt Altona* (1934–35), 11. See "Die Neuordnung," for individual members of the city's administration.

11. *Verwaltungsbericht* (1933–34), 11, 15; *Verwaltungsbericht* (1935), 12.

12. BAK NS25/346, bl. 280–6: Der Gaufachberater Kompol. f. Flensburg, 8 Feb. 1934: "Tätigkeitsbericht."

13. BDC: Personal File Saß, membership no. 67,846; StAH 421–5 Kc1a Bd.II, file Saß.

14. BDC: Personal File Sieh; StAH 421–5 Kc1a Bd.II (1933–1935), Sieh: "Lebenslauf."

15. Personal files in the BDC: freelance violinist Werner Schmalmack (Pg.7,543) Ratsherr and Gau musical director; Ratsherr, bank director and grain merchant Heinrich Hartwig (Pg. 477,738); Friederich Utermarck (Pg 177,390), a

clerical employee, later administrative director in the personal office of the Oberbürgermeister, and Bürgermeister of Bad Bramstedt in Dec. 1934.

16. StAH 614–2/5 A5a, for names and addresses.

17. His membership number, 4,179,309, however, dates from May 1937.

18. Sieh, Protz and Hartwig. Members of sub-committees were no longer
elected but appointed by Brix, and ratified by the *Gau* leadership.

19. StAH 424–2 IVe Städtische Kollegien, nos. 45, 46, 47, 48 (1929–32). Cf.
Priamus, ed., *Deutschlandwahn,* 53, 55; Rennspieß, *Aufstieg des Nationalsozialismus,* 182, 184, 186.

20. Brix interview, *Norddeutsche Nachrichten* 304, 30 Dec. 1933: "Altonas Weg
ins neue Jahr." *Verwaltungsbericht* (1933/34), 14.

21. Der Gaufachberater, "Tätigkeitsbericht."

22. RGBL (1935) 1:49; Matzerath, *Nationalsozialismus,* 132–64; Engeli and
Haus, eds., *Quellen,* 673–98. Carl Goerdeler, "Die Gemeinde als Teil des Reichs-
ganzen," *Der Städtetag* 27 Jg. (1933); Fritz Markmann, "Die Aufgaben der
Gemeinden im nationalen Staat," *Reichs- und Preußisches Verwaltungsblatt* 54
(1933); Carl J. Friedrich, "The Development of the Executive Power in Germany,"
in *American Political Science Review* 27 (1933): 185–203.

23. StAH 421–5 Kc 1a Bd.II 1933–35, Der Staatskommissar mit der Führung
der Geschäfte des Oberbürgermeister und des Magistrat beauftragt an den Herrn
Regierungspräs. Schleswig, 13 Apr. 1933, Betr. Wahl der Magistratsmitglieder.

24. StAH 421–5 Kc 1a II, Bez. Absrchift bl. 2–4: Verhandelt in der Sitzung der
Stadtverordnetenversammlung zu Altona, 13 Apr. 1933. *Amtsblatt* 10, 8 Mar.
1933, for the quote. Brix's position as Oberbürgermeister was confirmed in the
autumn, StAH 421–5 Kc 1a Bd.II, Der Regierungspräs. to Pr.M.d.I, Aug. 1933,
Betr. Einweisung des Oberbürgermeisters und 2 Bürg. [Berichterstatter Reg. Ass.
Schröder].

25. StAH 421–5 Kc 1a II, Der OB -10- to Regierungspräs. In Schleswig, 30
Apr. 1934, Betr. Besetzung der Beigeordnetenstellen, zur Verf. v. 10 Apr. 1934 -IG-
4000 Altona 12; and Regierungspräsident, IG 4000 Altona 12, 25 Apr. 1933 to
Staatskommissar [Brix], Betr. Wahl der Magistratsmitglieder 13.4.33. See also
Amtsleiter Schön, "Nationalsozialismus und Gemeindepolitik."

26. *Verwaltungsbericht* (1933–34), 15. Jane Caplan, *Government without
Administration: State and Civil Service in Weimar and Nazi Germany* (Oxford,
1988), 139.

27. StAH 421–5 Kc1a, Kb3 and StAH 421–5 DK 1–46 (Akten der Dienst-
strafkammer Schleswig).

28. Stolz, "Schutzpolizei," 62, 68.

29. One hundred and forty were appointed by the end of 1933, 207 by the end
of 1934, and 259 by the end of 1935, *Verwaltungsbericht* (1933–34): 15; *Verwaltungsbericht* (1935): 14; *Tatsachen,* no. 9 (10 Oct. 1936): 1–3; McElligott, "Municipal Politics," 149; Matzerath, *Nationalsozialismus,* 79–81.

30. BAK NS25/123, NSDAP Gauleitung Rheinpfalz an die Oberste Leitung
der PO, 10 Oct. 1933.

31. BAK NS25/123, Schriftwechsel des Stableiters des HAfK, Bürgermeister
Treff, Bd.4 (1933–34), bl. 81.

32. StAH 421–5 Kc 1a II, OB -10-, An den Regierungspräsidenten Betr. Ortsabwesenheit des Oberbürgermeisters, ohne Verf., 4 Dec. 1933; BDC: Personal File Brix, SA-Führer-Bogen, to the question on "expertise," Brix had answered "finance and organization."

33. Brix, "Altonas Weg ins neue Jahr"; Ian Kershaw, *The "Hitler Myth": Image and Reality in the Third Reich* (Oxford, 1987), 96–104.

34. StJBDS 28 (1933), chap. 23: "Der Schuldenstand der deutschen Städte am 31.Dezember 1932," 539–42; StJbDG 31 (1936): "Die Schulden der deutschen Städte am 31.XII.1935 und ihre Entwicklung 1929–35," 578–79.

35. StAH 424–27 G7, Amt für Wirtschaft und Statistik to Wohlfahrtsamt Altona, 12 Nov. 1935, Anlage. Deutsche Gemeindetag, *Gemeinden und Statistik* 10 (20 Oct. 1933), table 1: "Personenkreis und Kosten der gesamten öffentlichen Fürsorge im zweiten Kalendervierteljahre 1933," 98–99.

36. RGBL. (1933) 1:23–29; StAH 424–2 IVe 49 (1933), Drucksache 1670, Baukommission 14 Jan. 1933, Betrifft: Arbeitsbeschaffungsprogram. Avraham Barkai, *Das Wirtschaftssystem des Nationalsozialismus* (Frankfurt a.M., 1988), 151–55; Dan P. Silverman, "National Socialist Economics: The *Wirtschaftswunder* Reconsidered," in B. Eichengreen and T. J. Hatton, eds., *Interwar Unemployment in International Perspective* (Dordrecht, Boston, and London, 1988), 185–220, here: 190. Birgit Wulff, "Arbeitslosigkeit und nationalsozialistische Arbeitsbeschaffungsprogramme in Hamburg 1933–34," in Herzig et al., *Arbeiter in Hamburg,* 529–39; Michael Schneider, "The Development of State Work Creation Policy in Germany, 1930–1933," in Peter Stachura, ed., *Unemployment and the Great Depression in Weimar Germany* (London, 1986). Richard Overy, *War and Economy in the Third Reich* (Oxford, 1994), 37–67.

37. BAK NS 25/346, bl. 235, Abschrift: Der Oberbürgermeister, Drucksache 1794, Arbeitsbeschaffungsstelle -103- to Ratsherren, 18 Jan. 1934; and bl. 237, Gaufachberater Kommunalpolitik, 9 Apr. 1934, Betrifft: Tätigkeitsbericht zum Rundschreiben vom 26.Sept. 1933, 2–3. See *Norddeutsche Nachrichten* 12, 20 Jan. 1934; and no. 87, 14 Apr. 1934.

38. StAH 424–15 (Bauamt Altona) XXX Lit. B, no. 28 Z.1; and no. 28 Y1 vol. 3; no. 28 Z.2, vols.2–4. StAH 421–5 Kb 3V and 3VI, ZAS, 1933–37, for numerous press reports of these. Although Silverman, "National Socialist," 188, plays down the "specifically National Socialist imprint" of the work creation scheme at a national level, the *"Sonder-Aktion"* identified the program with National Socialist endeavor at the municipal level. See David Welch, *The Third Reich: Politics and Propaganda* (London, 1993), 59, on the political importance of the propaganda value of the "Battle for Jobs."

39. StAH 424–24 32:3, has a number of *Bittschriften* (begging letters).

40. StAH 424–15 XXIII, Lit. A no. 23: Rex to Piwitt, 10 Oct. 1933. The following cases are taken from this file.

41. Ibid., Oberbürgermeister -103-, Arbeitsbeschaffungsamt, Vfg. 13 Oct. 1933, and 21 Oct. 1933.

42. Ibid., Butenschön. This section is based on correspondence dated Feb. and Mar. 1934.

43. Ibid., Wenzel to Arbeitsbeschaffungsamt der Stadt Altona, 21 June 1934.

44. Ibid., Wolpert to Oberbürgermeister, 24 Nov. 1934. Wolpert seems to have been assigned mostly to the unpopular *Landhilfe* program.

45. For example, the case of Franz Bachmann, in StAH 424–24 32:3, Gesuche der NSDAP in Unterstützungsangelegenheiten 1935–1936. Adelheid von Saldern, *Mittelstand im "Dritten Reich." Handwerker-Einzelhändler-Bauern* (Frankfurt a.M., 1979); Ian Kershaw, *Popular Opinion and Political Dissent in the Third Reich. Bavaria, 1933–1945* (Oxford, 1983), chap. 3.

46. This is why Brix was not prepared to reduce welfare benefits as recommended by the municipal auditors, *Altonaer Nachrichten* 128, 1 June 1933: "Oberbürgermeister Brix über die Altonaer Schuldenlast" ("Unterstützungen werden nicht gesenkt!"); StAH 424–24 32:2, Erwerbslosenselbsthilfe (1931, 1933), for alleged cell of Communist unemployed organized by Andreas Soltau in the vicinity of the Langenfeldestraße. Barkai, *Wirtschaftssystem,* 159–60.

47. StAH 424–15 XXIII, Lit. A no. 23, Bonne to Brix, 23 Sept. 1934.

48. Ibid., Bonne to Altona's chief medical officer, Dr. Trendtal, 24 Oct. 1934.

49. Ibid., Bonne to Brix, 9 Oct. 1934, and Brix to the branch Employment Office of the Nordmark, Altona (Dr. Ahrens), 12 Oct. 1934.

50. Ibid., Bonne to Brix, 23 Sept. 1934; Kershaw, *Popular,* 95–110.

51. Bonne to Brix, 23 Sept., op. cit.

52. Brix to Bonne, 27 Sept. 1934 and 12 Oct. 1934; Oberbürgermeister to employment office, Dr. Ahrens, 27 Sept. 1934

53. StAH 614–2/5 A5b, NSDAP Kreis Altona, Der Kreisgeschäftsführer, Rundschreiben no. 56/1935, Betrifft: Arbeitsbeschaffung, 9 July 1935.

54. Ibid., Rundschreiben no. 107/1936, Betrifft: Arbeitsbeschaffung, 5 Sept. 1936.

55. StAH 424–27, G8, "Feststellung im Wohlfahrtsamt Altona, Hauptstelle Statistik am 21 März 1935 [mit Herrn Peters]"; StAH 424–27, G6, Amt für Wirtschaft und Statistik (Kirchhoff), "Abschrift: Zur Arbeitslosenstatistik," 3 Aug. 1932; StAH 424–37 G7. On the quality of the statistical material, see Silverman, "National Socialist," 204–8; Overy, *War,* 46, 50; and especially, Rüdiger Hachtmann, "Arbeitsmarkt und Arbeitszeit in der deutschen Industrie 1929 bis 1939," *Archiv für Sozialgeschichte* 27 (1987): 177–237.

56. *Altonaer Nachrichten,* 14 May 1935: "Altona und die Arbeitsschlacht." StAH 424–27, G7, Arbeitsamt Hamburg I/3 an die Oberbürgermeister Amt für Wirtschaft und Statistik, "Zahl der HUE, WE in Altona und Blankenese, Stichtag 28 Feb. 1935," 15 Mär. 1935.

57. Industrie- und Handelskammer Altona, *Jahresbericht* (1933), 3ff. *Ruhr und Rhein* 14 Jg., no. 11 (17 Mar. 1933): 178.

58. Max Stampe, the journalist who interviewed Brix: "Altonas Weg ins neue Jahr."

59. *Norddeutsche Nachrichten* 126, 1 June 1933: "Oberbürgermeister Brix verkündet sein Altonaer Aufbauprogramm für ein neues Altona." Brix was following the recommendations made by an external auditing body, Wirtschaftsberatung deutscher Städte A.G., which had been asked by the provincial authorities in 1932 to carry out a thorough examination of the city's finances (StAH 421–5 Kb 8b, "Bericht Nr 229." James, *German Slump,* 105–8).

60. *Norddeutsche Nachrichten* 87, 14 Apr. 1934: "Oberbürgermeister Brix: Neue Finanzpolitik in Altona"; *Altonaer Tageblatt* 143, 22 June 1934: "Altona schafft Ordnung."

61. *Altonaer Nachrichten* 128 (Beilage), 1 June 1933: "Oberbürgermeister Brix über die Altonaer Schuldenlast"; *Norddeutsche Nachrichten* 283, 4 Dec. 1933: "Das Schulwesen," has the quote; *Altonaer Tageblatt* 281, 1 Dec. 1933: "Aus der Magistratssitzung." On the other hand, Lurup and Osdorf were each to get a new primary school in 1934, "Altonas Weg ins neue Jahr."

62. StAH 424–15 XXX 28 Y2 (Arbeitsbeschaffungsprogramm), "Fragebogen für Gemeinden und Gemeindeverbände, Angaben nach dem Stande vom 1. Januar 1933"; 424–15, XXX 28 Y1 Bd.II, bl. 81–82, "Fragebogen . . . nach dem Stande vom 1. April 1933." StAH 421–5 Kb 8d, Brix to Regierungspräsident, 4141 S/Pfa, n.d. Details of the budget were published in the local press, e.g., *Altonaer Nachrichten* 128, 1 June 1933.

63. McElligott, "Municipal Politics." 141 n. 110.

64. StAH 424–27 AI 4d, Statistik über die Bautätigkeit in Altona.

65. *Tatsachen* 6, 30 July 1936: "Schulden der deutschen Großstädte am 31. Dez. 1935," 1–3; ibid., "Arbeitslosigkeit und öffentliche Fürsorge in Altona," 7–8; See "Die Schulden der deutschen Städte am 31.XII.1935 und ihre Entwicklung 1929–35."

66. *Norddeutsche Nachrichten* 304, 30 Dec. 1933; Preller, *Sozialpolitik,* 434.

67. StAH 424–15 XXX 28 Y1 Bd.1, Notstandsarbeiten der Stadt Altona, Mag. Besch[luss] Billigung des Arbeitsbeschaffungsprogramms, 6 Jan. 1933; ibid., Magistrat -40- to Regierungspräsident, Betr. Arbeitsbeschaffungsprogramm, 9 Jan. 1933; ibid., Magistrat, Ausz. Sitzung, Notstandsarbeiten, 11 Jan. 1933; ibid., Magistrat -40- to Regierungspräsident, 26 Jan. 1933; ibid., "Zusammenstellungen der bisher von der Stadt Altona gestellten Anträge"; StAH 424–15 XXX 28 Y2 Bd.2, Brix to Oberpräsident [Betr. Arbeitsbeschaffung], 6 June 1933.

68. StAH 424–15 XXX 28 Y1 Bd.4, Deutsche Gesellschaft für öffentliche Arbeiten to Brix [XI 932 Wf/Ne], 13 June 1933.

69. StAH 421–5, BA 2b III; *Norddeutsche Nachrichten* 283, 4 Dec. 1933 and Nr 304, 30 Dec. 1933. On party efforts to provide help to small businesses: StAH 614–2/5 A5d, NSDAP Kreis Altona, Rundschreiben 126/1934, 10 Dec. 1934.

70. StAH 424–20 [Rechtsamt] A4, bl. 16: Oberbürgermeister to Treuhänder der Arbeit für das Wirtschaftsgebiet Nordmark, Dr. Völtzer, 7 June 1934.

71. Wirtschaftsberatung, "Bericht," 28, 34.

72. StAH 421–5 Kb 8e, Regierungspräsident to städtische Sparbank Weimar I.G. 3250/Altona, 27 Feb. 1933. StAH 421–5 Kb 8d [Zwangsvollstreckung], Regierungspräsident I.G. 3250/Altona.12 to Prussian MdI [Berichterstatter Reg.ass. Schröder], 3 July 1933. This file has numerous cases of non-payment.

73. Wirtschaftsberatung, "Bericht," 30.

74. StAH 421–5 BA 2b II, Magistrat [Kämmerei] to Bezirksausschuss, 202/33, 18 Mar. 1933. "Altonas Weg ins neue Jahr"; *Norddeutsche Nachrichten* 65, 17 Mar. 1934; Matzerath, *Nationalsozialismus,* 96.

75. StAH 421–5, Kb 8e, "Finanzlage der Stadt Altona 1933, Verzeichnis per

31. März 1933," and Der Kommissarische Oberbürgermeister, Magistrat Käm-merei 60, 9 May 1933.

76. *Altonaer Nachrichten* 128, 1 June 1933.

77. StAH 421–5 KB 8d, for copy of the agreement, 18 July 1933. Barkai, *Wirtschaftssystem,* 192–93.

78. StAH 421–5 Kb 8d, for details.

79. Ibid., letter to Magistrat, 28 July 1933.

80. This section is based on her file in: StAH 421–5 Kb 3V.

81. See, for instance, the individual cases and reports in StAH 421–5 Kb 3; StAH 421–5 Kb 3v; StAH 421–5 Kb 41 II.

82. Unpaid rents came to half a million marks, or one-fifth of expected rent roll, StAH 424–15 Lit. L 13 SAGA "Geschäftsbericht" 1927–1933; StAH 424–18 (Wohnungsamt) 14/2, "Ausstellung ü.d. Stand der Einnahmen und Ausgaben des W.A."

83. The auditors from the Wirtschaftsberatung deutscher Städte estimated that at the time of their report (late 1932), the city had amassed between four and five thousand unpaid bills from small contractors, Wirtschaftsberatung, "Bericht," pt. 1, 37; StJBDS 28 Jg., NF7 (1933): 541.

84. Rittner's case is documented in, StAH 421–5 Kb 3V.

85. StAH 424–20 B5 and F9 [Fritz Kölln], especially the correspondence between Kölln and Brix in early 1933.

86. Matzerath, *Nationalsozialismus,* 326–28, has 1,100 regulatory decrees affecting municipal financial administration between 1933 and 1939. Municipal finance was also heavily regulated by the central authorities during the Weimar era, Gerhard Ritter estimates by as much as ninety-seven percent, Ritter, *Goerdeler,* 35. Wysocki, "Die Kommunalfinanzen," 35–59.

87. StAH 421–5 Kb 3VI, Walter Brockmann to Regierungspräsident, 15 Mar. 1936.

88. *Norddeutsche Nachrichten* 126, 1 June 1933; and Nr 283, 4 Dec. 1933: "Altonas Weg in die Zukunft. 9 Monate nationalsozialistisches Altona."

89. *Deutschland Berichte der Sozialdemokratischen Partei Deutschlands, 1934–1940* (= *Sopade*) 7 vols. (repr. Salzhausen, Frankfurt a.M., 1980), 4 Jg., no. 11 (Nov. 1937): 1611.

90. StAH 421–5 Kb 3 a, and Kc 1a I, for details.

91. "Altonas Weg ins neue Jahr."

92. *Sopade* 1 Jg., no. 3 (June–July 1934): 240.

93. BDC: Personal File Alwin Schröter, member no. 1,113,459, 1 May 1932, for embezzlement of funds.

94. StAH 424–24 32:3, Unterakte SA-Heim in der Allee 257, 1934: report by Rechtsamt to Stadtrat Schumann, 6 Apr. 1934.

95. See the cases cited in: StAH 614–2/5 A5a, NSDAP Kreis Altona, Liste [. . .] über Ausschlüsse aus der NSDAP, sowie Gliederungen und betreute Organi-sationen, Liste no. 2/1936, 26 Oct. 1936; Liste no. 1/1937, 1 Feb. 1937; Liste no. 2/1937, 4 Mar. 1937; Liste no. 3/1937, 23 July 1937.

96. StAH 614–2/5 A5a, Kreisverordnungsblatt 13/33, 24 Nov. 1933, 4–5.

97. *Sopade* 3 Jg., no. 2 (Feb. 1936): 222–23.

98. BDC: Personal File Brix, "Lebenslauf," 6 Feb. 1935.

99. BDC: Personal File Brix, Oberste SA-Führung Gerichts-Rechtsamt SA—Disziplinargericht II Kammer, Aktzeichen B2/N/1938, excerpt from Lohse's letter to Hess, dated 14 June 1935. The following quotes are from this document.

100. He thus escaped the purge of the S.A. on 30 June, and of the party organization by barely four days (Dietrich Orlow, *A History of the Nazi Party*, vol. 2: *1933–1945* [Newton Abbot, 1973], 123–25).

101. Brix's removal was made to look like a resignation in order to take up the post in Kiel. BAK NS25/346, bl. 409, Gau Schleswig-Holstein, Gaufachberater f. Kompol., Flensburg, "Tätigkeitsbericht," 11 Mar. 1936; *Verwaltungsbericht* (1935), 11. Deputy mayor Dehning had already been removed under the "Law for the restoration of the professional civil service" in July 1935, *Verwaltungsbericht* (1933–34), 12.

102. BDC: Personal File, Brix, Oberste SA-Führung Gerichts-Rechtsamt S.A.—Disziplinargericht II Kammer Aktzeichen B2/N/1938, S.A. der NSDAP B 2/N/1938, Beschluss, P.G.2 3888/38 NfD. N/St; *Sopade* 4 Jg., no. 11 (Nov. 1937): 1611.

103. StAH 614–2/5 A6a, Der stellv. Gauleiter Rundschreiben 68/35, 2 Dec. 1935; ibid., Gau Hamburg, Der stellv. Gauleiter (Henningsen) Rundschreiben 37/38, 5 Oct. 1938.

104. StAH 614–2/5 A6a, NSDAP Kreis Altona, Anlage zum Rundschreiben 2/1934, 14 June 1934, "Betr. [Hess] Anordnung an den Gauleitungen des Reiches 1936."

105. StAH 614–2/5 A6a, Der stellv. Gauleiter, Rundschreiben no. 68/35, 2 Dec. 1935. Kershaw, *"Hitler Myth,"* 97–103.

106. Karl Dietrich Bracher, Wolfgang Sauer, Gerhard Schulz, *Die national-sozialistische Machtergreifung. Studien zur Errichtung des totalitären Herrschaftssytems in Deutschland 1933/34* (Cologne, 1960), 619. Peter Diehl-Thiele, *Partei und Staat im Dritten Reich. Untersuchungen zum Verhältnis von NSDAP und allgemeiner innerer Staatsverwaltung 1933–1945* (Munich, 1971), 138–39 n. 10, 141 n. 18; Jeremy Noakes, "Oberbürgermeister and Gauleiter: City Government between Party and State," in Gerhard Hirschfeld and Lothar Kettenacker, eds., *Der "Fuhrerstaat": Mythos und Realität. Studien zur Struktur und Politik des dritten Reiches* (Stuttgart, 1981), 194–227, here: 207. See the biting comments on the *Gau* Schleswig-Holstein leaders by Hamburg's ex-*Gauleiter* Albert Krebs, *The Infancy of Nazism: The Memoirs of Ex-Gauleiter Albert Krebs 1923–1933*, ed. and trans. William Sheridan Allen (New York, 1976), 270.

107. BAK NS25/97, Dr. K. H. Patutschnick, Reichshauptstellenleiter HAfK, "Sinn und Aufgabe der kommunalpolitischen Arbeit der Partei" (1940).

108. Peter Longerich, *Hitlers Stellvertreter. Führung der Partei und Kontrolle des Staatsapparates durch den Stab Heß und die Partei-Kanzlei Bormann* (Munich, 1992), 84.

109. StAH 614–2/5 A6a, Rundschreiben des Kreisleiters (Piwitt) no. 65, 17 Aug. 1936; 614–2/5 A5c Rundschreiben nos. 28–36, 3 Nov. 1936.

110. StAH 424–27 BI 1, "Bevölkerungsbewegung in Altona, Gliederung der HJ" (16 Feb. 1937). For the PO structure, StAH 614–2/5 Ac5 Rundschreiben der

Kreisleitung Altona, Kreisorganisationsleiter 1935–1940 [Zimmerling] Warnke, Vogt 1938/39, Rundschreiben no. 28/36, 3 Nov. 1936, Anlage zum Rundschreiben Nr 28/36. See also the entry for NSDAP Gau Schleswig-Holstein in *Altonaer Adreßbuch* 1934, pts. 1–6; Diehl-Thiele, *Partei,* 164–65.

111. Orlow, *History,* 2:92–93, 136–37.

112. StAH 614–2/5 A5a, NSDAP Kreis Altona, Der Kreisleiter, Rundschreiben 53/1935 29 July 1935; ibid., NSDAP Kreis Altona, Der Kreisleiter, 13 Mar. 1937, "Betrifft: Veranstaltungen. Verabschiedung des Kreises Altona am 30. März 1937 durch den Gauleiter Parteigenossen Lohse, Anlage: Aufmarschskizze." For the *Frauenschaften,* see StAH 614–2/5 A5b, NSDAP Kreis Altona Geschäftsführung (Bannier), Rundschreiben no. 17/34 22 Mar. 1934. The reference to "technically able cadres" is from Hitler's speech on 1 Jan. 1934, Orlow, *History,* 2:98.

113. NS 25/2134, Gauschatzamt, 4 May 1937.

114. StAH 614–2/5 A5c, NSDAP Stadtkreis Gross-Altona, Anlage zum Rundschreiben Nr 28/36 des Kreisorganisationsamtes (n.d.). Personal details from entries in the *Altonaer Adreßbuch* 1933.

115. StAH 614–2/5 Ac5, Kreisorganisationsleiter, Rundschreiben no. 28/36, 3 Nov. 1936, Anlage zum Rundschreiben no. 28/36.

116. BDC: Personal File Piwitt, for details.

117. Orlow, *History,* 2:90–91, 134, 145–46, points out that the purge was also the occasion to rid the party organization of corrupt officials. Matzerath, *Nationalsozialismus,* 229ff.

118. Orlow, *History,* 2:152.

119. Ibid., 2:153–54.

120. StAH 614–2/5 A5a, Rundschreiben no. 11/1934, 14 May 1934. Diehl-Thiele, *Partei,* 167.

121. StAH 614–2/5 A5a, NSDAP Kreis Altona, Der Kreisleiter 2 Feb. 1937, Rundschreiben no. 12/1937. Diehl-Thiele, *Partei,* 161–69; Robert Gellately, *The Gestapo and German Society. Enforcing Racial Policy, 1933–1945* (Oxford, 1990), 130ff.; idem, "The Gestapo and German Society: Political Denunciation in the Gestapo Files," *Journal of Modern History* 60 (Dec. 1988): 645–96.

122. StAH 424–24 32:3, Unterakte: "Berichte des Kampfbundes des Gewerblichen Mitttelstandes Gross-Altona über Wohlfahrtsempfänger." Dieter Rebentisch, "Die 'politische Beurteilung' als Herrschaftsinstrument der NSDAP," in Detlev J. K. Peukert, J. Reulecke, eds., *Die Reihen fast Geschlossen. Beiträge zur Geschichte des Alltags unterm Nationalsozialismus* (Wuppertal, 1981), 293–313; Peter Hüttenberger, "Heimtückefälle vor dem Sondergericht München," in Martin Broszat, Elke Fröhlich, Anton Grossmann, eds., *Bayern in der NS-Zeit,* vol. 4 (Munich and Vienna, 1981), 435–526. This is brilliantly captured by Anna Seghers, *Das siebte Kreuz* (Berlin, 1962), 92–100, where old Mr. Mettenheimer is interviewed by the Gestapo, and his innocent remarks misconstrued.

123. Finkenhäuser and Iwersen, "Die Juden," 130, 140–44, 153–54; Robert Gellately, "Enforcing Racial Policy in Nazi Germany," in Thomas Childers and Jane Caplan, eds., *Reevaluating the Third Reich* (New York and London, 1993), 42–65.

124. *Altonaer Adreßbuch* 1929, pt. 1, p. 11: "Schulen"; Finkenhäuser and Iwersen, "Die Juden," 138–40.

125. E.g., Julius Neumann of the Holsatia Werke discussed in chap. 4. Finken-hauser and Iwersen, "Die Juden," 126–57.

126. StAH 614–2/5 A5a, Der Kreisleiter, Rundschreiben 41/1934, 23 Aug. 1934; StAH 421–5 G2, G5, G7ii, G9ii ("aryanization"); StAH 614–2/5 A6a, NSDAP Gauleitung Schleswig-Holstein, Der stellv. Gauleiter (Sieh), 15 Jan. 1937, Rund-schreiben no. 3/37. Krebs, *Infancy,* 270.

127. StAH 614–2/5 A5e NSDAP Altona, Der Kreisleiter, 15 Oct. 1935, Rund-schreiben no. 83/35: "Betrifft: Jüdische Geschäfte, Anlage: Vorläufige Liste." Cf. StAH 614–2/5 A5a, NSDAP Kreis Altona, Der Kreisleiter (Kreisamtsleiter Zim-merling) 24 Sept. 1935, Rundschreiben no. 78/1935.

128. StAH 614–2/5 A5a, NSDAP Kreis Altona, Der Kreisleiter 11 Mar. 1937, Rundschreiben no. 26/1937: "Betrifft: Jüdische Geschäfte."

129. StAH 614–2/5 A5a, Der Kreisleiter, 2 Sept. 1935, Rundschreiben no. 72/1935: "Betrifft: Judenfrage."

130. StAH 614–2/5 A5d, NSDAP Kreis Altona, Propagandaamt Sch/Mey, Der Kreispropagandaleiter (i.V. Schläfer), 14 Dec. 1935, Rundschreiben no. 92 (1935).

131. *Sopade* 5 Jg., no. 12 (Dec. 1938): 1357. On the insidious nature of adminis-trative ghettoization, Raul Hilberg, *The Destruction of the European Jews* (New York, 1985), 27.

132. StAH 421–5 Kb 3V, complaint from Frau Herta Lorf to Oberpräsident, 7 Apr. 1936; and correspondence between Regierungspräsident and Oberpräsident, 10 June 1936, IG 2031 Altona 12, containing report by OB Daniels, and copy of statement by the informant, Dennert, 8 May 1936. On this latter aspect of the *Block* and cell system, see Rebentisch, "politische Beurteilung," 121–22.

133. "Bericht des Kampfbundes des gewerblichen Mittelstandes Gross-Altona über Wohlfahrtsempfänger," 25 Aug. 1933. For the street-traders: StAH 424–24 32:2, letter from Paul Z. and Karl S. to Stamer, 26 Mar. 1933. Both files contain numerous denunciations.

134. LAS 309/22721 and IML/ZPA St.3/622, for examples of political terror in the Altstadt in early 1933. For judicial terror, McElligott, "Authority." Detlev J. K. Peukert, *Inside Nazi Germany: Conformity, Opposition, and Racism in Everyday Life* (New York, 1987), 197ff.

135. See IML/ZPA St. 3/622, bl. 20ff., bl. 328ff. Peter Hüttenberger, "Vorüber-legungen zum 'Widerstandsbegriff,'" in J. Kocka, ed., *Theorien in der Praxis des Historikers* (Göttingen, 1977), 117–39; Reinhard Mann, *Protest und Kontrolle im Dritten Reich. Nationalsozialistische Herrschaft im Alltag einer rheinischen Groß-stadt* (Frankfurt and New York, 1987), 236–51.

136. Kershaw, *Popular,* 72ff., 128.

137. RGBl. (1934), 1:1269. This point has been explored by Peter Hüttenberger in his study of the special court in Munich, Hüttenberger, "Sondergericht."

138. StAH 424–111, C3, Robert S.

139. *Sopade* 3 Jg., no. 8 (Aug. 1936): 1036.

140. StAH 614–2/5 A5a, NSDAP Kreis Altona, Der Kreisleiter, Rundschreiben no. 80/1935, 28 Sept. 1935, point 2.

141. StAH 424–111 C6; BAK NS25/346, bl. 432, Gau Schleswig-Holstein, Der Gauamtsleiter für Kommunalpolitik, "Tätigkeitsbericht," 8 Oct. 1936.

142. StAH 614–2/5 A5a, NSDAP Kreis Altona, Der Kreisleiter, Rundschreiben no. 29/1935, 13 June 1935, "Betrifft: Lokal Elbschlossbrauerei-Ausschank (Pächter Hans Thun)"; ibid., Rundschreiben 34/1935, 20 June 1935, "Betrifft: Aufhebung des Lokalverbotes des Elbschllossbrauerei-Ausschankes."

143. StAH 614–2/5 A5a NSDAP Kreis Altona, Der Kreisleiter, Rundschreiben no. 10/1937, 1 Feb. 1937: "Betrifft: Lokalverbote," listing fifty-three taverns in Hamburg, mostly in the St. Pauli/Reeperbahn area bordering Altona.

144. StAH 424–111, C4, Bruno R.

145. StAH 421–5 Kb 3a: *Norddeutsche Nachrichten* 60, 11 Mar. 1933: "Eine Mahnung an die Beamtenschaft"; *Kieler Zeitung,* "Die große Saüberungsaktion: Die Neuordnung in Altona," op. cit.

146. StAH 421–25 Kb 3V, Der Oberbürgermeister Schulamt, 25 May 1936.

147. *Sopade* 3 Jg., no. 8 (Aug. 1936): 1029. Diehl-Thiele, *Partei,* 161.

148. StAH 424–111, C5. See StAH 614–2/5 F1, F2, F21, for further examples. According to the reports of the municipal department of the *Gauleitung,* there were no cases of resistance to the introduction of the Four Year Plan, BAK NS25/347 bl. 117, Gauleitung Schleswig-Holstein, Gaufachberater Kompol. "Tätigkeitsbericht," 12 Jan. 1937.

149. StAH 614–2/5 A5a, NSDAP Kreis Altona; BAK NS25/347 bl. 116, Gauleitung Schleswig-Holstein, Gaufachberater Kompol. "Tätigkeitsbericht," 12 Jan. 1937, gives the membership of the Deutsche Arbeitsfront in Altona as 132,000.

150. BDC: Personal File John Wohlers, subfile Akten des Obersten Parteigerichts Kammer III (Ortsgruppe Nienstedten). For more personal rivalry and conflict, see BDC: Personal File William Käselau.

151. StAH 614 2/5 A5a NSDAP Stadtkreis Gross-Altona, Abschrift: Nationalsozialistische Deutsche Arbeiterpartei, Gauleitung Schleswig-Holstein, Der stellvertr. Gauleiter P/Hp, Rundschreiben no. 21/36, 4 Mar. 1936: "Betr. Politische Beurteilungen." Rebentisch, "politische Beurteilungen," 122; Diehl-Thiele, *Partei,* 165 n. 86.

152. StAH 614–2/5 A6a, Der stellv. Gauleiter, 17 Aug. 1936, Rundschreiben no. 65/36.

153. Rebentisch, "politische Beurteilungen," 107. Diehl-Thiele, *Partei,* 157.

154. Diehl-Thiele, *Partei,* 159.

155. Patutschnick, "Sinn und Aufgabe"; BAK NS22/572, Helmut Jahn, "Kulturpolitik am Feierabend," unidentified newspaper cutting, 1934.

156. BAK R36/2438, Deutsche Gemeinde Tag, Beigeordnete Dr. Benecke to OB Prof. Dr. Dr. Weidemann, Halle, V394/40, 20 Mar. 1940: Dr. Goetz, "Die städtische Kunstpflege im Kriege," 1–53.

157. BAK NS25/346 bl. 319, Gau Schleswig-Holstein der NSDAP, Der Gaufachberater für Kommunalpolitik to Hauptamt für Kommunalpolitik der Obersten Leitung der P.O. München: Tätigkeitsbericht" (June–July 1934), 13.

158. Goetz, "Die städtische Kunstpflege," 6.

159. BAK NS25/346 bl. 297–98, Gau Schleswig-Holstein der NSDAP, Der

Gaufachberater für Kommunalpolitik to Hauptamt für Kommunalpolitik der Obersten Leitung der P.O. München, report for May–June 1934, 2–3; and bl. 361.

160. "Tätigkeitsbericht," July 1934, 13.

161. Ibid., 13–14.

162. See for example, Hitler's arrival at a rally in Munich in Mar., *Sopade* 3 Jg., no. 3 (1936), 281–83. Allen, *Nazi Seizure,* chap. 17; Adelheid von Saldern, "Cultural Conflicts, Popular Mass Culture, and the Question of Nazi Success: The Eilenriede Motorcycle Races, 1924–39," *German Studies Review* 15, no. 2 (May 1992): 317–38.

163. StAH 614–2/5 A5a, Der Kreisleiter, "Richtlinien zur Durchführung des 1 Mai 1934," 21 Apr. 1934.

164. Ibid.

165. StAH 614–2/5 A5a, Rundschreiben "Betr. Nationalfeiertag des deutschen Volkes 1.Mai 1934," 26 Apr. 1934; NSDAP Amt für Handel, Handwerk und Gewerbe (NS-Hago) Kreis Altona [Boge], Rundschreiben 32/1935, 27 Apr. 1935; ibid., Der Kreisleitung [Piwitt], Rundschreiben 18/1935, 25 Apr. 1935.

166. StAH 614–2/5 A5a, Rundschreiben 80/1935, 28 Sept. 1935.

167. StAH 614–2/5 A5a, Der Kreisleiter, Rundschreiben 89/1935, 31 Oct. 1939; Rundschreiben 77/1936, 3 Nov. 1936; Rundschreiben 80/1936, 6 Nov. 1936. The anniversary of the deaths of the two S.A. men, Koch and Büddig on 17 July 1932, was also solemnly kept, ibid., Der Kreisleiter, Rundschreiben 45/1935, 15 July 1935.

168. StAH 614–2/5 A5b Der Kreisgeschäftsführer [Bannier], Rundschreiben 59/1934, 14 Aug. 1934.

169. StAH 614–2/5 A5a, Kreisverodnungsblatt 13/33, 24 Nov. 1933, 5.

170. StAH 614–2/5 A5d, Der Kreispropagandaleiter [Schläfer], Rundschreiben 81/1935, "Betrifft Tag der nationalen Solidarität 7.Dez. 1935," 28 Nov. 1935.

171. StAH 614–2/5 A6a, Gaupropagandaleiter 83/1936, 20 Nov. 1936.

172. Ibid., Rundschreiben 83/1935, 2 Dec. 1935; ibid., Rundschreiben 85/1935 4 Dec. 1935.

173. Rebentisch, "Politische Beurteilung," 118–19.

174. BAK NS 25/346 bl. 287–89, Der Gaufachberater für Kommunalpolitik to Stabsleiter für Kommunalpolitik der Obersten Leitung der P.O. Berlin, 9 Apr. 1934, 2. BAK 25/347 bl. 116–7, Gauleitung Schleswig-Holstein, Gaufachberater, report on the Winter help for 1936–37, 12 Jan. 1937, in which an *improvement* in collections is mentioned and put down to a recovery in the economy.

175. See the reports filed in IML/ZPA St. 3/622.

176. For the Führer plebiscite on 19 Aug. 1934, Altona returned one of the lowest "Yes" votes (73.8 percent) in the country, Bracher et al., *Stufen der Machtergreifung,* 487–88, 496.

177. BAK NS25/346 bl. 51, Gau Schleswig-Holstein der NSDAP, Der Gaufachberater für Kommunalpolitik (Dr. Sievers) Flensburg, to Hauptamt für Kommunalpolitik der Obersten Leitung der P.O. München, 8 Nov. 1934.

178. BAK NS25/346 bl. 341, Gaufachberater, report 8 Oct. 1834, 15. *Verwaltungsbericht,* 1934ff.

179. Orlow, *History,* 2:91.

180. BAK NS25/347 bl. 116, Der Gauleitung Schleswig-Holstein, "Tätigkeits-bericht," 12 Jan. 1937.

181. StAH 614–2/5 A5a, Der Kreisleiter, Rundschreiben 73/1936, Betr. Deutscher Gruß: "Heil Hitler," 20 Oct. 1936; ibid., Der Kreisleiter, 18 June 1934; ibid., Der Kreisleiter Rundschreiben 66/1934, 22 Nov. 1934.

182. Ibid., Der Kreisleiter, Rundschreiben 20/1936, 23 Nov. 1936.

183. Ibid., Der Kreisleiter, Rundschreiben 2/1935, "Betr. Ausbildung der Pol.Leiter," 7 Jan. 1935.

184. Ibid., Der Kreisleiter, Rundschreiben 23/1934, 25 June 1934; StAH 614–2/5 A6a, NSDAP Gau Schleswig-Holstein, Der Gauleiter, Rundschreiben 2/36 (K), 4 May 1936.

185. StAH 614–2/5 A5a, Der Kreisleiter, Rundschreiben 71/1935, 2 Sept. 1935.

186. Ibid., Der Kreisleiter to members of the Kreisleitung, 18 June 1934.

187. Ibid., Der Kreisleiter, Rundschreiben 65/1935 26 Aug.1935; ibid., Rund-schreiben 9/1935 to Kreisleitung and Ortsgruppen, 6 Nov. 1935.

188. Allen, *Nazi Seizure,* 255, and chap. 19. See the rather dim picture of life by 1937, painted in the reports for the Gau Schleswig-Holstein in BAK NS25/347 bl. 125ff. (10 Feb. 1937) and compare it to the more upbeat, report from Jan., ibid., bl. 117, Der Gauleitung Schleswig-Holstein, "Tätigkeitsbericht," 12 Jan. 1937.

189. Bürgermeister Velthuysen, in *Worte des Abschieds von Altona, gesprochen von . . . in der letzten festlichen Ratsherrensitzung in den Räumen des Jenischhauses Altona am 19.März 1938* (Altona, 1938).

Chapter 8

1. Orlow, *Weimar Prussia 1925–1933,* 272. Hagen Schulze, *Otto Braun oder Preußens demokratische Sendung. Eine Biographie* (Frankfurt a.M., Berlin, and Vienna, 1977).

2. Exceptions are: Gerhard Schulz, "Die kommunale Selbstverwaltung in Deutschland vor 1933," *Franz-Lieber-Heft* 2, no. 3 (1959): 14–31; Peter Steinborn, *Grundlagen und Grundzüge Münchener Kommunalpolitik in den Jahren der Weimarer Republik* (Munich, 1968); Christoph Engeli, "Städte und Staat in der Weimarer Republik," in Bernard Kirchgässner and Jorg Schadt, eds., *Kommunale Selbstverwaltung: Idee und Wirklichkeit* (Sigmaringen, 1983); Jeremy Leaman, "The 'Gemeinden' as agents of fiscal and social policy in the 20th Century—local government and state-form crisis in Germany," in Eve Rosenhaft and Robert Lee, eds., *The State and Social Change in Germany, 1860–1960* (New York, Oxford, and Hamburg, 1989), and in spite of its faults of uncritically reiterating the arguments of the DNVP, Harold James, *German Slump,* chap. 4; idem, *The Reichsbank and Public Finance in Germany, 1924–1933. A Study of the Politics of Economics during the Great Depression* (Frankfurt a.M., 1985); idem, "Municipal Finance in the Weimar Republic," in Rosenhaft and Lee, *State;* Priamus, *Deutschlandwahn,* is a critical assessment in German of the interface between national politics and munic-ipal policy in the crisis. See also the works by Peukert and Harvey, cited in chap. 3; the important study by George Steinmetz, *Regulating the social: the welfare state and local politics in imperial Germany* (Princeton, N.J. 1993), and two forthcoming

studies by David Crew at Austin, Texas, and Hong Young Sun at Stony Brook, New York.

3. Robert Gellately, "German Shopkeepers and the Rise of National Socialism," *Wiener Library Bulletin* 28, nos. 35–36 (1975): 31–40.

4. LAB 142/1 StB 2376, [Albert] Meyer-Lülmann to Oberbürgermeister Mitzlaff, "Kämmer der Selbstverwaltung" (11 Jan. 1921). Heimann, "Zur Demokratisierung," 506; Koch-Weser, "Die Stadt," 20.

5. Quarck, "Die Demokratisierung der Gemeindeverfassung," 345; *Mitteilungen der Zentralstelle des Deutschen Städtetages* 6, nos. 16–17 (1918): 380–98; and 6, nos. 18–19 (1918): 404–11. See Bessel, *Germany,* for the failure of the central authorities.

6. Schulze, *Otto Braun,* 192, 312; Johe, "Territorialer Expansionsdrang"; Hans-Dieter Loose, "Groß-Hamburg, Hansestaat oder Republik Niedersachsen? Territoriale Neuordnungspläne für Nordwestdeutschland in der Revolution 1918–19," *Zeitschrift des Vereins für Hamburgische Geschichte* 66 (1980): 95–116; Ehni, *Bollwerk Preussen?* 15–24.

7. LAB 142, StB 4935 bl. 3: Der Königliche Kommissar für Vorbereitung der Verwaltungsreform (Drews) to Vorstand des Preußischen Städtetages, 9 Feb. 1917; and StB 2934: "Vorbericht für die Vorstandssitzung des Preußischen Städtetages am 15. Oktober 1920" (Mitzlaff); *Ursachen und Folgen. Vom deutschen Zusammenbruch 1918 und 1945 bis zur staatlichen Neuordnung Deutschlands in der Gegenwart* (Berlin, n.d.), vol. 1: "Die Wende des Ersten Weltkrieges und der Beginn der innenpolitischen Wandlung 1916/17," doc. 141, 256–74, for a further report by Drews; Schulz, *Zwischen Demokratie und Diktatur,* 258–60.

8. Matzerath, *Nationalsozialismus,* 29.

9. Terhalle, *Die Finanzwirtschaft des Staates,* 298.

10. Schacht's speech is reprinted in *Ursachen und Folgen,* 6:220–28; see also the speech by von Eynern (DVP), 2 Mar. 1926, against municipal expenditure, "Sitzungsberichte des Preußischen Landtags," 2. Wahlperiode, vol. 697, col. 9278f., printed as doc. 1278, in *Ursachen und Folgen,* 6:162–63; LAB StB 270 II, Oskar Mulert, "Der deutsche Reichsbankpräsident gegen die deutschen Städte," 22 Nov. 1927, for a rebuttal of Schacht's arguments. On the "crisis in confidence": LAB StB 435, "Vorbericht für die Sitzung des Preussischen Vorstandes am 7 Februar 1931"; Ernst Forsthoff, "Die Krise der Gemeindeverwaltung im heutigen Staat," *Zeitschrift für Politik* 21 (1932): 248ff. Mabel Newcomer, "Fiscal Relations of Central and Local Governments in Germany under the Weimar Constitution," *Political Science Quarterly* 51, no. 2 (1936): 185–214.

11. Richard Lohmann "Kommunale Selbstverwaltung oder nicht?" *Die Neue Zeit* 40, 23 Jg., no. 1 (3 Mar. 1922): 529–33. LAB 142/1 StA 327 I, Oberbürgermeister Dr. Jarres, "Die Behandlung der Gemeinden in der Heutigen Gesetzgebung und Verwaltung."

12. Heffter, *Selbstverwaltung,* 731ff.; Peters, *HKWP,* 100ff.; Engeli, "Städte und Staat," 163–81.

13. Der Städtetag, *Mitteilungen des deutschen Städtetags* 21, 28 Oct. 1927 (special issue: "Reichspolitik und Städte"), 26.

14. Gustav Boß: "City and Self-Government."

15. LAB 142/1 StA 603 I u. II, report of the Annual General Meeting, 27 Sept. 1929, 50.

16. This can be charted through the material deposited in LAB 142/1 StB 3778/I–II.

17. *Akten der Reichskanzlei:* Kabinett Brüning, vol. 3, doc. 655: "Besprechung vom 1. Feb. 1932"; docs. 660, 689 n. 6, 720, 746. On the debate in general: Jochmann, "Brünings Deflationspolitik," Borchardt, "Zwangslagen," Holtfrerich, "Alternativen," all cited in chap. 5; see Jürgen von Kruedener, "Die Überforderung der Weimarer Republik als Sozialstaat," *Geschichte und Gesellschaft* 11 (1985): 358–76.

18. Luther, "Die Stadt als Teil des neuen Staates," 23–24; Hofmann, *Zwischen,* 75, 188.

19. Gerhard Schulz, Ilse Maurer, and Udo Wengst, eds., *Staat und NSDAP, 1930–1932. Quellen zur Ära Brüning. Quellen zur Geschichte des Parlamentarismus und der politischen Parteien. Dritte Reihe: Die Weimarer Republik,* vol. 3 (Düsseldorf, 1977), doc. 177, 511.

20. Gerhard Schulz, Ilse Maurer, Udo Wengst, eds., *Politik und Wirtschaft in der Krise 1930–1932. Quellen zur Ära Brüning. Quellen zur Geschichte des Parlamentarismus und der politischen Parteien, Dritte Reihe: Die Weimarer Republik,* vol. 4/1–2 (Düsseldorf, 1980), doc. 238, pp. 286ff.; Brüning, *Memoiren,* 372, 389; Ehni, *Bollwerk,* 214–21; Werner Conze, "Die Reichsverfassungsreform als Ziel der Politik Brünings," *Der Staat* 11 (1972); James, *German Slump,* 108.

21. Carl Schmitt, "Die Verfassungsmäßigkeit der Bestellung eines Reichskommissars für das Land Preußen," *Deutsche Juristen-Zeitung* (1932): col. 958; *Akten der Reichskanzlei:* Kabinett v. Papen, doc. 84: "Der Vorsitzende der Deutschnationalen Volkspartei Hugenberg an den Reichskanzler. 23 Juli 1932," 314. Rudolf Morsey, "Zur Geschichte des "Preußenschlags" am 20.Juli 1932," *Vierteljahreshefte für Zeitgeschichte* 9 (1961): 430–39; Trumpp, "Franz von Papen, der preußisch-deutschen Dualismus und die NSDAP in Preußen; Gerd Schwerin, "Wilhelm Frhr. v. Gayl, der Innenminister im Kabinett Papen 1932" (Ph.D. diss., Friedrich-Alexander University, Erlangen-Nuremberg, 1972); Orlow, *Weimar Prussia,* chap. 9; see Gerhard Schulz, "Sand gegen den Wind: Letzter Versuch zur Beratung einer Reform der Weimarer Reichsverfassung in Frühjahr 1933," *Vierteljahreshafte für Zeitgeschichte* 66 (1996): 298–319.

22. Schwerin, op. cit., 128, 225–31. Forsthoff, *Lehrbuch,* 444; *Akten:* Kabinett v Papen, doc. 97, 357–74.

23. Fritz Morstein Marx, *Government in the Third Reich* (New York and London, 1937), 144.

24. BAK NS25/123 bl. 17–36: Gau Schlesien Amt für Kommunalpolitik an die Oberste Leitung der P.O. Abtlg. Kommunalpolitik (Der Stabsleiter), 10 Oct. 1933, 4, 6.

25. BAK NS25/123 bl. 81: NSDAP Gauleitung Rheinpfalz an die Oberste Leitung der P.O.: report: 10 Oct. 1933; ibid., bl. 4–9, 103, 113–14, for reports on the problems outlined here from *Gaue* München-Oberbayern, Süd-Hannover-Braunschweig, Gauleitung Thüringen. Matzerath cites the Main Office of the

Party Chancellory complaining of the "inflation" of decrees, *Nationalsozialismus,* 327; Caplan, *Government without Administration,* chap. 5.

26. Pollock, *Government of Greater Germany,* 139–43; Matzerath, *Nationalsozialismus,* 121ff., 154ff. and chap. 3. Martin Broszat, *Der Staat Hitlers Grundlegung und Entwicklung seiner inneren Verfassung* (Munich, 1969), chap. 7, for general background.

27. *Sopade* 2 Jg., no. 1 (1935): 128ff. 131, 133; Marx, *Government,* 140ff. Schulz, *Zwischen Demokratie und Diktatur,* 601, 612–26.

28. *Sopade* op cit., 129; Peters, *HKWP* 1:103; Marx, *Government,* 236–37.

29. Ribhegge, "Systemfunktion," 18; Schulz, *Zwischen Demokratie und Diktatur,* 447; Schultz, "Grundgedanken nationalsozialistische Kulturpolitik."

30. Heffter, *Selbstverwaltung,* 788; Matzerath, *Nationalsozialismus,* 353; Ribhegge, Systemfunktion, 15.

31. Hegel's "Monarch," *Philosophy of Right and Law,* para. 275.

Chapter 9

1. Inge Döll-Krämer, Gerd Krämer, Andreas Rieckhof, "Zwischen Hunger und Hoffnung, Nachkriegsalltag und Politik in Altona," in Stadtteilarchiv Ottensen, ed., *"Ohne uns,"* 172–99, here: 172–74.

2. IfZ, OMGUS Ed122/Pollock Papers, vol. 65, "Elections 1945–48"; and Ed122/34, Konrad Mommsen, "Political Observations of a Berliner after Four Months' Cessation of Hostilities (1945)," 25 Aug. 1945, 1–6. See also OMGUS 45/1/1 1945–46, secret report of General Clay to Secretary of State of War, U.S, 14 Oct. 1945.

3. StAH 424–88, Nachlaß Brauer, box 8, curriculum vitae (ca. 1936), and curriculum vitae (ca. 1955); Lüth, *Max Brauer,* 40–45; Christa Fladhammer and Michael Wildt, *Max Brauer im Exil. Briefe und Reden aus den Jahren 1933 bis 1946* (Hamburg, 1994).

4. Holger Christier, *Sozialdemokratie und Kommunismus. Die Politik der SPD und der KPD in Hamburg, 1945–49* (Hamburg, 1975), 241, for the quote; 188–89, 242, 255–56, 259–60, for Brauer's politics toward the middle-class parties; 261–66, for the return of the Socialist tradition in municipal politics. Cf. Lüth, *Max Brauer,* 6–9, 36–39, 46–48, 57–63, 135–42; Döll-Krämer, Krämer, Rieckhof, "Zwischen," 183–94.

Archives and Sources

Staatsarchiv Hamburg

A. Bestand 424—Dienststelle Altona
   —series nos. 1–111
B. Bestand 614 2/5 NSDAP und ihre Gliederungen
   —A 3 Verzeichnis v. Nationalsozialisten in Altona (Ortst.716)
   —A 5 Rundschreiben der Kreisleitung Altona: A–G, 1933–39, 1941
   —A 6 Rundschreiben der Gauleitung Schleswig-Holstein: A–F, 1934–38
C. Bestand 421–5 Regierung Schleswig
   —Kb Kommunalverwaltung der Stadt Altona, Allgemein
   —Kc Einzelne Dienststellen und Bedienstete der Stadt Altona
   —Yb Produktive Erwerbslosenfürsorge
   —BA a Kommunalangelegenheiten der Stadt Altona
   —BA d Verwaltungsstreitverfahren
D. Staatliche Pressestelle 1–4
   —Zeitungsausschnittssammlung: A752, 71c Max Brauer (press cuttings)
E. Bestand 215–2: Ausserordentliches Gericht
   —Series C, D (October Uprising 1923/Altona)
F. Bestand 122–3: Arbeiterrat Groß-Hamburg
   —312: Groß-Altona Frage

Landesarchiv Schleswig

Rep. 301   Oberpräsident
Rep. 309   Regierungspräsident
Rep. 352   Sondergericht Altona
Rep. 384   Akten der politischen Parteien
Rep. 454   NSDAP Gauleitung Schleswig-Holstein
Rep. 456   NSDAP Verschiedenen Dienstellen

Landesarchiv Bremen

Bestand 4,65 Polizeidirektion Bremen

Bundesarchiv Koblenz

Slg. Schumacher 208 I,2: bl.139–351 Gau Schleswig-Holstein

NS-1   (Gau Schleswig-Holstein, Vermögensausstellung)
NS-22   (NSDAP: Gau Schleswig-Holstein)
NS-25   (Kommunalpolitik)

Landesarchiv Berlin

Rep.142   Deutsche Städtetag

Stadtarchiv Kiel

Akten des Ausschusses zur Feststellung der Entschädigungen für Aufruhrschaden für Kiel und Umgebung Tumult-Schaden, files 28640–51

Institut für Marxismus–Leninismus beim Parteiarchiv SED

St.3   Reichssicherheitshauptamt
St.12 Bd.IIa/b Reichskomm. Überwachung d.ö. Ordnung
St.18   Preuß. Ministerium d. Innern
NFV.385   Anwaltschaft: Anklageschrift Mago u.Gen.
Vdf/9   Flugblattsammlung
V/SuF/40   Flugblattsammlung

Geheimes Staatsarchiv Preußischer Kulturbesitz, Berlin-Dahlem

Rep. 77:   Reichsministerium d. Innern
Rep. 84a   Preußische Justizministerium Bd.11
Rep. 87   Preußische Ministerium f. Landwirtschaft, Domänen and Försten
                (Teil 2, 6410: Die Groß-Hamburg-Frage 1922–27)

Berlin Document Center

Personal Files

Wilhelm von Allwörden
Max Böge
Emil Brix
Hans Bruhn
Edmund Dietze
Heinrich Hartwig
William Käselau
Kurt Lehnemann
Hinrich Lohse

Heinrich Piwitt
Emil Rüß
Hermann Saß
Werner Schmalmack
Ernst Schnackenburg
Alwin Schröter
Wilhelm Sieh
Bruno Stamer
Friedrich Ütermack
John Wöhlers
Herbert Zimmerling

Interviews

Julius Kammern, 9 November 1981
Walter Stolte, 17 and 24 March 1982
Helmuth Heins, 17 December 1982
Erich Lüth, 5 January 1983
Dr Emilie Kiep-Altenloh, 29 January 1983
Anni Staudinger, 2 February 1983
Harry von Bargen, 16 February and 6 March 1984
Albert Stenwedel, 19 March 1984

Election Data

Hamburger Echo: Nos. 88, 22 February 1921; 122, 5 May 1924; 338, 8 December
    1924; 266, 26 September 1927; 140, 21 May 1928; 319, 15 November 1929; 255,
    15 September 1930; 101, 25 April 1932; 1 August 1932; 7 November 1932

Index

Abegg, Waldemar (*Regierungspräsident*), 44, 141, 146
Abegg, Wilhelm (state secretary, Prussian interior ministry), 141
Adickes, Franz (mayor of Altona), 55
Adult Education College (Volkshochschule), 92*ff.*, 211
aerodrome, 231
Ahrendt, Heinrich, 36*ff.*, 40, 103, 122, 145
alcohol, 78*ff.*
Allen, William Sheridan (historian), 2, 235, 237
Alltagsgeschichte, 2
Allwörden, Wilhelm von (NSDAP), 46
alte Kämpfer, 204
Altona, 1*ff.*, 19, 50, 76, 87, 95, 194*ff.*, 200*ff.*, 211, 217, 220, 225, 228*ff.*, 232, 235, 241, 243; "Abruzzenviertel" (slums), 68, 164*ff.*, 171, 192; "Abruzzenviertel" and ungovernable people, 227; administration, few women in, 25; Altstadt, 4, 11–12, 26, 55*ff.*, 62*ff.*, 91, 109, 150, 163*ff.*, 171, 176, 221; bankruptcy proceedings, 214; and "Bloody Sunday," 166, 191*ff.*, 194; and bolshevization, 140; council, 201; deficit, 153; development of industry, 3*ff.*; DNVP support compared with DVP, 34*ff.*; economy, 126, 128, 134*ff.*, 137, 139*ff.*, 143, 145*ff.*, 151, 153, 160, 205, 213; elections, 10; Greater Altona, 36, 40, 100, 116*ff.*, 119, 170; incorporated into Hamburg, 3; incorporation of suburbs, 11, 40, 95*ff.*, 104, 107, 109*ff.*, 112*ff.*, 115*ff.*, 117*ff.*, 120, 123, 238; KPD stronghold, 28*ff.*, 185, 188*ff.*,

192*ff.*, 233; "little Moscow," 26, 172–77; "New Altona," 40, 56; NSDAP support, 159, 178, 182; Office for Art and Culture, 230; religious denominations, 3; revolution, 20, 239; socialist stronghold, 159; violence, 163, 171*ff.*, 174, 181; VSB, 47
Altonaer Kai und Lagerhaus A.G., 224
Altonaer Nachrichten, 51, 131, 210
Altonaer Tageblatt, 44, 143, 153
Altona House and Property Association, 36, 38, 142
Altona-Kiel railway, 97
Angell, James (economist), 125*ff.*
anti-Semitism, 135, 224–26
Armin zur Treue und Einigkeit, 46
Association of Industry and Commerce, 142
Association of Tavernkeepers and Assembly Room Owners of the Elbe Communities, 104
August Wilhelm (prince), 50

Bahrenfeld, 3*ff.*, 11–12, 26, 34, 64*ff.*, 97, 215, 227
Bannier, Eric (NSDAP *Geschäftsführer*), 210, 225*ff.*
"Battle for Jobs," 205, 210. *See also* unemployed
Bauermeister (honorary senator), 41
Baumann, Egbert (head of welfare office), 77
Becker, Erich (political scientist), 5, 7*ff.*, 10, 237
Becker, Mattheus (head of press office), 89
beggars, 76